Governing Cross-Sector
Collaboration

Governing Cross-Sector Collaboration

John J. Forrer
James Edwin Kee
Eric Boyer

JB JOSSEY-BASS™
A Wiley Brand

Published by Jossey-Bass
A Wiley Brand
One Montgomery Street, Suite 1200, San Francisco, CA 94104-4594—www.josseybass.com

Jossey-Bass books and products are available through most bookstores. To contact Jossey-Bass directly call our Customer Care Department within the U.S. at 800-956-7739, outside the U.S. at 317-572-3986, or fax 317-572-4002.

Wiley publishes in a variety of print and electronic formats and by print-on-demand. Some material included with standard print versions of this book may not be included in e-books or in print-on-demand. If this book refers to media such as a CD or DVD that is not included in the version you purchased, you may download this material at http://booksupport.wiley.com. For more information about Wiley products, visit www.wiley.com.

Library of Congress Cataloging-in-Publication Data

Forrer, John J.
    Governing cross-sector collaboration / John Forrer, James (Jed) Kee, Eric Boyer.
      1 online resource. — (Bryson series in public and nonprofit management)
    Includes index.
    Description based on print version record and CIP data provided by publisher; resource not viewed.
      ISBN 978-1-118-84593-6 (pdf) — ISBN 978-1-118-84592-9 (epub) — ISBN 978-1-118-75969-1 (paperback)
      1. Public-private sector cooperation.   2. Public administration.   I. Kee, James Edwin.
    II. Boyer, Eric, 1977–   III. Title.
    HD3871
    352.5'38—dc23

                                      2014017142

Printed in the United States of America
FIRST EDITION
PB Printing   10 9 8 7 6 5 4 3 2 1

The Jossey-Bass Nonprofit Sector Series

CONTENTS

ACKNOWLEDGMENTS

This book is the product of more than a quarter-century worth of teaching, writing, and thinking about cross-sector collaboration. We are indebted to our many colleagues and students who have informed our thinking on this topic, and it would be impossible to name everyone. However, there are a few individuals we want to especially mention and thank.

Eric Boyer joined the effort as a coauthor during our early stages of discussions with Jossey-Bass. He assumed the lead on several chapters and provided important insights and made contributions on theory and practice throughout the book. He expresses his appreciation to his parents, Paul and Susan Boyer, for their support and love.

George Washington University (GW) professor Katherine E. Newcomer, director of the Trachtenberg School of Public Policy and Public Administration, has supported the project throughout this process; she read and provided valuable comments on several draft chapters and was a coauthor on two foundational articles in *Public Administration Review*. GW Professor Emeritus Michael Harmon sharpened our thinking on the question of democratic accountability. Mike Worth, GW professor of nonprofit management, offered comments on leading in the nonprofit sector relative to cross-sector collaboration. Georgia Tech Professor Gordon Kingsley provided useful feedback on issues surrounding organizational learning and cross-sector collaboration.

We have benefited from the assistance of several graduate assistants. At GW, Lydia Vollmann assisted with research on accountability and bureaucracies related to gender and communications issues. Samuel Clements assisted with research on network governance. Ridhima Kapur assisted with research on independent public-services providers. Satoru Yasutani, a visiting scholar from Japan, worked with us on numerous issues concerning public-private partnerships. Georgia Tech graduate student Arindam Das provided background research on collaboration. Patti Niles provided invaluable administrative support.

We also thank the many individuals who agreed to be interviewed for this effort and especially recognize Admiral Thad W. Allen, USN, Ret., Ron Carlee, Lori Kaplan, Pat Stillman, and Sue Russell. Terry Kee provided insights into organizational issues with independent public-services providers. We are very appreciative of several anonymous reviewers who examined the manuscript at various stages of its completion. They gave us valuable suggestions and advice as to both the content and organization of the book.

Professor John Bryson and Jossey-Bass editor Alison Hankey were strong supporters of the book and pushed us to broaden our topic to include all cross-sector collaborations. We appreciate the staff and editors of Jossey-Bass for their many suggestions and improvements of the manuscript.

Finally, we express appreciation to our spouses, Sharon Forrer and Suzanne Erlon Kee, who supported us with patience and love throughout the process. We dedicate this book to them.

Washington, DC   *John J. Forrer*
April 2014   *James Edwin (Jed) Kee*

FOREWORD

Society is indeed a complex system of interdependencies that we describe as different sectors—public, private, and nonprofit. As we live our lives, we are generally oblivious to the different sectors. We may, for example, have a notion that the government is somehow involved with trash collection, even though a private company collects it from our homes and takes the trash to wherever it goes. Yet we are mostly oblivious about how this simple service, which we take for granted, is managed and influenced by the different sectors: local, state, and federal governments; private haulers; public and private disposal providers; nonprofit environmental organizations; and others.

Nothing is simple. No aspect of modern society is the domain of any single sector. None.

Governing Cross-Sector Collaboration addresses the reality of today's interconnected society. The delineation of the different collaborative approaches in this book is illustrative, not definitive. As the authors write, the five "choices" they discuss "can be viewed as evolutionary." The authors do not claim "that these five options cover all possibilities"; they represent basic models. Thus, readers are encouraged to assess the different approaches critically and explore variations. Contracting, partnering, and networking will converge in unique and, it is hoped, creatively effective ways from one community to another. This book provides the valuable foundation on which creative cross-sector problem solving can occur.

While the book is targeted to public administration, it should be read across all disciplines, and not just the obvious ones of business administration and nonprofit management. Engineering, planning, health care, law, and a host of other professions are all part of and affected by our connected society. The leadership skills discussed in *Governing Cross-Sector Collaboration* are also not just for senior managers. Professionals at all levels of organizations are required to generate support from others, lead outside their formal roles, understand the wider system, and build trust—the four essential leadership skills that the authors discuss. In fact, collaboration occurs meaningfully and effectively only when people at all levels of our organizations understand, value, and nurture working together across organizational boundaries.

Consider my own field of city management. Local government does not exist solely for the purpose of providing services that cannot be efficiently or profitably provided by the private sector. Local governments serve a larger purpose. While the vision statements of cities vary, they essentially come down to the vision of creating great places where people can live, work, and play. Such places offer economic opportunity, excellent education, and safe and healthy environments. These societal characteristics cannot be provided by a single sector working in isolation. Can business in isolation provide economic opportunity? Can the board of education in isolation ensure that all students succeed? Can the police department in isolation make neighborhoods safe? And into what silo could community health possibly be placed?

It is not enough to be a good manager of the services that one's organization provides. Organizational leaders across all sectors must be concerned with the boundary-spanning activities discussed in *Governing Cross-Sector Collaboration*. Not only must leaders themselves see the wider system, we must proactively work to help others see the wider system and the ways in which our futures are all inextricably connected.

Jed Kee confronted these issues early in his career as a public practitioner and has studied them extensively over the years as an academic. The result is a book that is not abstract but of practical utility. Kee's perspective is also guided by his deep sense of shared responsibility for the public good. John Forrer brings a global business perspective to the project, and Eric Boyer brings the perspective of the current generation on public administration. The result is a book with actionable principles, illustrated by numerous examples from the field.

James Schwartz of the Arlington County Fire and Rescue Department was the incident commander for the initial response to the terrorist attack on the Pentagon on 9/11. He notes that in relation to emergency responses, people often ask, "Who is in charge?" Jim says that this is the wrong question. The real question is, "Who is in charge of what?" This is true for all that we do as a society. No one is or can be in charge of society or any major piece of it. Each sector and each organization has a role and a responsibility to the whole. Achieving effectiveness—livable communities where people can thrive and pursue their hopes and dreams—ultimately depends on the extent to which organizations can collaborate across sectors with a shared understanding of our connected relationships and connected future. *Governing Cross-Sector Collaboration* helps move us toward this goal.

Charlotte, North Carolina   *Ron Carlee, DPA*
May 2014   *City Manager*

INTRODUCTION

Today's twenty-first-century public leaders and managers are increasingly involved in cross-sector collaborations (CSCs)—a transformation of public governance as important as the one that began over a century ago. In the late nineteenth and early twentieth century, the United States evolved from a nation of small governments, largely managed through patronage, to a large public sector, run by professional civil servants. This increase in professionalism led to the development of schools of public administration and public policy, the creation of the senior executive service at the federal level of government, and the development of a bureaucratic model of management and accountability that until recently has gone unchallenged. A similar public sector development also occurred internationally, especially in Western nations.

Beginning in the 1980s, however, the traditional public administration orthodoxy was challenged in the United States and abroad. The challenge came from a mix of political and academic actors who felt that the public sector that had evolved by the 1980s was inefficient, oversized, and unresponsive. They argued for more private sector involvement and innovation in the delivery of public goods and services and the unfettering of the public sector bureaucracy to become more flexible and innovative. The debate over the wisdom of this movement, often labeled the New Public Management, continues. The reality, however, is that the public enterprise of today increasingly relies on third parties (states, private firms, and nonprofit organizations) to deliver services to the American public (Salamon 2002).

This book is designed for those who want to learn more about these forms of collaboration and for those in the public and nonprofit sectors who will increasingly find themselves involved in a variety of collaborative arrangements—contracts, partnerships, networks, and other independent relationships—as they fulfill their public and nonprofit missions. The private sector also will benefit from understanding how public managers approach collaborations and the options and practical trade-offs they face.

THE CHANGING NATURE OF THE PUBLIC ENTERPRISE

The nature of this broader governmental environment, what we label the "public enterprise," has fundamentally changed since our nation's founding.[1] While government remains at the center of the public enterprise, today it also encompasses a variety of private and nonprofit actors engaged in public service activities. This emerging dynamic requires us to rethink the basic governance structures and relationships within the public enterprise.

Government in the United States during the time of the constitutional debates was largely patterned after colonial administration. The major functions of government, such as the courts and the militia, were performed by people in their respective state or local governments (counties, parishes, or shires). These were farmers, lawyers, professionals, and laborers who supplemented their income through their government appointments. There was no such thing as a permanent civil service, which did not emerge in Western nations until the late 1800s. Government administrative appointments in the United States during its first century were largely based on whom you knew, not on your own skills.

At the time of the nation's founding, there was a blurring of distinctions between the public and private sectors. Government jobs were often part-time; associations of neighbors worked together to create "public" infrastructure; and private parties developed toll roads and canals to facilitate both public and private transportation. As the nation developed, and especially after the Industrial Revolution, the indistinct dividing line between the public and private sectors created significant problems. Major parts of the economy were unregulated and unsafe; urban areas were run by political machines whose supporters were rewarded with public jobs or contracts. In the late 1800s, there was a growing realization, reflected in the Progressive movement, that the nation needed a clearer distinction between the roles of the two sectors, and Progressive forces argued for the development of a professional civil service to manage the public's business. The professionalization of public administration began at the local level, but was then spearheaded by the federal government, which created a federal civil service system in the Pendleton Act of 1883.

The size of the current public enterprise as we now know it is primarily a result of the growth of the national government during the twentieth century, particularly during the Great Depression, World War II, the Cold War, and the Great Society eras that followed. National government spending as a percentage of gross domestic product rose tenfold from under 2.5 percent in 1930 to more than 25 percent in 2010. During this period, there was a dramatic increase in public employment through the development of professional civil service systems. However, federal civilian employment growth in the latter part of the twentieth century was limited by Congress through ceilings on full-time employees and the congressional practice of shifting the implementation of federal programs to state governments or federal contractors. There were actually fewer federal employees in 2009 than in 1980, even though federal government spending grew from $678 billion to $3.5 trillion. Even when new federal departments were created, such as Energy and Homeland Security, the employee ceilings meant that those new departments largely relied on private contractors to fulfill their public mission.

THE CURRENT STRUCTURE OF THE PUBLIC ENTERPRISE

The evolution of the current public enterprise over the last half of the twentieth century can be explained by five elements: the shift of actual program operations (to the extent possible) to state governments; the use of private and nonprofit contractors to perform any function that is not "inherently governmental"; the growing use of public-private partnerships to address public problems and needs, especially in the infrastructure area; the development of networks of public service providers that include private and nonprofit actors; and, finally, the growth of independent actors, composed of private and nonprofit organizations, which we refer to as independent public-services providers (IPSPs), delivering public goods and services. Four of these five trends involve cross-sector collaboration.

Government and the Expanding Public Enterprise

The result of devolution, contracting, partnerships, and networks is a public enterprise that is much different from the one that developed through most of the twentieth century. Some have labeled this the "hollow state" (Goldstein 1992; Milward and Provan 2000) because of the increasing inability of the government to effectively manage the public enterprise. Others have referred to it as the growth of "third-party government" (Salamon 2002) or "the market state" (Bobbitt 2002). Proponents and opponents have lined up to praise or decry these developments, but there is no doubt the public enterprise has dramatically changed.

In the latter half of the twentieth century, public governance included an expanded role of nonprofit organizations in providing public goods and services and the emergence of a private market for providing goods and services, from prisons to roads (Savas 2000). Despite the growth of networks and partnerships, the formal structures of government and how it is organized have remained largely unchanged, and yet the role of the public manager has changed significantly over that same period of time.

Public-Private Partnerships, Networks, and Independent Public-Services Providers

The focus of this book is on various collaborative arrangements—contracts, networks, public-private partnerships, and what we are labeling independent public-services providers—as vehicles for government action. IPSPs are a natural extension of a more networked delivery of services. They are self-directed entities composed of businesses and nonprofit organizations that collaborate, sometimes with government, in the production or delivery of public goods and services.

Government (federal, state, and local) remains at the heart of the public enterprise and continues as the dominant but not sole actor. Also included within the public enterprise sphere are contractors that generally operate within a governmental framework as agents of government. However, in contrast to contractors, partners and networks are sometimes within the governmental framework and at other times act with greater discretion and autonomy. Government must negotiate with other principals in networks and partnerships over the nature, scope, and delivery of public goods and services. IPSPs, the most independent of these organizational options, are created without any government involvement at all.

Governmental action is now largely framed through bureaucratic structures that dominated government activity for much of the twentieth century. The bureaucratic model works well in fairly structured situations, where problems can be compartmentalized and commanded by single governmental agencies, but that is not the nature of many of today's critical problems and issues, such as climate change and health care cost reform. Instead, public servants must look to multiagency, multisector solutions that involve multiple organizations in a network of policy actors and implementers, or IPSPs, which are much different from the current government bureaucratic hierarchy.

This cross-sector world involves collaboration and mutuality and is organized around heterarchy rather than through the traditional government hierarchy. This heterarchy requires a different type of leadership and public management than the existing model does (Kettl 1997; Kee and Newcomer 2008). Instead of a public administration based on hierarchical notions of accountability, public servants must negotiate agreements with a variety of actors, with whom they may have little leverage or no direct control, but instead are connected through contractual or ad hoc arrangements in horizontal relationships that involve the development of reciprocal trust and mutual accountability.

ORGANIZATION OF THE BOOK

The book is organized into two parts and twelve chapters. Part 1 of the book, "Choosing Cross-Sector Collaboration," delineates the various forms of CSC—their advantages and disadvantages—and provides a framework to analyze their use in solving public issues or problems. Chapter 1 discusses the challenges to public managers and the current complicated governing environment, including political, social, and economic forces that are driving CSC. It describes the types of organizations that are emerging to address problems that traditional governmental structures seem unable or unwilling to address. It also introduces the concept of the IPSP.

Chapter 2 examines the rationale for the growing use of CSC by all sectors and provides a template for engaging in a more strategic approach to CSC. This chapter draws a clear distinction between government activity in a principal-agent environment and government negotiations with other principals in collaborative contracts, networks, partnerships, or IPSPs.

Chapters 3 through 6 examine the primary CSC modes: collaborative contracting, partnerships, networks, and IPSPs. Each of the chapters defines a form of CSC, examines its rationale, and provides specific examples and a framework for public managers to engage private and nonprofit actors in delivering public goods and services.

Chapter 3 covers contracting and examines how contracting is shifting from the traditional or classic contracts to contracts that require more interaction between government and the contractor. We are labeling these types of incomplete or relational contracts "collaborative contracting" to differentiate them from the more traditional type. In this chapter, we also provide a detailed assessment process for all types of contracts.

Chapter 4 covers partnerships with nonprofits and public-private partnerships: we use the term *cross-sector partnerships* when discussing both. Governments are increasingly engaging in partnerships with both the nonprofit and the private sectors. The nonprofit actors are particularly important in delivering a variety of health care and social services. Private organizations are seeking and entering into public-private partnerships, particularly to address public infrastructure needs. The chapter provides a framework for public managers to effectively engage partnerships.

Chapter 5 deals with network organizations, including their functions, types, and structures. These are illustrated through a variety of examples and case studies. Public managers are provided with a framework for working effectively with networks that deliver public goods and services.

Chapter 6 further explores the concept of IPSPs, addressing their growing use and potential as legitimate actors in the delivery of public services. It provides examples of IPSPs addressing the critical challenges raised in chapter 1.

Chapter 7 proposes an analytical framework for assessing these new forms of governance and when they should or could be used in particular situations or to solve particular problems. Using case studies, the chapter explores critical issues such as the nature of the public task or challenge, the location of necessary resources to address the challenge, the identification and allocation of risks, the analysis of best value for the public, and the importance of measuring performance and ensuring appropriate accountability.

The chapters in part 2, "Managing Cross-Sector Collaboration," examine a number of implementation factors that influence the effective use of CSC by public managers. They describe the current state of public administration with respect to these new forms of CSC governance and identify the stewardship and leadership requirements when public managers engage cross-sector collaborators.

Chapter 8 examines the current bureaucratic form of public administration, providing arguments in favor of and against the current model. The chapter argues for the need for a new model for the evolving heterarchy of actors. Chapter 9 describes the leadership requirements of public managers when working in a heterarchy rather than a hierarchy and examines techniques for public managers to coordinate the contributions of nonprofit and for-profit organizations in public service.

Chapter 10 stresses the importance of developing a system of mutual, democratic accountability and proposes approaches to achieve that accountability, providing public managers with four pillars to foster accountability in CSC. Chapter 11 discusses the need for public agencies to develop learning practices to improve their approaches to collaborating with the private and nonprofit sectors.

Chapter 12 concludes with a discussion of how we can close the governance gap by rethinking the role of public managers and the potential of increased action by the for-profit and nonprofit sectors. It addresses the key challenges for public managers, summarizes the advantages and disadvantages of CSC, and presents "public value" as an important consideration when assessing CSC success.

Within the chapters are various case studies, including a case study on state employment and training options, which will give readers an opportunity to apply concepts in the chapter to further understand choices available in CSC. Additional cases are on the book's website, www.wiley.com/college/forrer.

Public managers today face a variety of choices for solving public problems and delivering public goods and services. These new cross-sector collaborative choices offer promise for improving performance but require a very different approach to management and leadership from the current traditional approach in government agencies.

This book is aimed at public leaders and managers who are responsible for the effective stewardship of the public enterprise and for their partners in the nonprofit and private sectors. It provides a blueprint for analysis and a framework for ensuring public accountability in the public interest. We believe it will be useful for both students and practitioners, who understand we are living in challenging times and desire to better understand different modes of action and governance.

Governing Cross-Sector
Collaboration

PART ONE

Choosing Cross-Sector Collaboration

Dimensions of Cross-Sector Collaboration

For public managers, cross-sector collaborations (CSCs) allow governments to leverage funds, expertise, and risk sharing with other sectors that can provide key ingredients to the successful delivery of public goods and services. For nonprofit managers, collaborations allow their organizations to better meet their stated mission and possibly expand that mission to related areas of interest. For private sector managers, collaboration promises increased profits, enhanced reputation, and expanded business opportunities. All sector managers can benefit from a better understanding of the nature of these collaborations and how they are successfully led, managed, and governed.

This chapter begins by examining a dilemma facing all public managers: how to respond to global challenges with a public sector that lacks the resources and support to accomplish its public responsibilities. It also addresses the collaborative imperative, a confluence of factors that are driving governments toward networks and partnerships. Second, the chapter defines cross-sector collaboration and provides a framework of types and uses of such collaboration as well as key issues for the public manager. Each type of collaboration is explored in more detail in later chapters.

THE DILEMMA FOR PUBLIC MANAGERS

Governments at all levels—federal, state, and local, in both the United States and internationally—face enormous societal, governmental, and economic challenges that are likely to become even more complex. These challenges pose a dilemma for public managers: the gap between what citizens expect government to do and the resources and support to our governments have never been broader. Government is underresourced, undervalued, and underappreciated at the very time when there are so many challenges for efficient and effective government policies and programs.

The lack of confidence in government, built up over years of accumulated frustration, means there is scarce political support for enhancing government agencies and their performance. And the lack of resources that agencies receive, coupled with the expanding demand and the need for government responses to current and emerging challenges, means perpetuating ineffective government performance, which in turn reinforces the lack of confidence in government.

Governments at all levels frequently lack the expertise, capacity, or funding needed to identify emerging trends and adopt effective policies and procedures. As a result, public managers may need to depart from current governmental hierarchical structures and engage actors outside government, in the private and nonprofit sectors, to address the challenges we highlight in this chapter and other critical emerging policy concerns. Cross-sector collaboration is not the answer to all of today's challenges, but it can become part of the solution if managers understand when collaboration is an effective alternative to government-only solutions and when they recognize the underlying tensions that exist between competing values that are important for protecting the public interest.

THE CROSS-SECTOR COLLABORATION IMPERATIVE

Public managers confront a complicated and difficult governing environment in which they are expected to carry out their duties and responsibilities. Markets, politics, and societal expectations are rapidly changing. Some of the changes stem from forces outside government, some are a product of a public sector that often seems largely dysfunctional, and some are the result of new forms of organizations that are emerging and becoming actors on the public scene. Today's problems are more challenging than ever before, and yet governmental efforts to address those challenges seem more problematic than at any other time in recent memory. Thus, the challenges facing public managers "require concerted action across multiple sectors" (Kettl 2006, 13). A number of factors appear to be accelerating this cross-sector imperative.

Societal Transformations

Transformations in society and societal expectations often make it difficult for public managers to address new challenges, especially from a single agency or governmental perspective. Today we live in "a densely interconnected system in which local decisions and actions may trigger global repercussions—and vice versa—and the fate of communities in one region is bound to choices by decision makers elsewhere" (O'Toole and Hanf 2002, 158). Many different things move on globalized networks—people, products, data, money, flora and fauna, news, images, voices—faster, more cheaply, and to more places than ever before (Rosenau 1990; Scholte 2005; Wolfe 2004). Globalization compels public managers to look outside their traditional jurisdictional boundaries in an attempt to understand and solve the problems they face.

Increased global competition also is transforming what used to be thought of as a seller's market, where power was held by the producers of goods and services, to a buyer's market, where consumers have more choices. This has led many businesses to increase their focus on customer-centered practices. As a result, consumers have increased expectations of receiving excellent customer service from the firms and stores where they shop. When we order clothes, books, and household items online, we expect to receive what we wanted, and if we are not satisfied with the product, we expect to return it, no questions asked. With this growing expectation, public services that follow a more bureaucratic (and monopolistic) culture look even less satisfactory than before.

Major Challenges Require New Thinking

The list of major challenges for government is as numerous as at any other point in our recent history, encompassing such issues as deteriorating infrastructure, out-of-control health care costs, and climate change. Climate change provides just one clear example of a need for collaboration. The earth's temperature is rising. Although some may debate the impact human activity plays in the rising temperatures at the earth's surface and in the atmosphere (e.g., a combustion of fossil fuels for power and transportation, deforestation, and expanding livestock herds), none can debate that greenhouse gases in the atmosphere have sharply risen in modern times (Pachauri and Reisinger 2008). Figure 1.1 provides a dramatic illustration of the problem.

The consequences of climate change are alarming: greater melting of ice at the earth's polar caps and rising sea levels that threaten cities and nations.

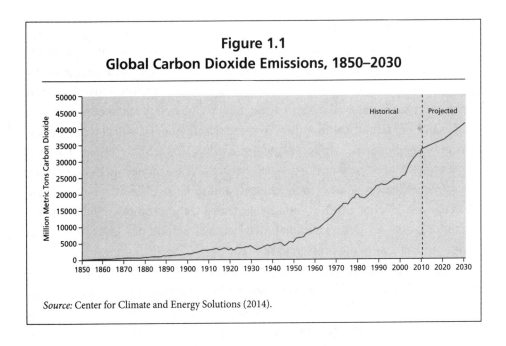

Figure 1.1
Global Carbon Dioxide Emissions, 1850–2030

Source: Center for Climate and Energy Solutions (2014).

Global ecosystems will be altered, threatening the health or even survival of flora and fauna. Weather patterns are changing, and hurricanes and other storms are likely to become stronger due to warmer ocean temperatures. Diseases could also migrate with rising temperatures, possibly spawning global pandemics. Rising temperatures could mean dramatic changes in crop yields and production, threatening food shortages (National Geographic 2011; US Environmental Protection Agency 2011). Public leaders and managers will have to find methods for involving all sectors in addressing the causes and consequences of climate change.

A Dysfunctional Public Sector Environment

Despite the obvious need for an effective public sector, public attitudes about government, caused in part by the dysfunctional behavior of public officials, and public fiscal constraints, make public-only solutions nearly impossible. Americans' confidence in their national government is at historic lows, according to Gallup's annual governance survey. A poll conducted in October 2013 found that 81 percent of Americans are dissatisfied with the way the country is being governed, equaling the highest share since Gallup first asked the question in 1972 (Gallup 2013). Fortunately, public satisfaction with state and local government is significantly higher than that of the federal government, with 74 percent expressing a good or fair level of confidence in local government and 65 percent in their state government (Gallup 2012).

Over the past twenty-five years at the federal level, the public has witnessed a retreat from building rational, bipartisan policy consensus. By almost all measures of partisan polarization, the divide between Democratic and Republican members of Congress has deeply widened over the past twenty-five years, reaching levels of partisan conflict not witnessed since the 1920s and 1930s. Even the appointment of officials to lead government agencies is a victim of such partisanship. Presidential appointees now take longer to get approval than ever before, and more positions remain unfilled for long periods of time. The very functionality of government agencies is weakened, and qualified executives simply pass on taking a government position, unwilling to face the partisan public scrutiny and politicking that is often the price to pay for public service.

The fiscal health of most US governments is not good. In 2012, government debt at all levels was at record levels and budget deficits were commonplace. While fiscal conditions improved somewhat in 2013, many state and local governments are at or near their borrowing limits. Standard & Poor's announced in August 2011 that it had downgraded the US federal credit rating for the first time ever, dealing a symbolic blow to the reputation of the world's economic superpower.

Hollowed-Out Government

More than twenty years ago Mark Goldstein (1992) observed how sustained budget cuts for US government agencies and the rollback of regulatory authority had severely reduced their capacity to govern. At the time he cited Department of Housing and Urban Development and Food and Drug Administration scandals, the savings and loan bailout, and the Hubble telescope failure as proof of the damaging legacy of severe government cutbacks. He used the term *hollow government* to indicate the lack of resources to carry out government's responsibilities. Figure 1.2 compares the growth in national spending and US population to the growth of federal civilian employees since 1948. Despite the increase in spending and population, federal civilian employment has not changed significantly since the post–World War II era. While increased government productivity due to technology may ameliorate this issue somewhat, much of what

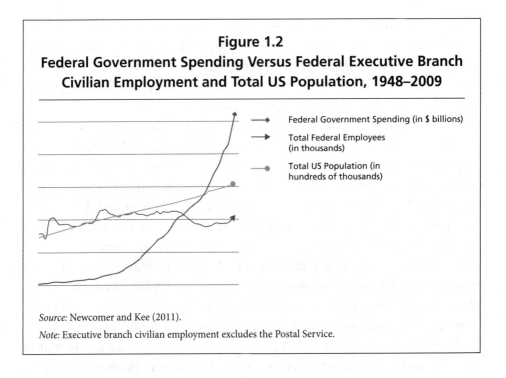

Figure 1.2
Federal Government Spending Versus Federal Executive Branch Civilian Employment and Total US Population, 1948–2009

Federal Government Spending (in $ billions)

Total Federal Employees (in thousands)

Total US Population (in hundreds of thousands)

Source: Newcomer and Kee (2011).
Note: Executive branch civilian employment excludes the Postal Service.

government workers do has limited potential for productivity gains. Of course, looking just at federal employment hides the full extent of federal government programs. More than a decade ago, Light estimated that the "true size" of government was substantially larger than the federal workforce when you counted federal contractors, state and local employees enforcing federal programs, and various grantees of federal funds (1999).

It was in the early 1980s and during the Reagan Revolution that public support began to ebb for maintaining the highest-quality workforce in federal government agencies. In the past thirty years, the nondefense federal workforce has remained at nearly the same level as it was during the period Goldstein was observing. Since that number includes significant increases for Homeland Security and Veterans Affairs, the workforce at other federal agencies has actually shrunk (US Office of Personnel Management 2011).

THE COMPLICATED ORGANIZATIONAL ENVIRONMENT

When governments struggle to find answers within their traditional bureaucratic structures, they often look to other sectors or new governmental forms to address the problem. The result of these emerging governance structures creates a more complicated organizational framework for public managers.

During the last half of the twentieth century in the United States, we saw three major trends:

- The creation of quasi-governmental structures that provide more latitude to managers than the traditional bureaucracy
- The growth of government contracting, in both the private and nonprofit sectors, as a method of delivering government goods and services
- Devolution of program responsibilities from the federal government to state governments

As we entered the twenty-first century, three new forms emerged to challenge traditional governmental structures: partnerships, networks, and a variety of independent actors, which we refer to as independent public-services providers (IPSPs). Some of these new structures complement and easily coexist with existing governmental structures, but many do not. Some networks and partnerships operate outside the traditional structures with a degree of independence that requires that public managers use nontraditional skills, such as in risk analysis and negotiations.

CROSS-SECTOR COLLABORATION: DEFINITION AND SECTOR ROLES

Cross-sector collaboration is the interaction of two or more of the three organizational sectors: the public sector (governmental units at all levels—local, state, and national), the private or for-profit sector, and the nonprofit or not-for-profit sector. Collaboration could include any combination of the three sectors, including public-private, public-nonprofit, private-nonprofit, or public-private-nonprofit. It is those collaborations involving the delivery of governmental goods and services that are the primary focus of this book. Many authors have articulated their own definitions of cross-sector collaboration. For this book, we build on the definition provided by Bryson, Crosby, and Stone (2006):

> *Cross-Sector Collaboration* is the voluntary linking of organizations in two or more sectors in a common effort that involves a sharing of information, resources, activities, capabilities, risks and

decision-making aimed to achieve an agreed to public outcome that would have been difficult or impossible to achieve by one organization acting alone.[1]

Intergovernmental collaboration, while important, is not included in this definition because it does not refer to collaborations between sectors. National governments use a variety of tools, including grants and regulations, to encourage state and local governments to implement federal policy. The changing dynamics of collaboration in the federal system of government in the United States have received a great deal of attention (see Conlan and Posner 2008; O'Toole 2006; Derthick 1996; and *Publius: the Journal of Federalism*). State and local governments also enter into a variety of compacts and interlocal agreements to coordinate service among state and local governments. There is a considerable literature on this type of collaboration (see Brown 2008; Kettl 2006; Provan and Milward 1995). Interorganizational coordination among governments is critical, and lessons from those collaborations can inform cross-sector efforts. However, the focus of this book is on interactions among the sectors, not within them.

Also excluded are collaborations that are forced, which is why the definition includes the word *voluntary*. A business implementing environmental regulations is not an example of collaboration. However, if federal legislation permitted experimental approaches to reducing pollution and those experiments involved actions by more than one sector, then that might be an example of CSC.

In addition, excluded from this discussion are social enterprise organizations, except related organizations involved in delivering a public good or service. A social enterprise organization applies commercial efforts to improve human and environmental well-being rather than maximizing profits for external shareholders (Ridley-Duff and Bull 2011). Social enterprises can be structured as either for-profit or nonprofit and may serve a public purpose such as sustainability or economic development, but their primary goal is to provide private gains for the individuals who are involved in the enterprise.

Cross-sector collaboration may take many forms, from ad hoc interactions to complex partnerships or networks that may be glued together with contracts or other sophisticated agreements. In some cases, private or nonprofit organizations provide public goods and services in lieu of government provision. It is essential to understand the scope of sector actors involved in CSC. While there are some commonalities among the sectors, there also are significant differences in their missions, how they operate, to whom they are accountable, and how they measure success.

Public Sector

The public sector consists of entities organized and governed through some type of government-sponsored structure. In the United States, eighty-nine thousand governments are tracked by the US Census and constitute the public sector. This includes "general-purpose governments": the national government, fifty state governments (and the District of Columbia), over three thousand county governments, nearly twenty thousand municipalities, and sixteen thousand towns. There also are fifty thousand single-purpose governments, such as school districts, utility districts, airport authorities, and miscellaneous quasi-governmental units. All public sector units operate under federal or state constitutional authority and applicable statutes. These governments range from the very small (e.g., a local community library district) to very large, such as the State of California, whose economy, if it were a nation, would rank eighth in the world, ahead of both Brazil and Russia.

Public organizations tend to be mission driven, and the process for the delivery of goods and services is an important element in their mission. Principles such as equity, citizen participation, and due process are sometimes as important as the final results. Public organizations are typically more constrained than either their private or nonprofit counterparts. Legislation, regulations, and judicial decisions all influence how public organizations operate. Public manager discretion is typically low, with too often an overemphasis on rules and procedures. Fortunately, some of the public sector reforms beginning in the 1980s have led to public organizations that are becoming more results driven as we shift from an emphasis on process to a greater emphasis on outcomes, as provided in the federal Government Performance Results Act, performance budgeting, and balanced scorecards (Newcomer 1997).

Private Sector

The private (or for-profit) sector consists of all individuals or organizations that provide goods or services with the goal of making a profit. In the United States, the Internal Revenue Service determines for-profit classifications, and there is an enormous diversity of organizations that operate within the private sector. Examples of for-profit entities include multinational corporations, such as Toyota, Marriott, General Electric, Apple, and Samsung; businesses designed to have a social impact (social enterprise organizations); family-run mom-and-pop stores; a variety of partnerships; and individual self-employed persons who generally provide a limited range of goods and services.

Private sector organizations are primarily driven by profit motivation; measures of success are typically financial measures such as profit, return on equity, dividends, stock price related to earnings, and market share. Financial measures are important because the private owners of these organizations are in competition for capital and customers. Private firms may exhibit corporate social responsibility by assisting their communities, becoming environmentally sustainable, and contributing to other worthy causes; but good corporate citizenship also is generally good for business. In the final analysis, however, private sector organizations are oriented toward a positive fiscal bottom line. They place a high emphasis on efficiency and entrepreneurial activity that can enhance their short-term and long-term fiscal situation and satisfy their customers, stakeholders, and shareholders.

Nonprofits

The nonprofit sector consists of organizations and associations that are organized for reasons other than to make a profit but are not governmental. A wide spectrum of organizations fits into the broad category of nonprofit organizations, and more and more public services are delivered through some type of collaboration with nonprofits. The trend is particularly prevalent in the area of human (or social) service provision. As of 2009, government agencies had approximately 200,000 formal agreements (contracts and grants) with about 33,000 human service nonprofit organizations (Boris et al. 2010). Working with government is the primary function of many nonprofit organizations, with over 65 percent of the overall revenue for human service nonprofits coming from the public sector (Boris et al. 2010).

Not all organizations classified as nonprofits in the United States provide human services, however. Nonprofits also consist of insurance companies, religious organizations, recreational clubs, arts organizations, business associations, cemetery companies, and a variety of other service organizations. This sector includes small neighborhood associations and churches, larger arts organizations (a local symphony orchestra, ballet, or opera company), and very large organizations such as the American Red Cross (in the United States) and the Red Crescent (in the Arab-speaking world). It also includes coalitions of such organizations. For example, the International Federation of Red Cross and Red Crescent Societies is the world's largest humanitarian organization, consisting of 187 members and a secretariat in Geneva (International Federation of Red Cross and Red Crescent Societies 2013).

Some nonprofit organizations are specifically created for educational and charitable purposes; in the United States, these organizations (nearly one million) are referred to as 501(c)(3) organizations (after the applicable section in the federal income tax code) and receive special tax status and are allowed to receive tax-deductible contributions from individuals and corporations. Internationally, nonprofit organizations are often referred to as NGOs. This sector collectively is also sometimes referred to as "civil society."

Nonprofit organizations have a more nuanced bottom line than the private sector does. They are typically mission driven (as is the public sector) and place an emphasis on numbers of people served related to that mission. For example, Meals on Wheels, an organization that brings food to homebound individuals, measures its success by the number of meals delivered and individuals served. Nonprofit organizations have to maintain a balanced budget to stay in business, but they do not think about making a profit. Maintaining some budgetary surplus, however, is good for the long-term sustainability of the organizations. Surplus earnings can help to build institutional capacity in nonprofit organizations, strengthening fundraising departments or administrative divisions devoted to monitoring and evaluation. The challenge for many nonprofit organizations is that the program funding that they depend on often prioritizes program delivery and leaves little room for the institutional capacity building that can sustain long-term operations (Boris et al. 2010).

Nonprofit organizations also must meet the needs of donors, members of their organizations, and the clients they serve. Donor organizations such as foundations generally pressure nonprofit organizations to professionalize by promoting operating procedures and reporting structures in consistent formats that align with funding objectives. While members and donors normally are committed to the mission of the nonprofit, they may have additional goals that must be met, for example, participation in decision making or delivery of the services. Efficiency is important, but more important is how effective the organization is in meeting its mission and whether it is conforming to the principles of the organization, such as fairness, or service to a particular population of citizens. Finally, the increasing reliance on user fees in nonprofit service delivery, as high as 24 percent from private sources in 2008, adds pressure for nonprofit organizations to respond to the populations they serve (National Center for Charitable Statistics 2012).

While it may seem that these sector definitions are fairly exact, there is overlap among the sectors in terms of functions, approaches, and interactions with the public. Figure 1.3 provides an illustration of the sector's roles and overlap.

While there are some roles that only the public sector performs (such as elections for public office, criminal trials, public health), other functions overlap the sectors. Thus, in the United States we have both publicly and privately operated utilities, as well as nonprofit cooperative utilities. Most housing is produced in the private sector, but we also have public housing authorities, and nonprofit

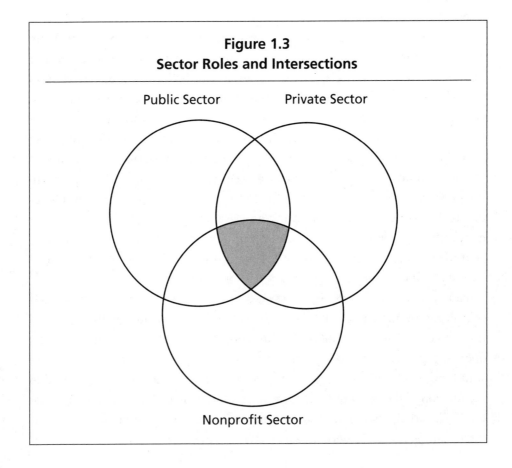

Figure 1.3
Sector Roles and Intersections

Public Sector   Private Sector

Nonprofit Sector

organizations are involved in producing or managing low-income housing. Most arts organizations are organized as nonprofits, but many entertainment activities of similar nature (e.g., Cirque du Soleil, Broadway shows) are operated for a profit. We have for-profit television and the nonprofit Public Broadcasting Service. Attempts to delineate some activities as "inherently governmental" or "for-profit only" have not been terribly successful, as we examine more closely in chapter 3.

EMERGING CHOICES FOR PUBLIC MANAGERS

As the nature and extent of the public enterprise have changed, so have the choices available to public managers. We no longer automatically assume that if government has a role, that role must include public production and provision. Choices for public managers are a continuum, from full public production and provision to full privatization (and regulation) of the function, with a variety of arrangements in between. Figure 1.4 displays that continuum of choices. The choices between total public provision and full privatization are examples of CSC where government engages either or both the private and nonprofit sector in the provision and delivery of public goods and services.

There are advantages and disadvantages with each choice for public managers. As we move to the right on the continuum, government gives up some control over the good or service produced; CSC involves creating more autonomy for the actors, with full private provision removing government altogether from the provision equation. At the same time, in moving across the continuum, public managers are involving more actors, often creating a more innovative environment. In partnership and network arrangements, private and nonprofit

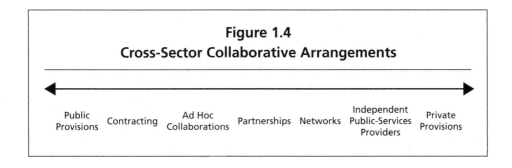

Figure 1.4
Cross-Sector Collaborative Arrangements

| Public Provisions | Contracting | Ad Hoc Collaborations | Partnerships | Networks | Independent Public-Services Providers | Private Provisions |

actors are not treated as agents of government but as principals deserving of a voice in production decisions.

While these terms and choices of CSC seem discrete, in actuality there is often a blurring of distinctions, with public programs provided through a variety of these frameworks, including a number of hybrid arrangements. Furthermore, book and journal authors sometimes use the terms loosely or use analogous terms, adding to the confusion for public managers. For example, partnerships and contracting out might be viewed as a type of collaboration or even types of privatization. Partnerships are sometimes referred to as public-private partnerships (PPPs or P3s). Privatization is sometimes partial, as when part of a function is devolved to the private sector, or might be complete, as when government sells off a state-owned enterprise.

As the world becomes more complicated and problems become more challenging, public officials and managers need choices to engage other organizations outside government in the delivery of public services. Those choices need to be innovative and more flexible than the conventional approaches, such as direct provision by government or contracting out. The creation of new methods of public service delivery gives public managers a choice among a variety of policy and delivery tools (Salamon 2002).

CONSIDERING THE CHOICES

Public managers currently can select from these seven choices for delivering public goods and services:

- Direct government provision
- Contracting out
- Ad hoc collaborations
- Partnerships and public-private partnerships
- Networks
- Independent public-services providers
- Private provision or privatization

Excluded from significant discussion in this book are two of the possibilities that are first discussed briefly. The first is the ad hoc collaborations that periodically occur when government calls on the private or nonprofit sector to assist in a temporary project or emergency (Donahue and Zeckhauser 2011); the second is private provision or privatization, where government essentially vacates a policy or public delivery area, allowing the private or nonprofit sectors to provide those particular goods and services (Savas 2000).

• *Ad hoc collaboration.* Public officials invite private or nonprofit actors to participate in some public project or program, or those sectors might volunteer to participate. An example might be the creation of a new local park, where the public sector provides the land and certain basic infrastructure and private or nonprofit collaborators voluntarily provide certain amenities, such as sports fields, music forums, and other enhancements. While these arrangements pose interesting questions, such as transparency and private influence (Donahue and Zeckhauser 2011), they do not involve the ongoing interactions that are the hallmark of the CSCs discussed in this book, which raise the most significant challenges for public managers.

• *Privatization (private provision).* Government exits a particular function in whole or part, allowing that function to be performed, if at all, by private and nonprofit sector actors. Government no longer owns or supervises the function except through regulations or taxation. An example is the sale of state-owned enterprises, such as occurred in Britain under Margaret Thatcher, when utilities, housing, airline companies, and other public assets were sold to the private sector. This option is largely a political decision to lessen the role of the public sector in the nation's economy. Although it is important in nations with a significant number of state-owned enterprises, it is not an option that most public managers will address or influence.

Primary Choices for Public Provision and Cross-Sector Collaboration

This section briefly describes and discusses the five choices representing the primary options available to public managers, ranging from the most traditional, direct government provision, to the latest incarnation of CSC, IPSPs. We do not claim that these five options cover all possibilities, but they represent basic models public managers may use, each with basic characteristics, differences, expectations, tensions, and implications.

Direct Government Provision Public officials develop a program and assign it to an agency or create an agency to deliver it. The program is therefore delivered primarily through public sector workers directly to citizens eligible for the program. Direct provision of public services by the government continues to be the mainstay for many government functions. Examples include government agency inspectors, such as food safety, and environmental regulation compliance; state and local safety and security functions, such as police, fire, and medical emergency; recreation and park services; water and water treatment; and public education (Bowman and Kearney 2011).

Contracting Out   Public officials determine that some or all of a public function could be provided at less cost by private or nonprofit actors. The public sector defines the parameters of the good or service, and the contractor provides the service based on those parameters. Examples of public contracting include such simple necessities as office supplies to very complex products such as the development and construction of major defense systems. Contracting out also has become more common in areas that used to be considered (and in some circles remain) the exclusive domain of government (Verkuil 2007). For example, some state department of motor vehicle functions are contracted out, and the Transportation Security Administration contracts out some security screening at sixteen US airports, the largest being San Francisco International Airport.[2] Contracting out is the topic of chapter 3.

Partnerships   Public officials engage a private sector organization or a nonprofit organization in the joint production of public goods and services where certain aspects of the production and provision are shared, such as planning, design specifications, risk, and financing. In a partnership, the public manager is working primarily with one other party. However, the variations in the types and forms of partnerships are numerous (Wettenhall 2003). Growing in popularity are partnerships involving infrastructure projects, where the private sector might agree to fund, build, own, and operate a facility for some period of time in exchange for a return on its investment—paid by either users or by the government. Partnerships and PPPs are discussed in chapter 4.

Networks   Public managers use "formal and informal structures, composed of representatives from governmental and nongovernmental agencies working interdependently to exchange information and/or jointly formulate and implement policies that are usually designed for action through their respective organizations" (Agranoff 2003, 7). The difference between a partnership and a network is the number of actors: networks involve the public sector with more than one other actor from the private or nonprofit sector. Many human services programs are operated through networks that include a variety of governmental and non-governmental organizations. Networks are a new and curious configuration of governance for most public managers and are organized in a variety of forms (Koliba, Meek, and Azia 2011) that are discussed in more detail in chapter 5.

Independent Public-Services Providers An emergent type of collaboration is the IPSP, a term we are using to describe entirely new entities that are attempting to meet unfulfilled public needs. Nonprofit and for-profit actors jointly develop an organization or framework to address public problems outside the traditional hierarchical structure in government. IPSPs are formed through a collaboration of principal actors; they are not agents of government.

Independent public-services providers are self-directed entities composed of businesses, nonprofit organizations, and governmental units that collaborate in the production or delivery of public goods or services but operate outside the sphere of government control and oversight. Increasingly they are being established out of a recognition that governments have become unable to respond adequately to serious public policy challenges. While individual characteristics of IPSPs may be familiar, it is their combined characteristics that make them singular and allow them to have a unique relationship with the government. We believe these are the most significant characteristics:

- They are largely self-directed and are able to act independently of government.
- They comprise multiple stakeholders who provide the organization a sense of legitimacy.
- They provide public goods and services, acting in place of government.

Consider these three diverse examples of IPSPs:

- *Bill and Melinda Gates Foundation: The Family Homelessness Project* (2013) consists of a network of public and private partners to address the long-term needs of homeless children and families in the Puget Sound region.
- *AidMatrix* (2013) helps coordinate humanitarian relief among more than forty thousand business, nonprofit, and government partners. It provides web-based, supply chain solutions that work in the harshest field conditions.

- The *Global Network for Neglected Tropical Diseases* (2013), an initiative of the US-based Sabin Vaccine Institute, works with international partners to break down the logistical and financial barriers to delivering existing treatments to the people who need them most.

Each of these IPSPs is distinctive in its mission, approach to solving problems, and relationship with its partners. In contrast to government employees and contractors, always enmeshed in the government hierarchy, IPSPs are sometimes linked to a traditional government framework, for example, through funding, and at other times have no specific linkage to government. In either case they act with a greater discretion and autonomy because they are outside the governmental bureaucratic framework, even when the government is involved. Because of the autonomy of IPSPs, public managers do not have the same control that they might over other arrangements.

Illustrating the Five Choices: Public Health Programs

To briefly illustrate those choices, we examine a common public service: public health.

• *Direct governmental provision.* Governments directly provide health services through a variety of programs. The federal Veterans Health Administration operates hospitals and clinics for veterans, states or counties have hospitals for those with mental health disabilities, and many cities operate public hospitals. All of these are funded with public dollars and staffed by public employees with the expectation that direct public provision is less expensive than private health care or that direct provision is necessary to provide services to a population that otherwise would not be served.

• *Contracting out.* Governments have determined that certain public health functions can be contracted out to reduce the cost of service. Some city hospitals have been contracted out to a private provider that operates and manages them. In these cases, personnel might be a mix of public and private sector workers. In instances where the local government has sold the facility to a for-profit or nonprofit health care provider, the workers are private (although many would be former employees of the hospital and therefore former government workers). Government may contract for certain services, such as care of indigents or emergency room operations, where the private or nonprofit sector may not be able to recoup costs; in this case, government might pay based on service provided.

• *Partnerships.* Partnerships in the health care industry are common. They range from the use by the federal government of private providers in Medicare (for seniors aged sixty-five and over) to the use by states of various health maintenance organizations to provide services for those eligible for Medicaid (the federal-state program for low-income individuals). Partnerships typically occur because expertise and functionality exist in the private sector, so it makes sense to use the private sector in the delivery of these services instead of maintaining or developing a separate public capacity to provide the same services. Such partnerships often provide greater choices for the citizens served.

• *Networks.* Networks in health care are common. The Small Communities Environment Infrastructure Group (discussed in chapter 5) is an illustration of a consortium of public, private, and nonprofit organizations designed to assist local communities in the design and funding of clean water and wastewater programs. Networks allow the combining of expertise from a number of different sources and sectors to bring to bear on the problem at hand.

• *Independent public-services providers.* IPSPs are emerging in response to health care needs that are not being met by government programs. The Global Network for Neglected Tropical Diseases, discussed in more detail in chapter 6, is an example of a program funded and operated by a consortium of private and nonprofit organizations to fight tropical diseases that do not receive much attention from government programs.

Examining the Trade-Offs

There are advantages and disadvantages with each method of collaboration. For example, government has complete control when it defines, produces, and provides the public good or service (public provision). As we move to the right on the continuum, there is less government control as other actors become involved. At the extreme right is privatization or private provision, where government is completely removed from the provision equation and only indirectly controls, if at all, through the regulatory and taxation process. In giving up control, government may achieve other important objectives, including greater efficiency, more innovation, greater targeted service, and growth of the private sector. As we move to the right, government also must operate in a greater collaborative environment, and the intensity of the collaboration is likely to increase. Thus, as with many other choices, public managers may have to decide which competing interest or value is most important and then decide whether and how to use the various approaches.

As public servants move to the right on the continuum, they also are embracing multisector solutions that involve multiple organizations in a network of policy actors or implementers. This new environment involves collaboration and mutuality and is organized around a heterarchy, or web of actors in a variety of horizontal relationships that exist outside the traditional government hierarchy (Kettl 1997; Kee and Newcomer 2008). Instead of a public administration based on traditional hierarchical notions of accountability, public servants must negotiate agreements with actors over whom they may have less leverage or no direct control, but instead are connected through contractual or other arrangements in horizontal relationships that involve the development of reciprocal trust and mutual accountability. In heterarchical relationships, government must exercise control through contract monitoring, performance measurements, after-action reports, citizen engagement and feedback, or other means to ensure that their contractors, network partners, and others involved are performing in a manner that meets public expectations.

Finally, moving from direct provision and a traditional contracting arrangement to CSC means moving from the traditional principal-agent to a principal-principal relationship. In public provision, public servants are agents of elected policymakers (the principals), and in contracts, contractors are agents of public managers; both of these are traditional principal-agent relationships. In partnerships and networks, however, private and nonprofit actors are principals with their own goals and objectives, and negotiations become more nuanced and balanced. While there may be some agency involvement (e.g., in developing a contract), the nongovernmental actors traditionally have more control over how they operate, and the development of goals, objectives, and measurements is typically a joint activity, not one in which government dictates to its agent. Finally, with IPSPs, public managers are dealing with fully autonomous organizations over which they may have little leverage and or control.

Table 1.1 provides an illustration of additional characteristics among the four CSC methods in contrast to public provision.

The descriptions provided in table 1.1 make clear that choosing the best option is based on a variety of factors. The relationship to the government takes into account the role it will play in directing and controlling the public services being provided. Direct provision gives government maximum control. As we

Table 1.1

Characteristics of Approaches to Delivery of Public Goods and Services

Approach	Government Provision	Contracting Out (Traditional)	Partnerships/PPPs	Network	IPSP
General approach	Direct provision by government-employed workforce	Government hires private or nonprofit provider	Mutual production, usually under a defined agreement	Varied production by members of the network according to individual strengths	Production by an independent organization with significant discretion
Relationship to government	Government provides funding, defines process, and hires personnel.	Government writes the request for proposal and issues a contract based on defined criteria.	Government is a partner, with a specific role that may include funding, monitoring, or even joint production.	Government may be the network administrator or central coordinator; it may provide funding; or it may simply play a supplemental role.	No relationship, or government may play a secondary role; it may be a funder but is not the exclusive source of revenue and the IPSP is not totally dependent on government.
Relationship to citizens	Government provides direct contact and provision.	Contractor may provide the direct contact and provision.	Either or both partners interact with the public, depending on their agreement.	Diffused, multiple contacts from network partners.	IPSP provides direct contact and provision as needed.
Trust required among actors	Low: traditional checks and balances	Low: contract monitoring	Medium: frequent interaction among partners under legal parameters set by the agreement	High: multiple points of contact and working together; limited government oversight	High: multiple points of contact and working together without government oversight
Key issues or tension	Efficiency, capacity, and government failure	Contract design and monitoring	Public interest versus interests of partners; agreement on outcomes	Convergence of multiple interests and outcomes	Ability to influence outcomes and protect public interests

describe more fully in chapters 3 through 6, each of the other choices in sequence reduces government's ability to specify and dictate the services to be provided and requires a different approach by public managers with respect to leadership and accountability. The choice of using an IPSP means that governments will play only a secondary role in defining and directing what services are provided, how they are provided, and individuals' eligibility to receive them.

Choosing an approach has implications for the relationship of the service provided with citizens as well. Except when government directly provides the service, all the other choices involve some entity other than the government that provides services to citizens. Having the service provided by public employees may best ensure that government is responsive to its citizens. When someone else provides a service, direct accountability is reduced. This can raise questions and potential protests by people who do not want to deal with government contractors or others.

The third factor that relates to relationships is trust. IPSPs and networks require a high level of trust between government and their collaborators. Since government has less influence in networks and IPSPs over the specifics of the service delivery, it must have great confidence that collaborators will carry out activities as expected and in good faith. Partnerships and PPPs also require trust, but there generally are legal provisions within the partnership agreements to ensure that performance meets expectations. Trust is a minimal factor in traditional contracting out, as it is assumed vendors will present their capabilities honestly in their proposals and adhere to their contractual obligations. The contract itself will ensure compliance.

Each of the choices poses significant issues for public managers. Public managers are more familiar with the issues and tensions around government provision and traditional contracting out. However, as public managers seek to choose collaborative options, new issues and tensions arise. Can the public manager ensure an outcome in the public interest? Can the managers recognize the legitimate interests of their private and nonprofit collaborators and still effectively articulate an overriding public value or result that is the expected outcome of the collaboration?

Private and nonprofit organizations are capable and credible actors in the provision of public goods and services. When collaborating with government, they present to public managers an important option for improving the quality of such goods and services and citizens' access to them. Of course, governments have long made use of the capacities of business and the nonprofit sector to help achieve government policy and program goals and objectives, typically through specific contracts for the products and services that government needs or wants to deliver. However, the growth and popularity of arrangements such as partnerships/PPPs and networks suggest that they also are expanding collaborative mechanisms of choice.

Today public managers have many options, and partnerships/PPPs and networks can be found at all levels of government:

- Yuma Desert Proving Grounds is a unique partnership arrangement between General Motors (GM) and the US Army Enhanced Use Leasing (EUL) Program. The public-private partnership resulted in GM constructing a new proving ground on federal land. GM and the EUL share use of the facilities and jointly advance vehicle testing (National Council for Public-Private Partnerships 2009).

- Indiana Economic Development Council is a 501(c)(3) nonprofit organization that serves as a statewide economic development agency. Its membership consists of a network of all entities within the state that are involved in economic development, including representatives from all sectors (Agranoff 2003).

- Rainforest Alliance uses the power of the market to ensure profit for both business and local communities through a variety of partnership arrangements with governments and business. The alliance strives to conserve biodiversity while ensuring sustainable livelihoods (Rainforest Alliance 2013). It operates outside governmental structures and directly with business and other nonprofits.

- Drug Abuse Resistance Education, created in Los Angeles in 1983, is a network advocating substance abuse prevention. The program brings police officers into classrooms to deliver necessary skills to students to prevent drug use, gang involvement, and violence (Milward and Provan 2006).

- City of Dallas/Dallas Public Library is a developmental partnership agreement between the City of Dallas and the Kroger Company, which developed a library in a strip shopping center. Library attendance rose while more people were similarly brought to the neighboring grocery store as they both benefited from shared services (National Council for Public-Private Partnerships 1999).

- Global Alliance for Improved Nutrition (2011), created in 2002, is an independent public-services provider that supports public-private partnerships to increase the amount of nutrients in the diets of people around the world. It has already worked with more than six hundred companies in twenty-five countries, reaching an estimated four hundred million people.

As government solutions move away from programmatic silos toward structures that involve the public, nonprofit organizations, and the private sector, public managers need different management skills from those honed in traditional hierarchical structures. Although the exact shape and extent of the emerging heterarchy is not fully defined, it is evident that public managers are moving toward a networked or partnership approach to service delivery that involves organizations from all sectors. In such a heterarchy, "authority is determined by knowledge and function—through horizontal linkages rather than the traditional hierarchical form of vertical authority" (Kee and Newcomer 2008, 10). Sometimes these horizontal linkages are forged through contractual arrangements with government as chief funder and coordinator. At other times, public managers must negotiate with entities over which they have little control.

CONCLUSION

Public managers have several choices in the way in which public services may be delivered. However, they face constraints as well: budgetary, legal, and political. As innovative forms of CSC have emerged to join the more familiar modes of direct provision and contracting out, it is critical that public managers understand how to choose among these options to provide the best public services possible.

In some ways, these five primary choices can be viewed as evolutionary and a reflection of broader efforts by practitioners, scholars, and public managers to innovate as new challenges present themselves and conventional public service delivery choices prove to be inadequate. The expanding number of issues public managers are trying to address, the complexity of both the problems and possible solutions, the limitations of available public funding, and the rapid pace of change have all motivated those inside and outside government to discover and invent more effective ways of providing public services and of providing those services in a way that is more responsive to people's preferences and circumstances.

An overview of the steady evolution of the five public service choices and their presumed advantages and potential disadvantages is provided in table 1.2 and will be discussed in more detail in succeeding chapters.

Deciding to contract out instead of directly providing services is based on a classic make-or-buy decision. It poses the basic question of whether it is better to rely primarily on the use of internal public resources to provide some goods or services (make) or rely on vendors outside the government (buy). While the services are intended to be the same, they are contracted out when they can be achieved more efficiently. However, contracting out results in some loss of control by government managers, and success is tied to how effectively the contract is written and monitored.

Table 1.2
Transition Through the Five Basic Options

	Capacity	Services	Presumed Advantages	Potential Disadvantages
From government to contracting out	Same capacity	Same services	Cheaper	Loss of control
From contracting out to partnership	Expanded capacity	Better services	Technical and management expertise	Capture by partner
From partnership to network	Expanded capacity	Responsive services	Technical and management expertise Local preference insights	Diffused accountability Difficult to gain consensus
From network to IPSP	Expanded capacity	Enhanced services	Technical and management expertise Local preference insights Innovative problem solving	Lack of government oversight Policies may conflict with government priorities

The need for additional capacity and access to greater technical and management expertise and access to capital has pushed governments to work in partnership with business, typically through various PPPs. Such partnerships are created to improve existing services or create new services that would be difficult for the public sector to manage alone. At the same time, private and nonprofit partners have different goals from government that must be reconciled. Private partners are primarily motivated by profit; thus the potential for capture by the private partner or excessive compensation must be addressed by the public manager.

PPPs often raise issues of fairness and whether a full representation of community interests has a voice in the PPP. When broader community expertise is needed, particularly information about local conditions and preferences, and when broader political support is sought, a network approach is useful and effective. Networks allow a variety of voices and multiple actors to address a public problem. But more actors also have a tendency to diffuse accountability. Managers must work to gain consensus on network objectives and measurements.

Finally, government may support an independent public-services provider when an entity exists that already is providing the services needed to solve a public problem. The independence of the IPSP can foster more creative and innovative problem solving. However, public managers often have limited oversight of IPSPs, and their independent nature may lead to policy directions that are contrary to existing government policy.

The five options offer public managers different approaches to delivering public services. Each of these approaches offers unique advantages but also places different expectations on the collaborators and different requirements for public managers to ensure success. Using these five options in a way that promotes the efficient and innovative delivery of public services means public managers must understand how to align public service delivery with the best option.

Some of these options are relatively new to public managers, or they may have limited experience in knowing how to use them successfully. This book is designed to encourage public managers to consider innovative options that could be beneficial in the public interest. The following chapters describe these choices in more detail, examining what they are, how they are different from the other choices, and their advantages and disadvantages. Public managers must learn how to analyze these tools effectively and under the right circumstances if they are to improve public service delivery.

Case Study for Discussion: State Employment Training

You are an assistant to the executive director of the Department of Social Services (DSS). The governor has campaigned on increasing job training in the state and moving individuals from receiving state welfare payments to working. Currently the Division of Employment Training (DET) (within DSS) provides that service; however, the governor and the state legislature are unhappy with the current results. At an annual cost of $20 million, DET has found work for only a fraction of those on welfare. The program is operated out of twenty local offices, and the current annual success rate is less than 10 percent of the 500,000 adult recipients on welfare placed in a job. Welfare payments cost the state over $2 billion a year (averaging about $4,200 a person per year plus administrative costs of program administration).

Questions and Issues for Consideration

1. Many states have job training programs; other states use private or nonprofit providers as part of their job training programs. What are the advantages and disadvantages of state provision versus provision through some type of cross-sector collaboration?

2. Does government have any special expertise for public provision?

3. What are the characteristics of the private and nonprofit sector that might argue for collaboration with government?

Note: This case will be continued in most of the following chapters addressing the specific topic issue.

The Rationale for Cross-Sector Collaboration

I n *Shrinking the State* (1998), Feigenbaum, Henig, and Hamnett classified rationales for approaches to privatization under three broad categories: pragmatic,
tactical, and strategic. This chapter outlines a similar set of rationales for why
public, nonprofit, and private sector managers might want to engage in cross-
sector collaboration (CSC). The three rationales are pragmatic, economic, and
strategic. Thus, some CSCs occur for very pragmatic reasons—perhaps a public
problem or service delivery issue that cannot be easily solved by one sector, so
finding collaborators in another sector makes sense. There also are some sound
economic reasons for CSC that revolve around the concept of comparative
advantage: some sectors are better able to address certain problems or deliver
certain services because that sector may have the skills, market know-how,
capabilities, or contacts necessary to do so. Finally, increasingly all sectors are
examining how CSC might address the long-term success of their organizations
and are beginning to address this issue in a more strategic fashion.

The chapter also examines a key governance pivot that occurs in CSC and
the implications of that shift. Most traditional government interactions with the
private and nonprofit sectors are characterized by a principal-agent relationship. Government defines what it wants out of the relationship and then designs
mechanisms to achieve that result, typically through a contract, a tax incentive, or imposition of regulations. In CSC, however, government moves from a
principal-agent relationship to a principal-principal relationship. While this
may occur for a number of pragmatic reasons, the effect is strategic, as other
sectors become partners with government in the delivery of government goods
and services. The consequences of this governance shift are profound. Sharing

power, decision making, and risk with private or nonprofit organizations creates a risk-reward governance environment. The potential rewards, such as bringing innovation and expertise to a public problem, are significant, but risks of this approach are also real, including capture by private or nonprofit interests, loss of control, and failure of democratic accountability.

PRAGMATIC RATIONALE

Salamon (2002) represents the pragmatic viewpoint. He examines the new array of methods for government to deliver public goods and services and refers to a variety of CSCs—contracts, partnerships, networks, and other approaches—as simply different possibilities in a toolbox of government options. In this view, governments are increasingly facing new challenges and entering new policy arenas where they are required to provide services but often lack sufficient resources or staff to respond completely to the new requirements or mandates. They may find that expertise and resources are available in other sectors.

Consider the case of communities affected by a large-scale natural disaster. In the immediate aftermath of Hurricane Katrina, the Federal Emergency Management Agency (FEMA) struggled with the logistical demands of coordinating supply chains in service delivery for such a large-scale disaster. In contrast, Walmart was able to step into the void and provide basic food and hygiene articles to citizens displaced by the storm.[1] Thus, it makes sense for FEMA to partner with organizations such as Walmart or Home Depot that have the capabilities to deliver the necessary supplies in an emergency. This is one major pragmatic reason behind the expansion of CSC; the expansive nature of these problems makes a solution without collaboration more difficult.

The complexity of social problems that public administrators must deal with now also demands new approaches to leading across public and private sectors and across multiple levels of government (Kettl 2006). Many of the issues facing government administration today cross the jurisdictional boundaries of state and local governments and often involve both the federal government and other sectors. For example, a social problem like childhood obesity is multifaceted and might be addressed by all sectors. The Centers for Disease Control (2013) estimates that 17 percent of children aged two to nineteen in the United States are obese. Making matters worse, the scale and scope of obesity has been increasing dramatically over the past thirty years, although a recent study found a reduction in obesity in children ages two to five, pointing to better nutrition and increased physical activity (Centers for Disease Control 2014). Any program directed at this problem inevitably draws heavily on local government and local school districts. Yet a wide spectrum of nonprofit providers also serves youths; corporations donate resources and time to youth causes as part of their corporate social responsibility efforts, and federal-level authorities have taken an interest in the issue, as evidenced by First Lady Michelle Obama's Let's Move campaign.

Problems like childhood obesity are wicked in the sense that they are difficult or impossible to solve because of their complexity, which often involves incomplete, contradictory, and changing requirements that can be difficult to recognize (Weber and Khademian 2008; Rittel and Webber 1973). Any effort at developing a solution is ongoing and iterative as responses to one aspect may reveal other problems. The various stakeholders in any kind of problem-solving effort are likely to view the issue in different ways. In the case of childhood obesity, these factors actually favor collaboration because we are still coming to terms with what this health condition means. Involving more collaborators may lead to innovative solutions to address this kind of emerging social problem. One such organization is the State of Washington's Childhood Obesity Prevention Coalition, a coalition of organizations—public, private, and nonprofit—working to improve Washington's overall environment so children can live a healthy, active lifestyle. Among collaborative approaches, they advocate for shared-use agreements between public and private or nonprofit organizations to provide space for after-school activities and provide a detailed tool kit for interested organizations (Childhood Obesity Prevention Coalition 2014).

Other complex, interdependent problems are apparent across other policy sectors in the United States, such as homeland security and emergency management, which include examples such as Hurricanes Katrina and Sandy and the Boston Marathon bombing. The BP Oil Spill provides another illustration of the need to address problems in a multisector framework. In these and similar cases, public leaders face emerging problems with very little precedence for how to adequately address them and a growing recognition that they are dependent on interorganizational structures for solutions—both within the governmental sector and across sectors. Organizations may not have worked together before and are often thrown together without adequate training and experience in collaboration.

On April 20, 2010, an explosion occurred on the Deepwater Horizon oil rig, killing eleven workers and releasing up to 228 million gallons of oil near the Gulf Coast. The long-term impact to fish and wildlife remaining in the area remains uncertain, but thousands of species were harmed. Responding to the crisis as it unfolded required coordination across all of the states bordering the coast, local government officials, and numerous federal agencies. Hundreds of public, private, and nonprofit entities responded to the disaster. British Petroleum estimated the full cost of the spill at over $40 billion.

Source: National Commission on the BP Deepwater Horizon Oil Spill and Offshore Drilling (2011).

PRIVATE AND NONPROFIT PERSPECTIVES

As we noted in chapter 1, the private and nonprofit sectors might want to collaborate with government for a variety of pragmatic reasons. For the private sector, government contracts or public-private partnerships provide additional revenue possibilities. Although the profit margins working with government are often less than other potential customers, there usually is less risk, and governments can provide a steady stream of revenue to complement other riskier (and potentially more lucrative) business opportunities.

More recently, we have begun to see business characterized as potential partners and collaborators with governments, nonprofits, and social entrepreneurs. Cast in this role, business is viewed as a positive actor that contributes to solving social problems, redressing or avoiding damage to the environment, and developing innovative solutions to persistent problems such as global poverty. Such portrayals reflect a dramatic change in how businesses are perceived and their impact on society (Nelson 2005).

This view is in stark contrast to a more conventional view of business presented by public management textbooks and frequently assumed in public policy analyses: businesses are fundamentally profit seeking—more succinctly, the business of business is business.[2] Of course, not all businesses are enlightened; many do take a narrow and self-serving view of their social responsibilities. However, more and more businesses are coming to believe that participating in collaborations with governments and nonprofits can be beneficial (Chandler and Werther 2014). A good illustration of this is private sector collaboration with government in emergency management situations, providing food, water, and other essential supplies. While often ad hoc, such collaborations provide goodwill that enhances employee and customer feelings about the company, which ultimately benefits the company in terms of new customers and less employee turnover.

For the nonprofit sector, collaborating with government is often essential for the organization to operate. Many nonprofits rely on funding, at least to some extent, from grants, contracts, or other forms of collaboration with the government. This provides revenue to nonprofits and assists them in fulfilling their mission. In addition, sometimes the nonprofit will be successful in a particular area and may see collaborating with government as a way to expand its mission to related areas of concern to its members, including employees and donors.

ECONOMIC RATIONALE: COMPETITIVE ADVANTAGE

As we noted in chapter 1, political support for government spending on public services, especially federal government spending, has declined, and arguments that the private sector and nonprofit organizations could do a better job than the government have become more popular (Sclar 2000). Academics such as Buchanan and Wagner (1977) supported this viewpoint, as did proponents of New Public Management (Osborne and Gaebler 1993; Pollitt and Bouckaert 2011). Underlying this argument is a set of economic ideas concerning the competitive advantage that the private (or nonprofit sector) may have over government. This notion gained force with conservative political leaders in the United States in the 1980s and is sometimes referred to as a neoliberal perspective. Neoliberalism is a political and economic philosophy whose advocates support economic liberalization, free trade and open markets, privatization, deregulation, and decreasing the size of the public sector while increasing the role of the private sector. This economic argument largely rests on the theory that, in general, private markets are often superior to public sector action in allocating resources.

Market Failure and Government Failure

Proponents of neoliberalism concede that sometimes markets fail, and market failure is a justification for government intervention in the economy. Market failure occurs when the private sector's pursuit of its own interests leads to an allocation of resources that is not considered efficient. Examples of market failure include public goods (goods that are nontrivial and nonexcludable and therefore cannot be produced by the private sector at a profit), externalities (positive or negative spillovers that may distort the price of a good—for example, not considering the costs of pollution when producing a private good), and information "asymmetry," where consumers do not have sufficient information to judge the value and efficacy of a private good (e.g., the safety of drugs). Market failure provides a rationale for government intervention, which might occur in many forms: public provision (national defense), regulation (amounts of allowable pollution), subsidy (certain health care programs), and prohibition (unsafe products).

At the same time, neoliberals and some other economists argue that governments also often fail to achieve their objectives. Governments may be inefficient for a number of reasons. They may be unable to overcome bureaucratic limitations to find an innovative solution to emerging public problems. They may fail because political leaders have conflicting goals and objectives for a government program, providing mixed signals to public managers and employees working on those programs. They may fail because even "benevolent" public managers and employees have weak incentives to invest in cost reduction or quality improvements because they are not owners and gain only a fraction of a return on their efforts. In addition, governments may fail because elected officials cannot always ensure that public managers will perform efficiently or to their maximum ability.

In an influential paper, Wolf (1978) provided a theory of nonmarket failure—the idea that individuals and institutions constituting the government often fail to achieve the results that policymakers seek when developing public programs. Some of the reasons he cited included the difficulty of describing the desired output or outcome of government programs; the inability to measure the quality of government goods and services; the lack of competition in government provision, leading to problems of monopolistic services; and reward structures that do not favor efficient resolution of problems. While nonmarket (or government) failure does not necessarily imply that government should never act, it does provide a cautionary framework suggesting that citizens may not always achieve a desired outcome from government provision of goods and services. Thus, in terms of CSC, it suggests the possible advantages of using the private or nonprofit sectors in achieving government objectives rather than a government-only approach.

Property Rights Theory

Property rights theory (or ownership theory) explores how various ownership structures affect incentives and behaviors of employees (Demsetz 1967; Hoffman et al. 1994). The two most common types of ownership are private ownership and public ownership. Private owners are able to transfer (or sell) their rights to another party; because of this, it is argued, private ownership leads to a more efficient allocation of resources and a superior incentive system for employees. The principal feature of this argument is that private ownership of resources will be concentrated on individuals who have a comparative advantage because of their knowledge, resources, or superior management ability. They are better able to prevent "employee shirking" because of their intense interest in productivity and making a profit from their ownership.

In contrast, government ownership is diffused. We all "own" our governments—federal, state, and local—but our individual interests are not strong enough to demand an efficient allocation of resources by the government. Tiebout (1956) theorized that people vote with their feet and will locate in a jurisdiction that best meets their willingness to pay taxes and desire for services. Tiebout's theory has significant limitations, including the lack of mobility for some taxpayers and incomplete information on the fiscal circumstances and productivity of various governmental jurisdictions where people might reside.

Property rights theory, however, has limitations. Often the management of a private firm is separate from ownership (corporate officers versus stockholders) and management may have its own interests, such as larger salaries and bonuses, which may end up diverting a portion of the owners' profits to the managers' own ends. Private ownership itself may be diffused, especially in large corporations, with individual stock owners having limited interest in monitoring corporate efficiency. Stockholders do of course monitor stock prices and dividends, one indirect indication of whether a firm is using its resources efficiently.

The Principal-Agent Problem

The principal-agent problem, or agency dilemma, concerns the difficulty of ascertaining whether an agent is acting in the best interests of a principal rather than in the agent's own interests. Most private firms and all governments are characterized by the separation of ownership and management. This results in an agency situation, where the owners (the principals) delegate the work to others (the agents). The principal-agent problem is centered on the issue of how or whether the principals can ensure that the agents carry on the work in an efficient manner that will maximize gains for the principals. The two major issues with the principal-agent problem are asymmetrical information and diverging goals and objectives. Because the agents are closest to the customers or clients and the public issue or the problem, they are much more likely to know whether they are responding to that customer or client or to that issue or problem in a cost-efficient manner. Agents also may hide information for their own purposes or may have their own goals and objectives, such as shorter work hours, higher pay, and bigger budgets, which may run counter to the interests of the principal. This last argument is at the core of the public choice school of economics, whose scholars argue that it is in the public managers' or employees' best interest to maximize the agency's budget, not to find the most cost-effective solution (Downs 1967; Niskansen 1971).

In order to solve the principal-agent problem, principals attempt to design mechanisms and incentive structures that both monitor and encourage behavior that is in the interests of the principals. Because of extensive employee protections and limited incentive structures in the public sector, many argue that it is difficult, if not impossible, to overcome the principal-agent problem in government. The private sector, it is argued, has more tools for owners or principals to induce their agents to work toward efficient outcomes. But again there are limitations to that justification. Many public employees join government because of their commitment to some public cause or activity and thus may be motivated in the public interest beyond their own self-interest. In addition, the asymmetry of information can be a problem in both the public and private sectors. Private agents may find that it is in their interests to hide information to maximize their own self-interest within the firm.

An additional issue in principal-agent relationships stems from transaction costs. In order to get the agent to conform to the principal's objectives, the principals have to design employment contracts or provide other incentives to ensure compliance with the intent of the principals. This is one reason that some nations, such as New Zealand, have moved toward performance contracts with their top public managers: managers are rewarded based on achieving predefined goals or outcomes. The design of such contracts is not simple and does not necessarily ensure best efforts. If a public manager is to be judged based on performance, it would be in his or her best interest to set the performance targets as low as possible, and because the public manager may have more information on what is possible, the principals (elected officials) may not know enough to set the performance bar high enough. In contrast, private principals and agents may have a stronger incentive to reduce costs and raise quality because agents are more likely to achieve personal gains that they view as significant and worth their effort. Agents may receive bonuses, pay increases, promotions, profit sharing, stock options, or other personal gains that reward them for innovative and efficient behavior.

Competition

Classic microeconomic theory also stresses the role of competition in achieving allocation efficiency. Competition is prevalent in the private sector and to some extent in the nonprofit sector, but virtually nonexistent in the public sector. Similar to the effects of property rights theory, competitive forces push prices toward their optimal marginal costs, thereby allocating resources to their highest value. Weak firms with poor management or that lack innovation will find their products are noncompetitive. They either will go out of business or be bought by others who believe they can operate the firm more efficiently.

Public sector provision is essentially monopolistic. Government decides what it will provide and typically has a one-size-fits-all attitude toward their clients/citizens/taxpayers. It is true that citizens can vote their elected officials out of office and vote in a new group of officials whom they hope will be more responsive to their needs. Elections, however, except perhaps at the local level of government, are seldom about the efficient operation of government programs. Elections are more likely to be about ideological policy disputes, such as national health care, or referenda on the likability of the candidates.

While competition is a compelling force in achieving efficiencies and innovation, public managers cannot always ensure that this will occur with collaborations with the private or nonprofit sectors. A classic problem in collaborations with defense contractors (through contracts or partnerships) is the oligopolistic nature of the defense industry. Replacing a public monopoly with a private monopoly will not achieve the desired competitive environment. Similarly, governments may reach out to nonprofits for their local knowledge or experience with a given clientele. However, since there may be few nonprofits working in a particular area, competitive forces are unlikely to exist.

The Nonprofit Competitive Advantage

Nonprofit service delivery organizations also may have a competitive advantage in addressing specific social needs that may not be covered by government.

The public sector is under pressure to provide social programs that meet the needs of the "median voter," or the dominant coalition influencing legislation (Steinberg 2006). Because of this, the interests of specific minorities may not receive specialized attention from the government. Nonprofits fill in this role by offering smaller coalitions the opportunity to mobilize resources for causes they deem important. In this way, nonprofits have the potential to address social needs that may be overlooked or underresourced by the government.

The reliance on private donations and, in many cases, fees for services in the nonprofit sectors also creates more opportunities for constituents with a direct interest in a given set of goods or services to devote their own resources to those programs. While there is contention over the extent to which nonprofits serve the needs of their donors or exhibit "downward accountability" to those receiving their services (Baur and Schmitz 2012), the very nature of nonprofit governance brings attention to their constituents in ways different from their private sector counterparts. For-profit firms are governed by shareholders who prioritize the generation of profits and influence organizational behavior with that goal in mind. Nonprofits are governed by a board of directors who generally share a commitment to the social or cultural needs that the organization is working toward (Steinberg 2006). The implication for government leaders is that the existing social commitments of human service nonprofits may argue for creating a collaborative relationship that directly aligns the nonprofit actions with government priorities. This also is true for other nonprofit actors in other areas, such as protecting the environment, where nonprofit goals align with government policies and priorities.

A STRATEGIC APPROACH TO CSC

Increasingly all three sectors—public, private, and nonprofit—are striving to move beyond ad hoc or pragmatic forms of collaboration to more strategic approaches that have the potential to significantly assist organizations and managers from all sectors. *Strategic collaboration* has been defined as "an intentional, collective approach to address public problems or issues through building shared knowledge, designing innovative solutions and forging consequential change" (Norris-Tirrell and Clay 2010, 2).

The increasing prevalence of collaboration across levels of government and sectors suggests important strategic objectives to such collaborations. Norris-Tirrell and Clay (2010) categorize those strategic objectives under three major areas of impact:

- *Deliverables and outcomes:* This might include enhancing operations, attaining goals, or achieving better overall results.

- *Increased capacity and competence:* This might result in greater capacity for individuals, the organization, or the community.

- *New resources and opportunities:* This might lead to new funding opportunities for new markets or program areas and the potential for further cross-sector collaboration.

In viewing CSC as a strategic rather than a pragmatic or economic choice, managers can see collaboration as part of their overall organizational strategy that could help them to better meet organizational needs.

Strategic Considerations for the Private Sector

Businesses have long used strategic alliances to improve their competitiveness and advance their own strategic goals (Uddin and Akhter 2011). Strategic alliance success requires cooperative behavior from all partners. More specifically, alliance success depends on several factors, such as active involvement of all parties in problem solution, building trust, creating value by combining partner resources and capabilities, and cooperating in and coordinating activities to promote compatible organizational behavior (Mowla 2012). Large and fast-growing enterprises such as Microsoft, Philips, and Unilever rely heavily on alliances to support their growth strategy. The data clearly show that companies are becoming more and more dependent on strategic alliances to sustain global competitiveness (Kale and Singh 2007; Kanter 1994; Steensma et al. 2005). Collaborations with governments and nonprofits have become a logical extension of this experience, and firms seek out such collaborations with the same goals as they do in other strategic alliances: increased competitiveness.

Corporate Social Responsibility   Corporate social responsibility (CSR) is a concept supporting the idea that businesses should act in a way that contributes to society and its inhabitants. The principal assertion is that business has an obligation to take actions that have a positive effect on the communities where they operate. This may require that businesses forgo full profit maximization in order to uphold their responsibilities to society. Optimally a firm can achieve both its CSR obligations and maximize profits (Baron 2013). Among the reasons given to firms that it is a good idea to be active in CSR activities include these (Lawrence and Weber 2014):

- Bolsters business reputation
- Improves stakeholder relationships
- Promotes long-term profits
- Discourages government regulations

CSR activities can take many forms: encouraging employees to develop and implement local community projects (IBM); reducing the firm's carbon footprint through energy efficiency practices and addressing climate change (Walmart); reducing water use through recycling and replenishing water sources in developing countries with water shortages (Coke); and using recycled products that comprise 85 percent of materials used in automobiles to take pressure off landfills (Ford). These and other CSR activities can be controversial because such programs generate benefits for the firms as well as society. Some view such programs as self-serving for the firms since the efforts may be carried out only to improve the reputation of the company among potential customers; others, however, see them as simply good business that fits into the company's overall mission (Baron 2013).

Shared Value   Beyond CSR, Porter and Kramer (2011) argue that businesses can advance their strategic business goals and create social value at the same time. The central premise behind creating shared value is the mutual dependence of the competitiveness of a company on the health of local communities near its locations. Recognizing these connections between economic and social progress and business competitiveness has the potential to stimulate local and global growth.

Companies can create shared value opportunities in three ways (Porter and Kramer 2011):

1. *Reconceiving products and markets.* Companies can meet social needs while better serving existing markets, accessing new ones, or lowering costs through innovation.

2. *Redefining productivity in the value chain.* Companies can improve the quality, quantity, cost, and reliability of inputs and distribution while

simultaneously acting as a steward for essential natural resources and driving economic and social development.

3. *Enabling local cluster development.* Companies do not operate in isolation from their surroundings and can assist their communities. To compete and thrive, for example, they need reliable local suppliers, a functioning infrastructure of roads and telecommunications, access to talent, and an effective and predictable legal system.

Standard approaches to CSR can be seen as a cost of doing business, with concerns over program costs and the loss of potential profits. Creating shared value acknowledges the trade-offs between short-term profitability and social or environmental goals. However, it also emphasizes the opportunities for competitive advantage that can come from building a social value proposition into a broader corporate strategy. The increasing numbers of companies that are incorporating CSR imply that many private sector organizations (particularly potential partners for government) do not care about profit alone; they may also have social objectives underlying their overall strategy. Given such changing attitudes, there are more opportunities for governments to participate in cross-sector collaboration that can advance public and private interests in ways that are not only compatible but also mutually reinforcing.

Strategic Perspectives of the Public and Nonprofit Sectors

Just as private sector organizations are beginning to think of CSC as a strategic initiative, the same dynamic is beginning to occur in the public and nonprofit sectors. While most public and nonprofit managers currently view CSC as a pragmatic approach to leverage resources and expertise to address particular problems, some managers are trying to be more proactive, seeing CSC as a fundamental part of their organizational strategy.

To assist public and nonprofit managers, Norris-Tirrell and Clay (2010) identify a five-step process or "life-cycle of collaboration" critical for strategic implementation of CSC:

1. *Exploration:* Setting the stage for strategic collaboration

2. *Formation and implementation:* Shaping the strategic collaboration

3. *Growth and evaluation:* Strengthening the collaboration

4. *Maturity:* Achieving results, achieving shared value, making a difference

5. *Endings or renewal:* Letting go when you have achieved your objectives or renewing the collaboration with existing or new partners

While a triggering factor in CSC may be some event or crisis, such as a loss of funding, a new state or federal mandate, or a natural disaster, public and non-profit managers might effectively use that event or crisis as a basis for considering CSC as a strategy for the long-term success of the organization.

The process of strategic thinking about CSC is applicable to all sectors, with some differences. The private sector begins the process by thinking about how to create shared value or become more competitive through corporate social responsibility as ways of boosting the organization's bottom line. The nonprofit sector begins by thinking about how it can leverage its resources, stabilize its fiscal environment, and expand its impact on behalf of its constituencies or its members. Thus, it is clear that the motives of private organizations will differ from those of nonprofit organizations. Nonetheless, CSC can both improve the financials of for-profit and nonprofit organizations and at the same time create value for the general public, improving the capability of both public and nonprofit organizations to meet their public missions.

The public sector necessarily starts with the question of what is in the public interest. While public managers may find that they must collaborate to be successful, they may be limited in terms of the types of collaborations that are possible. However, by exploring options with private and nonprofit organizations, public managers may find new approaches to better achieve the results the public desires. The evolving nature of many companies' approaches to CSR, and the overall social orientation of many nonprofits, suggests there are many areas of full convergence among public, private, and nonprofit organizations for working together collaboratively.

Whether collaborative results or outcomes meet the diverging objectives of private or nonprofit organizations is not the critical issue for the public manager as long as the collective results are in the public interest. Thus, it does not matter if different organizations are engaging in a CSC for different reasons (such as a private firm pursuing profits on a toll road or a nonprofit youth services organization serving a particular demographic in the community) as long as the overall effect of the effort improves collective social value. Collaborations will not last long unless the needs of all organizations are met, and much of the work of the public administrator in a CSC is to understand what those different needs are and how individualized incentives need to be incorporated in order to serve the wider public interest.

FROM A PRINCIPAL-AGENT TO A PRINCIPAL-PRINCIPAL RELATIONSHIP

Overseeing the governance of CSCs is complicated because it draws the public sector into a relationship that portends more power sharing and more discretionary authority to nonstate actors. The significance of these two complementary governance conditions of public-private-nonprofit relationships can be better understood when considered in respect to the principal-agent problem.

Traditional public administration operates within the framework of principal-agent relationships. With government provision of services, public managers and their employees are agents of the elected officials (the principals) who establish policy through legislation and executive actions. Elected officials are themselves agents of the general electorate. There are some good reasons for this relationship: elected officials are responsible to the general electorate; public managers are responsible to the elected officials; public employees are responsible to the public managers. A clear line of democratic accountability provides affirmation to public administration scholars and the general public. There is a long-standing debate over the degree of discretion to give public managers and a concern that public managers might become too entrepreneurial (Moe 1994, 2001). However, there also is recognition that administrators—from the street level on up—in fact have a significant amount of discretion in the execution of policy (Lipsky 1980; Lynn 2006). That discretion is traditionally thought to exist within the scope of authorities delegated through vertical lines of accountability.

The Principal-Principal Relationship

Collaboration, whether in certain types of contracting, partnerships, networks, or IPSPs, changes the governance dynamics of principal-agent relationships as they are traditionally conceptualized in public administration. In many ways, collaboration involves interactions between two principals: the public manager (acting for government) and the collaborator—the entity or entities involved with the public manager in providing public goods and services. All parties to the relationship act more as principals since they each influence the terms of

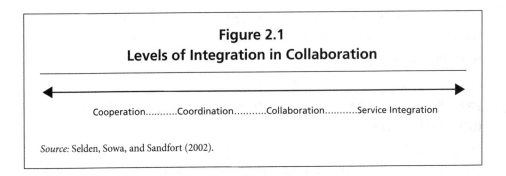

Figure 2.1
Levels of Integration in Collaboration

Cooperation..........Coordination..........Collaboration..........Service Integration

Source: Selden, Sowa, and Sandfort (2002).

the relationship. As a consequence, public sector organizations involved in collaborative efforts are more susceptible to the influence of stakeholders outside their traditional boundaries (Agranoff 2012), since nongovernmental actors weigh in on the content and conditions of the policies and programs jointly implemented.

The very nature of CSC is that there are varying levels of integration through which two or more parties agree to work together. The possibilities could be considered along a spectrum of options (Crosby and Bryson 2005), since in some agreements, members have very little influence over one another while in others they have more. Numerous factors affect the level of integration in collaborative structures, such as the depth of interaction or the overall level of cooperation. The extent of collaboration is conceptualized in figure 2.1.

In moving from coordination to collaboration, the actors accept a greater degree of mutual influence over how they will operate. Collaboration transforms the nature of a principal-agent model through the formalization of the relationship among public and nongovernmental entities and the sharing of power among parties in the relationship. In the most explicit structure of a principal-agent relationship (as in a traditional contract), a principal determines the most specific elements of an agent's behavior. These specifications of behavior are detailed in the terms of the agreement, offering more leverage for a supervising principal to correct the work of an associated agent. The reality of many forms of CSC is that the specification of expectations is left rather open-ended, with more room for the relations among the partners to the agreement rather than written rules to govern the collaboration. To varying degrees, personal relationships fill the void of formal role definitions, and informal understandings become more important than legal contracts to guide the communications and decision making among organizations in the collaboration (Gazley 2008). The less formalized the specifics of the agreement are, the more discretion each party is able to exercise in the collaboration and the more influence they have in determining what is produced.

The second characteristic that shapes the characteristics of CSC is related to the extent of relational governance: the amount of power sharing among the involved members (Donahue and Zeckhauser 2011; Huxham and Vangen 2005). In the most explicit form of principal-agent relations, a principal is assumed to have superior influence over the participating agent. In CSC, a single authority is replaced by a model of cogoverning (Agranoff 2012), a more reciprocal set of relations among the parties to the collaboration (Bryson, Crosby, and Stone 2006).

The extent that power is shared can be considered with respect to vertical and horizontal relationships. The former defines relations where one party holds more explicit, formal authority over the other, and the latter indicates relations where power is more evenly distributed among the parties. The horizontal linkage necessitates a different type of management skill and the ability to negotiate with other principals. Put in the context of public administration, the public manager remains democratically accountable in a vertical fashion to the elected officials (or other relevant stakeholders), as well as horizontally to the other organizations in the collaboration, which act not as agents of government but as principals with their own set of goals and objectives that must be blended with government objectives.

Taken together, these two characteristics, formalization and power sharing, can differentiate levels of integration achieved in various structures of CSC, displayed in table 2.1.

The more formalization there is, the greater the degree of control public managers are able to exert in the relationship. The more power sharing there is, the greater the potential is for innovative solutions, but the greater the necessity for public managers to engage in nontraditional communications and negotiations with the collaborators. In the top-left quadrant of table 2.1, where there is high formalization and limited power sharing, collaboration is minimal; about all that is expected is coordination or consultation. All of the other quadrants involve various degrees of collaboration, with the lower-right quadrant (low formalization and reciprocal power sharing) requiring the greatest degree of collaboration, communications, and trust building.

Table 2.1

Dimensions of Integration in CSC

	High Formalization	Low Formalization
Limited power sharing	Traditional contracting	Block grants
	Traditional management in public provision	Foundation grants for nonprofits
	Formula and competitive grants to nonprofits	Service delivery networks (noncentralized)
Reciprocal power sharing	PPPs for infrastructure	Government-nonprofit partnerships
	Emergency response networks (under FEMA's Incident Command System)	Nonprofit advocacy networks
	Collaborative contracting	Emergency response networks (ad hoc)
	Centralized service delivery networks	Independent public-services providers

THE GOVERNANCE CONSEQUENCES OF CSC

As more and more governments engage the private and nonprofit sectors in various forms of CSC, there are very real social, political, and structural challenges that make it much more difficult for the public sector to ensure that the public is well served. Much of this concern has been investigated through the literature on government accountability (Behn 2001 and Lynn 2006) and that of collaborative governance (Forrer et al. 2010). The more collaborative forms of cross-sector exchange challenge norms of traditional government administration; they also challenge the norms of how public managers should engage the private and nonprofit sectors (Entwistle and Martin 2005). They move out of their reliance on rule-bound governance to an environment that depends on acting outside those guidelines and creating more discretion for and power sharing with the collaborators (Agranoff 2012). The increased discretion afforded the nongovernmental parties involved in CSC, however, creates a number of potential problems that the public manager must manage.

Challenges of Private Sector Involvement

Engaging the private sector in government programming is very much a double-edged sword. The private sector offers incentives, resources, and capabilities that can transform the work of government programs. However, a focus by the private sector on profit can create an "excludability" problem, where portions of a population who desire access to a product or service are denied access by their inability to pay. A prime example is the impact of congestion pricing in roadway design, which prices out consumers who are unable to pay the fees necessary to access the higher-speed lanes.

Challenges of Nonprofit Sector Involvement

While it also is clear that nonprofits have certain competitive advantages in serving certain populations, nonprofits, by their very nature, also involve a number of challenges that can inhibit the successful delivery of public goods and services. Salamon (1987) explains the administrative challenges of nonprofit management in respect to "voluntary failures." These failures are illustrated in respect to four areas: philanthropic insufficiency, philanthropic particularism, philanthropic paternalism, and philanthropic amateurism.

Philanthropic insufficiency relates to the danger that attention to specific issues by nonprofits might crowd out the resources that organizations from other sectors provide for those same needs. A well-established nonprofit child care provider in a community, for example, may encourage government authorities to invest less in the same types of programs. This issue is particularly problematic in low- and middle-income countries where public agencies operate in already fiscally constrained environments and may ignore certain problems if they believe nonprofits are addressing them.

Philanthropic particularism explains the tendency of nonprofits to address the needs of narrow constituencies, in contrast to government, which must respond to issues that affect the entire populace. HIV and AIDS prevention programs in many parts of Africa, for example, have long been a priority of international nonprofits, but some research suggests that these programs address the social needs of a relatively small segment of the society and are gaining attention at the expense of wider health goals such as basic services (Shiffman 2008).

Philanthropic paternalism refers to the problem that nonprofits may adopt a "we know best" approach toward services for their key constituents, which can distort an understanding of what constituents really need. Philanthropic amateurism explains the tendency of many nonprofit organizations to attract professionals who care more about the programs that they are supporting than the administrative resources to deliver those programs effectively (Salamon 1987); thus, they may ignore building staff with technical and managerial abilities.

Negotiating Divergent Interests

Administrative action is purposive in that it is goal driven and directed around objectives that relate to some central vision or guidance (Senge 2006). The challenge in any form of cross-sector exchanges is that organizations that operate under much different motivations are tasked with cocreating some form of shared purpose. Collaborators will often pursue a common objective or result for different reasons, that is, they may have differing overall individual goals. Negotiating a common aim or result out of these individual aims creates a level of complexity that is absent in more authoritative and formal modes of exchange (O'Leary and Vij 2012; Huxham and Vangen 2005). Organizations are driven by different motivations and aims based on the institutional logics inherent in their legal status or designation as a public, private, or nonprofit organization (Bryson et al. 2006). An inherent challenge in public-private collaborations is ensuring that private sector values, such as profit maximization or protection of intellectual property, do not compromise public sector values, such as equal access and transparency (Hodge and Coghill 2007: Bozeman 2002, 2007).

Overcoming the divergent motivations in collaborations not only involves developing a common vision across sectors, but also one that relates to both the individual and collective interests of the parties. The literature on organizational missions and visions, for example, emphasizes the cultivation of internal working norms to drive collective behavior (Senge 2006). CSC requires considering not only one's own mission, but also the mission of the wider collaborative structure. Thus, working in CSC requires attention to shared as well as individual goals (Wood and Gray 1991). This often requires an iterative process of managing the needs of one's internal responsibilities with those of a wider network or partnership (Milward and Provan 2006). A shared orientation is particularly important to encourage the sharing of information across the parties in the collaboration (Thomson and Perry 2006).

Operating Under Different Legal Constraints

The founders designed the US federal system of government to control its various constituents. The elaborate system of checks and balances across three branches of government and between the federal and state governments laid the foundation for overlapping authorities designed to control administrative behavior. There is little question that the American desire to limit bureaucratic self-interests comes at a cost to efficiency. The bureaucratic red tape of public administration often drives up the costs of managing programs, stifles innovation, and develops redundancy. Yet that very framework also scrutinizes the behavior and actions of government in an effort to ensure the public's interests are met.

Nonprofit and private sector organizations operate outside these institutional checks and balances (Schooner 2001). Government contractors, for example, are not under the same human resource restrictions as their public sector counterparts. The same is true for nonprofit organizations, which serve primarily under the standards that their donors put in place and those of their boards (Axelrod 1994; Brooks 2002). Public managers may need to create their own system of institutional controls within the context of the collaborative agreement.

THE LOSS-OF-CONTROL PROBLEM

One of the most-cited problems with delegating responsibility to private or nonprofit organizations is that government loses control over the public good or service once it is "outsourced" to a partnership or network. The issue of control is important; under traditional public administration, control is exercised through a hierarchical system of delegation, approvals, reporting relationships, and audits. In reality, control under traditional hierarchical relationships is often illusory. Why? First, we know that street-level bureaucrats often have significant discretion in how and to whom public goods and services are delivered (Lipsky 1980). The public servant who interacts directly with the public does need flexibility to interpret the public interest in a way that is consistent with the legislative framework and also makes common sense. Second, we know that public program delivery is affected by the so-called principal-agent problem. The principals may have a difficult time in monitoring the actions of their agents in order to "maintain control."

It is true that when public managers engage collaborative contractors, partnerships, networks, and independent public-services providers in the private or nonprofit sector, they give up some control. The public manager's focus there-fore must be on the results desired and less on the process of how to get there. By becoming more results oriented, managers are governing what is most impor-tant. By relinquishing some control, they recognize that other organizations and actors might have a more innovative and superior approach to achieve the results desired. However, some processes, such as ensuring equal employment opportunity, may remain essential. Thus, a blending of control based on process and legal regulation with control based on results achieved may be more impor-tant and consistent with the public interest. Where process is important for equity or other legitimate reasons, those elements themselves can be addressed as one of the measurable results.

This is a challenging area for public managers. The danger is that in the rush to collaborate, the manager may be captured by private or nonprofit interests or the manager may not have the management skills necessary to balance the com-peting needs of the collaborators while protecting the public interest. In addition, effective collaboration takes time to develop, and public managers often are torn between the need to address the problem now, perhaps appearing more responsive to their political principals, or spending the time and effort to build a collaborative structure that might be more effective in the long term.

HOLLOWED-OUT GOVERNMENT

One of the challenges for public managers working with organizations outside government is the danger of hollowing out expertise within government (Milward and Provan 2000). That is, the more that the functions of government are carried out by organizations outside government, the greater potential there is for public managers to decrease their own internal expertise in program areas. The question any public manager must ask when choosing among in-house or collaborative solutions is the potential impact over time that the decision will have on main-taining the expertise of government employees.

The National Aeronautics and Space Administration (NASA) provides an illustration of how important governance systems are to CSC. NASA is one of the great public success stories, despite the tragedies. The United States was first to land a man on the moon, and the success of that effort and the many technological spin-offs are an example of American entrepreneurship and drive. However, NASA was, in reality, operating through a series of contracts and partnerships. The number of federal workers in NASA was dwarfed by the contract employees. In 1966, at the peak of the program, there were 36,000 federal employees and about 300,000 private contract employees often working side by side with their public sector counterparts (Adams and Balfour 2004). Private sector contractors and partners produced rockets, satellites, and even the space shuttle. It would have been impossible for NASA to have succeeded otherwise.

We also know that the two shuttle disasters, and perhaps the earlier *Apollo One* fire tragedy, happened in part because of an organizational culture and a disjointed leadership style that ignored or overlooked important safety information that could have and should have prevented the deaths of those astronauts. "How many different groups of professionals," ask Adams and Balfour, "most of whom would think of themselves as embodying professional ethics—were nonetheless drawn into actions and nonactions that led first to unacceptable risk and finally to the tragedy of fourteen unnecessary deaths?" (2004, 116–17). The death of an automobile passenger in the new Boston I-90 tunnel (referred to as the Big Dig) resulted from similar failures to take action in the face of a clear design flaw (US National Aeronautics and Space Administration 2008). The critical question in both cases is whether government lacked the technical expertise to understand and address the potential risks appropriately.

CONCLUSION: ADDRESSING THE GOVERNANCE CHALLENGES IN CSC

Despite the challenges and risks inherent in CSCs, a number of administrative techniques are available to address them. Public managers must recognize the "normative, legal and regulatory elements" that set the norms for organizational legitimacy (DiMaggio and Powell 1983). Understanding the wider institutional environment helps managers to identify the value of structures and processes, as well as individual leadership capabilities, to make things happen in collaboration (Huxham and Vangen 2005). A short list of critical items is necessary for the appropriate and ethical use of private and nonprofit partners in public service (many of which are amplified in later chapters):

- Public organizations that use CSC for critical public functions should be led by individuals who are public stewards and encourage stewardship throughout the organization and by collaborators (Kee and Newcomer 2008; Kass 1990).

Such stewardship entails a commitment to the public interest and protection or conservation of ethical values (Cooper 1990; Terry 1995).

- One way to strengthen the protection of key public values is to develop an ethos or ethics of public service to govern all those who do the work of government, not just the civil service (Guttman 2011).

- Public organizations need to retain sufficient in-house expertise to appropriately supervise private partners and contractors, including both procurement and specialty professionals. Adams and Balfour (2004) identified the problem for NASA: they no longer had "sufficient scientific and engineering capacity to make sound judgments about myriad technical decisions and choices made by contractors" (114).

- Public organizations need to engage all interested parties in the decision-making process. The more complex the problem and the greater the number of actors (public, private, and nonprofit), the more important it is that public leaders engage and give voice to the general public (Allen 2010).

- Developing a clear accountability structure is essential (Forrer et al. 2010).

At first, working with collaborators might seem more problematic than the hierarchical principal-agent relationships in traditional public administration. However, regardless of the motivations or individual goals of CSC participants, if collaborators agree to specific objectives, outputs, or outcomes that benefit all parties to the collaboration, they are more likely to share information to achieve that outcome, eliminating a major problem with principal-agent relations. Collaboration eliminates some transaction costs—the development and monitoring of contracts or employment relations—but adds others, for example, time spent developing the collaboration and ongoing interaction with CSC participants.

Authentic collaboration may provide greater combined strength in attacking a public sector issue or problem. Nearly a century ago, Mary Parker Follett, an early American proponent of management reform, discussed the value of "power-with" or "collective power" versus "power-over" (Fox and Urwick 1973). Principal-agent relationships are essentially power-over relationships with the principal having the power over the agent, and perhaps not harnessing the full power (such as knowledge, effort, and expertise) of the agent. Collaboration is collective power; it encourages all parties to the collaboration to use their full knowledge and abilities and to achieve the outcome that the parties desire. For example, in a networked approach to social services delivery, collaborators, whether nonprofit, private sector, or government, can use their own strengths and abilities. For the nonprofit sector, that might be local knowledge or current relationships with a particular clientele. For the private sector, it might be their ability to be innovative or to interact with the private market. For government, it might be their ability to draw on service delivery systems and protocols already in place to ensure the equitable delivery of services.

Public managers must overcome some of the constraints in traditional public administration in order to engage the other two sectors by moving to a more devolved, networked, heterarchical approach to service delivery. This requires a move away from Madisonian checks and balances to one of power sharing, focusing on capacity building, collaboration, partnership engagement, trust building, and long-term results. In this fashion, public managers can take advantage of the strengths of the private and nonprofit sectors in rethinking the delivery of public goods and services.

No matter how good the administrative solutions designed for addressing CSC are, however, there will always be risks for the public sector. Much of the reason that the public sector operates the way it does, after all, is to control for any malfeasance on the part of public officials and to more adequately provide for the public interest (Lynn 2006). The same mechanisms designed to control the delivery of government programs—from the intergovernmental system of checks and balances to the red tape of administrative approvals—serve important functions in our political system.

CSC is simply a means to achieve a government goal and is not a panacea for every type of problem the public sector faces (Bryson et al. 2006). As with any other administrative decision in government, it is critical that public managers do not view CSC as one of many strategic options. Adequately assessing the various options and addressing the potential dangers and problems in CSC are critical. The following chapters develop those issues in more detail.

chapter THREE

Contracting and Collaborating

Empires were one of the earliest forms of government collaborations. Rome maintained its power through a variety of collaborative arrangements with individuals and vassal states. The Roman Empire used mercenaries in its armies, lured with the promise of loot and land if they came home alive. Rome even contracted with private tax collectors to fund its state.[1] Similarly, Britain maintained its hold on its vast empire over three centuries by using the East Indian Company (among others) to raise armies, collect taxes, and bring the riches home to Mother England.

In this chapter, we discuss contracting as a form of cross-sector collaboration.

CONTRACTING

In contracting, a government makes agreements with private and nonprofit organizations to provide some good or service that it cannot or does not want to produce itself. Some contracts, however, are more collaborative than others. We first distinguish traditional or classic contracts from a form of contracting that is collaborative. Although some contracts have aspects of both, they tend to fall within these two categories.

Traditional Contracts

At one end of the spectrum, with little or no collaboration, are contracts that we identify as classic or traditional. This form of contracting has three defining characteristics: (1) contracts are complete, in that they specify the rights and obligations of the involved parties across future contingencies (Gietzmann 1996; Tirole 1999); (2) they are transactional, in that the terms of the relationship are clearly spelled out in writing or clearly understood in the transaction (Cooper 2003; Savas 2000); and (3) they are usually short-term agreements, one-off exchanges or contracts for a discrete, definable item such as constructing a building. Examples include contracts for basic materials and commodities that governments routinely use, such as office supplies, automobiles, computers, and concrete. Often a purchasing department establishes central state- or government-wide contracts for these types of goods with one or more vendors. Government departments buy from those lists with the designated vendors. There is no collaboration. It would be the same as if an individual went to Staples, Office Depot, or Best Buy to make a purchase. In return for an agreed-to (or negotiated) dollar amount, we receive the good that we want. Our interaction is momentary. While the purchase itself is "voluntary," there is no "sharing" of resources, risk, or the other attributes of a true collaboration. These are sometimes referred to as spot or on-the-spot transactions.

Another example of a short-term classic or traditional contract might be the construction of a governmental office building. There is an ongoing interaction between the parties to the contract during construction, but that interaction is largely defined by the legal contract. There is little collaboration in the terms we have discussed in chapter 1, for example, no sharing of decision making and limited sharing of risks. Of course the private contractor assumes the risk of not completing the project within the agreed-to budget or time frame, and failure may lead to penalties depending on the contract.

In traditional or classic contracts, the focus is on the formal legal documentation and the requirements and remedies detailed in the contract that govern how both the government and the contractor will act. In a competitive, contracting-out approach, government dictates the terms and conditions for service production and delivery. The government agency (the purchaser) defines what it needs, specifies the desired product or service, and then issues a request for proposal (RFP) to allow those in the private or nonprofit sector to bid on the good or service being sought. Potential vendors are invited to offer proposals for providing the good or service in the most cost-effective or efficient manner, given the constraints and specifications imposed by the government in the RFP.

Collaborative Contracts

At the other end of the spectrum, representing true collaboration, are contracts that require ongoing interaction between government and representatives of the sector organization receiving the contract. These complex modes of contracting generally adhere to one or more of the following characteristics: (1) they involve incomplete specifications of expectations, as the involved parties modify their requirements over the course of the exchange (Brown, Potoski, and Van Slyke 2008, 2009, 2011); (2) they are relational, as they involve aspects of governance that stretch beyond the formal or written terms of agreement (Bertelli and Smith 2009; Zaheer and Venkatraman 1995); and (3) they are generally long term in nature, with repeated interactions (Johnston and Romzek 2005; Gazley 2008). An illustration of such a contract is a state social services agency contracting with a local nonprofit to deal with a particular social problem—perhaps child care, sheltering battered women, or teaching basic parenting skills. The government might contract with the nonprofit not knowing the best approach to address these issues, instead relying on the nonprofit's local knowledge and mission to achieve success. The approach of the nonprofit and procedures in the contract might evolve gradually as both the government and nonprofit adapt to changing circumstances. This type of contract is often referred to as relational because both the nonprofit provider and the government need significant discretion to adjust services to meet the needs of the population identified (Sclar 2000; Van Slyke 2009).

Similarly, government might want to contract for something not yet in existence (the ultimate in an "incomplete" specification), yet it feels that if the private sector could produce something like it was envisioning, it would be beneficial for government. For example, the US Defense Department saw the need for a stealth bomber without having a very good idea of what it would look like, how much it would cost, or how to make it. A contract with a defense firm to produce such a weapon necessarily required ongoing dialogue and coordination to achieve a successful outcome. This type of contract is sometimes referred to as an incomplete contract because government cannot specify in advance the final product; therefore, the success of the contract hinges on good collaboration between government and the private contractor (Van Slyke 2009). The nature of the product or service delivered by a contractor in these kinds of complex agreements is often asset specific. There is a mutual dependence in the relationship since government would be at a loss if the contractor exited the agreement, and so would the contractor since the product is so specific to the needs of this one purchaser (Lonsdale 2005; Domberger and Jensen 1997; Brown and Potoski 2003).

This chapter provides a framework for analysis and management of government contracting—both traditional and collaborative—from the perspective of a public manager. We start with a definition of basic terms, then provide a rationale for contracting, and offer a brief history of contracting in the United States.

Definitions

Often there is some confusion between the terms *contracting out* and *outsourcing*. While some authors use the terms interchangeably, there is a subtle distinction between the two terms:

- *Outsourcing* refers to the transfer of a function or service from government to the private sector. Government turns over the control (or ownership) of the process and simply tells the supplier what products or services it wants to receive and makes the purchase in the private marketplace. Outsourcing has been a key area of governmental reform under the theory that governments should not do functions that are commercial in nature and could easily be provided by the private sector. Targets for outsourcing have included areas such as printing, lawn and building maintenance, auto maintenance, and cafeteria services. These activities are readily available in the commercial marketplace, and there may be no need for government to duplicate those services; instead government should purchase them from the lowest qualified bidder. Many studies report that this saves government substantial funds (Savas 2000).

- *Contracting out* is a government decision to have a private or nonprofit sector organization produce something (or an input into something) that is essential to a government function and therefore should be controlled by government. Government has a far stronger stake in the specifications, the process, and the outcome of such a contract. An example might be the construction of an aircraft carrier, where government is interested in the capabilities of the ship, or contracting out data processing, where government needs the output of that processing to fulfill critical missions.

Managed competition is another term used in conjunction with contracting and outsourcing and has a specific meaning. It is a defined process through which government decides whether to outsource or contract a given function or service.[2] In managed competition, government workers, currently producing a good or service (but perhaps not as efficiently as some would prefer), are given the opportunity to compete with private sector bidders to see whether the government or private sector can more efficiently and effectively provide that good or service. Managed competition was introduced during the presidency of Bill Clinton and supported by Vice President Gore's National Performance Review (1993) and has waxed and waned with various national administrations. The Obama administration currently is not a supporter of the concept, but the process is still widely used in state and local governments and widely advocated by Indianapolis's mayor, Stephen Goldsmith (Sclar 2000). The federal Office of Management and Budget concluded during the presidency of George W. Bush that the process had saved the national government significant dollars, including over $7 billion from 1,375 competitions during a five-year period from FY 2003 to FY 2007. Government savings occurred even when public sector employees won the competition, which they did in over 70 percent of the competitions in FY 2007 (US Office of Management and Budget 2008).

Rationale for Contracting

By contracting, public managers acknowledge that a private or nonprofit organization can be more efficient or effective than government in the production of some good or service. This may be due to potential vendors' greater experience and expertise; they may have invested in equipment and technology that is more productive than that used by the government; they may use management processes that are more efficient; or their total labor costs (including health insurance and pension benefits) may be lower than those of the government.

Commercial activities are usually better performed in the private sector because competition and ownership drive innovation and cost reductions. This certainly is the case in most spot transactions, as well as activities where there is a large commercial presence, such as office maintenance, auto repair, or other common commercial activities.

Government may also lack the in-house capacity for some critical functions and, even if politically possible, it may not be cost-effective to build those capacities within government. Specialized types of expertise, such as computer security, may be a skill that is difficult for most government agencies to develop through a government workforce. Government does not have the ability to pay the same salaries as the private sector or provide the same range of professional challenges that might exist in a larger private computer security firm.

Contracting also may reduce the principal-agent problem in certain cases where competition forces the contractor to reveal the most cost-effective way to achieve a certain outcome. Critical to this result is good design of the request for proposal (the RFP), the criteria for selection of the contractor, and the ongoing government-contractor relationship.

Contracting in the United States

Contracting has a mixed history in the United States, dating from the time of the Revolutionary War, when George Washington complained about the poor quality of arms, food, and clothing received by the Continental Army and condemned the "mercenary Spirit" of those supplying his troops (Mayer 1999). The Continental Congress formed committees to look into the supply problems, including the waste, fraud, and abuse of contractors to the army, a problem that would plague contracting practices throughout the nation's history, especially during wartime. The term *shoddy* derived from contracting in the Civil War and referred to material that looked like cloth but consisted instead of pressed cloth scraps (Cooper 2003, 30).

The Continental Congress contract to create a postal system revealed another common issue with contracting: price versus reliability. There was no requirement that the contract go to the lowest bidder, and the question soon arose as to how to prevent price gouging and at the same time ensure that service could be provided effectively by the low-priced bidder (Cooper 2003). Price overruns also plague contracting. The now-famous ship the USS *Constitution* (known as *Old Ironsides*) was one of six ships contracted for in 1796 under the new government of the United States, but only three were completed at the agreed-to price. They were excellent ships, but a question that would plague military and defense contracting is whether contractors and their military overseers opted too often for a "Cadillac" approach rather than focusing on price effectiveness.

The national government used contracts not just to secure public goods and services but also to support new industries, including rail and airlines, which received contracts to transport the nation's mail. The interstate highway system established during the Eisenhower administration resulted in a massive increase in infrastructure investment in the United States, most of it provided by the private sector through contracts with government.

Contracting reform is an issue that has received constant attention throughout the nation's history, especially during the Progressive movement of the late nineteenth century. Reform efforts were aimed primarily at requiring open, transparent processes, avoiding corruption through checks and balances and conflict of interest statutes, and preventing cost overruns. Many of the reform efforts began at the local level of government, led by such organizations as the National Municipal League and the International City/County Management Association.

The balance between public production and private production through contracts has always been an issue. Out of necessity during World War II, the United States largely shifted from government-produced armaments to the use of the private sector for the research, development, and production of the war machine. The success of such programs as the Manhattan Project, by which the United States became the first nation to use atomic power, was the result of the use of private contractors working under broad federal direction. At the close of the war, a deliberate decision was made to continue to use contractors, both private and nonprofit (such as universities), for federal activity. The increasing success with contracting led presidents from both parties to declare that "commercial activity" and anything not "inherently governmental" should be contracted to the private or nonprofit sector.

As the outside contractor force blossomed, some urged caution that the blurring of the boundaries between public and private raised troubling questions about the constitutional premises of our government (Bell 1962; Price 1965; Guttman 2000, 2002). Following President Eisenhower's 1961 warning of a growing military-industrial complex, various concerns were identified in a 1962 cabinet-level report to President Kennedy. The Bell Report warned that without corrective action, a brain drain from government into the contractor workforce would result.[3] However, political leaders saw contracts as a way to reward friends without building up the federal bureaucracy.

Starting with President Reagan and continuing through the administrations of President George W. Bush, reliance on outside contractors has accelerated. Between 2000 and 2010, federal contracts grew from about $200 billion to over $550 billion with virtually no growth in the federal contracting and acquisition workforce. This growth in contracting has been undertaken with political camouflage to give the impression that the federal government remains "small" while federal activities continued to expand. While contracting was initially confined to purchasing commercial activities or major weapons systems, many contractors now sit side by side with the federal workforce in government offices, often outnumbering that workforce, and perform functions that are among the most important core functions of government. The military even relied on a private contractor, MPRI, to prepare a manual to govern the employment of contractors operating in the battlefield (Moten 2010).

MOVING TOWARD COLLABORATION

Contracting has become so integrated with other government activities that contracts account for nearly half of all federal spending (excluding payments to individuals and interest payments) and typically account for one-third of all spending by state and local government. Increasingly these contracts involve complex relationships between government and the private or nonprofit sector, requiring collaboration. In moving to contractors (whether traditional or collaborative), in lieu of public production, government gives up strict hierarchical, vertical accountability. Contracts are horizontal agreements between government agencies (as principals) and contractors (as agents). The issue in all principal-agent relations is how the principal can ensure that the agent is performing effectively to meet the terms of the contract. Unlike government provision, where public employees are agents, in contracting, public employees (as principals) negotiate with other agents—the contractors. Traditional contracting is different from collaborative contracting and other forms of cross-sector collaboration (such as partnerships and networks) for a variety of reasons that are outlined in table 3.1.

Contracting involves a number of trade-offs: price versus quality, price versus timeliness, price versus risk, and process versus results. The higher the requirements in terms of quality and the speed of production, the more risks assumed by the contractor, and the more government controls the process of production, the higher the cost to government of the contract. Thus, public managers must decide what is most important in the contractual relationship.

Except for the simplest purchases, public managers need to understand that their role is not passive acceptance of bids with a simple low-cost selection process. Rather, public managers increasingly need to understand their role in the marketplace in relation to the private and nonprofit sectors as potential collaborators in the production of public goods and services. This must come with an eyes-wide-open realization of the different motivations of the other sectors and

Table 3.1

Traditional Contracting Versus Collaborative Contracting

Traditional Contracting	Collaborative Contracting
Detailed specification of good or service needed	Description of output desired, flexibility on process
Arms-length, RFP, and bidding process	Negotiated process with multiple possible partners
Bidding selected on best price (traditional), though now includes more factors	Decision based on best value for money
Government's role: monitor contract compliance	Government is a partner, monitors results
Risk mostly with government; contractor assumes risk of completing project on time and within the agreed-to budget	Risks shared between private sector and government

the reality that any successful collaboration necessitates a strong public presence as well as a strong collaborator.

Collaborative Contracting and Public Managers

The most collaborative type of arrangement has been labeled a complex or relational contract. This type of contract is based not on a detailed set of standards, processes, and specifications, but on a relationship of trust and collaboration between the parties. The explicit terms of the contract are just an outline or framework of the collaboration, which is built on ongoing interactions, not just a one-time transaction. A variety of implicit terms and understandings determine the behavior of the parties and the actual production of the contracted good and service. According to Van Slyke (2009), relational contracting does not happen by default; rather "it is a deliberate decision about contract design and management" (148).

Public managers engage in this type of contracting when it is difficult, if not impossible, to describe the specific output or quality of services desired or when they have developed a level of trust in the contractor. The advantage of a contract that contains less detail is that the parties can have an ongoing dialogue concerning the best approach to the service or issue. The disadvantage is that only the specifics in the contract are legally enforceable. Relational contracts place more responsibility on the public manager to have regular discussions with the contractor as to how the service is provided and what is occurring in terms of results.

Relational contracting is often used when the parties to the contract have a mutual interest in an ongoing relationship. An example might be a contract between a state human services agency and a local nonprofit organization whose mission is to provide certain social services to a needy population. There is an advantage to both parties to develop a collaboration of trust rather than try to spell out every possible detail or contingency in the contract. In these types of arrangements, "reputation, trust and custom can play an important role in 'completing' a contract, especially longer term and repeated contracts where parties have an incentive to develop a reputation for fair dealing" (Petrie 2002, 120).

A collaborative contract in some ways resembles a partnership with the aspects described in table 3.1. Such contracts tend to be more results oriented, with less detail on process and specifics. There often is ongoing negotiation as to the specifics of the performance. Public managers are more concerned with the results of the contract, whether the contractor is meeting the needs of the population being served, and whether the public perceives that it is receiving good value for the contracted funding.

There are some important differences, however, between a collaborative contract and a partnership. For example, in most cases, the contractor is not assuming any significant risk (other than the contract not being renewed). Nor does the contractor finance the project, as might occur in a partnership for developing public infrastructure. In addition, most governmental contracting relationships leave most of the significant decision making to the public agency. There are good reasons for this. It is the public agency that is responsible for ensuring the success of the contract and its consistency with the public interest. In contrast, partnership success is the responsibility of both partners.

No contractor, however public spirited, will have the same level of attention to the public interest as a public manager. At the same time, allowing some independent decision making by the contractor may result in a better outcome than if the public manager tries to micromanage the process. As the private or nonprofit contractor assumes more risk and decision making, the contract begins to resemble a partnership instead of a simple principal-agent relationship. Partnership issues are discussed in more detail in chapter 4.

THE PUBLIC MANAGER AND SUCCESSFUL CONTRACTING

In recognition of the expansion of contracting for public service delivery, Kettl (1993) identified the "smart buyer problem." He argues that governments have embraced the approach of engaging business and nonprofits for an expansive set of public services, but at the same time, governments have not developed the ability to conduct the most basic contracting analyses and assessments: what to buy, from whom to buy, and what was actually bought.

Successful contracting entails a number of discrete phases designed to determine the need for the contract, the process and criteria for selection and award, and the monitoring and evaluation of the outcome of the contract. Kelman (2002) argues that successful contracts must have three goals: to get a "good deal" for the government, to prevent corruption and promote integrity in government operations, and to be "fair" with prospective vendors who enter the contracting system.

Figure 3.1 provides an illustration of the essential phases of contracting, both traditional and collaborative, to address Kettl's concerns and achieve Kelman's three goals.

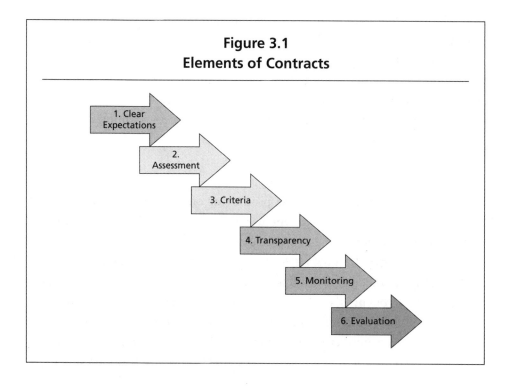

Figure 3.1
Elements of Contracts

1. Clear Expectations
2. Assessment
3. Criteria
4. Transparency
5. Monitoring
6. Evaluation

Clear Expectations

Contracts often fail at the very beginning of the process, when a government agency decides to outsource or contract out a function. If public managers cannot clearly articulate what they want, they are not likely to assess options effectively or develop good criteria for the contract—essential for attaining a "good deal" for government. This is important in developing the RFP that defines what it is that government desires to contract for. When there is uncertainty, it is worth the up-front planning to clearly define the governmental need. One approach in such uncertainty is to issue a request for information (RFI) and allow potential vendors to explain options and potential solutions to particular problems or needs. This was the approach one of us used during Utah's development of a new telecommunications system for state government. Although the state had some idea of its needs, the options available and what might best serve the current and future interests of the state were unclear. The RFI produced a variety of potential solutions, with various features and options. From this information, the state was able to craft an RFP with more specific features, both mandatory and optional, that provided vendors with clear expectations of the state's needs and desires.

This also is the time to decide whether the contract will be "complete" or whether an ongoing dialogue is necessary with the successful bidder, creating a more collaborative contract. Thinking about that process and the nature of the likely collaboration is critical at this stage. As government agencies engage in strategic planning, contracting should be part of a larger strategy about the role of contracting in relation to their agency human resources within the context of the mission of the agency (Walker 2002; Bryson 2011).

Assessment

Once they have a clear sense of the product or output desired, public managers need some process to assess whether government should do this in-house (make) or contract for it in the marketplace (buy). There is no perfect assessment methodology: the one we look at is based on an analysis of a number of authors, under the heading of COMPARE before contracting out a function (the acronym is spelled out in table 3.2). The list of illustrative questions in the table provides a framework to assess the pros and cons of in-house production versus contracting out. Of course, in some cases, the need to contract out is clear, as it was in the case of the new telecommunications system for

Table 3.2
The Assessment Method: COMPARE

Cost efficiency and competitive dynamics	1. Will contracting be less expensive? 2. Is there a competitive market in the private sector that will reveal the best-value approach? 3. Are there economies of scale in the private sector?
Organizational impact	1. Is the function inherently governmental and therefore should not be contracted out? 2. Will contracting be consistent with the agency mission? 3. Are services/functions intermingled (e.g., fire and emergency medical technicians), or are they discrete?
Management issues	1. Does the government agency have sufficient contract management skills? 2. Are you contracting for expertise that government does not have? If so, would it be better to develop those skills in-house? 3. Will contracting out discourage the public workforce?
Political considerations	1. Is there a strong legal environment for contracting? 2. Can you minimize political interference in the selection process? 3. Are there union considerations?
Accountability issues	1. Can you hold the contractor accountable for measurable results? 2. Can you prevent waste, fraud, and abuse in the contracting system?
Risk assessment	1. Can you identify and allocate risks in an appropriate manner? 2. What are the consequences of contractor failure?
Equity and effectiveness concerns	1. Can you take into account issues of equity and other socioeconomic factors? 2. Will the contractor be effective in achieving the public purpose?

Sources: Compiled by Kee (2005) from multiple sources including: Commercial Activities Panel (Walker 2002); Cooper (2003); Savas (2000); DeHoog, Hoog, and Salamon (2002); US General Accountability Office (2004); and Kelman (2002).

Utah. Even in this case, however, going through an assessment tool may reveal issues or problems that will have to be addressed during the purchase.

Since efficiency is often the primary reason for contracting, an assessment of the costs and benefits of contracting versus in-house production is essential, though not always easy to conduct. The true costs of a function to government are not always clear because of a number of factors (Sclar 2000):

- Some employees perform more than one function or may support another function. For example, emergency medical personnel may also support firefighters, or an army cook who also is trained as a soldier.

- Overhead costs are not easily allocated. Looking at marginal costs and the use of activity-based accounting may assist in appropriately costing a function.

- Political interference and contract modifications can result in higher contractor costs than originally anticipated.

Contracting is often sold on the expectation that competition will drive down cost; however, in many areas, especially military systems and hardware, there may be a limited number of potential vendors with the skills necessary to bid on the contract.

All of these illustrative questions could easily consume several pages of discussion and analysis, which is beyond the scope of this chapter. In addition to the cost issue, however, there is one other critical threshold question: Are there any functions that are inherently governmental and should not be contracted out, no matter whether it might be more cost-efficient to do so? The federal Office of Management and Budget (2011) defines an "inherently governmental function" as one that "is so intimately related to the public interest as to require performance by Federal Government employees."

In the United States, the Supreme Court has ruled that government has the authority to contract, but cannot contract out certain basic governmental powers or functions. Various federal administrations have attempted to interpret this mandate, and it is incorporated into federal regulations and circulars, but defining the terms has been problematic. The federal Office of Management and Budget's current list of "inherently governmental" powers and "critical functions" powers is fairly narrow and is summarized in the box.

This is a much debated area. Nationally we have contracted out prisons, security for ambassadors, and even security for our troops overseas. We have contractors who draft testimony for public officials testifying before Congress and contractors who sit side by side with federal employees drafting regulations that affect businesses and individuals. As noted earlier, the military even relies on a private contractor to prepare a manual to govern the employment of contractors operating in the battlefield. All of these arguably fall under the inherently governmental functions in the latest OMB Policy Letter (2011), and yet federal agencies contract out these functions because they have not been given authority to hire the number of federal employees necessary to carry out their missions. While federal officials might be nominally in charge to ensure "regularity," the reality might be quite different (Guttman 2000).

It is at this stage that the decision must be made as to whether the contract will be a competitive or a sole source one. Since a major reason for contracting is to take advantage of competitive market forces, it would seem that most contracting should involve multiple bidders. But there may be important reasons to approach only one or a few vendors. The expertise desired may be very specific, with few firms able to provide what is desired. In US Department of Defense contracting, we now have an oligopoly with few vendors for most defense systems. At a state or local level, contracting may entail working with local nonprofits or faith-based organizations that have particular access to the client population that government wants to support. In these cases, a full, competitive sourcing may not make sense. Since competition is a major factor in reducing costs to government, there must be other counterbalancing advantages to contracting if competition is not present.

Criteria

At the heart of good contract design are the criteria government develops to make the selection and measure the success or failure of the contract. Selection criteria enable the public manager to make the best choice among competing contractors. In traditional contracting, government states exactly what it wants and then selects solely on low price—that is the main reason governments decide to buy in a competitive market. However, contracting has moved beyond price considerations to a broader list of criteria that include both cost and various measures of value, such as past performance, reliability, flexibility, and the ability to take on risks that normally government might bear.

It is also critical for public managers to specify what constitutes success. There must be a clear specification of the goods or services to be delivered and the performance standards expected, providing for accountability. In short, what are the measurable results, outputs, or outcomes anticipated in the contract, and how will the government measure whether they have been met? If a certain quality of the product or service or if public satisfaction will determine whether the contract is successful, then those measures should be built into the criteria for selection. There has to be a relationship between the choice of a particular contractor and how to determine whether the contractor was a success.

Criteria might include design or other specifications (how the contract is fulfilled) or could primarily be based on performance (what the contract is to achieve). Traditionally government has relied heavily on design specifications, and those specifications, even for the simplest item, have pages of detail that draw derision from critics. It is now generally felt that performance criteria offer the best method of selection, as ultimately that is what government is trying to achieve. Sometimes a public agency might include both types of measures, where a certain design approach might be viewed as necessary or in the public interest.

Even in cases where a contractor is viewed in some respects as a collaborator, the core of the relationship is the contract itself, an enforceable document that sets out the responsibilities of both parties to the contract. As Cooper (2003) notes, "The contract relationship is, after all, a legal relationship" (95). Thus, public managers must recognize that no matter how collaborative the contract is, the only measures that managers can hold the contractor accountable for are those specified in the contract itself. In order to ensure impartiality, selection should be made by a team of analysts and not just the judgment of one person.

An important area is how the prospective contractor will be compensated. The two most common methods today are fixed price or cost reimbursement. In a fixed-price contract, the contractor bids a price that it is paid based on the delivery of a stated product or service. This may be used in either a competitive or sole-sourcing contract and might be adjusted with change orders or other specific factors in the contract (e.g., general inflation). In a cost-reimbursement contract, the vendor is paid for all legitimate direct and indirect costs to achieve the product or service in the contract. In addition, vendors are generally paid a fixed fee award in addition to the costs to provide the firm with a profit margin. Past practices of cost reimbursement plus a percentage of costs are no longer in use because of the obvious incentive for the contractor to increase base expenditures.

A key area of contract negotiation is how the public manager ensures good contractual success—that is, what types of incentives (for superior performance) or penalties (for lack of performance) are built into the contract and what performance benchmarks are used to make those decisions. So-called performance contracts are the latest manifestation of this issue. In one sense, of course, all contracts should be performance contracts. But it may well be that contract design can lead to a win-win superior performance by the contractor. An oft-cited example is the State of California's contract award to restore its infrastructure after a major earthquake, which included major performance bonuses for successful early restoration and penalties for delays. The freeway opened seventy-four days early and netted the contractor a bonus of more than $14 million—almost equal the original contracted amount (Cooper 2003). While some complained about the largess of the bonus, the savings to state residents and commercial firms in reduced delays likely exceeded the additional cost to the state.

Transparency

The clearest way to avoid contract fraud and abuse and promote integrity in government is transparency throughout the process of contracting. The federal government and most states have developed statutory procedures to improve the process of contracting, including publishing bid requirements and selection criteria, keeping all bidders informed throughout the process, an open selection process based on the criteria, and the ability of aggrieved parties to appeal to some independent arbitrator, such as the General Accountability Office in the case of the federal government. Transparency often is an issue in developing nations that do not yet have a legal system that supports fair and impartial contracting. The box provides a list of some of the more important factors in contract transparency that will assist public managers to avoid corrupt practices.

WAYS TO AVOID CORRUPTION IN THE CONTRACTING PROCESS

1. A clear, transparent process
   - Development of the RFP
   - Multiple bidders
   - A predetermined and clear selection process and criteria
   - Selection by a team of analysts, subject to oversight
   - A provision for the losing party to appeal
2. A legal system that ensures the process is carried out, including the ability of third parties (whistle-blowers) to identify and report contract fraud and abuse
3. A public or political system that does not tolerate corruption

---

From this list, it is obvious that developing nations will have difficulty in meeting the second and third items in the box to avoid corruption. One of the ironies of effective cross-sector collaboration is that governments often involve the private or nonprofit sector because of government failure, and yet effective contracting requires a government that has strong legal protections and due process—an area that many developing nations find problematic.

Monitoring

Contracts are not self-executing. Public managers often spend more time on selecting a contractor than they do on the operations or execution of the contract. This lack of effective government contract compliance, at least at the federal level of government, has resulted in the Government Accountability Office's consistently listing contract management as high risk (2011). Even when the contracts are well designed, it still is essential to monitor for compliance to contractual terms and specifications. Monitoring primarily includes an examination of the legitimacy of the costs of the contractor (in cost-reimbursement contracts) and the performance in achieving the results anticipated in the contract.

Good contract administration is a balance between developing good working relationships with the contractor and effective oversight to meet government expectations. Some agencies begin contract operations on major projects with a joint retreat designed to build an effective relationship between contract managers and contractors. The relationship does not have to be (and should not be) adversarial, but it also should not be so cordial as to risk the manager's cooptation by the private sector. Developing a trusting, collaborative relationship, however, will facilitate contract administration because it reduces transaction costs of repeated site visits or audits. Building on work by Hardin (2002) and Sako (Boston 1994) we identify three levels of trust:

1. *Contractual trust*—adhering to the legal agreement. There is little collaboration in this trust level. The public manager trusts that the contractor will complete the task according to the contract. Hardin refers to this as "encapsulated interest"—the contractor's interests align with the government's because it is in the contractor's interest to complete the contract according to terms. In many cases, nonprofits are dependent on the resources provided by the government contract, and the resource interdependency allows the public manager to have confidence that the contractor will fulfill its part of the bargain.

2. *Competence trust*—belief in the competence of the contractor. In this level of trust, the public manager recognizes the special expertise or local knowledge of the contractor and allows discretion within the confines of that competence area. This may come from past interactions with the contractor and may gradually grow with repeated collaboration. Although this is not yet a partnership, there is genuine collaboration and a respect for each party's expertise and judgment.

3. *Goodwill trust*—confidence that the contractor will go beyond the contract minimum in order to achieve mutual objectives. As a result of repeated interaction and collaboration, the public manager now views the contractor as a true collaborator in delivering a public good or service. The contractor will have considerable latitude on how to proceed and on daily decision making. The public manager focuses on the results of the relationships without the need for ongoing audits or detailed reporting and monitoring.

Public managers must recognize the tension that exists between developing trust with the contractor and holding the contractor accountable. Whatever the level of trust, it remains the public manager's responsibility to ensure that the public interest is met in the contract execution, and that requires monitoring the contract. The frequency and level of monitoring often depend on the level of trust that exists between the public agency and the contractor.

Sometimes contractors fail partially or totally. The fault may or may not be the contractor's. Conditions may change. The government itself may find that its initial needs assessment is no longer accurate. Thus, the contractual agreement must include mechanisms for both contract modification and, if necessary, termination. In some types of contracts (e.g., facility construction) contract modifications almost always generate additional costs; however, there may be cases where new technologies will give government an opportunity for more cost-effective solutions. A contract should not be so inflexible that it prevents such an accommodation.

Some contracts are not simple purchases but involve interdependent relationships between a government agency and the contractor. Many defense contracts fit this definition. In this case, government will often have a program manager that works on a regular basis with the contractor counterpart. A major problem in defense contracting has been cost overruns, a result not of a lack of monitoring but a lack of holding defense contractors accountable for the cost overruns (Kelman 2002).

Dispute resolution also is a necessary part of the contractual relationship. Ideally mechanisms in the contract allow low-level discussion and agreement on areas of concern. In the final analysis, the contract is a legal document, so disputes can be taken to the courts. However, it is always better to build into the contract arbitration approaches that might avoid lengthy and costly legal actions.

Evaluation

Evaluation during and at the conclusion of the contract should be a norm in contract administration. The key to good evaluation is the development of good criteria, performance benchmarks that can be monitored, and an after-contract review of what worked and what did not work well in the arrangement, so that the public managers can learn from successes and failures and can improve on the contracting function in the future. We spend more time discussing evaluation in chapter 10.

TRADITIONAL CONTRACTING ILLUSTRATION

US Environmental Protection Agency, Cyber Security Software

In July 2012, the US Environmental Protection Agency (EPA) decided to renew maintenance of its cybersecurity software. It put out a notice in the form of an RFQ on a public forum, GSA eBuy. The quote with the lowest price would be the winner. In this case, the government used a form of competition reserved for the purchase of commercial products: a buyer that gets three quotes can choose the one with the best price or can justify using the next lowest quote if there is a solid reason—perhaps the brand is better suited to the existing system and information technology staff are comfortable using it. The procurement was initiated as a firm fixed-price transaction, and there were no negotiations for the procurement, which put the bidders on notice to give their best and final price offer up front.

Services Provided and Award

The RFQ listed the following specifications: one-year maintenance renewal of a specific cybersecurity software brand and version or similar product, for between twenty-five thousand and forty-nine thousand end users. Bidders were required to provide maintenance and support for each end user consisting of upgrade patches and security patches without further charges to the government and also to provide telephone and e-mail technical support from a source located in the United States. The award was made to Guidance Software for a one-year period, from August 2012 to August 2013.

Choosing Contracting Out

The EPA had a clear sense of what it needed, and it knew it did not have the technical capabilities in-house; thus, it chose to continue to contract out the activity—in this case, cybersecurity software maintenance. Because of the sensitivity of this function, it might be argued that the EPA should develop its own workforce to maintain its software. However, hiring, training, and keeping software engineers is difficult and costly for government. The private sector is able to pay larger salaries and has a diverse group of clients that provides new challenges for their workforce. The EPA does not have this ability.

Kettl's concern about a "smart buyer" remains an issue with this procurement. If the EPA does not maintain some in-house analytical capability, how will it know that it is getting a good deal on the contract or that the contractor will deliver in an effective and efficient manner? Good contract management and the establishment of measures of contract performance become critical components for this choice.

COLLABORATIVE CONTRACTING ILLUSTRATION
Kansas Foster Care and Adoption

State governments in the United States have used collaborative or relational contracting for many years, primarily in the social and human services delivery areas. Such contracts include health maintenance organizations for Medicaid managed care (the joint federal-state program of health care for low-income populations); employment services as part of state programs under the 1996 welfare reform (the Personal Responsibility and Work Opportunity Reconciliation Act); and a variety of individual social services such as child care and preschool programs. The Kansas foster care and adoption program (FCA) is an example of one such program that put the state on the cutting edge of foster care reform but also generated controversy (Freundlich and Gerstenzang 2002).

In 1996–1997, Kansas became the first state in the nation to fully privatize its adoption, foster care, and family preservation services. Its Department of Social and Rehabilitation Services (SRS), previously the state's largest provider of adoption and foster care services, now is strictly a purchaser of services and contract monitor with respect to child welfare services (Foster Care Kansas 2013). The Children's Alliance of Kansas plays a critical role in the process by contracting with the state to serve as the initial point of contact for foster and adoptive parents. The Children's Alliance assists with matching families with agencies that are in their area.

Assessment

Johnston and Romzek (2005) examined several case studies of Kansas collaborative contracting, including the FCA, along three dimensions: contract specification, contract design, and accountability design. These dimensions are somewhat similar to three elements suggested in this chapter: clear expectations, criteria, and evaluation (though accountability is somewhat broader; we discuss this issue in chapter 10). They rated FCA as fairly high in terms of clarity of relationships and suitability of performance measures, obligations, and deliverables—all critical factors in thinking through what government desires out of a contract. However, they rated FCA low on contract design because it used five principal contractors for foster care services, and those contractors in turn substantially dealt with a variety of subcontractors, thereby blurring lines of accountability. They also viewed this approach as high risk for government because of the cost volatility of some services provided by FCA, such as mental health services. Furthermore, the state relied on technology to monitor the data from the private contractors, but contractor capacities in this area varied widely. However, FCA was rated high on its accountability designs, including legal, professional, and political accountability.

ASSESSING THE ADVANTAGES AND DISADVANTAGE OF CONTRACTING

Contracting is now an essential management function for public managers. In some cases, the decision to contract out or outsource a function is clear. There may be significant commercial capacity in the private sector and may be no inherent reason for government production. Thus, an examination of contracting as a lower-cost alternative to government production is clearly something public managers should consider. Traditional contracting works best when government has a clearly defined product or service that it wants to deliver and there is sufficient commercial activity in that area so that private sector production becomes a more cost-effective option than government production.

There may be other circumstances where the public sector lacks expertise and cannot hire public employees with that expertise because of either the cost or unavailability of individuals with that expertise. For example, a state government may be contemplating the sale of bonds for an infrastructure project. That is a specialized service, and most state governments do not retain in-house capacity because the need for that expertise occurs infrequently. Contracting becomes a way for the state to engage individuals or firms with that expertise for a specific project without a long-term commitment that a public hiring would entail.

In other cases, nonprofit or faith-based organizations may have access to a needy population that government does not have or could gain only through significant and costly new personnel. Given their proximity to the clients in need and their interests in serving those clients, these nonprofit organizations are likely to be more effective than government in delivering many types of social services.

Opponents to contracting would dispute many of these arguments. They note that often there is no competitive market, particularly in a substate geographical area, and thus no competitive advantage to contracting. They also argue that the evidence of lower cost and higher quality are overstated and do not materialize to the extent suggested by proponents (Sclar 2000).

There have been some spectacular failures in contracting. The Federal Bureau of Investigation had to scrap a $170 million data management project, including $105 million worth of unusable code. Various government and independent reports show that the FBI, lacking IT management and technical expertise, shared the blame with the contractor for the project's failure. In 2014, the State of Idaho had to take over a state prison whose management had been contracted to a major private corrections firm because of repeated problems uncovered in state inspections.

With any contracting, traditional or collaborative, the public manager gives up direct, vertical, hierarchical control of the production process of the good or service in exchange for a horizontal relationship over which he or she has only the control provided in the contract or that develops through the ongoing relationship with the contractor. Proponents of contracting argue that appropriate performance targets actually produce more real control than with the supervision of public employees who may have their own agendas, but the failures we have noted suggest that effective performance targets alone are not enough.

Contracts with the private sector also open up the possibilities of corruption. The steering of contracts to those who financially support elected officials is a constant danger. Even the best of processes can be undermined by a public manager with his or her own agenda, which might include employment opportunities with a prospective contractor after public employment. A well-publicized example was the selection of Boeing as the contractor for the US Air Force refueling tanker, a selection process that was fraught with political interference and criminal charges against the Air Force procurement officer who was in charge of negotiations; she eventually pleaded guilty to criminal conspiracy for secretly negotiating an executive job with Boeing at the same time that she was participating in the award decision. The enormous funds involved in these decisions raise the stakes for both companies and public managers. The larger the dollar amounts in the contract, the more that transparency and checks and balances are required in the contracting process.

GLOBAL IMPLICATIONS

Internationally, contracting out has become part of the general government reform movement that began in the 1980s and argues for the use of private sector efficiencies in the delivery of public goods and services. Petrie (2002) notes that member countries of the Organization for Economic Co-operation and Development (OECD) grew increasingly interested in the use of contract-type arrangements in the 1990s as a means of improving public sector performance. Many countries have pursued a strategy of developing a more performance-oriented culture in the public sector. Public sector reform has not taken an identical approach across OECD member countries. Different institutional arrangements, histories, and political circumstances have resulted in differences in reform efforts across countries. However, contracting out, and specifically performance contracting, has emerged as a tool of public sector reform (Petrie 2002). Emphasis on performance contracting also is strengthening in developing countries.

Since 2000, the countries of Eastern Europe, the Caucasus, and Central Asia (EECCA) have embraced private sector contracts and partnerships as a means to improve the operations of and attract capital to their water supply and sanitation sectors. Performance contracting has been one of the vehicles of reform adopted by some utilities in these regions. These contracts include performance targets within specified time bands against which the performance of the operator is measured. When designed properly, performance-based contracts align incentives, increase operating efficiency, close the gap between expectations and actual performance, and attract investment capital. As a result, performance contracting can help promote the long-term sustainability of utilities.

The OECD Environmental Action Programme (EAP) Task Force developed *Guidelines for Performance-Based Contracts Between Municipalities and Water Utilities in EECCA* (OECD 2010) as a means to support EECCA authorities and aid them in adopting the best performance contract design elements. The major elements usually include performance indicators, tariff-related issues, contract monitoring, mechanisms for conflict resolution, conflict enforcement, and risk mitigation. The guidelines address the key elements that should be considered in connection with the preparation, implementation, and periodic adjustments of successful performance-based contracts.

Examples of types of performance-based contracts that exist in these countries include a management contract for the Armenia Water and Wastewater Company with the French company SAUR; a lease contract for the Yerevan Water Supply Company with the French company Véolia Water (also in Armenia); concession contracts in Ukraine with domestic private operators in the towns of Berdyansk and Kupyansk; and (near full) divestiture in Kazakhstan, where the water utility in the city of Shymkent is owned by a domestic private operator.

The OECD report (2010) noted that implementing and instituting reforms like performance contracting can take a lot of time, effort, and political support. Success also requires other conditions: the right legislative authority, an appropriate regulatory regime, and the right administrative structure with sufficient resources. For example, monitoring performance standards through reporting obligations specified in the contract is an important element of contractual agreements. The OECD found that contracts from the examples in the EECCA region all had reporting requirement provisions but with different degrees of specificity. For example, in the case of the Armenian contracts, reporting requirements and the bodies responsible for overseeing contract implementation are specified in detail. By contrast, the Ukrainian contracts left the requirements vague and unclear.

CONCLUSION

Increasing amounts of public funds are going into contracts, and thus the role of the public manager in the delivery of public goods and services is shifting from program operations to contract management (Forrer and Kee 2004). Although the governments in the United States have used private and nonprofit providers since our nation's founding, the use of contracts through outsourcing or contracting out has expanded to the point where a variety of essential services are now provided not by government employees but by private and nonprofit providers working under a variety of contractual arrangements. Not everyone is pleased with this trend; public sector unions have been strong opponents, arguing that contracting out often results in higher costs, poorer service, increased opportunities for corruption, and diminished government flexibility, control, and accountability (American Federation of State, County, and Municipal Employees 2014). Even if this were true or sometimes factual, we are not likely to see contracting significantly reduced in the near future, for all of the reasons suggested in chapter 1.

Private sector organizations or nonprofits are capable of fulfilling a defined role in a cost-effective manner; however, it still is up to the government to define its needs appropriately, effectively engage those organizations, and monitor whether the tasks are being fulfilled to expectation. If government is to have a larger role and yet reduce its responsibilities as a public provider, public servants will have to become better public contract managers (Forrer and Kee 2004). Public managers also need to realize that they may be tasked with contracting in less-than-optimal market conditions and balancing a variety of competing objectives. This may be especially true in collaborative contracting where there may be limited competition for the contract and thus a heavier burden on the public manager to exercise leadership throughout the collaboration. This will require thoughtful analysis and decisions about with whom to contract, how those contracts will be analyzed, what ongoing interactions are required, and what criteria will be used to ensure the contract meets the public interest.

Case Study for Discussion: Contracting Out for Social Services (from Chapter One)

You are an assistant to the executive director of the Department of Social Services (DSS). You are considering contracting out the job training function that is not performing to expectations.

Initial Issues for Consideration

1. Is employment training an "inherently government" function?

2. What is the rationale for contracting out this function?

3. How would you go about the process of contracting for employment services?

4. What are the criteria that you should use in the development of the RFP and in the selection process?

After your analysis, you initiate a competitive sourcing RFP that results in the following four bids:

1. The Division of Employment Training has proposed to restructure itself as a "most efficient organization," a public corporation with greater flexibility in hiring, firing, salaries, and purchasing and reduce its annual costs to $15 million, with an incentive structure that would provide bonuses for each successful outplacement over a base of fifty thousand— bonuses would be shared by the employees.

(Continued)

2. Lockheed Martin's Public Services Division, with demonstrated success in other states, has proposed a straight pay-for-performance contract that would pay it three hundred dollars per successful outplacement, with a minimum guarantee of $9 million in the first year to cover start-up costs.

3. United Social Services (USS), a national nonprofit organization with no current offices in the state, has proposed a contract of $20 million with a suggested performance target of 100,000 successful outplacements a year. USS enjoys a good reputation nationally but recently suffered through a scandal involving the salaries and expenses of top administrators.

4. Urban Human Services, a local nonprofit organization that, under city contract, provides training to about ten thousand high school dropouts a year, is proposing to expand its operations to include welfare recipients. It has a good reputation for success and good customer service, but would have to expand its operations tenfold to handle the expected volume. It has proposed a contract of $15 million for training 100,000 welfare recipients a year.

How would you evaluate these public, private, and nonprofit options?

chapter FOUR

Cross-Sector Partnerships and Public-Private Partnerships

artnerships have existed in some form since the earliest forms of government. The Roman Empire developed partnerships in the form of toll roads to expand portions of its roadways. The US government authorized the use of privateers to harass the British Navy during the Revolutionary War. Much of the western US territory was developed through a combination of public-private partnerships, including the cross-continental railroad (Bain 1999). Today governments around the world develop intricate agreements with the private sector to develop physical infrastructure. International organizations such as the World Bank and the US Agency for International Development partner with business and nonprofits to operate development programs. US state and local governments collaborate with nonprofits to address problems as diverse as disaster recovery and human services.

The aim of this chapter is to help public and nonprofit managers understand cross-sector partnerships as forms of collaboration and to identify and differentiate a number of the forms of these partnerships that are present in public administration. The rationale for and performance implications of business alliances have been studied at length (Gulati, Lavie, and Singh 2009). The following sections summarize core issues concerning cross-sector partnerships, including their characteristics, rationales for formation, and techniques for managing them. Key to this discussion is a thorough understanding of different forms of one-to-one relationships that can form among public and nongovernmental organizations when different organizations come together around issues of mutual interest.

We use the term *cross-sector partnerships* to describe both public-private partnerships (PPPs) and government collaborations with nonprofits. Cross-sector partnerships involve at least one government partner and one partner from the nonprofit or private sector. The focus is on one-to-one organizational partnerships, although in some cases, one partner may serve as a master contractor, special-purpose vehicle, or key actor in a wider network. Like the other forms of cross-sector collaboration (CSC) discussed in this book, all cross-sector partnerships involve some relational elements of governance and necessitate greater sharing of power than more transactional approaches to government collaborations, such as a traditional contract.

In many ways, public sector partnerships with private and nonprofit organizations necessitate a different way of thinking about how the government should interact with entities from other sectors. The traditional approach to public-private engagement has been contracting, where the disciplinary role of the market is expected to yield operational efficiencies in public service delivery. The public sector describes the service it wants delivered and seeks out the market of providers to find the lowest-cost option for delivering it. Cross-sector partnerships are often established by selecting a partner that holds unique capabilities, not by choosing a partner through a competitive process. This approach can be considered a shift from prioritizing contestability (or competition among potential contractors) to prioritizing collaboration (or cooperation among partners) in these relationships (Entwistle and Martin 2005).

Consider the role of the United Way of New York City (UWNYC) in the immediate aftermath of the terrorist attacks on September 11, 2001. The City of New York and the New York Community Trust partnered with UWNYC to establish and manage the September 11 fund (Kapucu 2006). UWNYC was uniquely positioned to contribute staff, volunteers, and its fundraising network to the effort. The UWNYC was not selected through a competitive process but was chosen deliberately for the unique resources and capabilities that it could offer to the city. The decision to partner also reflected a wider interest among public officials to select nongovernmental partners based on the expected value they can offer to a public sector effort rather than the expected cost of their service (Boyer, Kingsley, and Weible 2013). In addition, such partnerships involve a governmental approach that replaces strategic control with mutual influence

(Bovaird 2004). The goal of these partnerships is to spend more time trying to nurture their relationship with one another instead of dictating the terms of the relationship (Kanter 1994).

TYPES OF CROSS-SECTOR PARTNERSHIPS

Cross-sector partnerships occur in a variety of forms and are formed for a variety of purposes. While a complete discussion of all partnership purposes and forms is beyond the scope of this book, we categorize the most significant as follows:

1. *Short-term, one-to-one partnerships* for a specific purpose or goal. These might include joint efforts of the private and public sectors to form a downtown business district or commercial development (Alexander 2012) or a partnership between government and a local community organization to fund and equip a local park. Sometimes a specific agreement is involved (perhaps a memorandum of understanding), but often these partnerships are ad hoc, with either party free to opt in or out of the collaboration.

2. *Intermediate-term partnerships* involving government and nonprofit providers to deliver specific public goods and services, as might occur between a state department of human services and a local shelter for the homeless. These types of arrangements (through either contract or grant) are often year-to-year but are typically renewed as long as the nonprofit provider is serving the population identified by the partnership.

3. *Long-term partnerships* involving the creation or renewal of major infrastructure projects. These PPPs, often termed P3s in North America (Boardman, Poschmann, and Vining 2005), involve the private sector in the financing and delivery of public infrastructure services, which transfers substantial risk to the private sector in return for an agreed-on payment (based on use or availability). These agreements are long term in nature, often extending thirty to forty years or more in length, and are structured through complex contracts (Grimsey and Lewis 2007).

Table 4.1 provides some examples and characteristics of the three types of partnerships.

Short-term partnerships include a diverse range of cross-sector partnerships that involve a one-to-one relationship between a governmental and nongovernmental organization. Examples could include a Habitat for Humanity partnership

Table 4.1

Characteristics of Different Types of Partnerships

Type of Partnership	Policy Areas	Structure of Relationships	Other Actors	Degree of Discretion
Short term: One-to-one relationships between government agencies and private or nonprofit providers for specific purposes	Natural disaster relief, site-specific development, community development	Range of formal, funded relationships and those less formal	Government may bring in other actors as partners but is the prime actor and decider.	Limited private or nonprofit actors generally acting within a narrowly defined agenda.
Intermediate term: One-to-one relationship between a nonprofit and a government agency to manage public services delivery programs	Human services, health, education, arts and culture, environment, education, economic development, disaster recovery	Highly formalized, structured by government funding Combination of formal and informal influence	Government may play the role of an administrator of a larger network of providers or may use a nonprofit in that role.	Varies; the longer the relationship, the more discretion likely afforded the nongovernmental partner.
Long term: One-to-one relationship formed between a public and private organization to build or operate public infrastructure	Transportation, water, energy, telecommunications, or other physical infrastructure	Highly formalized: long-term contracts with substantial private sector discretion	Private partners often through a consortium of private actors, including funders and contractors.	The contract generally spells out the areas of discretion, which may be extensive.

Sources: Andrews and Entwistle (2010); Suarez (2010); Whitaker, Altman-Sauer, and Henderson (2004); Kapucu (2006); Zhang (2005); Forrer, Kee, and Zhang (2002); Grimsey and Lewis (2007); Yescombe (2007).

with a local government agency to support housing needs for a community, or the work of a local energy company with local officials that aims to improve energy efficiency. The relationships can take on varying lengths or levels of integration across sectors, but they generally are of a short-term nature or for a defined project with limited duration. Short-term partnerships make sense when there is a specific action to be addressed or when the relationship involves limited commitments from either side.

Intermediate-term partnerships describe a variety of governmental relationships with nonprofit organizations, primarily in the human services area. Often government uses a preexisting group of nonprofits that are already serving a specific clientele and have contacts and expertise in the delivery of public services. Sometimes this is a one-to-one partnership; at other times, government may partner with a number of organizations in a network or use one organization as the primary contact, with other organizations acting as subcontractors to the primary nonprofit organization. This form of partnership is sometimes associated with federal aid for state and local governments or state aid to local government. Intermediate-term partnerships make sense when continuity of service and institutional memory are valued, balanced with keeping open opportunities for working with new partners with new ideas and approaches.

Long-term partnerships are commonly for delivery of infrastructure services and are highly formalized. On the private side, a separate legal entity is often established to represent a number of other partners who carry out roles in technical design, financing, construction, or operations and maintenance. The partnering relationship is established between a government agency (such as a state-level department of transportation) and the legal representative (or special-purpose vehicle), yet a host of other private sector organizations play a role. Long-term partnerships make sense when participants are heavily dependent on each other's actions for successful outcomes and when the cost of investments is recovered over a long period of time.

COMMON ASPECTS OF CROSS-SECTOR PARTNERSHIPS

The three types of partnerships also share a number of common attributes or aspects. For one, partnerships adhere to the core characteristics of CSC presented in chapters 1 and 2: power sharing and risk sharing. The more that decision making and project risk are shared, the more interdependent are the partners on each other. Klijn and Teisman (2003) suggest that relations among public and nongovernmental actors also are more equitable. The distribution of power within the partnership, however, actually increases partners' risks, since partnerships can create greater interdependence and leave partners more vulnerable than the arm's-length transactions typical in contracting (Chen and Graddy 2010).

Partnerships are dynamic, and relationships can vary across different stages of their development and operation (Velotti, Botti, and Vesci 2012). The California SR-91 roadway partnership is a good example. In 1995, the express lanes on 91 were opened using a variable pricing system based on the time of day. Operating responsibilities for the roadway were initially assigned to a private consortium. Later the Orange County Transportation Authority "repurchased" the roadway from the consortium (Ni 2012).

Cross-sector partnerships can involve a complex set of stakeholder relationships that go beyond the primary government partnership with a business or nonprofit; in some PPPs, a third-party nonprofit group may serve as an intermediary to foster more trust or legitimacy (Mendel and Brudney 2012). An example is the role the Cleveland Development Foundation played in bringing together the City of Cleveland and a steel company (Republic Steel) to create office buildings, housing, and commercial and retail business districts in Cleveland (Mendel and Brudney 2012). In PPPs for infrastructure, stakeholder relationships are particularly complex: involved parties often include a sponsoring public agency, private transaction advisers, auditors, regulators, and international construction and investment firms (Jooste and Scott 2012).

RATIONALES FOR CROSS-SECTOR PARTNERSHIPS

Governments seek out partnerships with private and nonprofit organizations for a variety of reasons, including their dependence on outside resources to carry out their work, the reduction of transaction costs achieved by working in a sustained, integrated partnership, and the expected reciprocity of social exchange inherent in partnerships.

Resource dependence argues that an organization can accomplish a given task only through the contributions of another (Pfeffer and Salancik 1978; Thompson 1967). A business may depend on a governmental partner for providing it legitimacy in working within a community, or a nonprofit organization could provide similar reputational value for a government working with a specific constituency (Provan and Kenis 2008). In other cases, organizations seek out partnerships because another entity has the skills that they desire (Gazley and Brudney 2007). The need for resources from other organizations is particularly prevalent as government agencies strive to address complex problems that are beyond the capabilities of a single organization (Rittel and Weber 1973).

Resource dependence among organizations is supported by the expectation that the sector identity of any organization contains qualities that organizations of other sectors lack. Since the legal classification of an organization (public, private, nonprofit) facilitates certain operational limitations and advantages (Rainey 2003), the very nature of an alliance that crosses sectors implies that one organization has the potential to contribute resources that another does not have. The government, for example, can bring public responsiveness, local knowledge, and equity concerns (Pongsiri 2002); the private sector offers unique approaches to efficiency, innovation, and financial capital (Savas 2000); and the nonprofit sector can bring access to a voluntary workforce, grassroots community connections, or a voice to marginalized groups in a community (Te'eni and Young 2003).

The costs of transactions when governments work with other organizations include monitoring the outcomes of nonstate providers. The possibility of reducing these costs prompts some governments to move from a contractual relationship to a partnership. As two organizations work with one another over time, trust often develops among the individuals involved. This trust can lead to greater reliance on shared norms for governing their interactions with one another. Over time, a formal, contractual relationship can develop into a relational partnership (Johnston and Romzek 2005). Long-term relationships can also reduce the costs of monitoring work, allow easier communication, and lay the groundwork for more agreement in collective decision making (Chen and Graddy 2010). For these reasons, PPPs often are a good option for public-private collaborations that involve long-term engagement and mutual dependence.

Social exchange theory provides a third reason for public managers to collaborate through partnerships. Most people are interested in contributing to a shared cause when they feel that there is some level of reciprocity, or return, for their contributions (Blau 1964). Throughout a partnership, each party is expected to exchange a combination of material and nonmaterial goods, like symbols of approval. In a structural agreement where many of the terms of exchange are ambiguous and evolve over the course of interaction, social exchange is expected to play an even more important role, since the terms of cooperation are often governed through informal means (Gazley 2008).

ISSUES OF WORKING IN PARTNERSHIPS

The two most prominent traits in partnerships are the high level of interdependence that is demanded by the unique nature of the relationships and the extent of shared power, which may create vulnerability for the public sector organization. A number of issues can arise from this vulnerability in ways that may compromise the public interest (Forrer et al. 2010). The same motivations that drive organizations to work with one another can also lead to conflict (Mendel and Brudney 2012). Potential problems include mission drift, a loss of public accountability, co-optation of actors, financial instability, difficulty in appropriately evaluating results, and the overall challenge of managing the costs of transactions necessitated by interdependent exchanges (Mendel and Brudney 2012).

The host of challenges created through cross-sector partnerships originates from two potential threats: the need for adequate government capacity to manage these relationships and the need to negotiate divergent interests in partnerships. Although these threats offer differing levels of severity in different types of partnerships, they are apparent to some extent in any cross-sector partnership.

Government Capacity

The importance of government capacity as an essential component of any agreement between public and private sectors is well documented (Kettl 2002; Brown, Potoski, and Van Slyke 2006). While government may defer various functions to the private or nonprofit sector through different formal or informal relations, it remains responsible for ensuring that the public is served. Ensuring appropriate service delivery through agreements with the private or nonprofit sector requires public management skills in areas such as developing project proposals, bargaining and negotiating with partners, and providing oversight and auditing of private vendors once a partnership has been created or an agreement signed (Van Slyke 2003).

The overall capacity for government to oversee projects with the private or nonprofit sector can be considered in terms of design (preparations for engaging the private or nonprofit sector) and implementation (ongoing oversight once a contract has been awarded or agreement reached). Preparations for engaging the private sector require skills in a host of activities that lead up to selecting a provider. As indicated in chapter 3, the basic tools require determining whether the government should deliver a product or service directly (the make-or-buy decision), specifying the scale and scope of the product or service desired, determining the market of nongovernmental providers for the item in question, and developing a bidding process to identify an appropriate partner (Brown et al. 2006). The issue of capacity is explored in more detail in chapters 7 and 11.

Managing the relationship in partnerships, once a partner has been selected, often requires government to oversee a set of agreed-on service standards. The overall steps draw on skills in codeveloping performance standards for a given product or service with a nongovernmental organization and overseeing their achievement. The sum of the tools required for designing and implementing partnerships, like any other form of cross-sector collaboration, represents the overall costs of transactions among public and private sectors and constitutes some of the most important factors in ensuring that the public interest is protected when goods and services are delivered by nongovernmental actors (Van Slyke 2003).

The challenge for public managers is that the skills for designing and implementing partnerships are different from traditional modes of government contracting and government-run provision (Forrer et al. 2010). Consider the following quote from a study of infrastructure-based public-private partnerships:

> Public agencies that seek PPPs for transport projects commonly lack productive, financial, or managerial expertise and capacity and, very likely, have no previous experience in managing a PPP. In contrast, private entities that bid for, and win, public contracts generally have long engaged in the business and have accumulated expertise in assessing risks, negotiating benefits, and crafting contracts. They may also demonstrate considerable experience in various aspects of developing the facility. (Ni 2012, 259)

Adding further evidence of this challenge, a survey conducted in 2008 found that numerous transportation departments identified knowledge gaps related to PPPs. The survey was administered to all fifty state-level departments of transportation and assessed PPP skill areas along a number of dimensions related to project experience, project conceptualization, bidding process, and overall management of PPPs (Buxbaum and Ortiz 2009). Almost all of the reporting agencies expressed the need for more knowledge of PPP concepts and trade-offs, necessary skills, using private capital, developing contractual terms, and effective measures and monitoring.

Managing Divergent Interests

The same issues that make partnerships attractive for the public sector also make them inherently difficult to manage. Much of the problem is due to the divergent interests that bring two organizations together within a single partnership. A nonprofit organization working with government, for example, may enter into a partnership with the goal of assisting a narrow portion of the community, while the public sector takes care to ensure that the entire community is well served. Or a private sector partner entering into a partnership for a toll road project may care first and foremost about its long-term profits, while the public sector wants to achieve good financial value for the traveling public (Grimsey and Lewis 2007). The reality is that while organizations from different sectors have some interests that align in a partnership, the institutional incentives driving their respective organizations put pressure on each of them to serve their own interests, even at a cost to the partnership.

The reason divergent interests in partnerships deserve so much attention is that they create incentives for noncooperative behavior (Ni 2012). Put in economic terms, the individual interests of partner organizations can lead a nongovernmental organization toward a moral hazard, or behavior that puts the partnership at risk for their own personal gain. In addition, a nongovernmental partner may be inclined to hide information (information asymmetry) in order to protect trade secrets or individual knowledge that increases its leverage in the relationship. These divergent interests often play out in the identification and allocation of risks. The more risks that either party bears with respect to the wider goals of the partnership, the more inclined each will be to cater behavior toward shared interests because it will be in both parties' interest to achieve the desired results. The challenge is that many of the risks inherent in a new project are difficult to define in advance, and the very open-ended and discretionary nature of partnerships often masks the extent to which either party is carrying project burdens.

Table 4.2 summarizes the major issues to consider before agreeing to work in cross-sector partnerships.

Table 4.2

Issues to Consider Prior to a Partnership

Government capacity	1. What knowledge capabilities are needed for the kind of partnership being developed?
	2. What knowledge capabilities does the agency already possess and which ones are needed?
	3. How will knowledge gaps be addressed to prepare the public sector for this work?
Managing diverse interests	1. What are the overall policy goals inherent in the proposed project?
	2. What are the expected interests of the private or nonprofit party to the partnership? How might these interests compromise those of the overall policy goals behind the project?

THE PUBLIC MANAGER AND SUCCESSFUL PARTNERSHIPS

The techniques presented in this section provide a broad framework for partnership engagement and governance that can be adapted to the particular circumstances of any cross-sector partnership. Figure 4.1 presents the essential practices for governing successful cross-sector partnerships.

Risk Allocation

The first dimension that is important in assessing cross-sector partnerships is understanding and allocating risk among the partners. Rigorous risk analysis can help to identify areas where partners are inclined to compromise shared interests for personal gain, and the proper allocation of those risks can improve the alignment of partners' goals. Negotiations between the partners should begin by explicitly identifying and defining the risks and agreeing on who is in the best position to bear the responsibility for the risks in the partnership. For the public sector, this process often means identifying project risks that they are not used to monetizing, such as the long-term operations and maintenance costs related to physical infrastructure facilities.

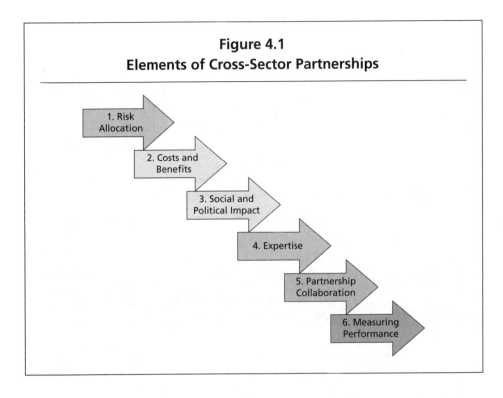

Figure 4.1
Elements of Cross-Sector Partnerships

1. Risk Allocation

2. Costs and Benefits

3. Social and Political Impact

4. Expertise

5. Partnership Collaboration

6. Measuring Performance

The goal of risk identification, allocation, and negotiation is "assigning risk to the organization that best understands and can control the risk and maximizes public benefit" (Eggers and Goldsmith 2004, 141). The objective is not to transfer all of the risks associated with a partnership onto a nonprofit or private sector partner. If the risks are not addressed properly, the partners may be tempted to avoid any relational interactions in order to minimize the risk of acting outside their prescribed contractual terms. Discovering the appropriate balance of risk allocation ensures a greater accountability for the services delivered and their conformance to public expectations.

Costs and Benefits

Cost–benefit analysis is critical for determining which projects are appropriate for cross-sector partnerships. While controlling the cost of a partnership is vital and also a major reason for government to enter into the partnership in the first place, it is also important to weigh the benefits in order to fully appreciate the overall value of the projects. Financial costs and benefits include both monetary expenditures and other gains and losses resulting from the partnership.

Opportunity costs, or those costs associated with the option of not entering the partnership, also should be identified. Saavedra and Bozeman (2004) find that cost–benefit analysis allows partners to determine whether a comparative advantage for a cross-sector partnership exists. Alternative approaches for examining collaborative value are presented in chapter 7.

There often are unanticipated costs and benefits in most cross-sector partnerships. For example, a study of one state's early childhood partnership with private firms (and local nonprofit childhood centers) indicated a decrease in center directors' focus on their education programs and a reduction in parent participation. Many of the forty-six center directors interviewed for the study said that the creation of the initiative led them to spend more time soliciting donations from their corporate partners and parents, which reduced their participation in center governance and policy. Yet there were also clear benefits from the partnership. The board members from the corporate world were thought by other members to add value through their critical thinking skills, orientation to innovation, and a strong valuation of efficiency that improved management and decision making at the centers (Patterson 2004).

In most cases (at least in the United States) public financing is less expensive than private financing; therefore, the advantages to a proposed PPP must include cost savings and other efficiencies of operations that offset the return on investment required by private partners. Public managers need to be certain that such cost savings do not come at the expense of providing high-quality public services. Public managers also need to look at life cycle costs of the project. Initial yearly payments (whether based on use or availability) may seem low compared to large capital outlays for an infrastructure payment. However, if total costs over the length of the project are not clearly outlined to decision makers, policymakers could opt for a PPP because of the lesser short-term costs without a recognition of the long-term nature of this fiscal obligation.

Social and Political Impact

The social and political impacts of cross-sector partnerships should be considered to help anticipate political or public resistance that can inhibit the objectives of the partnership. In assessing impacts, issues of social equity, such as the differential effects of a project on different communities, should be considered. The final benefit to the citizens is the primary standard of success that deserves attention in any government endeavor. Evaluating the interests of key stakeholder groups, including specific citizen groups, is central to that process. If services do not meet the expectations of the public, political consequences may include civic disengagement and weakened chances of reelection for partnership backers.

Part of the process of calculating social and political involvement involves citizen engagement and public involvement strategies. Citizen engagement strategies can include activities that range from town hall meetings and public hearings (Nabatchi 2012b), to web-based forums where members of the community can express their views and rank service delivery options (Brabham 2009, 2010). Key to any stakeholder engagement activity, however, is the importance of not only communicating the goals of the intended program to be delivered through a partnership, but also allowing outside groups to weigh in and influence the terms of the project (Nabatchi 2012a; Whitaker 1980).

Expertise

The government's ability to serve the public in cross-sector partnerships is only as good as its internal capacity for developing and monitoring these relationships. The challenge is particularly relevant in government offices that are unaccustomed to engaging nonprofit and for-profit organizations in more collaborative agreements. A key question in assessing public sector potential for managing effective partnerships therefore is whether they have decided to dedicate some of their administrative staff to work on cross-sector partnerships. The US State Department's Global Partnership Initiative involves a separate office that generates support from the private sector to cultivate partnerships related to US diplomatic efforts overseas. Many state departments of transportation have created stand-alone offices for developing and overseeing organizational partnerships.[1]

The dedication of public sector staff for partnerships also assists the public sector in learning how to work more effectively on these projects. Much of the knowledge and expertise that the public sector develops for working on cross-sector partnerships originates from direct experience, so the development of ongoing learning systems, such as best practice documentation, is critical for improving public sector capacity (Boyer 2012). Building government capacity is discussed in chapter 11.

Partnership Collaboration

The relational nature of cross-sector partnerships depends on effective governance of partnership relations, including a focus on the critical interpersonal dimensions of public-private or public-nonprofit relations (Gazley 2008; Zaheer and Venkatraman 1995). Trust among partners is extremely important in cross-sector partnerships. The cultivation of trust takes time; it flourishes as members of the involved organizations get to know one another better. Open and candid communication and transparency with the internal and external stakeholders is essential for engendering trust. "The way the two organizations regard each other is crucial, and above all else there must be mutual trust or the relationship may break down" (Office of Government Commerce 2003, 4). However, as one PPP manager stated, this type of partnership is "not a marriage, but a business relationship" (Kee and Newcomer 2008, 88). Some level of trust is required, but mechanisms are also needed for verifying one another's contributions.

Measuring Performance

Program evaluation refers to the "application of systemic methods to address questions about program operations and results" and monitoring, and performance measurement refers to the ongoing collection of data about programs such as workload or services delivered (Wholey, Hatry, and Newcomer 2010, 5). Information collected during evaluations can indicate how well cross-sector partnerships are achieving desired results and inform decisions that can improve their performance.

Performance measurement can complement the process of risk assessment and risk allocation by helping the involved organizations understand the extent that shared objectives (interests) are being achieved. Due to the discretionary nature of cross-sector partnerships, performance measurement systems often evaluate more abstract, higher-level partnership outcomes such as traffic congestion or safety standards in the field of transportation. The challenge for public managers is agreeing on the nature of the outcomes that will be evaluated and building in appropriate measures for assessing their achievement.

PUBLIC-PRIVATE PARTNERSHIPS FOR INFRASTRUCTURE

This section reviews a specific type of a cross-sector partnership: a public-private partnership for infrastructure (PPP). PPPs are becoming an increasing reality for governments around the world as public leaders seek out more innovative project solutions and access to private financing for public sector projects (Robinson et al. 2010; Grimsey and Lewis 2007). The rising popularity of PPPs has been described as a "massive" increase in infrastructure procurement (Delmon 2010). Infrastructure specialists highlight a worldwide increase in private investment in infrastructure, rising from less than $10 billion in 2000 to more than $55 billion in 2008, including areas such as telecommunications, energy, transportation, and water provision (Abadie 2008).

Decreases in fiscal resources available to federal, state, and local governments are leading many public officials to seek out alternative sources for financing large-scale infrastructure projects (Rall, Reed, and Farber 2010). Interest in private financing options through governing arrangements such as PPPs is likely to become even more appealing as state governments deal with the most challenging fiscal years since World War II (National Association of State Budget Officers 2011) and as federal agencies continue to experience a constrained budget environment.

The quadrennial *Report Card for America's Infrastructure* of the American Society of Civil Engineers has become the accepted authority on quantifying the gap in US infrastructure investments. It examines eleven different public infrastructure sectors and claims the US investment gap will be $1.6 billion dollars by 2020 unless action is taken (based on its 2013 study). The size of the investment gaps has been spurring interest in PPPs and a closer look at how private investors could be attracted to invest in US roads, bridges, airports, water systems and water treatment, levees, and renewable energy (American Society of Civil Engineers 2014).

PPPs attract attention for the potential incentives they create for the private sector to operate them more efficiently than direct-government provision or through the outsourcing of design and construction responsibilities to individual private contractors (Yescombe 2007). PPPs involve collaborative partnerships that are long-term in nature (often extending thirty or forty years or more in length), involve both public and private financing, require private sector involvement in the provision of government services, transfer risks from public to private organizations, and outline the roles and responsibilities of the organizations through complex contracts (Forrer et al. 2010).

Examples of some long-term arrangements in the United States include the Chicago Skyway toll road and the Indiana Toll Road, both deals closed in 2005. The City of Chicago sold the operating rights of the Chicago Skyway to a private consortium for ninety-nine years for $1.83 billion. The total was provided up front to the city to address long-term budget shortfalls in transportation and other areas. The Indiana Toll Road PPP garnered $3.8 billion in up-front payments for the State of Indiana, providing funding for programs statewide.

Despite the initial windfall to governments, these exceedingly long-term arrangements limit the future discretion of political leaders. They may be stuck in a relationship that is difficult or costly to exit from even if future conditions warrant a change. In addition, without adequate controls on fees charged to consumers (or limits on profits of the private sector), these arrangements empower a private party to essentially "tax" citizens for the use of infrastructure that has been publicly paid for, a situation that can lead to a political backlash from the population served.

The Port of Miami Tunnel

When President Obama spoke on the need for investment in US infrastructure in March 2013, he chose an interesting venue to make his claims. His backdrop was one of the largest PPPs in the United States, the Port of Miami Tunnel Project (Goldfarb 2013). The Port of Miami Tunnel (POMT) was designed to create a new direct-access roadway connection from South Florida's interstate highway network to the Port of Miami. The POMT will direct much of the port-related cargo traffic directly onto nearby interstate highways and around the city's downtown. The total cost of the project was estimated at $1.4 billion. The private sector partner is responsible for designing, constructing, and financing the entire facility over a five-year period and then operating and maintaining segments of the facility over a thirty-year time frame. The State of Florida, through the Florida Department of Transportation, will repay the concessionaire for the cost of building the facilities through an availability payment, an ongoing transfer of funds linked to project performance standards and contingent on the government's approval.

A number of factors make the POMT an interesting example of a PPP for infrastructure. For one, there is a substantial amount of risk transfer from the public sector to the private sector, with the private concessionaire (the Miami Access Tunnel, a consortium headed by Bouygues of France) bearing substantial risks associated with the design, construction, operations, and maintenance of the project. The private consortium does not receive payments until the facility is open to traffic in mid-2014. The availability payments are distributed monthly to ensure adherence to government-set performance standards for the project. The availability payment offers a unique form of repayment for the facility, in contrast to tolls or user fees.

Table 4.3
PPPs Worldwide

Europe	46%
Asia and Australia	24
Mexico, Latin America, and Caribbean	11
United States	9
Canada	6
Africa and Middle East	4

Source: Istrate and Puentes (2011).

International Experience with PPPs

When compared to the level of international PPP activity around the world, the United States is a small-time player. Between 1985 and 2011, 377 PPP infrastructure projects were funded in the United States, only 9 percent of all PPPs for infrastructure around the world. Europe leads the infrastructure PPP market, with 46 percent of all PPPs (table 4.3).

Of course, there are numerous social, economic, and political differences between the United States and other regions and countries that help explain the greater popularity of PPPs in other countries. In particular, many would cite the access that US state and local governments have to the municipal bond market, a major source of public financing of infrastructure that is much less available, and even nonexistent, in many parts of the world. State and local governments in the United States have little incentive to approach the private sector for financing infrastructure when funds can be borrowed through government (tax-exempt) bonds at a lower interest rate.

However, access to public finance does not explain all of the disparity in the use of PPPs for infrastructure. Despite the fiscal struggles that have beset US federal, state, and local governments since 2008, interest in and use of PPPs around the world for infrastructure projects such as rail, airports, and roads eclipses that found in the United States. Countries such as India and subnational governments around the world have been developing institutional structures for the promotion, development, and management of PPPs. No fewer than thirty-one countries currently have a PPP unit at the national or subnational level (Istrate and Puentes 2011).

Table 4.4
Outstanding World Bank PPP Projects

Country	Project
Benin	Port of Cotonou
Bhutan	Bhutan Education City
Brazil	São Paulo Metro Line 4
Egypt	New Cairo Wastewater
India	CLIFF Community Sanitation
India	Punjab Grain Silos
Jordan	Queen Alia International Airport
Mexico	Atotonilco Wastewater Treatment Plant
Peru	IIRSA Amazonas Norte Highway
Russian Federation	Pulkovo Airport
Rwanda	KivuWatt Power
Zambia	Chiansi Irrigation Project

Source: International Finance Corporation (2013).

The International Finance Corporation (2013) of the World Bank actively promotes the PPP model to attract private financing for infrastructure projects in developing economies. It identified forty PPP projects for 2013. A subset of these projects, shown in table 4.4, demonstrates the array of possible PPP projects, each recognized to have demonstrated high levels of innovation, development vision, replicability, and positive social impact.

PPPs will continue to be an invaluable vehicle for attracting private financing to critical public infrastructure in developing countries that lack critical infrastructure.

COLLABORATIVE PRACTICES IN CONTEXT

The elements of cross-sector partnership success (figure 4.1) are actions that public managers can take to achieve the overall goals of their collaboration. They are the primary processes for influencing the partnership formation in a way that advances the public interest. The challenge is that these processes are influenced by external conditions, which may affect partnership-level outcomes and in turn affect operational outcomes. Understanding the link between partnership-level outcomes and operational outcomes is critical to appreciating the difference between judging the success of partnerships based on partnership qualities and the overall objectives achieved through the collaboration.

The model presented in figure 4.2 contextualizes these partnering processes by considering the influence of other factors: operating environment, organizational characteristics, partnership attributes, and operational outcomes. The operating environment includes relevant institutions and the legal, political, and economic conditions where the partnership takes place. The organizational characteristics identify the different interests, experiences, and capacities of each partner. The partnership attributes describe the characteristics that facilitate successful partnerships, and the operational outcomes are the desirable traits of the services provision by the partnership.

This systems model describes the importance of the external environment and organizational culture on the partnering processes and the consequences for forming partnerships that deliver on their promise. This same model, with some modifications, might also be considered when implementing a network approach to delivering public services and, to a lesser extent, creating or engaging an independent public-services provider.

Operating Environment

The legal options available to address disputes that can arise during collaboration are a good illustration of how the operating environment influences relationships in partnerships. For example, the greater the confidence in third parties for resolving disputes and in the enforcement mechanisms, the better the prospects organizations from different sectors will have in working with one another (Ostrom 2000; North 1990). The operating environment is particularly influential on public-private partnerships for infrastructure, since state law frames the parameters of project risk transfers to a private sector partner (Garvin 2010; Geddes 2011). In developing nations where the rule of law is not well established, private partners will be hesitant to assume certain types of risks or may demand a large risk premium if they are to participate in PPPs.

Economic conditions, such as a recession or fiscal stress, may place more pressure on governments to develop partnerships in order to attract private funding. Limited availability of alternative service providers (the thinness of

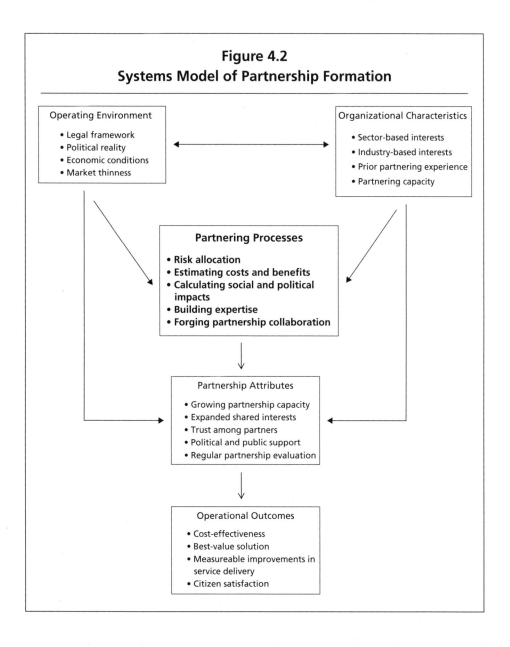

Figure 4.2
Systems Model of Partnership Formation

Operating Environment

- Legal framework
- Political reality
- Economic conditions
- Market thinness

Organizational Characteristics

- Sector-based interests
- Industry-based interests
- Prior partnering experience
- Partnering capacity

Partnering Processes

- **Risk allocation**
- **Estimating costs and benefits**
- **Calculating social and political impacts**
- **Building expertise**
- **Forging partnership collaboration**

Partnership Attributes

- Growing partnership capacity
- Expanded shared interests
- Trust among partners
- Political and public support
- Regular partnership evaluation

Operational Outcomes

- Cost-effectiveness
- Best-value solution
- Measureable improvements in service delivery
- Citizen satisfaction

the partnership market) can make finding partners difficult. When the United Kingdom began its public-private partnership program, the Private Finance Initiative (PFI), it had to help develop industry consortiums (financing, construction, and operations) that would ensure multiple bidders for PFI projects (Forrer, Kee, and Zhang 2002).

Organizational Characteristics

The skills, resources, and overall organizational culture that each partner brings to partnership formation influences its ability to collaborate. For example, private sector concerns about protecting intellectual property can conflict with public sector priorities of disclosure and transparency (Hodge and Coghill 2007). Different industries have their own practices and cultures that can influence the partnering process. Health care service organizations, for example, are likely to share a common concern with helping people and make them excellent prospective cross-sector partners with government agencies on a variety of health problems.

Prior partnership or networking experience and robust partnering capacity can be a significant factor in the government's ability to create and manage effective relationships in cross-sector partnerships. Organizations with a strong track record in partnering will be more likely to manage relationships effectively (Boyer 2013). Furthermore, the extent to which partner organizations have worked together in the past can create a foundation for information sharing and trust that can improve the terms of cooperation (Johnston and Romzek 2005; Gazley 2008).

Partnership Attributes

Durable capacities to collaborate and shared interests that have been identified and agreed to by partners are critical partnership attributes. They empower partnerships to take on the difficult yet essential tasks, effectively allocating risk to partners who are in the best position to manage that risk. This includes not only the ability to manage certain risks but ensuring partners are in a position to capture benefits from managing those risks well. These same durable capacities are needed to develop trust among partners. Effective partnership means a reliance on other partners, not only to carry out the actions they have agreed to take responsibility for, but also to have open and authentic discussions. Such arrangements and undertaking must be based on trust. Partnerships should recognize the importance of public outreach and stakeholder engagement. They can generate support from key political and community groups. Regular assessments and evaluations of partnership activities and operations provide an important basis for adjusting partnership decisions and arrangements. As partnerships learn about the relative effectiveness of their actions, adjustments can be made in both the outcomes and the approach to meeting outcomes.

Based on the description above, the interconnectedness of partnership attributes should be clear. Each attribute is not only important for the contribution it makes to effective partnerships, but the attributes are self-reinforcing. Strength in one attribute is a basis for strengthening others. Such interdependencies are a key feature of partnerships and of cross-sector collaborations more generally.

Operational Outcomes

The influence of the operating environment, organizational characteristics, and partnering processes on partnerships' attributes shapes the ultimate outcomes of collaborations. Understanding how these factors shape the opportunities for and limitations on partnering is helpful in setting reasonable expectations for what a cross-sector partnership might look like and what it could achieve. Areas most sensitive to these influences include the overall cost-effectiveness of the project, improvements in service delivery, and citizen satisfaction.

Those looking to form partnerships would benefit from thinking through the systems model from the bottom up. First, what type of public services do we want provided that meet the tests of cost-effectiveness, best value, improved status quo, and meeting citizen's expectations? Then ask, What type of partnership do we need to accomplish such outcomes? And next, what type of process should we put in place that will help us create just such a partnership?

With such aspirations set out, it is useful to ask, What conditions in the operating environment might support our partnering process? How reliable are those conditions, and how can we adapt to changes that may occur? What operating environment conditions could inhibit or derail forming a good partnership? Which firms or nonprofits have the characteristics that will support and facilitate the partnering process? Which partners might be less amenable to partnering? What could be done to improve the interest and participation of some reluctant partners?

The bottom-up approach sets out a clearer picture of the landscape within which partnerships will be formed. Some aspects will be positive and others will be negative. However, using the systems model in this way provides a useful diagnostic tool for anticipating the opportunities and the challenges faced in forming partnerships and achieving the desired operational outcomes.

ASSESSING THE ADVANTAGES AND DISADVANTAGES OF CROSS-SECTOR PARTNERSHIPS

Cross-sector partnerships, prevalent across policy sectors and levels of government administration, offer numerous advantages for government. Aligning with nonprofits and private sector organizations can capitalize on nongovernmental innovations and capacity for service delivery that does not exist within government. In many policy areas, organizations from outside government are the only ones with the potential for carrying out critical public services. Partnering also fosters more integration across sectors than more arm's-length exchanges, facilitating the cross-pollination of ideas and the creation of administrative solutions that government could not achieve on its own.

Similarly, partnering with organizations outside government can offer unique ways for managing risk in complex projects. PPPs for infrastructure shift significant construction, design, financing, and operational risks to partners, which can yield cost savings and improve innovation for government. The process of shifting risk also challenges the public sector to consider dimensions of project risk that are often not considered in traditional infrastructure projects, adding greater transparency to the costs and implications of project delivery. Transferring those risks to organizations outside government can reduce costs for projects by shifting those obligations to organizations that are better positioned to deal with them. Managing social outcomes in partnerships can also allow private or nongovernmental partners the discretion to develop innovations that the public sector could not have come up with on its own.

The same characteristics that offer potential in cross-sector partnerships can also cause problems for government. Working with organizations outside government to carry out core public service can create a level of independence that reduces public sector influence in collaboration. As risk is transferred to nonprofit or private sector providers, the public sector has fewer direct mechanisms for controlling that risk. Public managers need to pay special attention to the nature and the types of risks being transferred to ensure that the partnerships act in the public interest. For PPPs on infrastructure, this is especially the case. Long-term agreements lock governments into financial obligations that could have serious negative fiscal implications if they were not properly negotiated.

When the private sector is given more discretion for program deliverables, sometimes the public sector lacks the ability to properly monitor its contributions or do so too late, when it is difficult to turn programs around. There also are challenges in adequately developing public sector capacity for working on partnerships, particularly because the skills for partnerships differ from those in traditional forms of contracting. This capacity is particularly challenging in the more complex cross-sector partnerships, where the technical, legal, and financial expertise involved is beyond the capabilities of existing public sector employees.

Thus, as is true in most CSCs, public managers must examine and reconcile a number of competing values. Partnerships offer a promise of innovation, expertise, and additional resources. However, by shifting traditional government activities to the private or nonprofit sector, public managers give up some control, often relinquish direct contact with the citizens being served, and, in the case of long-term PPPs, reduce the discretion available to future political decision makers.

CONCLUSION

The increasing use, adoption, and potential of partnerships require more innovative approaches for public managers to learn how to create and support them. The need for developing a better understanding of partnership governance is particularly important given the potentials for partnerships to distribute risks in ways that can inhibit public interest. The shifting of risks to organizations outside government offers enormous potential for innovation and long-term operations and maintenance savings. Furthermore, the introduction of private financing in some models of infrastructure-based PPPs can fill in the gap of fiscal limitations in the public sector and help to accelerate projects that would otherwise prove impossible. The unique challenges and opportunities inherent in cross-sector partnerships require techniques for public managers to identify, capture, and transfer experiential knowledge related to their design and implementation.

Cross-sector partnerships create opportunities for the public sector to provide public goods and services in more innovative ways. The challenge is achieving an appropriate balance of control and flexibility, allowing partners from outside government the discretion to capitalize on their own comparative advantages while at the same time ensuring that overall outcomes meet the public interest. Considering the outcomes of cross-sector partnerships with respect to a system identifies the institutional, organizational, and environmental influences on partnership relations, as well as the achievement of partnership outcomes. This topic is explored further in the following chapters on other models of cross-sector collaboration.

Case Study for Discussion: State Employment Training

You are an assistant to the executive director of the Department of Social Services (DSS). The governor has campaigned on increasing job training in the state and moving individuals from receiving state welfare payments to working. Currently the Division of Employment Training (DET), which is within DSS, provides that service; however, the governor and the state legislature are unhappy with the current results: at an annual cost of $20 million, DET has found work for only a fraction of those on welfare. The program is operated out of twenty local offices, and the current annual success rate is less than 10 percent of the 500,000 adult recipients on welfare placed in a job. Welfare payments cost the state over $2 billion a year (averaging about $4,200 a person per year plus administrative costs of program administration).

Questions and Issues for Consideration

1. Many states have job training programs; other states use private or nonprofit providers as part of their job training programs. What are the advantages and disadvantages of creating nonprofit-public partnerships for this program?

2. What issues should the public sector consider before establishing a partnership for this kind of work?

3. What is the rationale for a partnership to improve the services delivered through this program?

4. What management considerations need to be addressed if a project like this is adopted as a public-nonprofit partnership?

chapter FIVE

Network Governance

Networks involving public, private, and nonprofit organizations are becoming a familiar form of collaboration through which public managers can more effectively address public policy issues. A logical progression in the evolution of the forms of collaboration, networks are more inclusive and diversified than PPPs and other cross-sector partnerships. They extend a long-standing approach to collaboration—informal government cooperation with private and nonprofit organizations—to more formalized multisector arrangements. Networks are more commonly found in the areas of human services delivery and response to disasters, but increasingly they are being used in other areas of public service delivery, such as job training and local economic development, and are increasingly adopted to address global issues (Hale and Held 2012).

Governments that use networks to deliver public services address a concern that is often expressed about PPPs where the principal participants in that type of collaboration are between government and the private sector. Critics have attacked the use of PPPs as being overly deferential to business interests and letting the private sector have too large a role in matters of public governance. One response by public managers to the negative public perceptions of PPPs has been to look for collaborations that expand the number of partners and engage networks that offer a more diverse representation of stakeholders and interests in the community, including nonprofits, community groups, schools and universities, and religious organizations. Private sector interests and values are counterbalanced by the more civic-minded culture of other organizations. As we have argued elsewhere, businesses will embrace a social responsibility mind-set and make decisions that advance the public interest, but the popular public perception typically casts business in a far narrower, self-serving role.

The attractiveness of networks as a form of collaboration for public managers is based on one assumption and one presumption. The assumption is that other organizations, in the private sector or the nonprofit sector (or both), have something of value to offer government in developing and delivering public services that are superior to what government could provide alone. Typically networks have the potential to offer public managers access to diverse and sophisticated sets of capacities, experiences, resources, and technologies that are not otherwise resident in most government agencies (Lee and Liu 2012). They also can contribute the experiences and expertise of private and nonprofit executives and managers. Finally, network members may be in a position to contribute to or directly fund activities, or the network itself may be able to attract funding support from charitable foundations or other sources of grant funding.

The presumption is that government can effectively coordinate its efforts with other organizations—private, nonprofit, and other government agencies—and work together more efficiently to deliver public services that are in the public interest. The presumption that public managers can effectively collaborate with networks is the chief subject of this chapter. In chapter 2, we described briefly how businesses and nonprofits have greater experience with collaborations and are highly motivated to establish further collaborations with government in the form of networks. Of course, many government agencies cooperate with other public organizations and have informal, if not regular, interactions with other entities outside government. However, most public managers have limited experience in the practice of using networks to meet their own program's goals and objectives. In this chapter, we discuss how public managers can examine potential networks, identify the unique characteristics of networks, and develop leadership and management approaches that can best support the network in achieving public purposes.

Moving beyond the bilateral relationships of cross-sector partnerships and engaging multiple participants to work together for a common cause has several implications for public managers. In a network, each member contributes efforts or resources, or both, toward a shared goal. Such an arrangement requires coordination of efforts between the network members, such that they share in discussions about what to accomplish and how to accomplish it, in what might involve a deliberative process. It also means creating mechanisms for open exchanges of information, emphasizing transparency so all parties in the network are able to voice their opinions and resolve issues to improve coordination and trust among members.

Of course, there also are instances of networks that public managers fall into and therefore have little voice in their design. In some areas of social services, the growth of the nonprofit sector in human services dictates that government engage a number of providers if they are to promote more holistic services. To effect change in childhood obesity, for example, federal authorities have taken a network approach by leveraging government and nonprofit youth services organizations that already serve targeted populations. In other cases, public managers must engage in ad hoc networks of local government agencies and departments to provide immediate relief, as in the immediate aftermath of a major natural disaster (Kapucu and van Wart 2006). Our focus in this chapter is on the purposive decisions that public managers take to develop and select network participants for specific types of public services.

DEFINITIONS

Working in a collaborative relationship with several organizations at the same time is easy to understand, but it is much less easy to define what constitutes a "network" as a formal arrangement of collaboration. According to Milward and Provan (2003, 2006), networks are collaborative, not bureaucratic, structures that involve autonomous organizations, often responsive to a broad range of nongovernmental stakeholders, while also working interdependently with both government and other network participants. Networks that governments use are collections of organizations that carry out activities on behalf of the public interest for a shared purpose. They are often orchestrated or coordinated by a public manager rather than directed by the manager. A key feature of network governance is the recognition that members work both collaboratively and independently at the same time. Our focus is on networks that involve government and are directed toward some public purpose rather than business alliances, policy networks, or nonprofit-to-nonprofit networks.

A network is a loose confederation; members join together to take collective action in which they share common interests but retain the primacy of their actions that will protect and advance their own interests. What actions a member is willing to take in concert with the others reflects in good measure his or her calculus of the consequences for his or her own interests and what can be gained through the collaboration. Working both collaboratively and independently makes perfect sense for members of networks, but it also renders network governance a tremendous challenge because individual members are continually weighing their own interests against the collective interests of the group.

For public managers, effective network governance means collaborating to formulate and implement government policies that are cost-effective or bring greater value to the constituents served. A distinctive nature of networks, where members' roles and contributions to the effort are a matter of negotiation, is that they are subject to change depending on the effectiveness of the network activities and alternatives available to members. Network governance requires good management skills on the part of the public managers and the creation of coordinating mechanisms across network members that are very different from those that are effective for managing programs in a government agency (McGuire 2002, 2006; Silvia and McGuire 2010).

Networks may present a double-edged sword to public managers: the more diverse the interests of the network members are, the richer the assets are to which public managers can gain access. At the same time, diverse network membership makes it all the more challenging to find common ground for action. However, much can be done to cultivate a shared purpose that unites network members despite their diversity. The key is identifying a fundamental value or desired result shared by all members of the collaboration and developing a method of validating it with one another through the collaborative process. The collaborative process (network governance) used to build agreement by members around what the network should do is itself a critical factor in building strong and committed networks. In some cases, that shared vision is facilitated and agreed on through the terms of the network's funding, such as a federal grant program that supports state and local actors addressing an at-risk community. In other cases, like emergency management, the vision is communicated as an overall need for a community to recover and prove resilient in the face of a major natural disaster.

One critical factor is the nature of the problem being addressed. When networks are formed to address a simple goal (albeit a critical one), the means for accomplishing the goal are straightforward, and shared expectations for the network members' contributions are clear so they can operate smoothly. Of course, the opposite is also true: governing networks that take on complex problems, where best practices are not confirmed and roles for members are unclear, can easily lead to problems. Similar to other forms of collaboration discussed earlier in this book, much of the challenge of network governance involves understanding the individual interests of different network members and how to negotiate those interests with respect to wider collaborative goals. Often the challenge is to communicate to network members how their individual interests can be better served by working together, such as the benefit to local businesses by cooperating with government to assist communities in rebuilding after a major disaster.

HOW NETWORKS FACILITATE COLLABORATION

Networks address different purposes for government and are organized with different types of structure out of either design or necessity. Understanding the role of the public manager and network governance involves first understanding the type of network that the manager is working with. The function or purpose of the network will influence the type of interest that individual members bring to the collaboration, the type of coordination required, and the overall measures for determining if the network is doing what it is supposed to be doing. The following sections review some of the different purposes that networks are organized around.

Types of Networks

Networks are formed in many ways and perform many functions. Four classifications capture dominant roles that drive different types of networks. While some networks may operate with more than one of these functions, one of these four typically indicates the dominant approach of the network (Agranoff 2007):

1. *Informational.* Partners come together almost exclusively to exchange information about agency policies and programs, technologies, and potential solutions. Any changes or actions are voluntarily taken up by the individual organizations themselves.

2. *Developmental.* Partner information and technical exchanges are combined with education and member services that increase the members' capacities to implement solutions within their home agencies and organizations.

3. *Outreach.* In addition to the activities of the developmental network, the network partners develop blueprint strategies for program and policy change that lead to an exchange or coordination of resources. Decision making and implementation are ultimately left to the agencies and programs themselves.

4. *Action networks.* Partners come together to make interorganizational adjustments, formally adopt collaborative courses of action, and deliver services, along with information exchanges and enhanced technology capabilities.

State and local governments have effectively used networks for decades to deliver a variety of human services programs. Examples include job training networks, health care and community care networks, community development networks, family and children's services networks, and local economic development networks (Turrini et al. 2010). The need for government agencies to coordinate the delivery of multiple social services for one person or family makes networks a natural form of governance in this arena. To illustrate the different ways networks can organize to deliver human services are four different types of networks providing social services for the homeless (Moore 2005) that align with the four types described above:

- *Informational*—Children and Homelessness Collaborative, Glendale, California. The primary focus of the Glendale Homeless Coalition is to have different agencies within the city work together to assist homeless individuals and families. Building on that focus, the collaborative has not only increased community awareness about the needs of homeless students but also fostered a better understanding of the different origins of homelessness through learning about different cultures and practices, leading to closer agency relationships and improved services for students and families. The information exchange improved service delivery by increasing understanding of homeless people's needs, but there was no joint action. Each agency acts on its own, based on its understanding of the information generated by the network.

- *Developmental*—Coalition for the Homeless, Pasco County, Florida. Several years ago, the Coalition for the Homeless of Pasco County recognized a lack of affordable transitional and emergency housing, as well as a need to disseminate information regarding available services for the homeless. Acknowledging that one agency could not provide all services needed, the coalition created the Housing and Urban Development Continuum of Care that now includes public, private, and faith-based agencies. It developed a formal memorandum of understanding with shared funding by the agencies. The collaboration supports ongoing services and specific projects such as the point-in-time homeless count. Each agency provides particular services as determined by its funding. The network increased its members' information and resource capabilities, but there was no pooling of resources in a joint program.

- *Outreach*—Perspectives, St. Louis Park, Minnesota. A nonprofit agency, Perspectives has served at-risk and homeless children since 1991. It offers an after-school program with academic, social, and nutritional components and a supportive housing program. Perspectives' staff approached the St. Louis Park School District and proposed a collaborative effort. The two entities coordinated their strategies and jointly applied for and were awarded a grant under the federal McKinney-Vento Act and then invited public, private, nonprofit, and faith-based social service agencies to partner with them. Those involved in health, housing, transportation, community education, parks and recreation, and the police were asked to join the collaboration. Target provides financial support, and General Mills supplies financial and volunteer support. Within the school district, the US Department of Education Title I coordinator and the homeless liaison were key participants, along with principals, teachers, and adjunct staff. In this case, Perspectives reached out to the St. Louis Park School District to develop a broader strategy for at-risk and homeless children, but implementation was addressed by each member of the network.

- *Action networks*—HEART Program, Spokane, Washington. Representatives of the Spokane School Districts sought to provide a quality academic atmosphere along with addressing other necessities such as housing, medical care, and clothing for their homeless students. They convened a task force to create a new vision for the program. The task force included representatives of the school district, YWCA, three universities, shelters, the school board, and the Spokane human services agency, along with the three teachers from the school. Based on the vision set out by the task force, the HEART (Homeless Education and Resource Team) Program was created as an integrated support model to refocus efforts on education. In this case, a fully integrated joint program was established.

The four models provide useful illustrations of how networks differ in the scope of their efforts and the scope and intensity of their collaboration. Some networks are more about cooperating (informational), while others involve deep integration (action). One advantage for the public manager in understanding the different types of networks and their functions is to set reasonable expectations for what participants should be working on and trying to achieve. Of course, it would be anticipated—especially when funding is uncertain—that networks change their activities and levels of collaboration over time in response to the demand for their services and the resources available to fund them. A network that begins as informational, for example, may evolve into one structured around action if the environmental conditions demand that type of transition.

Structure of Networks

Another way to understand how networks facilitate collaboration is to compare different structures for organizing networks and the implications of structure for the relationships among members. In the most decentralized structural form, participants are equal partners and have an equal voice in network activities. Even in such flattened structures, it is clear that some members of a network will be more influential than others and the relationships between participants and their exact roles will differ. For instance, members of a network who work part-time for a local nonprofit may feel intimidated or even offended by the business-style approach a participant from a large corporation might take at meetings. Network governance means identifying and accommodating different styles of the members and cultivating a governance approach that supports the overall aims of the network.

Network structure also has a direct impact on the overall effectiveness of networks (Turrini et al. 2010; Provan and Milward 1995). Along with the influence over shared goals and trust in the network, the structure can influence the stability of the network and how resilient the formal relations are to changes in the surrounding environment (Provan and Milward 1995). Three dimensions of structure that can be understood from formal relations are interconnectedness, cohesiveness, and centralization.

Provan and Kenis (2008) identify three distinctive structures (or modes) employed in network governance (see figure 5.1). Understanding these three forms can help public managers recognize the types of networks they are in and the associated implications for governments based on their structural characteristics. The three structures also present different models that can influence the design of networks for public purposes.

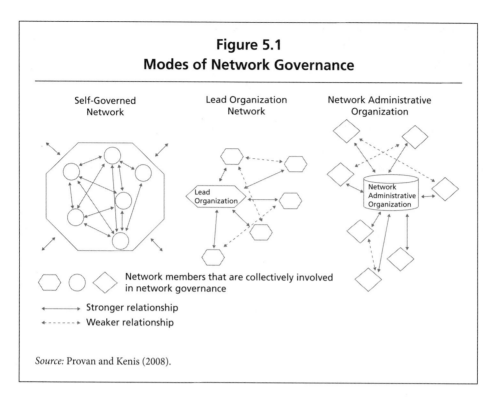

Figure 5.1
Modes of Network Governance

Self-Governed Network

Lead Organization Network

Network Administrative Organization

Lead Organization

Network Administrative Organization

Network members that are collectively involved in network governance

Stronger relationship

Weaker relationship

Source: Provan and Kenis (2008).

In some cases, public managers can promote a structure of network governance that best suits the needs of the government agency. For example, it is sometimes best for the government agency to offer leadership and direction for establishing the network's functions, as was the case of the National Incident Command in the weeks and months following Hurricane Katrina. Other times public managers will want to play the more limited role of convener and let the energy and interests of network members set the tone and ambition for the network. Whichever way it evolves, the structure of the network will have profound implications for the amount of influence a public manager will have in its governance.

A description of three examples of networks, each reflecting a different type of network structure, is provided in the following sections.

Shared or Self-Governed Network   In 1990, the Small Communities Environmental Infrastructure Group (SCEIG) was formed in Ohio as an association of federal and state agencies, local governments and groups, service organizations, and educational institutions in order to assist small communities in meeting their environmental infrastructure needs, such as safe drinking water and wastewater systems. Members include the State of Ohio Water Development Authority, Ohio Environmental Protection Agency, Ohio Department of Natural Resources, US federal-state Extension Service at Ohio State University, US Department of Agriculture/Rural Development, US Economic Development Administration, private lending representatives, university rural centers, nongovernmental organizations, and regional development districts.

This group of experts has quarterly meetings to discuss the needs of small communities and what responses or remedies are appropriate and feasible. In addition, the SCEIG has compiled a list of documents, publications, and Internet resources for the use of small communities in considering the financing, installation, repair, or expansion of environmental infrastructure. The goal of the network is to assist small communities in identifying the most appropriate resources that can help them with the difficult task of developing, improving, and maintaining their water and wastewater systems. To this end, the network established three committees to address the most pressing needs of small communities: Finance Committee, Curriculum Committee, and Technology Committee.

The network was convened by the State of Ohio Water Development Authority, which served as the initial lead organization for the network in its early days. Over time it has evolved into a shared governance model whose purpose is largely informational and outreach.

Lead Organization Network   The San Diego County Office of Education (SDCOE) and its school and community partners organized a network to address the response to and recovery efforts from wildfires. Strong Santa Ana winds channel through mountain passes in the area and create gusts approaching hurricane force. The combination of wind, heat, and dryness turns the chaparral found throughout the region into explosive fuel. Due to the winds, the wildfires are highly unpredictable, more so than wildfires that occur in other parts of the nation.

The October 2007 fires were the largest in San Diego County history; an estimated 515,000 county residents were evacuated. The fires resulted in ten civilian deaths, twenty-three civilian injuries, and ninety-three firefighter injuries. More than sixty-two hundred fire personnel fought to control the fires. In September of that year, the SDCOE had gathered resources to set up its Emergency

Operations Center (EOC). On October 22, 2007, the day after the fires started, SDCOE staff arrived in the EOC. The EOC served as a gathering place during the emergency, coordinated information resources and response and recovery actions across the school districts, and served as a point of contact for interfacing and coordination with other agency EOCs throughout the county. The SDCOE's superintendent had twice-daily calls with the forty-two district superintendents to generate a task list for the SDCOE. An SDCOE staff member served as liaison with the Operation Area Emergency Operations Center, the Red Cross, and sheriffs' departments for gathering information over the phone and using a real-time, web-based emergency management system.

The network was created to support a better approach to emergency response. The collection and distribution of information to network members and others improved reliability and timeliness. Access to the information facilitated quick decision making and the coordination of the decisions based on the information available. The network was supported by several staff, reflecting the need to use resources to ensure the efficient operations within the network itself. It is notable that the EOC was part of a larger regional network: a network within networks (US Department of Education 2008).

Network Administrative Organization   Fairfax County's Department of Systems Management for Human Services (DSMHS) was given the responsibility for facilitating the coordination of human services delivery in Fairfax County, Virginia. County leadership determined a need to streamline its social services during a time of rapid population growth, demographic changes, and expanded human resource needs, which included in-migration of refugees from other nations.

The original vision of county leaders was a fully integrated client intake system, with DSMHS serving as a lead organization in a broad network that would include federal, state, and county programs of assistance and available assistance through a variety of nonprofit actors in the county. The DSMHS failed to achieve that goal because of the difficulty of gaining sign-off from state and federal officials, concerns about privacy, and other issues that primarily involved protecting agency turf.

DSMHS implemented a coordinated service planning system that matched the needs of county residents with services available in the county from public, private, and nonprofit agencies, creating a network of human services providers.

It played more of a network administrator role, providing coordination and information but not fully integrating the actions of the various agencies in the network.

This effort was complex due to the number of actors involved, including county human services agencies, state and federal agencies, and both private and nonprofit providers of human services in the county. It was important to involve all key stakeholders in the planning and implementation effort. In this way, DSMHS was able to achieve widespread buy-in to the concept and improve overall delivery of social services to populations in need.

The Fairfax County case demonstrates two possible roles of government in a network-led organization: lead organizer and network coordinator. Rather than directing activities, determining what roles others might play, and ensuring these roles and responsibilities through contracts, governments can play many different roles, depending on the way the network is organized. Initially DSMHS sought to play a lead organizer role in the network, but practical and legal objections led to a network coordinator role that has worked effectively.

It is important to note that a network may evolve from one classification to another over time, as was the case with the Fairfax County network. Such was the case of the network established by the Federal Emergency Management Agency (FEMA) to address the emergency needs created by Hurricane Katrina, where the roles and influence of members changed over time. When the storm hit, the Department of Homeland Security (DHS) was only three years old, and FEMA had never before responded to a category 5 hurricane, which led many to argue that the system's infrastructure and individual expertise were not at all equipped for the storm. Due to the unprecedented nature of such a catastrophe, DHS and FEMA had little to no institutional knowledge to draw from in crafting a response, putting them at a disadvantage during the crisis (KSG 2006). The resulting intergovernmental network began as rather decentralized, and gradually assumed more of a lead organization model as federal authorities asserted more influence over the situation.

THE PUBLIC MANAGER AND SUCCESSFUL NETWORKS

We have grouped the factors of successful network governance from the perspective of a public manager under six broad categories illustrated in figure 5.2. The following sections describe each of these elements.

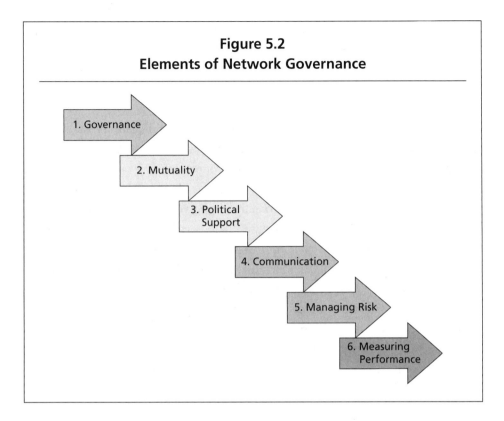

Figure 5.2
Elements of Network Governance

1. Governance

2. Mutuality

3. Political Support

4. Communication

5. Managing Risk

6. Measuring Performance

Governance

Networks may be designed in many ways. Provan and Kenis (2008) identified the three possibilities already displayed in figure 5.2. Whatever design is chosen for the network, it must accommodate the expectations of the network participants and facilitate the functions the network is to perform. Most often government is in a role of a lead organization or will act as network administrator, as in the Fairfax County Human Services case. Sometimes government assumes a lower-profile role, as in a self-governed network, where it is just one of many actors but can still exert its influence on the scope and activities of the network.

Regardless of the structure, network managers need to develop and communicate a common purpose that will encourage participants to act on behalf of the interests of all collaborators. Public managers may need to be directly involved in designing the networks to ensure that occurs. In either case, public managers must facilitate working relationships with external groups, recognizing their needs and interests. However, such relationships cannot be simply informal or convenient. The process requires more than monitoring, consultation, and reacting to proposals. It requires a recognition that the network will need to grow and learn together. It means public managers need to shift from being excellent "bureaucratic responders" to innovative "partner creators" (Agranoff 2012).

Mutuality

A public manager thinking about creating a network must consider the array of associations that might be involved: nonprofit organizations, small businesses and multinational corporations, local volunteer groups, substate planning agencies, public-private ventures, international organizations, and others. The question is how to find the right balance of organizations that bring value to a network yet have a shared interest in its efforts and outcomes. The participants must be convinced that the time and effort spent creating and developing a network is worth it; there must be a payback for them. The dilemma, however, is that sometimes it may be necessary to invest the time in building a network before the potential gains are clear.

When in a collaborative mode, public managers should account for the concerns of their own organization as well as those of potential collaborators. The shared purpose of the network is achieved in such a way that all participants can claim achievements for their own organizations. The achievements may be the kind that participants want to make public, such as an increase in the number of people receiving services. That type of publicity can improve an organization's reputation and help it with future fundraising. The achievements may be the type an organization would want to keep in-house, such as meeting influential people who might be contacted in the future and be a resource for other issues of importance to that participant. Successful networks find a way to achieve both the shared goals and the individual aspirations of individual participants.

Political Support

If participants harbor suspicions that the efforts of a network may be criticized by public officials or political support withdrawn, network governance may end up being more trouble than it is worth. The desire by elected officials for a strong government role in networks to ensure accountability is an understandable position, consistent with traditional views of public management. Yet the virtues of networks are their flexibility, innovativeness, and an expanded capacity over what government agencies can offer when acting unilaterally. Ultimately public managers need to represent the prospects for network success to elected officials by clarifying their expectation of how government participation in networks will improve public service delivery. Network members themselves can be effective lobbyists on behalf of the network and its cause. The support for the effort by well-regarded organizations and people in the community can be useful in allaying political concerns and building political support for the network.

The creation of networks also can be an initiative launched by a public official or government executive. Enthusiasm for networks among top managers may not reflect a full understanding of the complexity of the mission. Executives may not recognize gaps in skills or technical knowledge needed for effective network governance. The result could be an initiative that taxes public managers with an idea that sounds good but is difficult or even impossible to execute. In such cases, network participants can be a direct source of support for the public manager. They bring their own stakeholders and (sometimes) funding, which can be leveraged to garner the support of public officials.

Nothing breeds success like success. Garnering political support for a nascent network or managing the new responsibilities and expectations for a new initiative is a challenge. When there is clear interest in solving a problem, networks can be initiated and then mature as they operate. Other networks take time to develop, creating new working relationships, convincing people of the merits of collaboration, and discovering the shared goals and objectives among the participants. Delivering better public services and gaining support from participants is the best way to create political support.

Communication

Networks function best when there is an open flow of information among the parties (Zaheer, McEvily, and Perrone 1998). Deliberations are more successful when all of the parties are engaged and better informed. Public managers need to develop a variety of skills and procedures to facilitate that exchange. Communication protocols that are established help build trust among the network participants. Effective network governance is built on good relationships, which in turn are built on trust, and trust is founded on open and reliable communications.

In building high-quality relationships in networks through communities of linked professionals and practitioners, both inside and outside government, public managers face practical challenges. Learning to communicate openly in networks requires the capacity to create and use knowledge through informal exchange and mutual engagement. Information and communications technology are essential tools because partners often are situated in disparate locations.

However, they are not a substitute for face-to-face contact but a parallel to collaborative work, allowing not only the linkage of dispersed participants but also interactions with many potential and actual collaborators.

Managing Risk

Public managers are used to managing the risks associated with the activities of their agency. Certain procedures or precautions undertaken by public managers may seem unnecessary to those who work outside government, because they do not always understand how actions associated with a government agency may be viewed by elected officials or public media. Network members may not always act with the same sensitivities and considerations that public officials would employ, thereby putting public managers at risk of criticism of the network over which they may have no direct control.

As with any other collaboration, public managers share in the risk of a failure of others in the network to perform. It is useful for managers to understand the capabilities of the network participants and the challenges they face in maintaining their own operations and making long-term commitments of resources to the network. Will or can government step in to fill the void? Are other network partners available to substitute for the one that has been unable to fulfill its role in the network?

Public managers also must manage the risk that their own agency will not meet its promises to a network. Government budgets may not be approved or could be cut after they have been authorized. Everyone knows that bureaucracies move slowly, and public managers may have difficulty getting other government agencies to act quickly enough to meet network requirements. Networks that can align the activities of participants that are well established and funded will be easier to create and maintain.

Measuring Performance

Measuring network performance will depend on the purpose of the network's formation. For a network formed to respond to a natural disaster, performance could be based on meeting goals and objectives faster and with greater reliability. For example, SDCOE was successful in moving information about wildfires more quickly to those who could then pass it along to others and make decisions based on that information. When networks have a limited and clear role to play, measuring improvements in terms of outputs is best.

Networks that have more complex, integrative operations, such as Fairfax County's DSMHS, would choose factors that reflect their broader goals. The DSMHS chose percentage of needs met as one of its performance measures. It is also critical that performance measurements align with the functions the network was created to carry out. Agranoff's four types of networks—informational, developmental, outreach, and action—set expectations for what the participants want the network to accomplish, and performance measures should reflect that function. Public managers will want to deter others from assigning performance measures (and therefore expectations) to a network that has not been agreed to by the participants.

Turrini et al. (2010) suggests the following measures of network effectiveness: client level of effectiveness, network capacity of achieving stated goals, network sustainability and viability, community effectiveness, and network innovation and change. Thus, the performance of a network is not based on simply how well information is shared or that action is improved; it also depends on the overall operations and functions of the network itself. Network managers must address the needs of specific clients and the network's stated goals, but attention also needs to be paid to the viability of the network. Is the network vulnerable to changes in political priorities, research constraints, or other variables, or is it something that can adjust to these changes? The extent to which the surrounding community supports and assists the network also will influence its effectiveness. Finally, the ability of the network to innovate and adapt to change will influence both network longevity and the quality of services it delivers to the public.

Within the context of network effectiveness, the overall performance of networks should be considered in terms of both functions and institutional structure. Measuring the performance of networks in this way involves assessing their operational achievements in the short term, as well as their structural ability to integrate into communities and provide some lasting support to the clients they serve.

ADVANTAGES AND DISADVANTAGES OF NETWORKS

Networks are just one option among the choices public managers have for engaging in cross-sector collaborations (CSCs), and they have unique advantages and disadvantages compared to other forms of collaboration. As we have discussed, networks are diverse in the ways they organize, the types of problems they address, the complexity of those problems, and the extent to which government agencies participate in service delivery. As a result, the advantages and disadvantages we describe are not equally applicable to all networks.

Advantages

The advantages networks can offer public managers as a CSC are discussed throughout this chapter. We have consolidated some of the central ones and summarized them here. Of course, these advantages will be realized only when network governance is effective.

Cutting Across Silos Some types of public services are delivered using multiple programs or services that need integrating, such as those of Fairfax County's DSMHS. Others pose complex issues that call for analyzing and understanding multiple factors at one time, such as those of Ohio's SCEIG. Still others require rapid response times and precise coordination, such as those of San Diego County's SDCOE. In each instance, improving the delivery of public services required efforts that transcended one office, one mission, one sector.

Insular bureaucratic protocols often constrain public managers to operate within narrow silos and to direct their agency's efforts and resources toward a limited set of actions. Networks cut across these silos and facilitate a collaboration that helps participants see more clearly where their own organization's efforts contribute to achieving a larger impact. With such a perspective, it is easier for public managers and other network participants to adjust their approaches and activities in ways that result in better public services.

Leveraging Resources As governments find themselves under spending constraints, any one agency is unlikely to have all of the necessary skills, resources, and abilities to provide public services comprehensively and at the optimum level of quality. Businesses and nonprofits share the experience of government not always having enough funding or the right skills to meet their own organization's goals. At the same time, businesses, nonprofits, and government agencies have different ways of looking at issues; different mixes of skills, experiences, and resources available; and different approaches to addressing issues in their respective fields.

Collaborating in a network brings together organizations that can leverage their own resources with those of other network members and increase their overall capacities to take action. By unifying these varied skill sets, networks give all participants the opportunity to widen the scope and scale of their own organization's activities, particularly when engaging distinct cultures.

Greater Transparency and Citizen Participation   Networks thrive on the exchange of information among participants, which facilitates coordination among network members. In turn, that same cooperation and communication mean greater public access to information about agency operations, policies, practices, and performance. Many aspects of a government's operations remain a mystery to the public. Even simple requests for copies of government contracts seem nearly impossible without a great deal of effort and struggle. Sharing information within the network about past and future activities, performance successes and failures, and budgets and spending provides a greater chance of that information getting out to the public.

In contrast to PPPs, networks thrive on engaging and integrating many perspectives and leveraging diversity to provide better public services. The diversity of stakeholders and interests in a network can also translate into greater political support from public officials and citizens. Citizen participation is enhanced by networks in two ways. First is through the roles citizens play as volunteers for nonprofits. Nonprofits involved in networks provide a point of access for their members, who can learn about network activities through their own organizations. Second, as citizens express their views and preferences on the priorities of the organizations they are associated with, those same preferences are expressed in network deliberations.

Innovation   By bringing together diverse resources and perspectives, networks become centers of innovation where new ideas are offered and considered. Most large organizations, whether public, private, or nonprofit, tend to favor routines and established practices. Networks offer participants an opportunity to take a fresh look at how public services are being delivered and imagine how they might be improved, without the discussion being viewed as a direct challenge to accepted practices.

Thus, one of the attractions for people to participate in networks is the diversity of perspectives and experiences available. Networks can foster a sense of excitement about the possibilities of doing something new and different. They offer participants an easy way to learn about new ideas they can share with their home organizations.

Knowledge Transfer   Networks spread information faster and more easily than in other governance arrangements and provide many avenues for the transfer of information among participants. Learning from the experiences of others in networks can also lead to a behavioral change within the observing organization.

Networks are an invaluable source of program-related knowledge and experiences from other managers working in the field. Knowledge about past successes and failures also surfaces in network deliberations. Frank discussions of failures in public service delivery are a valuable learning experience and are more likely in a network, to the benefit of all participants and the network itself.

Disadvantages

Using networks as a form of collaboration, as with any other approach to governance, has disadvantages as well.

Less Accountability   A principal characteristic of networks is their decentralized operations, which allows them to be responsive and flexible. But networks are not always adept at providing the information or using a unified chain of command for accountability purposes. Networks may not have to confront difficult accountability issues when all is going well, but who becomes responsible for failing or underachieving networks? Who decides what the performance standards should be? When networks have volunteer organizations among their ranks—sometimes exclusively—how are they expected to respond to criticism from public officials or the media? Setting performance standards and collecting the data needed to make accurate assessments is challenging.

Less Stability   The very diversity that is a network's strength is the source of a possible lack of stability. Networks have to simultaneously balance external pressures from interest groups and internal pressures from within their organizations. Participants who are excited over forming a network might lose enthusiasm and decide to drop out, upsetting the balanced interests of the collaboration. Are there other participants to fill in? Will they have the same interests in outcomes? How will the change affect the network's group dynamics? Participants moving in and out of the network—particularly when one participant has been accommodated by the network, only to have it leave—disrupt network operations. The potential instability can be a deterrent to some organizations that may be considering joining the network.

Cost of Formation   One potential problem in forming networks is the intensive time and effort needed to create them. Many reform efforts involving networks can take years to create, and significant results may not be produced during the initial years. Every administrative hour spent on CSCs is an hour taken away from internal management issues. Government agencies may not have the personnel available or the free time to dedicate to the creation of networks. While the promise of better service delivery makes networks attractive, the time and effort have to be invested up front, without any guarantee of success. The time spent on a network that falls apart could be viewed, in retrospect, as wasted cost and effort.

More Complex Governance   The governance of networks is far more complicated than that of PPPs or cross-sector partnerships. The multiple organizations and their multiple goals, the diverse personalities of the leaders, the varied access participants have, and the willingness to share resources are only a few of the factors that public managers must try to align and direct toward a shared goal and its achievement. Of course, the conditions and circumstances under which these are done are themselves dynamic and subject to change, both gradual and sudden. The blending of interests together into a collaborative whole from such a diverse set of interests can overwhelm public managers as they attempt to institute good network governance. The key is understanding the level of involvement and intervention that is required by network members, particularly public managers, to coordinate network activities. Because networks are decentralized and often less formal, there is greater potential for dissensus among member goals. The less formal the relations of a network are, the more work public managers will have to coordinate and to align network activities.

Network Capture   Networks operate outside traditional government boundaries. If they are not governed properly, different interest groups could manipulate the goals and activities of a network for their own gains and to the disadvantage of people who have not organized a network or are excluded from it. Networks could use their access to government agencies to claim legitimacy for operations that are harmful or fraudulent. Just because a network has been formed to deliver public services does not mean it will act in the public interest. It is the responsibility of the public manager to ensure that networks are legitimate representatives of the relative community of interests and act in the broader public interest.

OVERCOMING CHALLENGES TO GOOD NETWORK GOVERNANCE

In the effort to explain networks and communicate their potential efficacy, public descriptions of how they are created and operate can be overly optimistic. We have described the advantages and disadvantages of collaborating using networks. In the real world, the number of successes using networks is likely matched by as many stalemates or failures to launch. We suggest some common-sense approaches public managers can take when creating networks that will assist them in overcoming barriers to their formation.

Lead with Purpose

Launching a network with a clear purpose and plan for government's role makes it easier to engage potential partners and bring them together in a shared cause and with a shared purpose. Leading with a clear purpose not only inspires people to do better, but sends a message that change is coming and it has the support of top leadership. Promoting a vision of change encourages people who want to see change and signals that they will be supported within the organization.

Secure Buy-In from Partners

Network participants need to believe that their interests and concerns will be given fair consideration. Uneven power relationships within a network are inevitable, but who has the power within the network to set agendas and make decisions is a critical issue for all participants. Mary Parker Follett's concept of "power with" (discussed earlier in the book) offers the best possible use of power in collaborative arrangements. If public managers see their role as blending their own power bases with those of their collaborators, the network will be stronger and more effective.

It is best not to identify network solutions too early or compel the network to reach a consensus too soon. Participants have their own ideas about the nature of problems the network could address and what actions could be effective. Allowing the network to endorse one approach supported by one participant before a full deliberation may undermine success. Establishing an open discussion and a deliberative process is critical to ensuring that participants have a voice and believe they will reap specific benefits for their organization and themselves. Such a process does not mean networks have to move slowly, but they do need to move deliberately with openness to pluralistic thinking.

Be Opportunistic

Networks present numerous challenges on how best to organize and govern. Building a network around an issue or problem that people agree needs immediate attention will make it easier to solicit cooperation. It is one reason that networks have been able to form so quickly around natural disasters. Once a network is formed and has proven itself useful to the participants and has a track record, it is easier to make the case for a long-term commitment to participating in the network and it opens up the door to expanding the issues that could be addressed collaboratively.

Pick Good Leaders to Participate

Not all executives who lead or work in organizations may be good candidates as participants in a network. Successful collaboration means a willingness to help advance the common purpose and interests of the network, sometimes at the expense of a more specific interest of a participant's own organization. Network leaders must convince others that support for shared network goals will end up advancing the goals of the individual participants, more so than if they operated on their own. Leaders who can take such an approach tend to recognize that trait in others, and there is a comfort in working with people who are perceived as "honest brokers" and "trusted partners." Networks need participants who are willing to act collaboratively and not use their role in the network to hinder its progress by seeking to retain the status quo or unfairly promoting their own organization's interests.

A public manager's decisions to participate in CSCs should include systematically thinking through whether they have the agency resources (e.g., staff time and budget) that will likely be needed and can afford to assign appropriately skilled staff to represent their agency and its interests. It may be helpful to use a memorandum of understanding, which clarifies the expectations and commitments associated with participation in a CSC.

> ## TEN ISSUES TO CLARIFY IN A MEMORANDUM OF UNDERSTANDING WITH CSC PARTICIPANTS
>
> 1. CSC mission
> 2. Expected outcome in quantifiable terms
> 3. CSC governance (such as leadership and decision-making procedures)
> 4. Participants (plus letter of commitment to participate)
> 5. Expectations for roles of participants
> 6. Length of commitment, including termination procedures
> 7. Financial commitments (if any)
> 8. Other resource commitments such as administrative or technical support
> 9. Reporting and monitoring format and time frame (if any)
> 10. CSC annual budget (if any)

GOING GLOBAL

Networks have gained rapid popularity as an approach to addressing some of the most difficult global policy challenges. The task of developing a consensus among national governments in the form of treaties or international protocols grows more difficult as globalization expands and intensifies the interdependence of nations. International organizations such as the World Bank and the United Nations confront these challenges as they look to design and implement programs and policies that address development issues such as described by the United Nations Millennium Development Goals.

The global governance landscape is becoming more crowded with expanded roles for multinational corporations and global nongovernmental organizations, which are becoming directly involved in solving global problems. Global networks have sprung up to fill a global governance gap across a range of policy areas. The absence of a global government that has full authority to regulate and enforce policies means that global networks tend to operate with greater independence and the government plays a less directive role. One example of a global network is the Global Fund (Hale and Held 2011).

The Global Fund is dedicated to attracting and disbursing resources for fighting HIV, tuberculosis, and malaria, supporting collaboration among governments, civil society, and the private sector. The Global Fund was established as a result of a 2002 UN General Assembly Special Session on HIV/AIDS, which underscored the need for increasing funding to combat HIV/AIDS. Since its creation, it has become the main source of funding for programs fighting AIDS, tuberculosis, and malaria. The directing board is composed of representatives from all sectors—businesses, donor and recipient governments, affected communities, and civil society. As an organization combating global disease epidemics, the Global Fund brings together many aspects of global society while it faces many challenges, such as funding and cooperation with participating countries.

CONCLUSION

Networks present a choice on collaboration that is very different from PPPs, partnerships, and contracts. The change from essentially a bilateral relationship to a multiparty collaboration expands the possibilities for aggregating interests across the private and nonprofit sectors in order to devise and implement a better way to deliver public services. At the same time, it adds layers of complexity involving network governance.

For many types of public services, PPPs and partnerships provide the right form of collaboration. When the type of public service needed has been clearly identified but the best way to deliver it is unclear, bilateral collaborations can achieve the innovation desired while developing a governance model that involves fewer transaction costs for public managers. However, preexisting conditions or the complex nature of a problem may necessitate a larger number of organizations in a given cross-sector collaboration. Many nonprofits already operate in areas of human service delivery, for example, and networks may be preferred over partnerships because of the reality that so many organizations already exist in the operating environment around the policy area of interest. In addition, networks may be necessitated by the complex nature of a social issue being addressed, such as childhood obesity, emergency management, or mental health care.

As we have illustrated in this chapter, networks have different structural characteristics and different purposes, which lead to different priorities for governance. They can address a straightforward problem—distributing information quickly to facilitate responses to natural disasters such as fires in San Diego— or a highly complex global problem—addressing the global threats of HIV, tuberculosis, and malaria. They can be launched as a high-level international initiative—like the World Commission on Dams (United Nations Environmental Programme 2001)—or as a practical effort to improve human services for the homeless in Pasco County, Florida, or social services in Fairfax County, Virginia. The complexity of the issue addressed has a direct impact on the structure of the network and the associated transaction costs of managing the relationships among the involved members. Understanding broad classifications of network structures and purposes can help public managers adapt their own governance approaches to coordinating action, trust, and overall effectiveness and performance within the network collaboration.

Managing networks calls on an administrative capacity that is beyond the typical set of management skills needed for working in government. The potential for networks to provide public services in more innovative and more responsive ways than direct government services, contracting, or PPPs demands attention to the types of administrative capacity needed to develop and coordinate these types of networks. Demonstrated successes of networks in any policy area are some of the most important means for sustaining political support for network approaches to service delivery. Recognizing network structures and functions, adapting elements of success in network governance, and measuring results will communicate successes and can lead to a better integration of network governance into the work of public administration.

Case Study for Discussion: State Employment Training

You are an assistant to the executive director of the Department of Social Services (DSS). The governor has campaigned on increasing job training in the state and moving individuals from receiving state welfare payments to working. Currently the Division of Employment Training (DET), within DSS, provides that service. However, the governor and the state legislature are unhappy with the results: at an annual cost of $20 million, DET has found work for only a fraction of those on welfare. The program is operated out of twenty local offices, and the current annual success rate is less than 10 percent for the 500,000 adult recipients on welfare who were placed in a job. Welfare payments cost the state over $2 billion a year (averaging about $4,200 a person per year plus administrative costs of program administration).

Questions and Issues for Consideration

1. If DET looked at creating a network to improve its impact, what types of organizations might be invited? Explain your choices.

2. Which of the three types of network designs would you choose, and why? Which of the four network functions would you assign the network, and why?

3. Which of the network partners has the potential to dominate, and what could be done to mitigate negative feelings in the network and harness the resources and interests of that powerful participant? Explain your answer.

chapter SIX

Independent Public-Services Providers

A New Potential Collaborator

Independent public-services providers (IPSPs) present the newest option for collaboration to public managers. These new entities at first appearance may look similar to networks or partnerships. Yet IPSPs have an approach to governance that makes them distinctive and offers a unique collaborative opportunity to public managers. All the other cross-sector collaborations (CSC) involve activities and relationships that advance the specific goals of a government program or policy. Collaborating with IPSPs is unique because the public service being provided is determined by the IPSP, not government.

Among all of the CSC considered here, IPSPs have two extreme conditions of collaboration for public managers. IPSPs can offer the most innovative approaches to delivering public services, since they are able to pursue their own priorities independent of the numerous constraints that govern public administration. They also thrive on designing and implementing public services that are more effective than conventional approaches employed by other collaborations that governments may engage. IPSPs, however, also operate outside government's sphere of control. Their independence can make them odd collaborators for public managers, who are used to setting agendas, directions, and deliverables in their collaborations.

Public managers need to learn how to engage IPSPs in a different manner from the conventional hierarchical, top-down approach used with employees and contractors. IPSPs hold a special status as collaborators with governments.

They are pioneering entities that are part of the emerging idea of new governance, a concept that is increasingly complementing the traditional concept of government. Governance includes not only governments but also other organizations that are providing public goods and services (Peters and Pierre 1998).

As potential collaborators, IPSPs have an obvious appeal for government. When IPSPs are providing services that are consistent with public policy goals and objectives, public managers may choose to support these operations through collaboration. It is an opportunity to meet a public agency's obligations at minimal cost. The lack of direct control over what public services are provided by IPSPs and how they provide them, however, raise serious worries about accountability and how to report on these collaborations to publicly elected officials.

DEFINING PUBLIC ENTERPRISE ORGANIZATIONS

In chapter 1 we defined IPSPs as self-directed entities composed of businesses, nonprofit organizations (often referred to as nongovernmental organizations), and governmental units that collaborate in the production or delivery of public goods or services.

IPSPs have unique characteristics that make them different from collaborations with the PPPs, partnerships, and networks discussed thus far. The defining characteristics of a IPSP are displayed in figure 6.1.

Although the individual characteristics of an IPSP by themselves are not unique, the combination of all three makes IPSPs distinctive collaborative partners and unique actors on the governance landscape:

- The multisector circle also represents organizations that do not provide public services and are not self-directed, such as alliances between nonprofits and business.

- The public services circle includes organizations such as national, state, and local governments and various quasi-governmental organizations that are within the traditional government hierarchy and provide services to the public but are not multisector.

- The self-directed circle includes both for-profit and nonprofit organizations that provide goods and services and exist in only one sector. One example is a company that has the freedom to make its own decisions (it is self-directed), sells goods and services for profit, and works solely in the private sector.

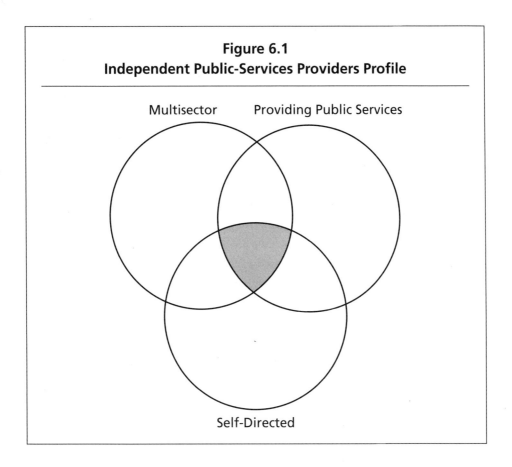

Figure 6.1
Independent Public-Services Providers Profile

Multisector   Providing Public Services

Self-Directed

IPSPs operate within the shaded part of the circles at the very center of the diagram where these three characteristics are unified. That is, IPSPs have all three characteristics:

1. *IPSPs are largely self-directed.* They do not operate within a traditional government hierarchy and often act independently of government. As a result, they have the freedom to think about issues and deliver public goods and services in a manner that may not necessarily conform to convention or only to those perspectives endorsed by government agencies. They also operate outside the constraints inherent in a federal system with its checks and balances. Because there is no direct oversight by public officials, they are able to act with greater efficiency, creativity, and purposefulness. Thus, IPSPs can offer new, innovative approaches that are more responsive

to the public and can address challenging public policy problems more effectively.

2. *IPSPs comprise multiple stakeholders.* They have diverse views and accommodate different perspectives and interests. In this way, IPSPs can claim a measure of legitimacy (when they properly represent the interests of appropriate stakeholders). Having multiple participants allows collaborations that combine the skills and experiences necessary to meet their goals and adapt to local circumstances in innovative ways.

3. *IPSPs provide public goods and services.* They serve in the place of governments and interact directly with the public. They often provide services that citizens might otherwise expect governments to provide, but they may provide a better option or the only option. Too often governments do not have sufficient funding to provide all the services that communities need.

In contrast to contractors, partnerships, and networks, IPSPs act with a greater discretion and autonomy in determining the types and methods of services they provide, a characteristic that places them outside the governmental framework, even when government may be involved. IPSPs are sometimes formed ad hoc; at other times, they are more permanent, structured through formal organizational structures or through contracts, memorandums of understanding (MOUs), or informal agreements; and often they are created without any government involvement at all. They provide enormous opportunities to supplement traditional governmental agencies to meet today's critical problems.

THE GROWTH OF QUASI-GOVERNMENTAL AND HYBRID ORGANIZATIONS

The idea of operating outside the usual administrative boundaries of government as a strategy to improve the performance of some functions thought important by government is not new. Throughout US history, the federal government, and more recently state governments, has created entities that operate outside government's conventional administrative structures to carry out specific public functions. These entities represent a diverse set of arrangements and responsibilities; however, they share the characteristic of conducting activities on behalf of the government but not being under the direct authority of a government agency. Examples at the national level include:

- Federal National Mortgage Association (Fannie Mae) and Federal Home Loan Mortgage Corporation (Freddie Mac)
- National Railroad Passenger Corporation (AMTRAK)
- National Dairy Promotion and Research Board
- The National Park Foundation
- Public Company Accounting Oversight Board

These entities and scores more represent what have come to be known as quasi-governmental entities. They are called quasi-governmental because they were created by the government and have ties to the executive branch but do not act as agencies as defined by the US Code. They carry out their mission, judged to be for a public purpose, but most often they do not have to operate under government procurement or personnel requirements. Although there is no clear-cut definition of *quasi-governmental* and they undertake a diverse range of functions, these entities conduct important government operations. An analysis by the Congressional Research Service identifies seven types of such organizations at the federal level. A summary review of some of the types of organizations demonstrates their variety (Kosar 2011):

- Quasi-official agencies, such as the Legal Services Corporation, the Smithsonian Institution, and the US Institute of Peace, are not executive agencies, but are required to publish certain information about their programs and receive direct funding from the federal budget.
- Government-sponsored enterprises, such as Fannie Mae, Freddie Mac, and the Federal Home Loan Bank System, are corporate entities established by federal law; they are privately owned and operate under a board of directors composed primarily of private owners.
- Federally funded research and development corporations, such as the National Laboratories at Oak Ridge and Los Alamos, are designed to address a federal need for research focused on specific topics through the application of private scientific and engineering skills. They are exempt from federal civil service rules and are operated under long-term (often sole-source) contracts initiated by government agencies, such as the Department of Energy.

- Agency-related nonprofit organizations have a legal relationship with a department or agency of the federal government in one of three ways: (1) adjunct organizations under the control of a department or agency (such as the Department of Agriculture's Agricultural Commodity Promotion Boards); (2) independent organizations created by federal statute that are dependent on or serve a federal department or agency (such as the nonprofit Veterans Administration medical centers of research and education); and (3) nonprofit organizations (created under federal law or state statutes) that are voluntarily affiliated with departments or agencies, such as nonprofit state park organizations.

- The other three quasi-governmental types that Kosar identified are federal venture capital funds; congressionally chartered nonprofit organizations, such as the Red Cross and the National Academy of Public Administration; and other entities that do not fit neatly into any category.

State governments also have created a number of quasi-governmental units. These include such organizations as airport authorities, building and housing authorities, and lottery commissions. Governments imbue these quasi-governmental organizations with a mission that contains a public purpose without hindering their operations with the typical governmental hierarchy and red tape.

Distinguishing IPSPs from Quasi-Governmental Entities

Despite their special status and their exemption from government procurement and human resources policies, quasi-governmental should not be confused with IPSPs. Quasi-governmental entities are created by an act of Congress or state legislatures; the very fact that they exist is a decision by government with a specific public purpose in mind. Their authority to act is vested in such legislation. IPSPs are not created by government (although there may be general authorizing legislation for them to exist and conduct their operations); they are arrangements that are formed voluntarily. IPSPs may, and sometimes do, collaborate with government through contracts or agreements, but not because the government created them. IPSPs "invent themselves" and can convene, change membership, or disband as the members decide.

In addition, the authority conveyed to quasi-governmental entities is specified, allowing a certain legal authority to act and limiting other kinds of actions. For example, regional airport authorities (sometimes multistate entities) have the authority to sell bonds without government approval, but the use of the funds from those bonds is restricted. The US secretary of energy cannot direct the specific research agenda or projects the National Renewable Energy Laboratory undertakes, but the laboratory is restricted to the general topics to which its research is directed.

In contrast, IPSPs choose their mission, and that mission is negotiated among its members. Of course, some IPSPs carry out missions that are consistent with government policy, but the choice to promote such policies comes from their own impetus. Therefore, IPSPs also are not subject to government oversight to the same extent as quasi-governmental organizations. In short, because IPSPs are not created by the power of the government, that same government has limited influence over them without engaging in an effective collaboration.

Distinguishing IPSPs from Other CSCs

Having defined IPSPs, it is easy to see how they could look similar to other CSCs. For example, nearly all IPSPs are formed as nonprofits. In addition, many organize as a network or join in partnership with other organizations. So what separates IPSPs from the partnerships and networks discussed earlier? IPSPs may look similar to these other organizations, but they act differently in important ways.

While IPSPs may share characteristics with other CSCs such as partnerships and networks, it is the combination of the three specific characteristics that makes them singular as a potential collaborator. First, IPSPs form with the intent to collaborate with stakeholders. The reason they form in the first place is to provide a different approach to delivering public services grounded in multisector collaboration. Some nonprofits also collaborate, but that is incidental to their mission and identity. That is, a nonprofit would still be a nonprofit whether it collaborated with others or not, but for an IPSP, collaboration is an important aspect of its core mission. Any nonprofit that embraces multisector collaboration as its primary approach to delivering public services might be considered an IPSP.

Second, IPSPs are self-directed and operate separately from government direction. In this way, they are distinguished from the networks discussed in chapter 5. Networks enhance and expand the resources and capabilities available to governments and are linked to a government organization. IPSPs create their own missions and determine their own operations for the very reason that they want to improve on the current practice. Since IPSPs act in collaboration with other organizations (including governments), their efforts may incorporate some government programs into a more integrated and comprehensive approach. In addition, IPSPs are not precluded from accepting grants from governments, but they do not let government funding or government policies guide their activities. It is the reason the IPSP was created in the first place: to be a self-directed operation that offers a new vision, a new approach to governance, and a new way to collaborate,

Third, IPSPs provide public services. Of course, all the other collaborations we discuss in the book provide public services as well. However, in the other CSCs, the services provided are those defined by government policy. Most public services have requirements for eligibility and other conditions that have to be met by those receiving the services. Government agencies have budgets and must put limits on the scope and scale of what they can do. The public services provided by IPSPs are the type they want to provide (within the law), and in this way IPSPs may offer public services that are distinctive or may be newly accessible to communities. While a great deal has been written on the role of the nonprofit (third) sector to address social problems outside government direction, we also bring to light private sector initiatives (often with a nonprofit) rooted in social entrepreneurship and corporate social responsibility that provide goods and services for the public.

IPSPs are distinguished not by being a nonprofit—although they usually are—or organizing their operations as a network—although they often do—but by also existing outside the purview of government direction, and often government funding, and yet still providing what would be considered public services. They are emerging as a new potential collaborator for the provision of public services, but at the same time they stretch the limits of government's ability to control or even manage the delivery of those public services. Therefore, they are the most challenging of collaborations for public managers.

IPSPs AND THE CHALLENGING GOVERNANCE ENVIRONMENT

Global climate change and related environmental challenges, our deteriorating national infrastructure, and perpetual health care crises are just three of many societal challenges that will require new thinking and innovative solutions by public managers. How do some IPSPs address these challenges?

Protecting the Environment: Climate Change and Sustainability

Climate change continues to be a hotly contested issue, with potentially disastrous long-term consequences for the planet and with no comprehensive solution in sight. Despite the Obama administration's recent Climate Action Plan (White House 2013) to reduce US greenhouse gas (GHG) emissions, the level of significant GHG reductions needed is so large, the sources of those emissions so diverse, and the cost of remediation so extensive that the scope of any solution that effectively addresses climate change will necessarily transcend sectors and political boundaries—domestic and international. Regulating air quality has been a priority of the federal government—in partnership with state governments— since the Clean Air Act of 1970. Yet even the authority of the federal government to regulate GHGs remains a political controversy. International agreements and protocols attempting to curb GHGs have resulted in over two decades of frustration, from Rio, Kyoto, and Copenhagen to Dubai, with governments unable to secure binding agreements on GHG reduction requirements and standards.

The diverse and serious effects of global warming stretch across sectors, regions, income classes, and states. The inability of governments to respond to concerns over climate change and sustainability has sparked action by private firms and nonprofits to begin to take action. Activities undertaken by concerned citizens, nonprofits, businesses, and community groups currently have surpassed the public sector efforts to reduce carbon footprints and develop alternative sustainability policies.

The Rainforest Alliance   The Rainforest Alliance was established in 1987 in an attempt to conserve biodiversity and promote sustainability by changing land use practices, business practices, and consumer behavior. The alliance uses the power of markets to arrest the major drivers of deforestation and environmental destruction: timber extraction, agricultural expansion, cattle ranching, and tourism. It builds coalitions with businesses, nonprofits, governmental entities, and individuals to support and develop guidelines for climate-friendly farming, and it links businesses that identify their goods and services as Rainforest Alliance Certified and Rainforest Alliance Verified to conscientious consumers who buy their certified products.

The Rainforest Alliance has worked with a coalition of more than two hundred organizations to promote sustainable tourism globally; it formed the Global Sustainable Tourism Council, which established minimum standards that any tourism business should aspire to reach in order to protect and sustain the world's natural and cultural resources, while ensuring that tourism meets its potential as a tool for poverty alleviation (Rainforest Alliance 2012). While the Rainforest Alliance works with governments and governmental organizations, its members are largely nongovernmental and are responsible for driving the agenda of the organization; thus their industry standards are not governmental. Their nongovernmental certification is sought after by private companies.

Joint Venture–Silicon Valley   Joint Venture–Silicon Valley (Joint Venture–SV) was born as an experiment to coalesce a multisector, collaborative group from the public and private sectors to create a neutral forum for leaders to discuss issues affecting the region. The group engages leaders in business, government, academia, labor, and the nonprofit sector to bring together the best strategies and reach a consensus on solutions. As Russell Hancock, president and CEO, put it, "We all work together, but we set our priorities." Part of the inspiration for its formation is preserving the image of the Silicon Valley region as a leader in innovation and entrepreneurship.

Joint Venture–SV collaborates to address issues of economic development, infrastructure, transportation, communications, education, health care, disaster planning, and climate change. Its new SEEDZ (Smart Energy Enterprise Development Zone) program attempts to create "the smart energy network of the future." The goal is, by 2020, to create the country's highest-performance two-way power network, supporting and rewarding active energy management and clean distributed generation on a sustainable economic scale. Reduced demand for energy corresponds to lower GHG emissions (Joint Venture–Silicon Valley 2013). To realize these ambitious energy efficiency dreams, Joint Venture uses its network of influential board directors representing business, nonprofits, and government. The group's collaborative culture facilitates its efforts to unify diverse stakeholders and provide faster, cheaper, and more efficient energy sources while simultaneously discovering new areas of profitability for its member firms.

The Oregon Environmental Council   The Oregon Environmental Council (OEC) reflects the mission of many IPSPs dedicated to promoting sustainability and addressing climate change. OEC was formed in 1968 by a group of citizens with the broad goal to protect Oregon's environment. Today as a nonprofit, membership-based organization, the OEC focuses on solving global warming, protecting citizens from exposure to toxic substances, cleaning up rivers, building sustainable economies, ensuring healthy food and local farms, and passing strong environmental policies. Its partners include individuals from or programs within Oregon State University, Zipcar–Portland, MKG Financial Group, Renaissance Foundation, Oregon Wine Board, and American Lung Association of Oregon.

OEC relies on a diverse membership and its engagement with other organizations to create a unique entity dedicated to improving the environment in Oregon (Oregon Environmental Council 2011). One of its main goals is protecting Oregonians from pollution, such as the level of exposure people face from toxic chemicals found in the environment. An example is the Green Chemistry initiative, which focuses on reducing the hazards of toxic chemicals and transitioning to less toxic renewable feedstock. The initiative began with the Oregon Green Chemistry Advisory Group in 2009, which brought together leaders of academia, industry, and agencies to identify and examine green chemistry options and opportunities. Following up on the findings, the OEC works directly with individual groups to share the research findings and help them develop greener and healthier practices for using chemicals.

Each of these IPSPs has formed a coalition to address climate change and sustainability in different ways. The Rainforest Alliance sets standards for forest conservation and has mechanisms for industry adoption. Silicon Valley–Joint Venture uses a business case approach to persuade its members to adopt sustainability practices that reduce their GHG footprint. The Oregon Environmental Council advances a shared stewardship vision of the environment in its state and promotes sustainability practices, including reduction of GHGs. Of course, the efforts of these IPSPs will not solve climate change problems, nor will the efforts of the scores of other IPSPs solve all environmental issues. Nevertheless, these three examples illustrate the types of actions IPSPs can undertake when addressing the problem of climate change, and they offer public managers many options to address climate change outside the parameters of current government policy.

Transportation Infrastructure: Reducing Travel Congestion and Improving Safety

The transportation sector in the United States is severely hampered by the fiscal challenges facing federal, state, and local governments. Government and transportation association reports have raised an alarm over the inability of government authorities at federal, state, and local levels to address the existing demands on our nation's transportation system. US roadways alone need a dramatic rise in investment over the next decades to address repairs and expansion needs (US General Accountability Office 2008). The failure on the part of governments to build and maintain an adequate transportation infrastructure has led to congestion in major urban areas and transit choke points for commerce across the nation. Despite the warnings, federal government spending on highways has remained largely steady during the past ten years and is projected to remain at that level for the decade ahead (Congressional Budget Office 2011).

With so much pressure on government to do more with less to address infrastructure capacity issues and with the related issues of safety and terrorism prevention, there is enormous potential for organizations from outside government to contribute to transportation financing, provision, safety, and maintenance. The private sector relies on transportation systems to move their goods; this need has sparked efforts to improve transportation infrastructure and ease congestion problems through the efforts of IPSPs.

Channel Industries Mutual Aid and the Houston Ship Channel The Houston Ship Channel is recognized as one of the most important routes of commerce for Texas. Infrastructure operators surrounding the channel and businesses dependent on this route for trade have long worked together to mitigate the risk of natural disasters and, more recently, terrorist attacks on the facility. In 1960, Channel Industries Mutual Aid (CIMA) was formed as a nonprofit and has worked collaboratively to join together firefighting, rescue, and first-aid manpower and equipment among Houston Ship Channel industries and municipalities for mutual assistance in case of emergency situations—either natural or man-made.

CIMA's current membership consists of approximately one hundred members from industry, municipalities, and government agencies covering Harris, Chambers, and Brazoria counties of Texas. It has numerous programs as part of its capacity to provide an organized response in times of disaster: a centralized dispatch system, a prearranged alarm list database for its members, a multicasualty incident plan, roadblock committees, and technical advice groups. CIMA maintains its preparedness for response by managing a well-detailed action plan, training, and formal reviews after each incident.

Although CIMA was established for the Houston Ship Channel area, it maintains agreements with several other mutual aid organizations along the Texas/Louisiana coast to provide assistance or receive it during major events. CIMA is recognized as one of the largest mutual aid organizations in the world and has shared its experience and procedures with other mutual aid organizations and countries, including the International Red Cross, Germany, Switzerland, and Australia (Channel Industries Mutual Aid 2014). What makes CIMA an interesting illustration of an IPSP is how the network developed out of the interests of the industry groups that depend on security at the Houston Ship Channel. They recognized the need for collective action to address security issues, and they have gradually incorporated more participation and contributions from the public sector. Public managers took advantage of the privately initiated organization to supplement government capabilities.

The First Response Team of America The First Response Team of America (FRTA) was founded as a nonprofit organization that works to supply emergency aid to disaster-stricken areas. Since its founding in May 2007, FRTA has helped US communities with postdisaster relief from tornados, primarily in northern Georgia and Alabama. It also provides hospitals, nursing homes, shelters, and command posts with electricity from Caterpillar equipment in disaster zones. The IPSP has assisted in reducing the time of emergency responses in forty disaster sites in the United States, providing emergency aid to thousands of disaster victims (Business Civic Leadership Center 2012).

One of FRTA's vital collaborators is the Caterpillar Corporation. Together they developed an innovative approach for clearing roadways after a major natural disaster in the United States to reduce the time for first responders and law enforcement officials to enter affected areas and gain access to victims. Working with the Caterpillar Corporation and other heavy equipment manufacturers, FRTA has been able to accrue a sophisticated collection of rescue gear and roadway clearance vehicles available for a response to disasters (Caterpillar 2012).

The interest of industry, nonprofits, and local communities in having open roadways and waterways after a disaster has prompted IPSPs to step in and act in the face of inadequate investment by the government in infrastructure. CIMA members coordinate industry-led efforts to secure access to waterways in Houston after a disaster. Similarly, FRTA anticipates the impact of natural disasters on roadway access and clears roadways so first responders can get to victims quickly. Both examples illustrate the value of investing in contingency plans and readiness, an approach many governments do not take. The combination of private and nonprofit interests around this issue created a unique opportunity for IPSPs in disaster response. IPSPs are providing a public service that is an assumed responsibility of local governments. This has implications for many other operations essential after a disaster.

Health Care Crises: Improving Access and Reducing Costs

As the debate in the 2012 presidential election over Medicare, Medicaid, the Affordable Care Act (popularly known as Obamacare), and health care costs illustrated, health care policy in the United States is at a critical juncture. While health care is state of the art in the United States, many residents lack essential health care coverage, and health care cost increases regularly exceed standard measures of inflation, placing this cost on an unsustainable path. In many other nations, especially in the less-developed world, health care is not available to a substantial portion of their population, and control of basic diseases, HIV, typhoid, and others is a primary health care need.

Public health is generally a responsibility of government, although the degree of government involvement in health care design and delivery is often controversial. Governments have used both the private and nonprofit sectors to deliver essential aspects of health care. That approach is predominant in the United States and, to a lesser extent, in other countries. Therefore, at least in the United States, it would seem logical for all sectors to be involved in developing and implementing solutions. Both private and nonprofit health care providers have an incentive to hold down costs: to be more competitive or serve larger markets or populations not yet served. Since health expenditures represent more than one-fifth of the US economy, the private sector has a strong profit motive to increase efficiency. Governments in developing nations may simply lack the resources to address some of their most critical health problems. Thus, it seems logical for the private and nonprofit sectors to develop alliances with and without government to address these issues.

Accountable Care Organizations   In the United States, one of the most promising initiatives to improve care and contain costs is the development of accountable care organizations (ACO). The term *ACO* was coined by Dr. Elliott Fisher and others in 2006 to describe the development of partnerships between hospitals and physicians (both private and nonprofits) to coordinate and deliver efficient care (Fisher 2006). The ACO concept seeks to remove existing barriers to improving health care, including shifting from a payment system that rewards the volume and intensity of provided services to one that focuses on quality and cost performance (Fisher 2009). Two illustrations of ACOs are Pathways to Health and Community Care of North Carolina.

In 2006, Blue Cross-Blue Shield of Michigan (BCBSM) developed the concept of integrated health partners that was later restructured into Pathways to Health, a framework that includes several local health care stakeholders such as insurers, consumers, and employers interested in reducing hospitalization and improving chronic care delivery in their area. Pathways to Health features key ACO concepts such as a patient-centered medical home (for primary care and case management), value-based purchasing, and community buy-in. The collaboration is currently developing a new payment structure and improving its patient data collection efforts. BCBSM reported that hospitalizations for conditions that can be prevented through better ambulatory care dropped 40 percent over the first three years of the program (Simmons 2010). While governments gain from the reduced program operating costs (especially Medicare and Medicaid savings), the cost reductions are being driven by IPSPs that are entirely nongovernmental.

Since 1998, the State of North Carolina has operated Community Care of North Carolina, a statewide medical program supported by the state's Medicaid program. Community Care evolved from an effort in 1983 by a local foundation to test approaches for improving primary care physician participation in Medicaid. The North Carolina Foundation for Advanced Health Programs, in partnership with state and county organizations, submitted a proposal to a private foundation to pilot North Carolina's first effort at developing medical homes for Medicaid recipients. This program has gradually expanded statewide and now consists of a community health network organized collaboratively by hospitals, physicians, health departments, and social service organizations to manage care. Each enrollee is assigned to a specific primary care provider, and network case managers partner with physicians and hospitals to identify and manage care for high-cost patients. In 2006, the program saved the state between $150 million and $170 million (Kaiser Commission 2009). Although government has been involved in Community Care, the driving force came from nonprofits and a private foundation. In this case, the IPSP began without direct governmental assistance, but is now integrated into the way government provides assistance to its low-income population, so it is beginning to look more like a governmental network. This example shows how IPSPs might morph into something with more direct governmental ties.

The success of the ACO model in fostering clinical excellence and continual improvement while effectively managing costs hinges on its ability to incentivize hospitals, physicians, post–acute care facilities, and other involved providers to form linkages that facilitate the coordination of care delivery and the collection and analysis of data on costs and outcomes (Nelson 2009). The ACO collaboratives must have organizational capacity to establish an administrative body to manage patient care, ensure high-quality care (including measuring outcomes), receive and distribute payments, and manage financial risk (American Hospital Association 2010).

The ACO model was initiated in the private and nonprofit sectors, and its potential led the Obama administration to include the concept in its national health care reform legislation as one of several demonstration programs to be administered by the Centers for Medicare and Medicaid Services. The ACOs participating in that program would assume accountability for improving the quality and cost of care for a defined patient population of Medicare beneficiaries. As proposed, ACOs would receive part of any savings generated from care coordination as long as benchmarks for the quality of care are also maintained. Initial analysis of ACO's pioneer and pilot projects has indicated savings of $380 million (US Health and Human Services 2014). ACOs are now being created nationwide and have a potential to expand beyond the Medicare and Medicaid populations.

Global Network for Neglected Tropical Diseases The Global Network for Neglected Tropical Diseases (GNNTD) was launched in 2006 at President Bill Clinton's Global Initiative Annual Meeting. The Global Network's job is to work with global partners to help deliver vital medical solutions to communities with the greatest needs. The Sabin Vaccine Institute Board of Trustees oversees its activities. Its board of trustees is composed of international leaders in business, civil service, academia, and philanthropy. Partners include academic institutions, foundations, and a variety of nonprofit organizations dedicated to addressing neglected tropical diseases. GNNTD seeks to achieve solutions through a three-pronged approach:

- Advocacy and policy change
- Resource mobilization
- Global coordination

Pharmaceutical companies are donating medicines to fight neglected diseases such as schistosomiasis; it costs approximately fifty cents to treat and protect one person for up to a year, but those funds are not available in developing nations. The GNNTD illustrates the importance of private and nonprofit actors in addressing global health issues. Governments can assist in facilitating treatment and funding, but the initiation and direction are outside the governmental bureaucracy, allowing flexibility in approach and funding (GNNTD 2013).

The GNNTD is a classic example of an IPSP: it was formed by a coalition of private and nonprofit actors. Although it collaborates closely with the World Health Organization and seeks and receives some support from governments, its policies and programs are driven by its nongovernmental board of trustees.

IPSPs and Their Approach

The examples demonstrate the diverse set of activities in which IPSPs have become involved. Earlier in the chapter, we presented a diagram that represented the unique characteristics of IPSPs. We have placed the IPSPs we have discussed in that same diagram (see figure 6.2). The differences among IPSPs

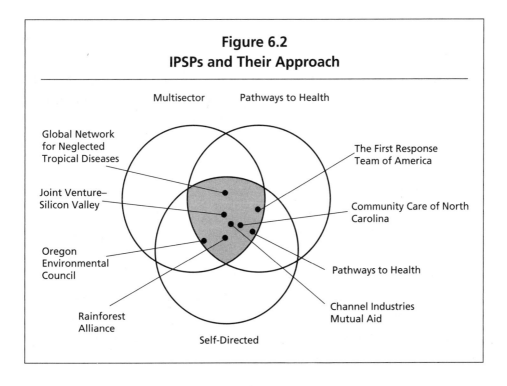

Figure 6.2
IPSPs and Their Approach

Multisector   Pathways to Health

Global Network for Neglected Tropical Diseases

The First Response Team of America

Joint Venture–Silicon Valley

Community Care of North Carolina

Oregon Environmental Council

Pathways to Health

Rainforest Alliance

Channel Industries Mutual Aid

Self-Directed

reflect their own unique approach to governance. The display of where different IPSPs fit in the diagram illustrates the variations public managers will find among different IPSPs.

Of course, not all IPSPs are exactly the same. They vary in the extent to which they reflect the three principal traits of IPSPs. Some have only a few partners but still represent multiple sectors. Some are more closely aligned with governments, although they remain self-directed. For example, the Oregon Environmental Council is self-directed and multisectored, but it might be considered limited in its direct provision of public services. Such differences are important for public managers to recognize and understand in order to make the most effective collaborations.

The placement of the IPSPs described in figure 6.2 demonstrates the variations in the characteristics and approaches IPSPs take, for example:

- The Oregon Environmental Council has members representing all three sectors, and it is strongly self-directed, but its direct public services are limited, providing information about what to do more than doing it themselves.

- First Response Team of America provides public services in the way of road clearing and acts independent of government policies, but its members are a relatively small coalition of community groups and industry partners.

- The Global Network for Neglected Tropical Diseases has a diverse set of members across national and international sectors and provides an obvious public service in the distribution of medicines. Its policies are consistent with government policies of the United States and international health organizations, although its approach to implementation is innovative and adaptive.

All IPSPs have their own unique profile and vary in the scope and intensity of the three defining characteristics. As we have noted, they are dynamic and evolve as organizations over time. Our presentation of IPSPs in figure 6.2 reflects a period of time, but it would not be surprising to see that IPSPs would migrate to different points in the diagram as they evolve.

THE PUBLIC MANAGER AND IPSPs

While public managers typically have limited influence over the creation and operation of IPSPs, they should have an understanding of what makes for a successful relationship with IPSPs. Figure 6.3 provides the elements that are most important for a successful IPSP collaboration.

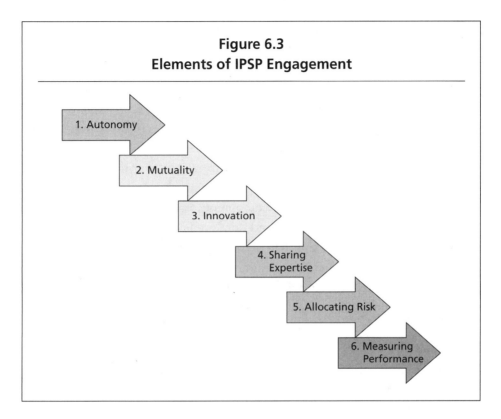

Figure 6.3
Elements of IPSP Engagement

1. Autonomy

2. Mutuality

3. Innovation

4. Sharing Expertise

5. Allocating Risk

6. Measuring Performance

Autonomy

IPSPs gain their flexibility from their autonomy from government. This does not mean they should not work with government; the whole premise of an IPSP is its freedom to engage a wide range of actors, both outside the government sphere of authority and potentially including government. From the public manager's perspective, the autonomy of the IPSP is valuable because it enables the organization to address areas that government may be constrained to address. The self-directing nature of IPSPs implies that government will have limited means to control or manage the operations of IPSPs. The more independent the nature of IPSPs, the greater the imperative for government managers to adopt a leadership style of accommodation and cooperation with nonprofit and private sector members of an IPSP.

Although public managers may be used to managing external relationships from a position of making the final decisions due to government funding and legal authority, it is not in the public interest for the pubic manager to attempt to co-opt an IPSP. A public manager may want to influence the IPSP to address particular public concerns or modify a program to avoid conflicts with existing public policy. The public manager should ask two questions: (1) Are the goals and objectives of the IPSP in line with current public policy? (2) Are they addressing a need not currently being addressed by government? If the answer to either question is yes, the public manager's role may simply be a facilitator or cheerleader for the actions of the IPSP. If the answer to both questions is no, or is ambiguous, the public manager will need to examine what sources of power or leverage the government has over the IPSP that may mold the IPSP more in the direction of government policy.

The Rainforest Alliance's globally autonomous nature allows it the flexibility to adapt to changing circumstances and develop new approaches and solutions that fit best at the time. The ability to try an approach and then discard it for an alternative one, when participants believe change is needed, is not what characterizes most government agencies. Innovative problem solving and adaptation make the Rainforest Alliance a useful partner for public managers.

Mutuality

Just as in networks, all parties in an IPSP must have something to gain from participation in the collaboration. Collaboration takes more time and effort than acting unilaterally. Members might participate for various reasons, but they will not stay engaged very long unless they believe they will benefit from their efforts. The benefits gained may be monetary, such as increased opportunities for financial support or increased sales, but the advantages participants believe they gain from participation in an IPSP can be diverse and not always obvious. The key is achieving a level of mutuality whereby the parties to the collaboration are able to maintain their respective identities and missions while contributing to the collaboration.

Public managers must discern the potential gain for their own involvement with an IPSP. The IPSP may be performing a governmental function that saves the government from providing such services to a particular community. If so, the public manager might examine whether it is possible to provide some governmental funding, for example, through grants or contracts, that would provide additional resources to the IPSP. The Obama administration's support of accountable care organizations, which clearly address a major theme of health care reform, is one illustration of ways government can support the actions of IPSPs.

As an example of the importance of mutuality in an IPSP, Joint Venture–SV's broad and diverse leadership provides the backbone to support its energy-efficiency goals. Without this unified approach to collaborating and directing their approach, the complexity in implementing their sustainability initiatives makes achieving their goals unreachable.

Innovation

An IPSP's strength is its ability to innovate. It can provide creative solutions that might otherwise never emerge from government agencies. Of course, not all ideas and innovations will work, but IPSPs, more than government, are able to take on the risk of failure and embrace innovative, systemic thinking and creative problem solving.

Successes by IPSPs can lead to new or revamped government programs to address public problems and issues. Public managers can benefit by learning what works and does not as IPSPs look for unique solutions—something that governments do not do so well. Public managers should encourage IPSP innovation through pilot project grants and other mechanisms. From an intergovernmental perspective, state governments often are referred to as "laboratories of democracy." IPSPs might be considered "laboratories of innovation." The North Carolina Community Care program is a good illustration of a laboratory of innovation that led the state government to incorporate the program's approach into how it delivers health care services to a particular population in the state.

Sharing Expertise and Resources

Transparency and openness are important aspects of successful IPSP operations. Hiding information, often a problem in principal-agent relations, is counterproductive in IPSPs, where the whole objective of the organization is to combine the capabilities of the various participants. Since the success of the IPSP will be measured in terms of shared goals and outcomes, there is little reason for its members to withhold their ideas or intentions that might be necessary for success. IPSPs that are successful in convincing partners to share information save everyone time and energy, which otherwise is too often spent and wasted on protracted negotiations and circular discussions.

From the public manager's perspective, government may have expertise and resources that would be useful to an IPSP and provide some leverage for public managers to influence the approach used by an IPSP to address particular problems. For example, government provides a certain legitimacy, so that government support might be useful for an IPSP to gain acceptance by particular constituencies. Government does have regulatory control over many areas, including health care, environmental protection, and workplace safety. The ability of public managers to help IPSPs navigate the regulatory bureaucracy or provide waivers to IPSPs may be an important power—one not to be used over the IPSP but to assist the IPSP in fulfilling its goals and objectives in line with the public interest. The Global Network for Neglected Tropical Diseases shows how combining resources and dispersing them in a well-informed manner can provide significant relief to disease-stricken regions around the world.

Allocating Risk

Just as in partnerships and networks, all members of an IPSP need to assume the risks they are best able to deal with. Thus, production costs might best be borne by a private sector member of an IPSP, whereas delivery systems might be better controlled by a local nonprofit that has contacts and experience dealing with a specific clientele.

From a public manager's perspective, government has little risk with IPSPs other than a risk of the IPSP actually making a problem worse. However, there may be some risks that would make sense for government to assume in support of IPSP activities. Government might be the insurer of last resort for certain types of liability, or it may use its legislative power to restrict the ability of individuals to take legal action if they feel they have been wronged by an IPSP. The only reason government might want to assume that role is if it felt that an IPSP was performing an important public function and believed the IPSP would be greatly hindered in its operations by potential liability. Clearing Roadways in Disaster Recovery provides an example in which significant monetary and implementation risks were divided and reallocated by combining the goals of publicly oriented nonprofits and financially interested firms to efficiently rehabilitate transportation to disaster areas.

Measuring Performance

As with any other well-run organization, IPSPs should have a mechanism to measure the performance of their operations. Measurements may include output measures (such as number of children receiving medication), outcome measures (such as overall health in a community), and organizational measures (such as cost of delivery per person served). Timely benchmarks and measurements are important aspects of effective organizational performance.

The public manager will want to weigh the performance measurements of an IPSP against public policy objectives. It may be that the manager is in a better position to collect the data necessary to assess whether an IPSP is meeting the public interest in its activities. Government might be the only party that can collect certain data because of privacy issues, and the ability of government to provide measurements may assist IPSPs in meeting their objectives while providing the public manager with assurances that the IPSP is operating in the public interest.

ADVANTAGES AND DISADVANTAGES FOR PUBLIC MANAGERS WORKING WITH IPSPs

Working with IPSPs can give public managers an opportunity to address policy issues and program implementation in a fresh way. They also can present challenges to public managers and may raise questions about whether they are the optimal form of collaboration.

Advantages for Public Managers

IPSPs offer public managers numerous advantages over other forms of collaborations because of the diversity of participants, their operations outside the basic realms of government, and their commitment to meaningful collaborations.

- *Additional resources.* IPSPs typically receive funding support from foundations, private donations, and fees for their operations. Public managers most often are constrained by their budgets. By learning how to collaborate with IPSPs, public managers can expand the resource base available to solve the problems their agency is charged with addressing.

- *Political sensitivities.* Trying new approaches to the delivery of public services can prove to be politically sensitive. Public officials and constituencies may object to changes in programs that have been routine, even if the intent is to bring about improvements, and especially if it involves untested approaches with uncertain results. IPSPs can serve as laboratories of innovation and advance new ideas without public managers facing the risks of being criticized.

- *Long-term view.* When IPSP collaborations are approaching issues of a long-term-view nature, such as adequate funding for maintenance of infrastructure or capital equipment replacement, public managers can use that perspective to consider issues beyond the typical government time frame of a one- or two-year budget cycle.

- *Social entrepreneurship.* Private organizations are interested in finding new business opportunities; nonprofits look to expand their member base and their impact. The drive to accomplish these goals encourages participants in IPSPs to look for innovative solutions and make something different happen. Change and urgency are the hallmarks of many IPSPs. Public managers can share in these entrepreneurial efforts, participating in the creation of new approaches that might be sustained, often without government funding support.

- *Adaptation and change.* Business has to change and modify approaches in real time when something is not working correctly. Markets can change rapidly, and firms have to adapt to stay competitive. When IPSPs have business partners, changing plans when the original approach is ineffective or when resources do not match requirements is viewed as a sign of strength and competence, not misunderstood as poor planning and ineptitude, as it can be in the government.

- *Leadership.* IPSPs often have the support and active engagement of community leaders. Typically volunteering their time, community leaders contribute their own professional experiences, harnessing their management, organization, and people skills for success. Public managers can leverage the leadership within IPSPs to build community support and help promote their own government programs.

Disadvantages for Public Managers

IPSPs present challenges to public managers that can be a disadvantage over other forms of collaboration. These disadvantages are rooted in the voluntary nature of IPSPs, which ensures a level of impermanence that permeates their actions and approach:

- *Difficult communications.* The decentralized organization of some IPSPs can create difficulties for public managers to communicate with and engage participants effectively. There is no mandatory requirement for IPSPs to submit reports, hold regularly scheduled meetings, request approvals, or write memos. Governments have their own administrative cycles around budgets or public hearings, and the need for information about IPSP activities may be difficult to obtain and validate in a timely fashion.

- *Unpopular politics.* The self-driven nature of IPSPs means that they do not have to conform to the political positions of parties or elected officials. IPSPs may provide public services in a way that is unpopular or may attract negative political attention. In such circumstances, public managers have to worry about guilt by association.

- *Impermanence.* There is little that holds an IPSP together besides the faith of its members and their commitment to a cause. Participants in IPSPs can disperse as easily as they come together. Funding for IPSPs can be uncertain, and if it dries up, there may be no alternative funding to support its activities. Public managers need to approach IPSPs with uncertain futures with caution and not overcommit government reliance on IPSP activities to achieve their own agency's goals and objectives.

- *Mission drift.* IPSPs are free to choose their own mission and the services they will provide. That mission can change at any time the participants feel that it is needed. IPSPs might change their mission because their participants have changed their priorities or based on the priorities of funders. Public managers should not always rely on an IPSP to provide the same services or provide them in the same way.

GOING GLOBAL

IPSPs have gained rapid acceptance as a preferred approach to address many global issues. The absence of global government and the difficulties associated with negotiating international agreements among many nations on problems that are highly interdependent and transnational make IPSPs an attractive alternative approach of global governance. A good example of a global IPSP that addresses global problems is the Global Alliance for Improved Nutrition (GAIN).

GAIN supports a vision of a world without malnutrition. Created in 2002, it is an alliance of governments, international organizations, the private sector, and civil society. Launched at a Special Session of the UN General Assembly on Children, GAIN supports collaborations to increase access to the missing nutrients in the diets of undernourished people. Its board of directors comprises leaders from government, industry, and nonprofits. An executive from the UN's Children's Fund is an ex officio member, but GAIN's priorities are not set by any government organization.

GAIN creates national and regional business alliances of leading companies, which are exploring ways to bring high-quality, affordable fortified foods to those most in need, including the base of the pyramid: the poorest people. GAIN has entered into direct partnerships with a select number of companies and organizations to implement concrete projects with clear and measurable objectives (Forrer, Kapur, and Greene 2012).

The IPSPs like GAIN, and scores more like it, fill a serious gap between public services that are needed globally and the lack of administrative capacity in many countries to finance, produce, and deliver such services. With so many problems in the world, IPSPs offer an exciting opportunity for people to bypass the crippling effects of failed governments and organize efforts that can work to solve some of our biggest global problems.

CONCLUSION

Public managers often choose IPSPs when autonomy and innovation are valued above control and clearly defined roles and responsibilities. In this chapter, we reviewed the core characteristics of IPSPs and their differences with quasi-governmental organizations. We also provided examples of how IPSPs operate in different policy areas to further a discussion of how public managers can leverage the potential of IPSPs to serve the public interest. When public managers reach out to IPSPs, they inevitably face challenges in learning how to cooperate effectively.

Engaging IPSPs successfully requires public managers to approach collaborations in ways that are different from when the government is working with contractors or even when it is involved in a partnership or network. The need for new rules of engagement presents a new challenge and a new opportunity for public managers. Because IPSPs provide public services, interacting directly with the public, it is more difficult for public managers to determine firsthand if the IPSP is providing services that meet public policy objectives. For example, is the provision of services by the IPSP politically acceptable to citizens, and how can public managers collect data that may be important to the relevant government agency but are not collected by the IPSP?

The increasing frequency with which IPSPs are providing public services highlights a primary reason for government managers to be interested in collaborating with them: IPSPs can complement or supplant government efforts to provide services for their citizens. The examples outlined in this chapter demonstrate how IPSPs help communities reduce their effect on global warming, improve the development of transit-oriented development in congested areas, and reduce the overall costs of health care for at-risk populations. In an era of increasing fiscal constraints at federal, state, and local government levels in the United States, IPSPs offer enormous potential for government managers to broaden the scope and scale of services to citizens. By drawing from the private and nonprofit sectors, IPSPs mobilize financial resources, expertise, and organized interests around emerging societal problems and issues.

IPSPs do not offer the full range or level of public services that government policy requires, but they may be effective in providing public services in an innovative way to a select group of citizens or a highly specialized service to a neighborhood or community. In this way, they may be especially useful in providing services to groups or individuals that may be particularly expensive because they represent a small proportion of the total population or in providing a service to a community requiring special types of services.

The multisector characteristic of IPSPs challenges governments to better recognize and reconcile the interests of specific constituencies. Since IPSPs operate in a self-directed way, outside government, they often form to address the interests of specific social groups within the broader society. In Oregon, groups of citizens allied with universities and key businesses to address what they saw as pressing needs for greater protection of the natural environment than the standards set by government. Equipment manufacturers and a nonprofit representing first responders teamed up to develop innovative ways to quickly reopen critical roadways so disaster and emergency relief vehicles could get through. Local health care providers teamed up with insurance companies to identify and eliminate waste in health care costs. It could be said that IPSPs do what people would want the government to do if only the government would or could.

Case Study for Discussion: State Employment Training

You are an assistant to the executive director of the Department of Social Services (DSS). The governor has campaigned on increasing job training in the state and moving individuals from receiving state welfare payments to working. Currently the Division of Employment Training (DET) (within DSS) provides that service; however, the governor and the state legislature are unhappy with the current results: at an annual cost of $20 million, DET has found work for only a fraction of those on welfare. The program is operated out of twenty local offices, and the current annual success rate is less than 10 percent of the 500,000 adult recipients on welfare placed in a job. Welfare payments cost the state over $2 billion a year (averaging about $4,200 a person per year plus administrative costs of program administration).

Questions and Issues for Consideration

1. A new IPSP, Shine Bright, located in the state's largest city, provides a range of social services to single mothers who never finished high school. How might the IPSP be a benefit to DDS?

2. Are there inherently governmental services associated with the DSS mission that government could not support were Shine Bright to provide them?

3. What risks would DSS managers face if they approved a local office to become a member of the Shine Bright IPSP?

chapter SEVEN

Analyzing Cross-Sector Collaboration Options

D eciding to collaborate with private and nonprofit organizations presents promising opportunities for government officials to enable them to provide better public services to their citizens. Contracts, networks, partnerships, and independent public-services providers (IPSPs) can provide a means for (1) leveraging public budgets and attracting funding from private sources or foundations; (2) tapping into valuable experiences and expertise on public policy issues from outside the government; (3) identifying modes of public service delivery that are more effective; (4) accessing better local knowledge about the needs and preferences of communities; and (5) using innovative, adaptive, and flexible problem-solving skills.

In considering options, the first question public managers need to ask is whether the apparent bureaucratic limitations of public employees are the only reason that contracting out, creating a network, forming a partnership, or using an IPSP option, appears superior to public sector solutions. Some argue that if we would only "free" the bureaucracy, giving public employees the same discretion as the private and nonprofit sectors, public agencies would be more productive (Sclar 2000). There is some evidence for this viewpoint. During the George W. Bush administration, where competitive sourcing was a key ingredient of its management agenda, federal agencies won a majority of the competitions, seemingly supporting the proposition that public employees can become high-performing organizations if only they are given the latitude to organize more efficiently.

There may be cases, however, where even a reformed government bureaucracy is insufficient to solve a public problem or concern, and public managers are looking at other solutions. There also are potential pitfalls with these new arrangements, and critical questions must be raised and answered. This chapter provides a framework to assist public managers in thinking through the options—to determine which is in the best interest of the public. It is not meant as a complete list of issues or questions, which will vary by the specific challenge and organizational proposal; but these questions are common to most decisions about whether and how to use cross-sector collaborations (CSCs). They are grouped under five headings:

- What is the nature of the public task or challenge?
- What resources are needed to accomplish that task or meet the challenge and where are those resources located?
- Can you identify and allocate the risks involved in the undertaking?
- Which approach creates the best value for the public dollars?
- How can you measure performance and ensure appropriate accountability?

CASE STUDIES

To illustrate the framework and analytical concepts, the chapter includes a number of illustrations and examines in more detail two case studies.[1] One involves a federal government agency, the US Coast Guard (USCG) and its use of a public-private partnership; the second case is about a local government agency in Fairfax County, Virginia, and its creation of a network of human service delivery providers.

Coast Guard Deepwater Program

In the early 1990s, the USCG was facing a daunting challenge: how to deal with its aging deepwater assets—those that operate beyond fifty miles from the US shore, including ships, aircraft, and other systems. These deteriorating assets threatened the Coast Guard's ability to meet its vital and expanding mission requirements. USCG leadership developed two key strategies to address the needs. First, leaders planned to design and build each new deepwater asset (ships and aircraft) to function in a coordinated, interoperable system that would extend the capacity of all of the Coast Guard assets—a "system of systems."[2] Second, recognizing the agency's lack of expertise and organizational structure to engage in an acquisition of this magnitude, leaders decided to use an innovative approach, a public-private partnership, to plan and coordinate the process, a first for the agency.

By the mid-1990s, the USCG had developed its overall strategy and elected to use a private sector firm to serve as the lead systems integrator (LSI) to plan, buy, and assemble the various components for their recapitalized deepwater assets. They lacked the in-house capacity to build the Deepwater system and did not believe that they could easily acquire that capacity. Furthermore, the USCG believed that a strong private partner would provide more influence with Congress, given the magnitude (in scope and dollars) of the expected acquisition. They secured initial funding from Congress and in 2001 issued a request for proposal for a private sector LSI. After discussion with several potential partners, the USCG encouraged two competitors, Lockheed Martin and Northrop Grumman, to form a joint venture, designated the Integrated Coast Guard Systems (ICGS), and awarded it a five-year contract to coordinate Deepwater Program acquisitions. The partnership had both successes (a new search-and-rescue HC-144 aircraft) and failures (a reconfigured patrol boat), but suffered from increased criticism both from within the Coast Guard and by Congress and the General Accountability Office, leading to a decision in 2007 for the USCG to take over the LSI role.

Fairfax County Human Services Delivery

The second case is about Fairfax County's Department of Systems Management for Human Services (DSMHS), which was given the responsibility of facilitating the coordination of human services delivery in Fairfax County, Virginia. County leadership determined a need to streamline its social services during a time of rapid population growth, demographic changes, and expanded human resource needs, which included an in-migration of refugees from other nations. While the original vision of a fully integrated client intake system was not achieved, DSMHS was able to implement a coordinated service planning system for matching the needs of county residents with services available in the county from public, private, and nonprofit agencies, creating a network of human services providers.

This effort was complex because of the number of actors involved, including county human services agencies, state and federal agencies, and both private and nonprofit providers of human services in the county. It was important to involve all key stakeholders in the planning and implementation effort. By drawing in these key actors, DSMHS was able to achieve widespread buy-in to the concept and improved overall delivery of social services to populations in need.

NATURE OF THE PUBLIC TASK OR CHALLENGE

Public managers must first consider, to the extent possible, the nature of the public problem or task before deciding on a specific tool or solution. If the solution is clear and there is agreement around the administrative approach or process required, then normally government would either act directly or, if it lacked the in-house skills, contract out the task to a third party that could deliver the desired result. However, in many cases, the nature of the problem may be somewhat obscure or the solutions murky. In those cases, developing a dialogue with private and nonprofit sector organizations might lead to a clearer perspective and options for action. Public managers typically face these major issues: determining whether a solution likely requires one-sector or multi-sector involvement, examining whether the problem is susceptible to a private market "business" solution or to a nonprofit solution, and analyzing the political factors that might inform a public manager's choice.

One or Multisector Solutions

Some problems lend themselves to one-sector solutions. For example, the national Social Security system provides uniform funding to retired and disabled individuals under rules set in legislation by Congress and interpreted and enacted by the Social Security Administration. This tax and redistributive program is clearly the responsibility of government (in this case, the federal government), and there would be little reason to involve another sector unless the policy issue becomes whether (or to what extent) we might privatize Social Security. Privatization, while advocated by experts in some parts of the world (Chile is often cited as an example), is opposed by a strong majority of Americans. Current issues regarding the long-term viability of the system need to be addressed, but Congress can play this role if it has the political will. Solutions include extending the retirement age, reducing or changing the way cost-of-living adjustments are determined, increasing the payroll tax, extending the range of income subject to the payroll tax (FICA), and increasing from 80 to 100 percent the taxation of Social Security on those who make over a certain amount of income. All of these solutions can be enacted by the federal government. There is no need to consider collaboration with another sector.

In contrast, Medicare, which is under a more serious threat of insolvency than the Social Security system, is already a collaboration with the private and nonprofit sectors. Rising health care costs are the primary driver of the US budget deficit (Congressional Budget Office 2011). Seniors sixty-five years and older are entitled to certain health care benefits (in-patient hospital care) and may opt for additional services (doctors and drug coverage) with additional payments. Although the system is financed and coordinated by the federal government, health care services are almost entirely provided by the private sector; providers are reimbursed based on rates established administratively (Centers for Medicare and Medicaid Services) and by Congress. There are some solutions that could be undertaken solely by the federal government: for example, increasing the eligibility age, reducing coverage of some services, increased fees or copayments for upper-income seniors, negotiated drug pricing, and reduced payments to providers. Other solutions will require active cooperation and involvement of the providers, both private and nonprofit. For example, the proposed Wyden-Ryan bipartisan plan would allow the private sector to compete with Medicare "in an effort to offer seniors better-quality and more-affordable health care choices" (Wyden-Ryan 2011). Regardless of whether this plan is adopted, it is clear that any long-range solution will require innovative ideas from both the private sector and nonprofit organizations. In addition to private option health insurance, innovative possibilities include shifting payments from one based on services to one based on outcomes and creating the accountable care organizations that were discussed in chapter 6.

If the likely solution requires an innovative approach to the problem, it probably argues for multisector involvement. The private and nonprofit sectors can be more innovative than the public sector simply because they have more flexibility and are not constrained by the same level of oversight and process requirements as is the public sector. Multiple sector involvement may encourage the innovation necessary to address the problem. If the task or challenge is clear and the solution is known, it may make sense for government to either directly provide or contract out (traditional or complete contract); however, if it is murky with an unclear solution, then a collaborative contract (incomplete or relational) or a partnership, network, or IPSP may be a better option. Alternatively, the federal government could work with states, which would become "laboratories of democracy," trying out various approaches to the problem that might then receive national application.

It also is important to match the likely longevity of the actors with the expected duration of the issue or problem being addressed. The longer the duration of the issue, the more important it is to have government participate in the solution, either as a prime actor or lead actor in a CSC, because it has the institutional memory that private and nonprofit organizations are not able to match. Short-term problems can more readily be addressed by other actors, leaving government to deal with the long-term challenges.

For example, global warming is not a problem that can be adequately addressed by a single sector, and yet governments are likely to play a lead role because of the long-term nature of the problem. However, the private and non-profit sectors are taking their own actions to deal with the problem, and because of the need for innovative solutions, it makes sense for government to take a multisector approach.

Many public issues or problems are already being addressed by public sector agencies. However, if the issues involve ebbs and surges of activity, it may not make sense for the public sector agency to be staffed to deal with all of the poten-tial peak needs. Contracting or partnerships with other sectors to deal with part of the problem or peak demand may make sense. This is one of the rationales for using private sector contractors to deal with security, base construction, and other ancillary activities for the military. It may not make sense for the military to maintain a continuing capacity in areas that may be needed only in times of conflict, where that capacity exists in the private sector.

In examining the options of "in-house" production versus contractors, one California local official noted the importance of maintaining a balance: "You need a tight sustainable group of in-source providers. In addition, you need good contract providers. Find a mix between the two. It is a great way to lever-age productivity with fewer dollars" (Way 2012). Similarly, relying on private or nonprofit sector partners to provide some critical supplies (such as water or health services) after a natural disaster, where those partners might have logistical advantages, can leverage the aid provided by government.

Susceptibility to Private Market Business or Nonprofit Solutions

Certain problems may lend themselves to a solution in a sector outside gov-ernment. Where markets can play a role in the provision of a good or service, involvement of the private sector makes sense. For example, where government has opted to increase transportation options or relieve highway congestion, one option is the development of toll roads. Government sometimes performs this function (e.g., in Virginia, the Dulles Toll Road from the Interstate 495 Beltway to Dulles Airport), usually through a quasi-governmental authority. However, where public financing is difficult, toll roads may provide an opportunity for private sector involvement through a public-private partnership (PPP), one of the fastest-growing areas of public-private cooperation. An illustration is the Greenway, a private toll road extending the Dulles Toll Road from the Dulles Airport to Leesburg, Virginia.

Public managers must recognize that business solutions are often controversial. Businesses charge fees for services in order to make a return on their investment. Fees may exclude some participants from the service unless government steps in to provide a subsidy or other mechanism to ensure access for all citizens. Where equal access is an important policy goal, public managers must ask whether a business solution is in the public interest.

Nonprofit organizations often close the gap between public and private sector actions, serving an underserved client group that often falls through the cracks and have needs that are not met by the other sectors. For example, N Street Village (NSV) in the District of Columbia, founded by Luther Place Memorial Church, has a mission of "empowering homeless and low-income women to claim their highest quality of life by offering a broad spectrum of services and advocacy in an atmosphere of dignity and respect" (N Street Village 2012). Its programs are funded through a variety of sources, including donors and foundations. Because of the nature of their clients' needs, NSV must provide a great deal of hands-on individualized services. By using volunteers as well as paid staff, it is able to offer services at a much lower cost than could either the private or public sector. Thus, to the extent that public managers want to provide services to that particular target group, it may make more sense to funnel public dollars to effective organizations, such as NSV, through grants, contracts, or other arrangements, rather than attempt to duplicate what this nonprofit is accomplishing.

Similarly, sometimes the nature of the problem requires local knowledge. This often is the case for many social services programs. Issues and client populations might not be the same in New York City and Salt Lake City. This is why the federal government often takes an intergovernmental approach, using state governments, through grants or contracts, for many of its social programs, to provide diversity of delivery in light of different state circumstances. Even within a state, social problems in a large urban area are likely to be quite different from those in rural areas; thus, states often partner or network with local government or nonprofits on social programs.

Political Factors and Considerations

Public managers also need to be aware of the political factors that may come into play as they examine choices beyond the traditional bureaucratic option. They may be empowered or constrained by such factors. Legal constraints may influence public manager choices among cross-sector delivery models. There may be no enabling statutes that allow PPPs, or acquisition statutes may set out detailed structures on contracting that may reduce public sector flexibility to use cross-sector options. Furthermore, the managers may not be able to engage IPSPs for concerns about conflict of interest or restrictions on working with private or nonprofit partners. Often new approaches will require legislative approval.

Unconventional approaches to public policy require political champions (US General Accountability Office 1997). Public managers often do not have the political capital to venture beyond the traditional approved approaches. While proponents of New Public Management encourage entrepreneurial public management, adherents to a more traditional public administrative framework are concerned about legal accountability. By involving political leadership in decision making, public managers protect themselves from possible criticism. When developing or using a particular instrument, managers should also be aware of the fine line between political support (and accountability) and political interference (e.g., in the selection process of a contractor). While it may not be possible for the public manager to fully insulate herself, the goal should be an appropriate flow of information and oversight, not micromanagement or interference.

Involving the private and nonprofit sectors in solutions brings an important interested party to the table, and this may prove to be a double-edged sword. On the one hand, the involvement may provide a significant voice in support of the program, as it did in the case of the USCG Deepwater Program. On the other hand, their political support may make it difficult for a public manager to terminate or amend the program, and such pressure may lead to suboptimal decisions.

Stakeholder analysis is a first step for any public manager in thinking through the political interests. Managers must reflect on the likely intensity of prospective stakeholder concerns in considering a network or partnership and the diversity of their perspectives. This recognition should lead to the structures and processes necessary to create a communication network to engage stakeholders throughout the process in order to create the trust necessary for effective collaboration (Kee and Newcomer 2008).

A choice to contract out an activity, engage in a partnership or network, or use an IPSP to address a public problem might have an impact on the rest of the public sector. Public managers need to consider what spillover effects might occur from their choice of options. Will it adversely affect agency morale? Will it create an incentive or disincentive to improve the public sector, consistent with developing high-performing systems? Will it conflict with human resource practices designed to attract, retain, and reward high-performing government workers?

Case Analysis

Of our two case studies, the Fairfax County example is more obviously a multi-sector problem. Government seldom (even across all three levels of government) meets the full needs of those who require a variety of human services, such as housing, health care, and job training. The nonprofit sector is a major provider to that clientele, and thus involving it in a broad solution made a great deal of sense. However, the county was looking at a long-range, holistic solution that argued for government involvement and leadership. In this case, county agencies actually strengthened their own capability. Social service workers, while first somewhat resistant to sharing information, were proud of the new approach because it allowed them to meet a greater percentage of the needs of the population they served.

In the Deepwater Program, the USCG could have stayed "in-house" or used other federal resources (such as the Department of Defense), but decided that it was in its strategic interest to engage a private partner. The USCG was used to replacing assets on an incremental basis with patchwork funding from Congress. It had neither the political support nor the in-house skills to undertake the massive upgrades needed. Its leaders felt that the private sector, already a provider of complex defense systems, would afford an edge in the innovation that was needed to create a system of systems and would assist in developing political champions in Congress. Thus, the USCG initiated a public-private partnership with Lockheed Martin and Northrop Grumman in an Integrated Coast Guard Systems (ICGS) approach. The corporate partners successfully lobbied Congress for the necessary funds, but there were other problems, including resistance among officers within the USCG, that ultimately led to the termination of the partnership.

RESOURCE NEEDS AND CAPACITY

Societal problems can be addressed only if organizations, whether government or from another sector, have the resources and capacity to address them. Today's most critical concerns—global warming, health care costs and access, deteriorating infrastructure—seem beyond the ability of any one organization or any one sector to address. Even the day-to-day challenges that public managers face may require a careful assessment of resources versus need or problem. Public leaders and managers must carefully consider the size, complexity, and scope of the issues they are addressing and then balance those against the resource constraints and capacity of their organizations. Resource constraints include not only funds, although clearly that is a major component, but also personnel, expertise, and ideas that may be critical for solving the problem. Two areas are the most important for public managers: (1) assessing the resource needs relative to the problem being addressed and determining in which sector they reside and (2) determining whether the public sector has the capacity to address the problem, the capacity to assist others in addressing the problem, and the capacity to learn and grow to better deal with the problem.

Resource Needs: Assessment and Planning

Public leaders and managers have a responsibility to accurately assess the strengths and weaknesses of their organization in relation to the tasks at hand. If there is a mismatch between available resources and the issue or problem that needs to be addressed, they must determine if they can secure the resources within government or need to go outside government through a contract or by partnering with a private or nonprofit organization. In this context, expertise and ideas may be as important as funding.

Governments generally have an advantage over other sectors in raising the funds necessary to address public problems. They have the power to tax and can borrow funds at interest rates lower than either the private or nonprofit sectors can (state and local bonds are generally exempt from federal taxes). However, government may lack the political support to raise the necessary funds because of public disenchantment with government, particularly at the federal level, and because many states are near their borrowing capacity as a result of constitutional limitations, rating agency concerns, or public unease over additional debt.

If a public sector organization is not likely to receive the funding necessary to fully address a public problem, then public managers and leaders need to determine where and in which sector the resources lie. There may be organizations, such as IPSPs, already addressing the problem. If that is the case, the public sector role might be more muted, perhaps as a cheerleader, integrator, or monitor of the efforts of the IPSPs—concepts we explore in chapter 9. Alternatively, it may be appropriate to partner or network with other organizations in the private or nonprofit sectors that can add value to potential solutions. Nonprofit organizations can bring a perspective and local knowledge that the public sector does not have.

Organizational Capacity

Organizations need the capacity to accomplish their missions, whether through traditional governmental structures or by involving another sector, through a contract, public-private partnership, network, or IPSP. Organizational capacity involves three aspects: (1) the ability to provide the public good or service (discussed above), (2) the capacity to examine and develop alternative strategies and to manage those choices, and (3) the capacity to learn and grow from those experiences.

The type of capacity and capacity issues or concerns vary depending on the choice of instruments to fulfill their mission. Table 7.1 provides an overview of capacity needs for each type of instrument and some issues and concerns that have to be addressed by the public manager or leader when considering instrumentalities for a major or complex project or program. We briefly describe capacity needs in this chapter and later, in chapter 11, discuss strategies on how organizations can best develop their organizational capacity to address today's challenging environment and work effectively in cross-sector collaborations.

Since this book is about cross-sector collaborations, this chapter spends less time on the first two categories—government provision and traditional contracting out—except to provide a contrast to the newer choices of public managers: collaborative contracting, networks, partnerships, and IPSPs. We argue that government leaders and managers must address a number of key capacity issues.

Planning While it may seem obvious, too often the public sector chooses a path without proper planning. Among critical elements of planning are a clear articulation of program goals, objectives, and results desired and a delineation of exactly what constitutes the program or project. This is important regardless of the instrument chosen. If a contract is being considered, there is a need to

Table 7.1
Organizational Capacity Needs for Major or Complex Projects or Programs

Approach	Capacity Needs	Concerns and Trade-Offs
Government provision	Planning Project design Construction and implementation Monitoring and evaluation	Higher costs as a result of production by government and no competitive bidding Control versus costs
Contracting out (traditional)	Planning Contract design Contract oversight Monitoring and evaluation	Specificity versus flexibility Is there a competitive market?
Collaborative contracting	Planning Communications Developing a common purpose Monitoring and evaluation	Integrating multiple goals of the collaborators Flexibility versus legal requirements Maintaining accountability
Public-private partnerships	Planning Partnership design Risk analysis and allocation Monitoring and evaluation	Proper allocation of risk Capture by partner Limited competition Flexibility versus control Agreement on key performance indicators
Networks	Planning Network design Network communications Network leadership Allocation of responsibilities Monitoring and evaluation	Potential gridlock among collaborators Flexibility versus accountability Agreement on measures of accountability
Independent public-services providers	Planning Communication skills Negotiations Leveraging support Monitoring and evaluation	Flexibility versus control Influencing behavior Protecting the public interest

understand whether there is a private sector competitive market for that particular product or service. Without competition, government may find itself at the mercy of the contractor, or it may be necessary to choose a more collaborative approach with other governmental units or across sectors with the private or nonprofit sector.

Similarly, public managers must have a sense of the capacity existing in the other sectors in terms of resources and skills necessary to successfully engage in a partnership or network. With respect to IPSPs, public managers need to understand what organizations are already acting within the program area and see to what extent it may be possible for government to become involved—as a funder, cheerleader, organizer of public input, or regulator depending on the situation. Strategic planning may include an environmental scan to examine available resources within and without an organization and to align organizational resources to address that problem. If resources are not solely available within the organization, it is incumbent on the leader or manager to involve key stakeholders in the planning that might provide those resources.

Determining the nature of the public interest also is a critical component of planning and the use of any of the approaches to delivering public goods and services. Sometimes the nature of the public interest is clear and may be spelled out in legislation or other policy documents; at other times, public managers must work with a broad set of stakeholders to craft a workable definition of the public interest.

Design   Public managers will want to be involved in the design of the project or program. When government is the provider or engages a traditional contractor, this involves detailed project or program design, setting forth benchmarks or a time frame for completion. With contracts, it is the contract design (in terms of process, timing, and deliverables) that often determines the success or failure of the contract. With partnerships and networks, a public manager will want to be involved in that design as well but in a more collaborative fashion. IPSPs are a special case, where the design is usually outside the control of the governmental agency; however, government might influence the design if it brings to the table funding or access to information that is useful to the IPSP.

Risk Analysis and Allocation   Public managers need to understand the risks posed in the approach taken, as well as those inherent in the project or program itself. When government is the provider, it bears the risks. At the other end of the spectrum, an IPSP bears the risk entirely outside government. The other instruments—contracts, partnerships, and networks—all involve the need for recognition and allocation of the risks. We discuss this issue in more detail below.

One additional risk that public managers must consider is whether a chosen instrument will strengthen or weaken the overall capacity of government to respond to this and other societal problems. A concern of many about the "hollow state" is that in contracting out so many functions, we are leaving government less prepared to deal with current and emerging problems (Milward and Provan 2000). In examining other instruments—partnerships, networks, and IPSPs— public managers must consider whether these options will ultimately strengthen or weaken their agencies and the ability of other governmental agencies to react to and address the complex challenges facing the public sector.

Communications Successful projects and programs require good communications skills by the public manager; however, the new instruments arguably require communications that are even more effective. In the cases of Fairfax County Human Services and the Coast Guard Deepwater Program, public leaders and managers made a major effort to communicate with various stakeholders during the planning and design phase, as well as during implementation of the programs. However, in both cases, there were some internal stakeholders who did not feel sufficiently involved despite the efforts of the leader. This led one person to remark, "You can never have too much communication." When assessing organizational capacity, communications systems are a critical aspect of any proposed partnership or network solution. If the organization lacks that capacity, it is important that it become a high priority before implementing a new strategy.

With IPSPs, communications also are critical, but in a somewhat more nuanced fashion. Here the goal is to share information and ideas rather than try to control the program or "get everyone on board." If public managers are uncomfortable with the approach taken by the IPSP, they should communicate their concern in a respectful way—as one principal actor to another—recognizing the independent status of the IPSP while trying to shape its direction if necessary.

Accountability Public managers are accountable for results, and when they are directly providing the program or project, accountability is clear and direct.

Accountability in government administration is primarily vertical: public managers report to their directors, who have the responsibility for reporting to the chief executive and legislature. In all of the other arrangements, accountability has both vertical and horizontal dimensions. Public managers are still responsible for the success of their programs, but contracts, partnerships, and networks all have horizontal dimensions of responsibilities.

In contracts, oversight, monitoring, and evaluation are the critical components necessary to achieve accountability. In partnerships, it is important to develop agreed-to measures, sometimes referred to as key performance indicators (KPIs), on which partnership success will be judged. In networks, the critical task is for all members to have a clear understanding of their role in the network and for what results or outputs each member will be held accountable. Public managers must be able to effectively negotiate those KPIs or responsibilities in order to monitor and evaluate the success of the partnership or network. With IPSPs, public managers have little direct control. If they support the broad goals and aims of the IPSP, they must leverage funding or other important resources the IPSP needs in order to achieve some degree of accountability. It may be that accountability is achieved more through quiet negotiations and discussions than with any direct control.

Monitoring and Evaluation All instruments need to be monitored and evaluated by public managers. The premise that concrete data on program performance or program metrics should guide public decision making has framed discussions in the public and nonprofit sectors, especially in the United States since the 1990s. Of course, the bottom line has long been the focus in the private sector. Monitoring and reporting on program performance focus the attention of public managers, their oversight agents, as well as the general public on the value of the program to the public (Newcomer 1997, 2002; Newcomer, Hatry, and Wholey 2010; Hatry 2007).

Case Analysis

The USCG in the 1990s recognized that it did not have the in-house knowledge or the capital budget to replace its aging fleet of ships and planes. In assessing resources and capacity, its leaders might have chosen a more incremental strategy—more consistent with past Coast Guard operations—but instead decided to engage private sector partners with the capability and political capital to push large-scale capital projects through Congress. They received the appropriations they needed, but also became dependent on their private sector partners for detailed decisions about the nature of the recapitalization. Complicating matters was the increased role given to the Coast Guard after the September 11, 2001, terrorist attacks, which enhanced the role of the service and gave it additional responsibilities to handle. Thus, they were involved in a major restructuring (both capital and systems) at the same time as their role and priorities were changing, a very difficult change environment (see Kee and Newcomer 2008).

In the Coast Guard Deepwater Program, Coast Guard leaders were heavily involved in the design of the partnership and the project's expectations. However, while convincing Congress of the programmatic needs and approach, they failed to fully engage their internal stakeholders in the design phase and experienced some resistance among the managers below the top leadership. In addition, the Coast Guard case illustrates that it is not enough to find partners that can bring in the resources and expertise necessary to address a problem or concern. Organizations also must build a capacity to effectively use outside actors. While the system-of-systems concept received strong support among the top echelon of the Coast Guard, the second level of leadership was more skeptical and felt they had not been fully included in the planning and decision making. The Coast Guard did create an office to provide liaison with the public-private partnership but may have lacked the capacity to use and monitor private partners effectively. Only after some highly publicized failures did they recognize the need to beef up their internal acquisition forces. Eventually they took over the leadership role, dissolving the partnership.

In contrast, the Fairfax County case involved developing a network of nonprofit providers that were already active participants in providing services for years to disadvantaged populations in the county, supplementing what government was providing and assisting populations that often fall through the gaps in terms of federal and state programs. Thus, in the effort to develop a more coordinated human services plan, engaging nonprofit service providers in the planning and implementation of a network of service was critical. Had the county ignored those participants rather than worked actively to include them in a collaboration, the county goal of creating a more integrated human services delivery system would not have occurred. On the other side, had nonprofits resisted the county's efforts, the county would not have been able to achieve its objectives.

Recognizing that the county could not address all of the needs of its population, it partnered with local nonprofit social services organizations in designing and implementing a new client information system. The state's Department of Systems Management and Human Services (DSMHS) engaged in extensive communications and information sharing with other nonprofits to assist it in creating a multiservice, multisector access point for citizens with social services needs. By creating a network and using its own strengths in data collection, intake, and analysis, the county developed its own capabilities as well as benefited the nonprofits active in the county. The network strengthened the capacities of all actors.

IDENTIFICATION AND ALLOCATION OF RISKS

One of the reasons for considering alternative approaches to government provision and delivery of a public good or service is the potential for shifting risks from the public sector to the private or nonprofit sector. If all risks are borne by the public sector, as is the case in government provision, there may be a tendency to stick to established processes and procedures in order to minimize risk, and public sector employees may be less cognizant of how those procedures may drive up the cost of provision. Of course, there may be valid reasons for why government does things in a certain way. One person's "red tape" is another person's "legal or equitable protections." However, it is possible that government may not be in the best position to judge and account for certain types of risks. For example, the private sector may have an economic incentive to finish a project on time and within budget, but there is no corresponding financial incentive in public sector provision. The two areas most important for public managers are (1) identifying the nature of and type of risks posed in various options and (2) determining whether risks can be appropriately allocated to the sector best able to deal with the risk.

Identification and Types of Risks

The first step in this analysis is to identify, to the extent possible, the types of risks inherent in the proposed program or project. Risks might fall into a number of categories, including these:

- *Political risks* include potential changes in legislation, appropriations, or policy that might affect the project or program; the potential backlash from stakeholders or citizens affected by the project or program; and the possibility that the involvement of the private or nonprofit sectors will create a blurring of roles that will confuse (or even anger) those constituents.

- *Financial risks* include the ability to fully finance the project at the expected rate of interest.

- *Economic risks* include the ability to accurately project use, inflation, and other such indicators that are affected by the general economy.

- *Complexity risks* include the magnitude and scope of the challenge (overall size and necessity for widespread change) and the fluidity of the socioeconomic environment.

- *Construction and operation risks* include site acquisition and planning, construction of the project or facility, operations according to plan, and results according to expectations.

- *Spillover risks* are impacts on third parties (or other areas of government) that were not initially part of the expectations of the partners. For example, project construction might result in adverse environmental impacts that one of the partners would have to address.

- *Modification and termination risks* include potential problems that might occur if modifications to the program need to be made and potential cost (financial and political) if the program or project needs to be terminated.

- *Uncontrollable risks* (often referred to as *force majeure*) are those which no participants can influence, such as war or a natural disaster.

- *Risks of failure* refer to the possibility that the network, partnership, or IPSP fails in its efforts and considers the consequences of such failure to the public sector. For example, if the public sector loses its capability to deliver a good or service and other sectors fail to accomplish it as well, there may be substantial costs for government to restart the provision.

In general, the larger the magnitude and scope of the project, the greater the uncertainty in the socioeconomic and political environment, and the more diverse the interests of the stakeholders, the greater the risk (Kee and Newcomer 2008). There are, of course, methods to ameliorate risks, but after identification of risks, the first consideration should be to determine which sector or which prospective partner can best manage that risk.

Allocation of Risk

Public managers should consider whether and to what extent risks can be shared with, or allocated to, other partners in a network, partnership, or IPSP. It may be that some risks cannot be shared with other sectors and need to be borne by government regardless of any partnership arrangement.

In general, risk should be allocated to the party that is best able to bear the risk. For example, in a PPP for a transportation project, financial risk might be borne by the private sector, while political risk (change of policy) should be borne by the public sector. Table 7.2 provides an illustrative set of risk factors in a PPP involving infrastructure and a possible allocation of those risks.

As illustrated in the table, most political risks, such as changes in law or policy, should be borne by the public sector. However, engagements with citizens and other stakeholders might be something that would be shared by both the public and private sector partners depending on the strategy of the partners to deal with specific stakeholder communications and citizen involvement. Most risks in the financing, construction, and operations phases are appropriately borne by the private sector because they are in the best position to manage those risks. However, a change in financing interest costs, which may be outside either government's or the private sector's control, might be something that is negotiated, with both interest savings (if there is a decline in interest rates) and interest cost overruns shared by the partners.

Another key area is economic risks such as projected use of the infrastructure. Normally the financing of an infrastructure project would be secured by the expectations of payments (either directly through tolling, or indirectly through government payments for accessibility or shadow tolls).[3] If payments are based on use, someone (either the private sector or public sector) must project actual use. If those projections are wrong, who should bear the risk? This is certainly a negotiable area and may depend on the reasons for the failed projections. Are they a result of actions by government, or is the failure because the private sector has not accurately assessed demand at a given toll charge? If the former, government likely should bear that risk, but if the latter, arguably the private sector should bear that responsibility. Generally government bears uncontrollable risks such as force majeure (e.g., war, flooding, or other environmental disaster) as the public sector (with its larger financial capacity) is thought to better bear that risk.

While government would like to pass off as much risk as possible to the private sector, in the long run that may not reduce its costs. If, for example, the risk

Table 7.2

Illustrative Allocation of Risk in a PPP Infrastructure Project

Risk Category	PPP Phase	Nature of Risk	Possible Allocation
Political risk	Planning, construction, and operations	Change in law	Public sector
		Political opposition	Public sector
		Stakeholder concerns	Public, private, or shared
Financial risk	Planning and construction	Interest rates could increase or decline	Shared
Economic risk	Operations	Inaccurate projections of project use, inflation, or other factors driving costs or revenue	Generally private sector unless government policy has contributed to the problem
Complexity risk	Planning, construction, and operations	Underestimation by partners on the difficulties of the overall project	Generally public sector as it is responsible for scope of project
Construction and operation risk	Construction and operation	Underestimation by partners of the cost of construction and operation, including subcontractors	Private sector, because that is the chief reason government entered into partnership
	Availability	Inability of private sector to keep facilities operable	Private sector
Spillover risk	Construction and operation	Effects on third parties not anticipated in negotiations	Negotiated, depending on the nature of spillover
Modification and termination	All phases	Project changes	Depends on who initiated change or who caused the default
		Project default	
Uncontrollable risk	All phases	Force majeure and other factors beyond either party's control	Generally public sector
Risk of failure	All phases	Project fails	Private sector may owe damages (or default on a performance bond) but public sector has to pick up the pieces

Source: Adapted from Yescombe (2007).

of interest rate fluctuations is borne by the private sector, that sector would have to engage in hedging or other risk-mitigation strategies and would have to build those costs into bids for the project.

An early infrastructure public-private partnership in the United Kingdom was the Dunford Bridge construction and tunnel reconstruction, the first use of private finance in the nation since 1945. In allocating risk, the private partnership agreed to assume the financing, construction, and operating risk. This was a private sector design-build-finance-operate project. The project was delivered on time and within the expected budget. It provided a reasonable return to the private partners with the expectation that all of the debt would be retired within the twenty-year time frame after the bridge opening (Parker 2009).

Case Analysis

The Coast Guard faced a number of significant challenges in developing its public-private partnership. Perhaps most important was the complexity of the overall proposal. The Coast Guard was trying to simultaneously alter its culture to create a system of systems and to recapitalize its entire deepwater assets (ships, aircraft, and systems). Thus, the scope and magnitude of the project was quite large. There was a great deal of uncertainty over whether interoperability standards could be met, and they were in a changing sociopolitical environment where the Coast Guard was taking on new antiterrorism responsibilities because of the September 11 terrorist attacks. This necessitated some modifications of the original designs, increasing the overall costs to the project. The USCG enjoys strong support on Capitol Hill, and its private sector partners provided additional clout when seeking major increases in appropriations—all very positive; however, changing vessel requirements over time and internal stakeholder reactions led to additional modifications.

Although the partnership had some successes—the HC-144A Ocean Sentry Medium Range Surveillance Maritime Patrol Aircraft—there was a major failure. The conversion, reconfiguration, and lengthening of the 110-foot Island Class patrol boats to become 123-foot boats failed to meet basic seaworthy and safety requirements, resulting in the scrapping of all eight modified ships, at a great deal of financial cost (approximately $100 million) and great embarrassment for the Coast Guard. In retrospect, one program manager suggested that the scope might have been too large given the Coast Guard's lack of an experienced acquisition staff for major projects.

In Fairfax County, the risks were largely political. The original goal was to create a central intake center for all human services. However, difficulties in matching various legal requirements (such as confidentiality), state agency concerns, and even discord among key internal players led to a modification of the strategy. While the original vision of full integration of client intake was not achieved, DSMHS implemented a coordinated service planning system to receive inquiries from prospective human services clients, prioritize the urgency of those requests, and direct clients to a network of governmental and nongovernmental agencies that could deliver the services needed.

BEST VALUE FOR THE PUBLIC'S DOLLARS

The fourth area of analysis is whether the proposed solution provides the best value for the public's dollars (see, for example, Her Majesty's Treasury 2008). While this may seem obvious, the calculation of exactly what constitutes "best value" is often problematic and requires assumptions about costs and projections about benefits that challenge even the best analyst. The following are the most critical issues for public managers to address: identifying the likely costs with a government solution, determining the appropriate analytical approaches to provide an answer to which option offers best value for the public, and understanding whether there are "value" issues that go beyond what can be quantitatively measured and determining whether and how to take those into account.

Government Cost Data

Generally, comparing alternatives starts with the current cost of government's providing the public good or service or with an estimate of that cost based on previous costs of delivering a similar program. The United Kingdom's PPP program, the Private Finance Initiative, introduced the concept of the public sector comparator to use as a baseline for analysis of PPP options. This approach has been widely followed by other nations and the World Bank in examining options to government delivery of goods and services, especially infrastructure projects.

A government uses a public sector comparator (PSC) to make decisions by testing whether a private investment proposal offers value for the money in comparison with the most efficient form of public procurement (Kerali 2012). The PSC estimates the hypothetical risk-adjusted cost if a project were to be financed, owned, and implemented by government. Thus, it provides a benchmark for estimating value for money from alternatives.

When evaluating options, cost must be examined wherever and to whomever they might fall. Thus, if a certain action saves government funds but raises the cost of those outside government, such as an affected clientele, those costs must also be considered. Developing or interfacing with one of these options also is not without costs to government. The transaction costs include developing contracts or networks and managing those new relationships. Transaction costs may be substantial, and therefore it seldom makes sense to examine alternative options to public delivery unless the gain in public value is significant.

Part of the cost analysis is to determine if going with a private or nonprofit provider will lead to competition in the provision of that good or service. Competition should drive down costs, spur innovation, and lead to better value for the taxpayers. When the United Kingdom began its Private Finance Initiative (now labeled PPP), its analysts found that it was necessary to help develop a competitive market in order to achieve the savings anticipated from the partnerships (Kee and Forrer 2008). Economies of scale also are an aspect of the analysis. Where the private (or nonprofit) sector already has substantial capacity for a particular function, economies of scale may argue for the public sector to outsource that function.

Analytical Approaches

Public managers have available a number of analytical approaches to examine various alternative instruments. The three most common approaches to analysis of options for governmental programs are cost-benefit analysis (CBA), cost-effectiveness analysis (CEA), and value-for-money (VfM) analysis. The choice of which approach to use (and sometimes more than one) depends on the exact nature of the options being examined and the public goal.

The three approaches have many uses but are frequently used to analyze capital or other large-scale investments and major programs and are useful when considering partnerships or networks. They help to answer a number of questions, for example:

- Does the gain to society justify the cost to society? The economic justification argues that only those projects or activities where benefits exceed costs should be undertaken.

- Will this project pay for itself? The budgetary or fiscal question addresses whether the costs exceed the available budget or expected revenue from the project or program.

None of the three approaches gives "the answer," but may permit reasonable comparisons of alternative means of accomplishing objectives.

Cost-Benefit Analysis   Cost-benefit analysis is a method for estimating in monetary terms the impacts of a policy.[4] Alternatives are generally weighed in terms of net benefits to society, where

Net benefits = Benefits (expressed in dollars) − costs (in dollars).

For example, if the benefits equal $2 million and the costs are $1 million, the net benefits equal $1 million.

Economists view CBA as the gold standard of analysis because all benefits and costs are put in monetary terms for ease of calculating net benefits. CBA often is used for major projects, such as those sponsored by the US Corps of Engineers or Department of Transportation; however, conducting such an analysis is costly and time consuming. It also involves assumptions about the dollar value of certain benefits that are sometimes problematic. For example, while reduced congestion and time saved are often benefits of new road construction (and can be valued in dollars), there may be spillover costs (such as pollution) or benefits (less anxiety) for which it is more difficult to place a dollar value.

Cost-Effectiveness Analysis   Cost-effectiveness analysis compares policy alternatives, based on the ratio of their costs to a quantifiable (but not monetized) effectiveness measure (or benefit). Results are expressed in terms of a cost-effectiveness ratio, where

CE ratio = $Cost/unit of effectiveness.

For example, if it costs $20 million to build five miles of highway and the measure of effectiveness is a highway mile, the CE ratio is $20 million divided by 5 (20/5 = 4), or $4 million per land mile.

CEA has a number of strengths relative to CBA. It allows the analyst to ascertain which option provides the maximum output (unit of effectiveness) for a given total cost or minimize the total cost of producing a given unit of effectiveness. It is useful when the decision maker is concerned with only one outcome or there is only one main benefit. It also is useful for comparing two or more projects of similar size. And it often is easier and less time consuming to conduct than CBA.

However, CEA has a number of weaknesses relative to CBA. It does not provide any information on how society values the unit of effectiveness. CEA ratios often hide differences in scale of two projects. It can focus on only one (or a few) main outcome. If the decision maker cares about multiple outcomes, CBA is better. CEA provides no bottom line on efficiency or value to society.

Value for Money Analysis

Value for money analysis examines the economy, efficiency, and effectiveness with which government has used its resources in discharging its functions (Her Majesty's Treasury 2006). It can be used as part of a prospective analysis to determine, for example, whether a public-private partnership is a preferred alternative to government delivery of a public good or service. VfM focuses on three critical components of value:

- *Economy*: minimizing the cost of resources used while having regard for the appropriate quality.

- *Efficiency*: the relationship between outputs in terms of goods, services, and results and the inputs (resources) used to produce them.

- *Effectiveness*: the extent to which objectives have been achieved and to which the outcomes achieved are those expected.

VfM is arguably different because of its multidimensional approach. It values qualitative as well as quantitative aspects of value. It approaches the issue from a variety of philosophical perspectives. Some believe it is more outcome oriented, as both CBA and CEA tend to focus on outputs that can be measured in units or dollars. Its weakness, however, is that it provides no bottom line to judge whether a project or program creates net value to society. Table 7.3 provides a comparison of the three analytical approaches.

Other Value or Public Interest Considerations

Despite the usefulness of the three analytical approaches, there is still the question as to whether it is possible to measure all of the values that are important for the public interest. There may be some issues other than a bottom line of efficiency or effectiveness. Government must always be concerned about equity issues. The "hot lanes" proposed for some interstate highways involve pay-per-access highway lanes on major roadways where some travelers are willing to pay more in tolls to escape traffic. Their fee-based structures have been labeled "Lexus lanes"

Table 7.3
Comparison of CBA, CEA, and VfM

Approach	Cost-Benefit	Cost-Effective	VfM
Analytical question	Which alternative yields the highest level of benefits to costs?	Which alternative yields the highest level of effectiveness divided by costs?	Which alternative provides the public with the most value divided by cost?
Measurement of costs	Total costs, including opportunity costs to whomever	Total costs, including opportunity costs to whomever	Total costs, including opportunity costs to taxpayer
Measurement of benefits	Total benefits to whomever; measured in dollars	Benefits measured in terms of units of effectiveness	Total benefits to whomever, measured in dollars and other means
Decision criteria	Efficiency: benefit/cost ratio or net benefits	Effectiveness: units per dollars or dollars per units	Multiple: cost/effectiveness; long-term outcomes, values

because pricing is based on congestion and could lead to very high costs to maintain an expected sixty miles per hour performance, which only the very wealthy could afford. At the same time, these lanes often provide discounts for carpooling, achieving another public policy objective. In social services networks or partnerships, government will have to ensure that all of its partners maintain the same notion of fairness in treating those with needs.

Government is expected to provide services equitably and with due process, providing avenues for appeal if a person feels he or she is not receiving what is due based on legislation and existing policy. Private or nonprofit sector partners may not pay the same attention to process details.

Even if it may be more cost-effective for government to deliver a good or service, if government lacks the resources, it may have to appeal to potential partners to fill the resource gaps. Using an existing nonprofit or IPSP that is already active in a policy area may provide government with the additional resources needed to address a particular problem.

The State of Florida Department of Transportation (FDOT) used a VfM approach to examine alternatives for the I-595 corridor improvements. It compared the present value dollar of the estimated cost of FDOT provision through a traditional design-build approach with financing by the state to a design-build-finance-operate-manage approach through a private concessionaire. State officials attempted to consider not only the quantitative results of the analysis (which favored the private concessionaire) but also such issues as long-term service quality and safety controls, locking in life-cycle costs, use of incentives to accelerate the construction timetable, and transferring appropriate risk. They ultimately opted for a PPP with a private sector concessionaire.

Source: Yasutani (2010).

Case Analysis

Neither Fairfax County nor the Coast Guard conducted a cost-value analysis before deciding on the approach to deal with the issues they faced. In the case of Fairfax County, the influx of new immigrants and fiscal constraints necessitated changes in the ways of operating. The strategy was designed both to leverage limited county dollars more efficiently and better coordinate the response of all agencies (public and nonprofit) to better serve the human resource needs of their growing population.

The Coast Guard did use a traditional best-value analysis in developing the contract for partnering with the private sector on the recapitalization of their deepwater assets. Unfortunately, there were limited bids, and the complicated nature of the task made comparative analysis problematic. The USCG eventually urged two private rivals, Lockheed Martin and Northrop Grumman, to form a private partnership, which would then partner with the Coast Guard.

MEASURING PERFORMANCE AND ENSURING ACCOUNTABILITY

Effective performance measurement is critical for ensuring the accountability of any alternative chosen by public managers and is becoming an increasingly important part of management responsibilities. In examining alternative strategies for delivering public goods and services, public managers must consider what type of performance measurement is appropriate, how it will be used, and whether it will be effective in ensuring appropriate accountability—both vertical and horizontal—for the results anticipated. The most important issues for public managers to address are determining how performance measures will be used to keep the selected solution on track, determining what types of performance measures make sense with the particular instrument or option chosen, and determining how to use performance measures to ensure accountability in the public interest.

Uses and Types of Performance Measures

Performance data have both internal and external use. Internally they can inform stakeholders (in the partnership, network, or IPSP) about levels of performance and areas needing improvement, provide trend data, motivate participants, and perhaps assist in making resource allocation decisions. Externally measures can be shared with funders and citizens, showcase successes, and provide illustrations of best practices. Appropriate performance measures depend on the solution and instrumental option chosen. However, certain approaches or rationales for performance measurements may be more salient than others.

Waste, fraud, and abuse are a trifecta of concerns that are common to all programs funded with government money. Public managers have vertical accountability for the funds entrusted to them, whether those funds are spent in a traditional government program, provided in return for a contract or partnership agreement, funneled into a network of service providers, or used to support an IPSP. Thus, some performance measures will need to ensure that funds are spent under appropriate controls and checks to avoid fraudulent spending or other spending not meeting public purposes.

Developing KPIs is a useful exercise to identify the critical indicators of success and hold the collaborators accountable. For example, in a road PPP, a key indicator might be the "percentage of time the road is fully available for traffic." By looking only at the key indicators that matter, partners can focus their efforts and government can use those results to reward success or punish failures (e.g., through withholding of payments or levying fines).

Another approach is the balanced scorecard, a strategic performance management tool managers use to keep track of the execution of activities and monitor the consequences arising from these actions. It focuses on both financial and nonfinancial measures such as customer service, internal processes, and organizational learning. The balanced scorecard framework has been widely adopted in English-speaking Western countries and Scandinavia since the early 1990s. Since 2000, the use of the scorecard, its derivatives (e.g., the performance prism; Neely, Adams, and Kennerley 2002), and other similar tools (such as results-based management) has also become common in the Middle East, Asia, and Spanish-speaking countries. Public, private, and nonprofit organizations worldwide extensively use the scorecard to align their activities to the vision and strategy of the organization, improve internal and external communications, and monitor organization performance against strategic goals to give managers and executives a more balanced view of organizational performance (Balanced Scorecard Institute 2012).

Evaluating performance may use numerous measurements. Several are suggested and described in table 7.4.

Table 7.4
Criteria for Evaluating Performance Measures

Relevance	Measures are closely linked to the mission or purpose of the partnership, network, or IPSP.
Timeliness	Measures are available when decisions need to be made or the program needs to be modified.
Vulnerability	Measures provide a fair assessment of the CSC activity and are not affected greatly by external factors (beyond the control of collaborators) that render the measures unusable.
Legitimacy	Internal and external stakeholders will find the measures reasonable and related to what they expect from the partnership, network, or IPSP.
Understandability	Internal and external stakeholders understand what is being measured and why.
Reliability	Consistent measurement procedures are used to collect data across time and areas of activity.
Comparability	When feasible, measures are similar to measures used elsewhere to benchmark performance.

Source: Adapted from Kee and Newcomer (2008).

Ensuring Accountability

Developing good performance measures is only the first step in ensuring appropriate accountability. Those measures need to be part of an overall strategy of accountability that we discuss in more detail in chapter 10. However, there are a few general comments that we think are important. Measures need to be developed in advance of any negotiated partnership or network and in conjunction with all key partners. This collaborative up-front agreement on accountability is essential but often neglected in the rush to develop the collaboration. Broad consensus on the measures will assist in using them to correct problems before they become critical. Measures may need to be adjusted in the course of a program's implementation, but knowing where you are going and having broad agreement on key measures is a good first step.

A decision also has to be made as to who will collect the data and how often. Measures need to be routinely collected and shared in a transparent fashion with all partners. "Bad numbers" should be used to hold partners accountable, not in a vindictive manner but as a process of encouraging continuous improvement in the program or project. Measurement results can be shared with key stakeholder groups, funders, and citizens generally.

Case Analysis

The key to a successful partnership or network is the development of KPIs before the consummation of the partnership or network. In the Fairfax County case, the DSMHS involved nonprofit social services organizations as well as their own staff in the design and implementation of a performance measurement system. They hired a process coordinator to retrieve and manage the data, which was made available to all key partners on a routine basis. As a result, everyone agreed to the metrics and used the information in their own efforts.

In the Coast Guard case, the PPP was awarded to ICGS without the prior development of performance metrics. This became a priority during the implementation phase and resulted in a balanced scorecard approach, which was widely praised. However, the key measures were not written into the contract with the private partner, and the effective use of the measures was still largely unresolved when the partnership was dissolved.

CONCLUSION

Public managers now have the opportunity to examine a number of options when addressing a difficult governmental challenge. In order to do so, however, they need a framework to fully consider the choices and their need to manage those options. It may be that an option such as an IPSP will present itself that a manager has not considered. We believe the preceding approach will assist managers in assessing their options. The chapter appendix provides a summary of the framework for use by public managers.

The framework is useful anytime a public manager is assessing options to a traditional governmental provision of public goods and services. Because particular issues will lead to different options, it is impossible to argue that answering a question one way or another will provide a definitive answer as to the best option. Each situation is unique. However, the following discussion looks at the general strengths and weaknesses of the four collaborative alternatives to government provision and traditional contracting: collaborative contracts, networks, partnerships, and IPSPs.

Collaborative Contracts

Collaborative contracts are becoming more common as issues become more complex and government may not know how to specify exactly what it wants or the best way to deliver a public good or service, at least in terms of the typical specifications in traditional contracts:

- *Strengths.* Public managers should consider collaborative contracts when governments can take advantage of the strengths of the private and nonprofit sectors by approaching contracting from a collaborative rather than a directive approach. The private and nonprofit sectors may have access to expertise or clients that the public sector lacks. They may be in a better position to determine how best to use that expertise, local knowledge, or relationships with the population targeted by government. Even a collaborative contract, however, has to have clear and measurable objectives or results by which to measure the success of the contract.

- *Weaknesses.* Collaborative contracts involve a leap of faith because important details and specifications that might be included in a traditional contract are not in a collaborative contract. Rather, public managers must rely on developing trust with the contractors. Public managers should not opt for this alternative when trust does not exist or the development of trust is problematic. In the final analysis, the only requirements that are enforceable are those in the contract. The ability of public managers to design these contracts with specific output or results measures is critical.

Partnerships and PPPs

Partnerships are collaborations where both parties have equal (or nearly equal) stakes in the outcome. Each partner has something significant to lose if the partnership fails. Thus, there should be strong incentives for sharing of information and close working relationships to jointly address the public problem or issue at hand:

- *Strengths.* A partnership option is attractive under numerous circumstances: government does not possess the resources and solutions to address the problem; the private sector has a potential market or business solution, or the nonprofit has special local knowledge; it is possible and desirable to share risks; the costs of the partnership do not outweigh the value to the public; government has or can develop the capacity to manage the partnership; and government can establish KPIs to assess partnership success and hold partners accountable for results.

- *Weaknesses.* A partnership option should not be considered when the politics are difficult (no authorizing legislation, no champion, potential for interference); the potential private or nonprofit sector does not bring much to the table in the way of expertise or resources; there are strong accountability issues (difficulty of measurement, inability to hold partners accountable); sharing risks is difficult or inappropriate; and the costs of creating and managing the partnership may exceed the additional public value created.

The DC Capital area I-495 Beltway Hot Lanes represents an effective use of a PPP in many respects. Private financing of $1.2 billion was committed (matching state and federal government financing) and was seen as essential for adding new lanes. The private sector partner (a Transurban-led consortium) took on the risk that the fees and tolls they collected from managing the road would be sufficient to provide an attractive return-on-investment. Transurban has experience managing other highway projects and brought that expertise to this project.

The expansion of that portion of the beltway meant the repair and replacement of numerous overpasses along that stretch, a significant and pressing capital improvement cost that the State of Virginia shifted in part to other partners.

The political acceptability of this PPP remains to be seen. The congestion fares took many drivers by surprise despite public relations efforts to inform the public. Paying a fee for what some may consider a decent commute time may seem a burden to many drivers—one they are likely to feel they have already paid for through their taxes. However, even for those who do not use the Hot Lanes, the expansion should reduce overall commuting time, taking some travelers off the existing lanes and on to the Hot Lanes. This PPP structure is similar to many under consideration nationally and internationally; tolls are critical to cover the interest and principal on the borrowed funds, whether publicly or privately financed, that paid for the expanded highway.

Networks

Networks are common in state and local governments in delivering a variety of social services. They also are increasingly being used in such areas as emergency management and homeland security:

- *Strengths.* A network option is viable under numerous circumstances when multiple actors and sectors have resources that they can employ to address the issue; government does not need to control every detail; innovation is highly regarded or expertise to solve the problem is widely dispersed; the costs of creating and managing the network do not exceed the public value created; network partners agree to manage the risks in their area of expertise; and network partners agree to a mechanism to measure performance and ensure accountability.

- *Weaknesses.* A network option is likely not viable when vertical accountability is an issue; the transaction costs of creating the network exceed the public value of the network; government cannot share the risk or the risks inherent in the network are substantial; measurement of results is problematic; or blurring the distinctions between governmental and nongovernmental actors will create problems for the public.

Hurricane Katrina is a clear illustration of both the promise and pitfalls of networks. The network was used in the effort to coordinate government (multiple levels), business, and nonprofits in the post-Katrina recovery. No one government agency was in a position to control the entire response to Katrina, and the resources that needed to be directed to the region and its victims were dispersed locally, regionally, nationally, and even internationally. As different organizations sought to mobilize resources and respond, there was a shared recognition that managers needed to manage the operations and risks within their immediate control in their own organization while seeking to integrate their efforts into a broader scope of activity and priorities. The challenge was to do so with limited communications and awareness of others' actions and decisions. Although the specific response activities encompassed high levels of complexity, there was a fundamental understanding among those operating within the network of the mission to provide safety, food and water, power, and shelter to the affected population. The shared understanding of what actions were required fits well with the network model.

Despite the best (and sometime heroic) efforts of many, analysis of the effectiveness of the post-Katrina response found substantial evidence of extensive miscommunication and delays in deployment of materials and goods (Koliba, Meek, and Zia 2011). Lack of awareness of the actions across sectors resulted in some turf wars that hindered efficient operations. Business offers to help were underused. All of these experiences reflect a potential downside to the network approach. Better upfront planning and scenario exercises, with an understanding of the roles and responsibilities of the various potential actors in an emergency and greater communication capability, would improve a network governance approach when responding to natural disasters. The use of such planning by District of Columbia metropolitan emergency organizations resulted in an improved response to the attack on the Pentagon on September 11, 2001, a positive example of intergovernmental and cross-sector collaboration.

Independent Public-Services Providers

Independent public-services providers are a bit different as an option because they may exist entirely outside government. A public manager's role may be one of deciding whether and to what extent the public sector should interface with the IPSP, as a funder, cheerleader, provider of information, or even a regulator to protect the public interest:

- *Strengths.* The greatest strength of an IPSP is its ability to act outside a government framework so it can be innovative and flexible, where government often is more rigid and process driven. Public managers should attempt to make use of IPSPs whenever their mission and goals align with the public sector or the outcomes sought are the same as (or similar to) those sought by the public sector.

- *Weaknesses.* The strength of an IPSP also is its greatest potential weakness from a public manager's viewpoint. Because of their independence, IPSPs are difficult to hold accountable in the same sense as other options. Public managers must first determine how the IPSP itself is measuring its results and determine if there is some legitimate accountability structure (such as a board of directors). Public managers also may have to find a mechanism for citizen input.

The self-direction and financial independence of the Global Network for Neglected Tropical Diseases (GNNTD), discussed in chapter 6, is a reflection of the benefits offered by IPSPs. The GNNTD established its own mission and goals consistent with its members' view that the diseases they wanted to investigate had not received enough attention from global health care funders. Federal programs directed at global diseases and pandemics had settled on the priorities of HIV/AIDs, malaria, and tuberculosis. The GNNTD has received funding support from the Gates Foundation and is implementing in-country programs that will lead to curing these diseases. The program efforts are consistent with the global health community's recognition of the importance of neglected tropical diseases (NTDs), but GNNTD supports programs well beyond those that the US government supports. For those who advocate greater attention to NTDs, an IPSP approach fits very well.

However, GNNTD's relative independence also means its efforts may be seen as separate from a larger global policy context. Would the funding generated by GNNTD have been better spent on priorities already recognized by the United States and the global health community? The GNNTD also strives to be the strongest advocate for NTD support, but other organizations (such as the UK Coalition against NTDs) remain active, and it is not clear how to resolve mission overlap among the different groups.

In considering the choices for public managers, a number of important questions arise that we will address more fully in part 2 of this book, "Managing Cross-Sector Collaboration":

- Is the current model of bureaucratic public administration adequate in this new age of partnerships, networks, and IPSPs?

- How can public managers lead in this new heterarchical environment?
- Can we maintain appropriate accountability in the public interest?
- What is the best approach to developing capacity in public agencies to prepare public managers to engage these new options?

For public leaders and managers, collaborative arrangements such as collaborative contracts, partnerships, networks, and IPSPs offer alternatives to public production that may provide value to the public. However, good analysis should precede any decision about whether such alternatives should be pursued.

Appendix: Summary of Analytical Framework

Area	Key Questions and Issues
Nature of the public task or problem	
One or multisector solution	1. Is the solution available in one sector? 2. Does the need for innovation argue for more than one sector? 3. Is this a short- or long-term problem? 4. Are we dealing with the whole problem or just part of the problem?
Susceptibility to a private (business) or nonprofit solution	1. Will a business approach help relieve the problem without creating equity problems? 2. Is the problem already being addressed in the nonprofit sector? 3. Does a need for local knowledge suggest the need to involve a local private or nonprofit partner?
Political considerations	1. Is the proposed option legal, or does it require new legislation to go forward? 2. Is there a political champion for the proposed solution? 3. Will the solution lead to more or less political interference? 4. Has a stakeholder analysis been done to examine how various parties will be affected by the proposed solution? 5. Will the involvement of a private or nonprofit partner help with additional resources or make it more difficult for the public manager to control the outcomes?

Appendix: Summary of Analytical Framework

Area	Key Questions and Issues
Resource needs and capacity	
Resources needed to solve problem	1. Does government have the resources (funds, staff, and innovative ideas) necessary?
	2. In which sectors do those resources lie?
	3. Are those sectors potential partners in addressing the problem?
Organizational capacity	1. Have you sufficiently analyzed the environment and know the capacities available in each sector to address the problem?
	2. Have you involved all appropriate stakeholders?
	3. Do you have a risk assessment and allocation methodology in place?
	4. Do you have a communications strategy?
	5. Do you have a process in place to achieve both vertical and horizontal accountability?
	6. What are the ways you will hold all actors accountable?
Identification and allocation of risk	
Identification of types of risk	1. Have you identified the types of risks that might be present in the proposed alternative: (a) economic risks, (b) political risks, or (c) force majeure?
	2. Will a proposed solution create a blurring of sector roles?
Allocation of risks	1. Which types of risks can be shared?
	2. Are any risks inherently governmental?
	3. Which partner is best able to bear the risk?
	4. Will the "risk premium" be excessive?
Other considerations	1. What are the consequences to government of failure of the option chosen?
	2. Are there spillover costs to other parts of government or other sectors?

Appendix: Summary of Analytical Framework

Area	Key Questions and Issues
Best value for the public's dollars	
Government cost data	1. Are government cost data available to compare with alternatives? 2. Can a "public sector comparator" be created?
Analytical approaches	1. Which analytical approach is most appropriate? (a) cost-benefit analysis, (b) cost-effectiveness analysis, or (c) value for money analysis?
Other value considerations	1. Are there equity issues that need to be addressed? 2. Does this approach help leverage public funds by bringing in additional resources? 3. What will be the impact on government agencies if the alternative is chosen—for example, agency morale or consistency with creating high-performing public agencies?
Political considerations	1. Should public sector agencies be given an opportunity to "compete" with the alternative?
Measuring performance and ensuring accountability	
Uses of performance measurement	1. How will you use performance measurements: to inform and track progress, to make corrections, internally and externally?
Types of measures	1. What type of measurement system is most appropriate given the nature of the problem and proposed alternative: (a) key performance indicators, (b) balanced scorecard, (c) preventing waste, fraud, and abuse? 2. Is the measurement clear, transparent, and realistic? 3. What other measurement criteria are important?
Methods to hold partners accountable	1. Can partners be held to a specific performance target? 2. Can you achieve both horizontal and vertical accountability? 3. Who will collect the data?
Other considerations	1. Does governmental capacity exist to develop an appropriate measurement system for the desired alternative? 2. Is flexibility needed to accommodate changing situations? 3. How are citizens involved in assessing performance? 4. Can the approach be altered or terminated if necessary without undue hardship to government?

Case Study for Discussion: Cross-Sector Collaboration in Job Training

You are an assistant to the executive director of the Department of Social Services (DSS). The governor has campaigned on increasing job training in the state and moving individuals from receiving state welfare payments to working. Currently the Division of Employment Training (DET), within DSS, provides that service. However, the governor and the state legislature are unhappy with the current results: at an annual cost of $20 million, DET has found work for only a fraction of those on welfare. The program is operated out of twenty local offices, and the current annual success rate is less than 10 percent for the 500,000 adult recipients on welfare who were placed in a job. Welfare payments cost the state over $2 billion a year (averaging about $4,200 a person per year plus administrative costs of program administration).

Questions and Issues for Consideration
1. If the goal is to make the DET more cost-effective, which option of a CSC would you choose?

2. Explain how that CSC choice would achieve cost-effective training better than any of the others.

PART TWO

Managing Cross-Sector Collaboration

The Need for a New Model of Public Administration

This chapter raises the issue of whether the current model of public administration, centered on a bureaucratic approach to management and leadership, is sufficient for today's cross-sector collaborative challenges. The chapter first examines the characteristics of the current model and various reactions to it, including New Public Management, and then explores alternative concepts. The chapter concludes with a tentative framework for creating a new model of public management that can better address our current challenges in a multisector environment.

The bureaucratic model has served modern governments fairly well, especially in developed nations (Wilson 1989). It has provided a degree of certainty in terms of how programs are delivered and protections against cronyism, fraud, and abuse, and it has achieved many noteworthy accomplishments in providing public services to large populations of citizens. However, the model may be unable to deal with today's major challenges, such as climate change, deteriorating infrastructure, and a costly and inadequate health care system. There are some common elements to these challenges:

- They are multijurisdictional, crossing local and state and even international borders.
- They are multiprogrammatic, often involving several different types of government programs and agencies.
- They do not lend themselves to command-and-control types of solutions.
- Citizens often interact indirectly with government; their chief contacts are with private or nonprofit organizations.

209

- Leadership is diffused and must be coordinated to achieve the best results.

- Rules and procedures may provide a framework, but flexibility is the key to success.

- Roles are determined by knowledge and ability in a heterarchy, not by positional authority in the hierarchy.

The nature of these problems is thus much different from those that occurred during the twentieth century when the bureaucratic model flourished.

HISTORIC ORIGINS OF THE BUREAUCRATIC MODEL IN US PUBLIC ADMINISTRATION

Understanding the influence of the bureaucratic model requires an examination of its origins and growth over time. Since the inception of the United States, public leaders have debated the appropriate structure for carrying out the work of government. John Rohr (1986) has noted that although the word *administration* does not appear in the US Constitution, "the word *administration* and its cognates appear 124 times throughout *The Federalist Papers*; more frequently than *Congress, President,* or *Supreme Court*" (1). Clearly the founders were keenly interested in the role of public administration in achieving the responsibilities of the newly proposed national government. Initially the approach of the new nation to governing was largely through local government; however, by the mid-twentieth century, the federal government began to exert a dominant administrative role.

The origins of the current model of public administration gradually emerged in the United States during the early twentieth century—a bureaucratic form, first studied and analyzed by Max Weber (1864–1920). Weber, a German sociologist, political economist, and administrative scholar, made significant contributions to the study of bureaucracy and administration, including the examination of such issues as the specialization of jobs, merit systems, uniform principles and rules of procedure, structure, and hierarchy. Contemporaries such as Frederick Taylor, Henri Fayol, and Elton Mayo also examined these issues, as did later US scholars, such as Herbert Simon and Dwight Waldo, early proponents of professional public administration.

Weber described many ideal types of public administration and government in his 1922 book, *Economy and Society* (1947, translation), including a type he labeled bureaucracy, and his works popularized the term. Many aspects of modern public administration go back to Weber, and a classic, hierarchically organized civil service of the "Continental" type is called "Weberian civil service" (Hooghe 2001). Weber believed bureaucratization was the most efficient and rational way of organizing government.

Of course, in the United States, bureaucracies developed not because of Weber but because increasingly complex policy problems, in scope and scale, demanded a more organized public administrative response. Goodsell (2004) argues that the heyday of centralized American bureaucracy occurred during the mid-third of the twentieth century—the 1930s to the 1960s—when the nation was grappling with the Great Depression, World War II, civil rights, consumer safety, and environmental protection. The administrative structure in government today was largely forged during this period.

What constitutes the current model? Bureaucratic management is a formal system of organization based on clearly defined hierarchical levels and roles in order to maintain efficiency, effectiveness, and accountability. With respect to government, it has certain clear characteristics:

1. Public programs established by acts of the legislative body responsible for policy, eligibility, and processes for the delivery of those programs

2. Public programs housed and implemented in specific public departments, divisions, or other units of government

3. Public programs delivered by a cadre of professional civil servants using traditional bureaucratic delivery approaches, characterized by (Allan 2005):

   - A hierarchical organizational reporting structure
   - Delineated lines of authority in a fixed area of activity
   - Action taken on the basis of and recorded in written documents
   - Rules implemented by neutral officials with expert training
   - Career advancement on technical qualifications judged by the organization, not individuals

4. Impartial civil servants who directly interact with the citizens or other clients served by those programs, with services provided equally to all who are eligible

5. Strict vertical democratic accountability

Advantages of the Bureaucratic Form

The bureaucratic organizational form has the potential to produce desired results. In a democratic government with competing citizen needs, bureaucracy generally serves to ensure the equitable distribution of goods and services. Because of its rational character and nonparticularistic method of organizing client needs, the bureaucracy can ideally serve all within a given community or client population at an equally efficient level. The bureaucratic form has often provided a foundation for effective as well as equal services.

The US Social Security system is an example of a bureaucratic success story, and it perfectly fits the bureaucratic model. Congress developed the program, established eligibility standards and the distribution formula, and created an agency to manage it. The Social Security Administration (SSA) opened offices around the country to provide direct contact with its citizen clients. The public interacts with the SSA either directly at a local office, by phone, or through a website. Determinations of eligibility and payments are made according to established rules and procedures, by impartial civil servants, with an appeal process for those who are not satisfied with the initial determination. Accountability is maintained through the SSA hierarchy to the administration's commissioner, who is appointed by the president and confirmed by the Senate. The system works quite well and public opinion is strongly supportive: SSA is reputed to have better customer satisfaction over the phone than such private sector exemplars as Nordstrom and LL Bean (Goodsell 2004).

While it is easy to lambast faceless bureaucrats, public attitude toward specific agency bureaucracies at the federal, state, and local levels is often quite positive—receiving higher ratings than many private sector counterparts. Among public agencies getting high marks are the US Postal Service, the Coast Guard, the National Institutes of Health, the Centers for Disease Control and Prevention, NASA, local fire departments, public health clinics, and both state and local parks and recreation departments (Amy 2011; Goodsell 2004). Bureaucratic success stories include greatly improved health care for most Americans, cleaner air and water, better predictions for weather disasters, protection of bank and savings and loan deposits, and safer food and drugs. In fact, much of what we take for granted today is made easier because federal, state, and local bureaucracies have worked in the public interest to produce policies and results that benefit all Americans.

These programs have succeeded for a number of reasons. Congress and state legislatures passed effective laws. Public agencies, often at more than one level of government, created the rules and regulations to implement the programs. Dedicated civil servants oversaw and managed the programs effectively. Some of these programs fit the traditional model of public administration, relying on a hierarchical bureaucratic model; others relied on other actors, nonprofit organizations, and even private organizations to fully implement the programs.

Critiques of the Bureaucratic Form

The bureaucratic model is frequently criticized, and the opposition to this model often coincides with criticisms of government itself. Goodsell (2004) finds three predominant typologies of antibureaucratic criticism: unacceptable performance, serving elite interests over the interests of all citizens, and oppression through formalism and a general lack of concern for particular needs of clientele. A fourth critique has arisen from scholars of gender relations and those examining communications patterns in organizations.

Of these criticisms, the focus on the unacceptable performance and the rigidity of bureaucracies seems to dominate the majority of the literature. Identified ills in bureaucratic practice include "unresponsiveness," "rigidity," "arbitrariness," "trained incapacity," "occupational psychosis," and "professional deformation" (see Wilson 1989; Osborne and Gaebler 1992). Additional critical thought on bureaucracy comes largely from contemporary organization theorists who have concerned themselves with the impact of bureaucratic structure on employees' motivation and attitudes. Adler and Borys (1996) point out that organizational research presents two conflicting views of motivation and bureaucracy: "According to the negative view, the bureaucratic form of organization stifles creativity, fosters dissatisfaction, and demotivates employees. According to the positive view, it provides needed guidance and clarifies responsibilities, thereby easing role stress and helping individuals be and feel more effective" (61). Wilson (1989) argues that the major reason for bureaucratic failure is rigidity: if we would only "deregulate the government," we would "liberate the entrepreneurial energies" of its members (369).

The critiques from gender scholars primarily center on their rejection of the rationalist-modern form of organization as decidedly male centered. Feminist scholars have argued that bureaucratic structures privilege male forms of communication, deemphasize intuitive and experiential knowledge, diminish the creative capacities of employees, and encourage conformity with historically male, hierarchical institutions such as government.

Hierarchical communication traces its roots to the scientific management movement, which sought to systematize and clarify roles and responsibilities within an office in order to increase efficiency. The structure prescribes an ultimate chain of command for making decisions and institutionalizing relationships. However, the workplace has changed greatly since the early 1900s when this model was introduced: organizations are more diverse as women and men from different cultures have joined the workforce, and bureaucracy is now more complex than ever before due to increasing partnerships across sectors. An alternative model to this system is a collaborative approach that promotes participation and inclusion. Collaborative communication "encourages participation, shares information and power, and enhances the self-worth of others" (Mumby 1996, 271), whereas hierarchical communication encourages workers to "compete for the floor in order to establish a winner" (Syed and Murray 2008, 419).

Researchers from communication, management, sociology, and gender theory have identified negative effects of top-down communication styles and argue that these structures need to adapt as organizations evolve. First, this communication style excludes both male and female workers who are uncomfortable with a hierarchical model. The inadequacies of this approach were articulated by Mary Parker Follett in the 1920s. She believed that the issuing of orders is surrounded by many difficulties; that to demand an unquestioning obedience to orders not approved, not perhaps even understood, creates a disincentive for effective problem solving by workers (Follett 2003, 2007). In her view, the hierarchical communication model inhibits proactive decision making: orders become depersonalized to such an extent that workers lose sight of how to find innovative solutions (Follett 2003, 2007). Ultimately women and men who do not like the rigidity of the top-down structure become "marginalized and [their] communication styles remain undervalued in organizational and group interactions" (Syed and Murray 2008, 419).

REFORMING THE BUREAUCRATIC STATE

Efforts to modify or reform the bureaucratic, administrative state occurred repeatedly during the twentieth century. Reform efforts largely focused on how the growing government bureaucracy could become more effective and efficient in its operations. For example, the 1912 Taft Commission on Economy and Efficiency led to the adoption of the federal budget, and the 1947–1949 Hoover Commission (on the Organization of the Executive Branch) led to an extensive reorganization of the executive branch to improve the efficiency and effectiveness of government. Most of the reforms in the first part of the twentieth century were designed to facilitate the centralization of federal functions, allowing more hierarchical control by the executive branch. That trend toward centralization began to shift somewhat during the second part of the century.

Concerns about the growth of the federal government led to the Second Hoover Commission (1953–1955), which recommended the curtailment and abolition of federal government activities that are competitive with private enterprise. The Kestenbaum Commission on Intergovernmental Relations (1955) addressed the need to improve intergovernmental relationships between the federal and state governments as more and more program administrations began to be shifted to the states. The 1982 Grace Commission (President's Private-Sector Survey on Cost Controls) examined private sector practices and, contrasting them to public sector practices, found widespread waste and inefficiency in government. Many state governments appointed "little" Hoover or Grace commissions that mirrored the effort at the federal level.

However, none of the reform efforts questioned the basic Weberian principles of bureaucratic management. Reforms sought to increase accountability (usually to the chief executive), streamline operations, and allow the bureaucratic model to work more efficiently and effectively. That changed in the 1980s. Over the past twenty-five years, antibureaucratic forces have coalesced and argued for a new model of public management exemplified by those who want to create a more entrepreneurial, competitive public sector (Osborne and Gaebler 1992). To these reformers, the public sector today is bogged down in endless red tape, driven more by process than results (Gore 1993).

The New Public Management

What emerged in the 1980s was reform under the broad label of New Public Management (NPM), a "tidal wave of government sector reform" that has swept the world (Kettl 1999). The widespread adoption of NPM ideas reflects their advocacy by a number of international organizations, including the World Bank. NPM largely is a reaction to a perception that government agencies have become too large and ineffective. After years of state growth and promotion of welfare state policies, many began to question both the level of state operations and the method of state intervention. Rather than questioning the fundamental principles of hierarchy and authority, however, the NPM movement suggested integrating market-based principles into its mode of delivery and in general reducing the size of government.

While the roots of NPM reach back to the anti-welfare-state writing of Friedrich Hayek (1944), Milton Friedman (1962), and others, New Zealand and the United Kingdom were the first nations to embrace, in the 1980s, the concepts of NPM on a significant scale. New Zealand began a systematic restructuring of its government with the passage of the State Owned Enterprise Act in 1986, the State Sector Act in 1988, and the Public Finance Act in 1989. In addition to the privatization of some functions, it created a number of semiautonomous state-owned enterprises (SOEs) and broke up the remainder of its departments into smaller, more focused units. New Zealand's ministers enter into agreements with chief executives heading SOEs, specifying the output to be produced during the year. The chief executives are appointed under term contracts and need not come from the career civil service. They are given flexibility to hire staff, purchase supplies, and select the mix of inputs to produce the agreed outputs within the limits set by the budget and the law.

In the United Kingdom, Margaret Thatcher first seized on privatization as a pragmatic response to a budget problem and then adopted NPM in a broader context. The Conservative government launched the "Next Steps" initiative in 1988, in which they divided policymaking and strategic direction from implementation and service delivery and organized those involved in service delivery into "executive agencies." Each agency is headed by a chief executive who negotiates a framework agreement with his or her respective minister, setting out the agency's performance goals, responsibility to the chief executive, and other operational arrangements. In order to make the agencies more responsive to the public and raise their standards (quality) of service delivery, the government started the Citizen's Charter program in 1991 whereby public agencies set and publish service standards, in which they commit to meet specific performance goals.

When Tony Blair's Labour Party took office in 1997, they continued many of the policies of the Conservative regime, especially the use of the private sector to deliver some critical public facilities. Originally labeled the Private Finance Initiative and relabeled Public-Private Partnerships (PPP) by the Labour Party, PPPs enabled the country to extend services without further public sector debt.

New roads, schools, and hospitals were built and managed by private sector consortiums (Forrer and Kee 2008).

The reforms suggested by NPM do not challenge the basic presumptiveness of the bureaucratic model, except insofar as they urge more creativity, flexibility, and innovation in government approaches to delivering public goods and services. However, the reform efforts were the first major effort challenging the bureaucratic model on the grounds that it was failing to meet today's public sector responsibilities.

While the nature of its reforms differs from nation to nation and even within nations at various levels of government, NPM's reform agenda contains the following elements: reducing or redefining the role of government, encouraging privatization and competition, using private sector expertise, becoming more customer focused, decentralizing authority to local levels of government, becoming more outcome oriented, and creating more transparency and accountability for results.

Ascertaining the underlying philosophy or ideology of proponents and opponents of NPM is not easy. At the heart of the problem are the dual, and in some ways conflicting, ideas or goals behind NPM. One broad goal is to reduce the role of government. This conservative, or neoliberal, objective views market mechanisms as superior in most cases in the delivery of goods and services. A second broad goal, which at least in part contradicts the goal of less government, is to "reinvent" government to work more effectively and efficiently for the citizens and other customers. This "managerial" objective is influenced by "best practices" in the business world, such as W. Edwards Deming's total quality management movement (Deming 1986).[1]

NPM proponents argue for a reassessment of the growth of government and a rethinking of how government functions—distinguishing between government responsibility and government provision. Thus, government might be responsible for public health, but without providing for solid waste removal; government might want to ensure that every child is educated, but without operating public schools; government might publish regulations, but without operating a printing press; and government might ensure access and reasonable electric rates, but without operating a power plant.

The Reaction to New Public Management

Critics of NPM focus on both effects and processes. The effects of reducing the role of government through privatization and contracting out, they argue, are a diminished government that is unable to care for the poor and those who cannot adequately compete in the market economy. In addition, NPM processes, with their emphases on efficiency and the entrepreneurial activity of government managers, interfere with democratic governance and with other values that are highly prized, such as fairness, justice, and democratic participation.

Terry (1998) argues that underpinning NPM's concepts are a "managerial ideology" or "managerialism" whose wild-eyed entrepreneurial styles are "a threat to democratic governance" because NPM threatens the hierarchical control inherent in the bureaucratic model (197). By *managerialism*, Terry means too much of an emphasis on business management principles at the expense of democratic values and clear accountability.

For Terry, the managerial ideology combines "liberation management" and "market-driven management." Liberation management was popularized in books by Paul Light (1997) and others. Their arguments centered on the notion that managers are "good people caught in bad systems" (Gore 1993). It is the bureaucratic system that leads to poor government performance. Terry and others (e.g., Moe 1994) assert that the managerial ideology creates a number of problems for public administrators' legitimacy. They argue that it changes the role of public managers from implementers of previously defined government goals to entrepreneurs who invent public policy without adequate democratic controls or accountability. "Public managers are, after all, public servants," argues Colin Diver (1982). "Their acts must derive from the legitimacy from the consent of the governed, as expressed through the Constitution and laws, not from any personal system of values, no matter how noble" (404).

In contrast, proponents of NPM argue that managers must lead (Behn 1998) because legislative and executive direction often lacks specificity. Without leadership, public managers can be held accountable only for faithfully following approved processes, not results. Thus, the democratic accountability that opponents argue will disappear with NPM is in reality, suggest the NPM advocates, an illusion. Furthermore, it is not as if the entrepreneurial public manager is free to act as he or she desires. Budgets, executive and legislative oversight, annual audits, and the public press all constrain public managers. They must continually justify in the public arena their actions as in the public interest. Rather than resisting the label of "managerialism," NPM advocates such as Brazil's Bresser Pereira and Spink (1999) accept the term, contrasting managerial public administration, with its focus on results, with bureaucratic public administration, with its focus on processes. To improve government performance, NPM advocates argue, public managers must be unshackled from red tape and allowed to be entrepreneurial agents of change, focusing on results, not processes. Market-driven management is influenced by the notion that markets are efficient and that the creation of internal markets and use of business technologies and processes will increase service and efficiency (Peters 1996).

Just as the proponents of NPM argue from different assumptions about human nature (empowerment versus forced accountability), the opponents also find themselves in a similar predicament. Thus, opponents fear empowerment because they see it weakening democratic accountability (NPM managers will act in their self-interest). Yet they oppose forced accountability because it runs counter to public administration's aims of "fostering an image of the public manager as trustworthy, ethical agents who administer the public's business with the common good in mind" (Terry 1998, 198). This conflict in beliefs about human nature (and the nature of public managers) results in an ideological stalemate.

Striking the right balance between administrative capacity and control remains a controversial aspect of public management, however, and failure to do so often defeats efforts to achieve public management reform. Tensions continue to exist between "making managers manage," that is, imposing substantial controls over managerial discretion, and "letting managers manage," that is, holding public managers accountable for their performance rather than for their compliance with formal rules and procedures (Kettl 1997; Lynn 2003). These two strategies, Kettl notes, "require culture shifts in opposite directions" (1997, p. 449), a reality not always fully appreciated by advocates of public management reform.

ALTERNATIVE APPROACHES TO REFRAMING PUBLIC ADMINISTRATION

Over the past decade, public administration scholars have attempted to examine other frameworks or paradigms. One attempt to offer a viable alternative is the concept of "new public service" (Denhardt and Denhardt 2011), which focuses on the values and ideals of public service. Another administrative approach applicable to many public problems is network management (see Goldsmith and Eggers 2004). Lester M. Salamon (2002), who edited an influential book on the use of the many "tools of government," calls for a "new governance," and Kee and Newcomer (2008) argue for "transformational stewardship." In these and other cases, contemporary authors challenge the notion that vertical chains of authority can best (or at least solely) carry out the work of government.

New Public Service

Whereas traditional public administration seeks to neutrally enact the policies of elected officials, who are responsible for determining the public interests, Denhardt and Denhardt (2011) argue for a much more activist role for public managers. They see the importance of engaging citizens (as coproducers, not customers or recipients) as the critical element of democratic governance. The public interest is thus determined through a dialogue; it is not simply an aggregate of self-interests or the sole province of elected officials as implied by the bureaucratic model.

The goal for Denhardt and Denhardt is not to find the quick solution but "the creation of shared interests and shared responsibility" (42). In their chapter "Think Strategically, Act Democratically," they suggest that public managers must develop collective efforts and collaborative processes. They also urge a "values-based leadership," where public managers need to:

- Help the community and its citizens understand their needs and their potential
- Integrate and articulate the community's vision and that of the various organizations in any particular area
- Act as a trigger of stimulus for action (141)

Network Management

There is a growing literature on the importance of networks in the delivery of public services (Goldsmith and Eggers 2004; Agranoff 2007). The role of networks emphasizes the importance of horizontal links between individuals and organizations, challenging the tenets of hierarchy inherent in the bureaucratic model. Of course, like many other things touted as new, governments have been using networks for years. Many state governments deliver social services through a network of local government and nonprofit providers. Law enforcement, whether federal or local, often cooperates with sister agencies in chasing malefactors or protecting the public.

Network management involves designing and activating the network; making sure the network actors' goals are congruent and agreeing to a strategy to achieve those goals; determining what human skills are necessary to fulfill the goals of the network; creating the information technology and other enablers so the network can get its job done; and developing and monitoring a set of performance measures to make sure the network is on track. Developing trust among the network partners is perhaps the most critical role of public actors. Others are risk management, negotiation and conflict resolution abilities, and communication across agencies and sectors—all critical skills for any new framework.

The New Governance

Salamon (2002) argues that public problem solving today has become a "team sport," spilling beyond the borders of government to other social actors—public as well as private, for-profit as well as nonprofit—whose "participation must often be coaxed and coached, not commandeered and controlled" (600). However, the resulting system of governance is not self-executing. He continues that it poses "immense management and organizational challenges, but challenges that differ from those characteristic of direct government, and that consequently they must be approached in a new way" (600). Those issues include management challenges, accountability challenges, and legitimacy challenges.

The new governance requires public managers to understand the motivations and incentive structures of the other actors and the ability to negotiate with largely independent partners in an interconnected system. It also requires the development of accountability structures that go beyond the traditional notions of accountability embodied in administrative law and procedures (at the heart of the bureaucratic model). Public managers, according to Salamon, need to better understand the tools available, be adept at design (to match the tool with a specific problem), and be effective enablers, that is, with the ability to bring multiple stakeholders to the table. This requires three important skills:

- *Activation skills*—the ability to mobilize and activate complex partnerships
- *Orchestration skills*—the ability to blend the partners into an effective network or system
- *Modulation skills*—the ability to find the right mix of rewards and punishments to elicit the necessary cooperation without providing windfall benefits to one actor or another

Transformational Stewardship

Kee and Newcomer (2008) argue that public managers must be transformational stewards in the public interest. While their book deals primarily with transforming public and nonprofit organizations, there are some important lessons for governing cross-sector collaborations. Governments, they note, are moving away from hierarchy and silo program administration toward a "heterarchy of systems (resembling a network or fishnet) that interact to meet the needs of citizens" (10). This network approach to service delivery depends on coordination and cooperation among multiple organizations from all sectors—public, private, and nonprofit—and various levels of government—federal, state, and local. The change is a departure from the insular, hierarchically organized organizations carrying out priorities, to one where multiple organizations cooperate with one another in shared roles.

In major natural disasters, for example, the organizations that respond most effectively, such as the Coast Guard, are used to operating in a multisector, multiorganizational environment. The Coast Guard even teaches the value of "pre-need networking" to develop the relationships and contacts that might be needed prior to an emergency in order to respond more effectively—as the Coast Guard did during Hurricane Katrina by rescuing more than twenty thousand people.

Managing networks requires the development of trust with those in the network. As trust accumulates, it creates social capital that allows networks to function more effectively without having to develop contracts or understanding for every possible contingency or situation. Trust is critical in light of the voluntary, nonhierarchical nature of networks. Leaders, lacking bureaucratic or positional power, must rely on personal and shared power to make these relationships work. Follett (2003) referred to this type of power as "power with" rather than "power over" and believed that it can be more effective and broader than trying to act alone.

Twenty-First-Century Government Management

In his reflections on twenty-first-century government, Kettl lays out a core of concepts that he argues must be part of any new approach to government management:

- A policy agenda that focuses more on *problems* than on *structures*
- Political accountability that works more through *results* than *processes*
- Public administration that functions more *organically*, through heterarchy, than *rigidly* through hierarchy

- Political leadership that works more by *leveraging action* than simply by making decisions
- Citizenship that works more through *engagement* than *remoteness* (Kettl and Kelman 2007, 9, italics in original)

The concept of governing through cross-sector collaborations, advanced in this book, is a new, consolidated approach regarding the role of public servant leadership and management and draws from governance concepts in traditional public administration as well as those of New Public Management, Denhardt and Denhardt's new public service (2011), network management, Salamon's new governance (2002), Kettl's twenty-first-century government management concepts (2007), and Kee and Newcomer's concept of transformational stewardship (2008). Its focus is on collaboration, not just between public managers and citizens but also with the private and nonprofit sectors, as the strengths of each sector are used to address problems. Table 8.1 summarizes the major leadership and management characteristics that we draw from these approaches and provides some tentative ideas concerning the most effective approaches to cross-sector collaboration.

Table 8.1
Leadership and Management Concepts for Governing Cross-Sector Collaborations

Origin of Concepts	Effective Concepts	What to Avoid
Traditional public administration	Democratic accountability	Rigidness
	Equity and fairness	Reliance on hierarchy
	Clear expectations	Command and control
	Controls over waste, fraud, and abuse	Process orientation
New public management	Flexibility	Too much reliance on markets
	Market mechanisms (where appropriate)	Private sector exploitation
	Transparency	
	Customer service	
	Outcome oriented	

(Continued)

Table 8.1
Leadership and Management Concepts for Governing Cross-Sector Collaborations (*Continued*)

Origin of Concepts	Effective Concepts	What to Avoid
New public service (Denhardt and Denhardt 2011)	Citizen engagement Collaboration Values-based leadership	Too much reliance on the public sector Difficulties in reaching consensus
Network management (Goldsmith and Eggers 2004; Agranoff and McGuire 2003; Agranoff 2007)	Flexibility Innovation Speed Specialization	Risks Lack of accountability Lack of tie-in to public interest or policy
New governance (Salamon 2002)	Multiple tools Use of private and nonprofit sectors Activation, orchestration, modulation skills	Notion that you can always control other actors Relating all actors to the governmental hierarchy
Twenty-first-century government (Kettl and Kelman 2007)	Problems over structure Results over process Organically, through a heterarchy Leveraging action Citizen engagement	Ignoring the hierarchical accountability that is still required
Transformational stewardship (Kee and Newcomer 2008)	Stewardship Heterarchy, not a hierarchy Risk assessment and management Mutual trust and accountability Power without power over	Constant change Too much idealism

CONCLUSION

As the short excerpt in the box on Hurricane Katrina notes, public managers often are faced with daunting challenges that can be addressed only with flexible organizational structures that respond to the problem at hand. Bureaucratic structures often get in the way of the cooperation and alliances that are needed.

KATRINA: FLEXIBILITY TRUMPS BUREAUCRACY

The failure of governments at all levels, and especially the federal government, to respond effectively to Hurricane Katrina in 2005 is well documented. However, within the turmoil, there were success stories, including a six-person squad from the sheriff's office of Hennepin County, Minnesota. Alongside them were sheriffs' deputies from Massachusetts and Kentucky, National Guard troops from New Mexico, and countless other contingents. All were linked by the Minnesotans' high-tech command van. And very few of them had been sent by the Federal Emergency Management Agency. These helpers came to Plaquemines and places like it from no single source, through no comprehensive organizing process, at no national leader's command. They came from across America, as officially or as ad hoc as they had to, because they wanted to help.

Source: Freedberg (2005).

The bureaucratic model provided an invaluable service to citizens by establishing the organizational structure and processes that support control over the actions of public employees. Public policy decisions made by elected legislatures and executive offices should be carried out faithfully by government agencies. Disputes over what policies may mean for the production and delivery of public services, eligibility to receive such services, how quickly to implement, and how to judge success are best resolved through the pluralistic structures of traditional governance that mediate diverse interests within communities and the nation.

At the same time, public managers do not always work in such an ideal system of government. We have discussed in some detail the constraints and challenges that public managers face when working in government agencies today, such as insufficient resources and outdated policies and assessment of problems.

The globalized world calls for rapid, informed responses to complex, "wicked problems." Many public administration scholars have identified the same issue: the frustration of trying to deliver public services in an effective, efficient, and equitable manner while working within the confines of a bureaucratic model of government that has survived for over a century. The emergence of CSCs and their growing popularity can be seen as a response to the shortcomings of the traditional approaches to public service delivery.

On the one hand, we think CSCs should be celebrated as innovative approaches to problem solving—a chance to improve public services when CSCs are designed and managed the right way. On the other hand, successful engagement of CSCs requires public managers to act and think in ways that can directly contradict the expectations for government employees as called for by the bureaucratic model. Innovation, flexibility, sharing, and adaptability, all traits required of public managers to thrive in CSCs, are values that are discounted within large public bureaucracies.

In recognition of a growing rift between wanting government to be more responsive and accountable to the public's needs and the expected norms of the bureaucratic model, this chapter has described recent scholarly ideas for modifying and, in some cases, overhauling the bureaucratic model. However, public managers should bear in mind that to get the full public value out of CSCs, traditional norms of bureaucratic behavior and values must continue to transform.

In the following chapter we describe the type of leadership required to enable public servants to effectively use cross-sector collaborations (collaborative contracts, networks, partnerships, and IPSPs), including issues such as accountability and organizational learning. We are not going to "banish" or "break" bureaucracy even though some have made that argument (Barzelay and Armajani 1992); it will be with us well into the future for very practical reasons and to ensure democratic accountability. However, other forms of organizations are needed to complement the current structures. The effective use and leadership of cross-sector collaborations are becoming critical responsibilities of today's public administrators. Combining elements of new public management and other new ideas on public service, while retaining essential accountability measures valued by all public administrators, leaders and managers of partnerships, networks, and IPSPs can provide the public sector with important mechanisms to address today's problems.

Assignment for Discussion

Contrast the US Social Services Administration with the Department of Homeland Security. Which department will function better under the current bureaucratic structure, and why? Which department might benefit from a different approach to public administration? What elements would that approach include? How might you apply this reasoning to our case dealing with state employment and training services?

Leadership Implications in Cross-Sector Collaboration

Good leadership skills are critical in any organization. However, leading organizations involved in cross-sector collaboration (CSC) require an emphasis in certain skill areas that perhaps are not as critical in more traditional hierarchical organizations. For example, all leaders must be good communicators, a common attribute cited in the leadership literature. But CSCs require more than just good communications; they require the ability to forge a common purpose or aim among actors who have their own organizational agenda. Public and nonprofit managers in CSCs also must see the larger system beyond their organizational niche. This may mean taking on roles not in their traditional job description and investing time in activities that at first glance may appear not directly related to the success of their own organizational mission. This is even more critical in CSC leadership because collaboration allows a variety of viewpoints and approaches to solving a particular public problem or issue. Finally, CSC requires the development of trust among the collaborators. The level of that trust may vary depending on the nature of the CSC, but trust plays a critical role in the success of all collaborative programs, much more so than traditional programs run by one public agency or nonprofit organizations.

This chapter describes nonprofit and public leadership in CSCs. It first introduces the concept of heterarchy as a different way of organizing activities from a traditional hierarchy. The chapter identifies four leadership strategies that are extremely important in CSC and views those strategies through discussions with four leaders involved in CSC: two from the public sector and two from the nonprofit sector. The chapter concludes with an examination of the implications for managing CSC.

HETERARCHIES AND HIERARCHIES

Hierarchies and heterarchies are two organizational designs that represent different approaches to consolidating authority to achieve organizational purposes. Hierarchies, which are the design structure in most large organizations in all sectors, represent the most centralized form of control by concentrating authority at the apex of organizations. Heterarchies, which are common in CSC, are the least centralized form of control by dispersing authority across divisions or even organizations.

Public managers are used to operating in hierarchies. However, as we have discussed in earlier chapters, managers across federal, state, and local levels of government increasingly find themselves engaged in partnerships and networks to coordinate collective action for social purposes (Provan and Lemaire 2012; Agranoff 2012). Similarly, nonprofit managers increasingly build relationships with other organizations to carry out their programs (Johansen and LeRoux 2013), involving partnerships with both governments (Gazley 2010) and businesses (Austin 2000). Thus, it is important for public and nonprofit managers to understand the distinct characteristics of these two methods of organizing.

Hierarchies generally are characterized by formal structures that clearly define boundaries around employee functions and establish authority in layers, with the most powerful people at the top and subordinates positioned below in pyramids or treelike distributions. The essential characteristic of hierarchies is authority through vertical relationships (Kettl 2006), whereby functions and priorities are determined from the top down and direction for collective behavior is determined from the higher levels of the organization (Senge 2006). Decision making within hierarchies is generally based on the specific authority assigned to an employee's professional position within the organization (Reihlen 1996). The inherent value of hierarchies is that they allow specialized, narrowly defined responsibilities among multiple units at the lower levels of organizations, while senior leadership deals with the complexity of coordinating the varied activities throughout the entire organization.

In contrast, heterarchies, which characterize CSC, cultivate integration and have less clearly defined structures of authority. Stephenson (2009) refers to heterarchies as "nonrandom aggregation[s]" of "human connections" with less direction provided from a central source (4). While some heterarchies may adopt formal rules and procedures, actors within a heterarchy operate on a more level playing field, where knowledge and ability are more important than positional authority (Kee and Newcomer 2008). In addition, the scope and scale of responsibilities are less clearly delineated among multiple parties in heterarchies. In a network, for example, it is common to find multiple organizations responsible for similar functions within a given environment. Examples of heterarchies include many forms of disaster response, where jurisdictions rely on "consultation and cooperation" to coordinate roles among multiple actors (Jenkins 2006, 32). The structural distinctions in the distribution of authority between hierarchies and heterarchies are illustrated in figure 9.1.

In the illustration of a centralized hierarchy, a state highway administrator would be responsible to the governor and the legislature. In turn, the administrator would oversee all transportation functions, including such functions as highway engineering and construction, and intermodal transit. Assistant state administrators for those functions would have various managers, specialists, and project or team leaders working under their direction. Accountability and direction flow vertically throughout the organization. In contrast, a CSC illustration is a decentralized network associated with a state government agency, such as a Department of Health Services. It might consist of the state agency as a hub of a network that might include federal agencies; city, county, and public school districts; and a variety of nonprofits (some serving as lead contractors, with other contractors working with them), and possibly for-profit organizations that are providing certain services.

The inherent advantage of cross-sector heterarchies is their potential for adaptation and flexibility, whereby multiple members can shift roles and duties in response to external conditions and to the knowledge and skills of one another. Cross-sector collaborations involve more symmetrical balances of information and knowledge among members, so that independent parts continue functioning even if some ties or members are discontinued, preserving the collaboration's resiliency.

Communication in Hierarchies and Heterarchies

Within any formal organizational structure, including the organizational chart or standard operating procedures, social interactions among individuals complement and often deviate from the order established. Even in a defined hierarchy, the informal elements of organizations (Barnard 1938), such as social and cultural norms (Schein 1992), often describe the behavior of employees in the workplace and are usually determined from outside the formal procedures and

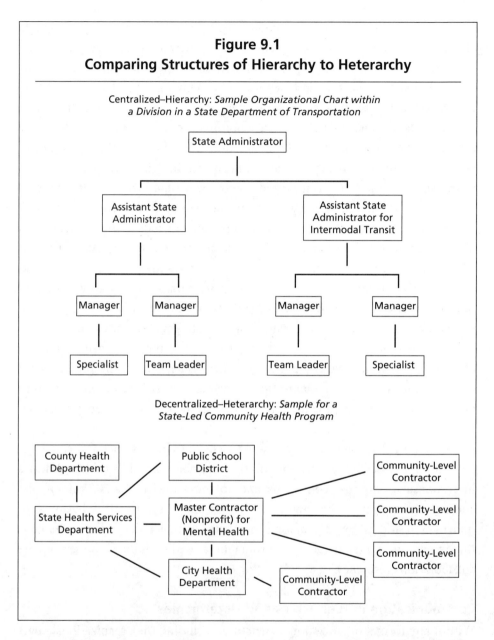

Figure 9.1
Comparing Structures of Hierarchy to Heterarchy

Centralized–Hierarchy: *Sample Organizational Chart within a Division in a State Department of Transportation*

State Administrator

Assistant State Administrator

Assistant State Administrator for Intermodal Transit

Manager   Manager   Manager   Manager

Specialist   Team Leader   Team Leader   Specialist

Decentralized–Heterarchy: *Sample for a State-Led Community Health Program*

County Health Department

Public School District

Community-Level Contractor

State Health Services Department

Master Contractor (Nonprofit) for Mental Health

Community-Level Contractor

Community-Level Contractor

City Health Department

Community-Level Contractor

staffing charts of organizations. However, within hierarchies, communication is more likely to follow vertical chains of command that lead to more siloed forms of information exchange, which create narrow flows of information within the organization and offer little opportunity for information sharing across different organizational units. As a result, communication among employees is restricted since potential interactions are constrained by each person's formal position of authority within the organization (Reihlen 1996).

Heterarchies in CSC, in contrast, thrive on information exchange. There are greater opportunities for individuals to interact and share ideas with one another and to generate solutions to problems collaboratively. In the most open case of a CSC such as a self-governed network, there are few barriers to communication, and ideas are shared openly and frequently among all members. Unlike limitations on reporting structures in formalized hierarchies, heterarchies foster work flow relationships that involve "supporting, consulting, and information exchange-oriented, task-based relationships" (Soda and Zaheer 2012, 758).

Understanding the implications of hierarchical and heterarchical designs is important as public and nonprofit managers turn to more horizontally based organizational structures (collaborative contracting, partnerships, networks, and independent public-services providers) for delivering public services (Agranoff and McGuire 2001). Each form of cross-sector collaboration calls for indirect tools of administration, such as contracts, memoranda of understandings, or informal relations that facilitate horizontal collaboration among organizations, and necessitates different leadership strategies for achieving effective outcomes (Kettl and Kelman 2007). In addition, nonprofit leaders who are accustomed to achieving their targeted missions within a community are challenged through heterarchies to consider wider social issues in the communities where they operate. The defining characteristic of collaborative, heterarchical work structures is that governance, accountability, and performance among members of a collective effort often depend on relational (or informal) modes of influence as a replacement for, or in addition to, any explicit (formal) terms that can be enforced with incentives and penalties (Bertelli and Smith 2009).

LEADERSHIP IN HETERARCHICAL STRUCTURES

A great deal has been written on the types of leadership and management skills that are needed to lead in more heterarchical structures of public services delivery. The overarching tension in adapting to this changing administrative environment involves balancing the advantages of top-level control offered by vertical channels of authority with the operating-level flexibility necessary in

CSC (Kettl 2006). Some effective concepts to address this issue were discussed in the previous chapter: Denhardt and Denhardt's (2005) citizen engagement, collaboration, and values-based leadership; network management concepts, such as flexibility and innovation (Goldsmith and Eggers 2004); and Kee and Newcomer's (2008) concepts of stewardship, power sharing, coalition building, and creating mutual trust and accountability.

Milward and Provan (2006) highlight the importance of building accountability, establishing legitimacy, mitigating conflict, adapting designs, and fostering commitment to improve collaboration. Similarly, Moynihan (2005) highlights the importance of "activating" relevant stakeholders, "framing" the rules of cooperation, "mobilizing" actors toward shared objectives, and "synthesizing" patterns of ongoing collaboration. Kettl (2008) discusses the importance of fostering teamwork, clearly defining missions, focusing on results instead of process, and inspiring action among fellow peers. Salamon (2002) advocates the collaboration of private and nonprofit sectors with government through the skills of activation, orchestration, and modulation.

The Four Critical Elements for CSC Leadership

While all of the attributes cited above are important, a review of the literature, an examination of elements of success in various CSC approaches, and interviews with leaders in the public and nonprofit sectors suggest that four general areas of leadership are the most critical when engaging heterarchies to address complex problems in a cross-sector environment:

1. Generating support from other actors

2. Leading outside of one's formal role

3. Understanding the wider system

4. Building trust

To better explore these CSC leadership strategies, we conducted interviews with senior executives leading collaborations (two in the public sector, two in the nonprofit sector). One of the great advantages of this kind of interview is the potential to target discussions around the specific areas of experience and expertise of the interviewee (Berry 2002). The goal of this inquiry is to explain what a "set of people think" and to more accurately reconstruct an understanding of key events (Tansey 2007). Also, the responses from the interviewees are not considered in isolation, but in respect to documentation related to the crises or events they were involved in (George and Bennett 2004).

The Four Interviewees

Thad W. Allen   Admiral Thad Allen is one of the most respected leaders in public service. He recently retired as the commandant of the US Coast Guard and is best known for his performance directing the federal government response to Hurricanes Katrina and Rita from 2005 to 2006 and as national incident commander of the unified command for the Deepwater Horizon oil spill. From his many roles in the US Coast Guard and related roles in crisis response, Allen has confronted some of the most complex problems our country has faced by leading widely diverse governance networks and partnerships.

On April 20, 2010, Deepwater Horizon, a deepwater oil rig drilling an exploratory well for British Petroleum (BP) in the Gulf of Mexico, experienced a catastrophic explosion, killing eleven workers (Berinato 2010). The incident would become the largest accidental marine oil spill in history. Hurricane Katrina hit the city of New Orleans in 2005, causing a storm surge that breached the city's levee system and caused up to 80 percent of the city to be flooded (Cooper 2005; US Government Accountability Office 2005; Kennedy School of Government 2006; Landy 2008). The impact of the storm left much of the city's communication systems in disarray, including the cellular towers. After stepping in to replace Michael Brown as the principal federal official in the government response, Allen found himself at the intersection of a host of federal, state, and local governments and nongovernmental stakeholders involved in response and recovery.

Ron Carlee   Ron Carlee is currently the city manager for Charlotte, North Carolina; he recently served as the chief operating officer at the International City/County Management Association; and he has served in local government for thirty years, including as county manager for Arlington County, Virginia. As county manager for Arlington on September 11, 2001, he played a central role in coordinating emergency response efforts following the terrorist attack on the Pentagon. Carlee faced the complications of supporting responders from not only different levels of government but from different agencies and from different cultures and with different priorities.

The physical location of the Pentagon added to the complexities of the emergency response on 9/11 (Varley 2003; Titan Systems 2002). Located in Arlington, across the river from Washington, DC, the Pentagon depends on local fire departments to take the lead on structural emergencies. Among the many complications of the immediate aftermath, federal officials in the Pentagon wanted to get back into their building, the Arlington County Fire Department wanted to put out the fire, the Federal Bureau of Investigation wanted to preserve the crime scene, and the District of Columbia wanted to offer assistance. The abilities of the parties to achieve agreement and collaborate in the aftermath of the incident reflect many of the values that Carlee instilled in his colleagues in Arlington County.

Sue Russell   Sue Russell is the president of the Child Care Services Association (CCSA) in North Carolina. Headquartered in the Research Triangle, she leads a variety of efforts aimed at nonprofit advocacy and service delivery to improve the condition of child care services in her state and across the nation. As an association, CCSA coordinates efforts across groups, individuals, and volunteers to improve the rights of children and their families. It also provides a range of services, including referral services for families seeking child care, salary supplements for child care professionals, and technology support to child care businesses.

CCSA develops relationships with a list of more than thirty businesses, foundations, state and local governments, and service delivery nonprofits to fund their programs. It also lists more than seventy partnerships with other nonprofits and public sector organizations in their state. The multiple alliances and relationships structured around the work of CCSA in a field as complex as child care services is indicative of the broad network and many stakeholders required to influence social programs in this area.

Lori Kaplan   Lori Kaplan is the president and CEO of the Latin American Youth Center (LAYC), a nonprofit located in Washington, DC. Its mission is to "empower a diverse population of underserved youth to achieve a successful transition to adulthood, through multi-cultural, comprehensive and innovative programs that address youth's social, academic, and career needs." The organization provides support to youths in the Washington, DC, metropolitan region through education programs, family counseling, workforce training, health services, and artistic expression. Leading and facilitating collaborations is central to Kaplan's work in the LAYC. Among her responsibilities is representing the organization through a variety of executive boards and nonprofit associations in the metropolitan region.

The four areas identified as critical in CSC shed light on the ways that public and nonprofit managers can achieve greater cooperation and coordination among semiautonomous actors mobilized around public issues. Although there is much that can be done to improve collaboration in heterarchies through the design of formal structures, by creating chains of command and reporting structures, individual leadership is the primary driver of cross-sector collaboration.

Generating Support

Managing the delivery of successful outcomes requires greater attention to leadership and the overall need to garner contributions from members and individuals across the sectors. The balanced roles of authority in heterarchies require building consensus among disparate members and building overall respect and commitment to common purposes. Rather than compelling others to take action, leaders need to generate participation and commitment among potential actors, each contributing to the shared purpose, while recognizing that individual member goals may vary. The leadership role is likely to be more akin to a conductor of an orchestra (Salamon 2002) than a CEO.

Thad Allen explains the coordination challenge in networked environments as the need for cultivating a "unity of effort" in place of a "unity of command" (Allen 2010; Berinato 2010). During the government response to Hurricane Katrina, for example, local governments, state governments, and federal authorities exercised various levels of independence in their contributions to the cleanup of New Orleans. Cultivating a shared vision (Senge 2006) or shared purpose built the commitment of all those involved in the cleanup effort.

In discussing the inherent challenges of reconciling the interests of a number of semiautonomous actors in a disaster response as complicated as the aftermath of the Deepwater Horizon oil spill, Allen explained one approach for generating the support of others: "If you don't have legal control or direct control, you need to come up with a 'value proposition' that allows you to have a basis for cooperation." He defined a value proposition as a statement about the benefit that another party will receive for carrying out a given course of action. In the case of public services, it could refer to the need to improve safety standards for frontline staff on the coast dealing with the Deepwater Horizon oil spill. He stated, "I put out a directive. It was not done through rulemaking. My responsibilities allowed me to do it. I created the standards by working with OSHA [Occupational Safety and Health Administration] [and] we came up with a MOU [memorandum of understanding] of how to work together [and strengthen the safety standards]." The improved conditions of the workers involved in the oil spill provided an indication of the added value that would be achieved by strengthening these rules. Because of this initiative, the frontline workers on the beaches achieved greater personal protection—not through the existing governance structures but through a directive that Allen initiated and was accepted because of its value.

Another example of Allen's efforts to generate support from multiple actors around a single effort was evident during his immediate tenure as incident commander for the cleanup after Hurricane Katrina in New Orleans. Arriving at one of the primary command centers, and standing before an all-hands audience of over one thousand frontline responders from federal, state, and local agencies, he communicated a simple purpose for their work: "Treat any storm victim that you encounter as a member of your family." The simple request helped them to unify responders around a straightforward mission that helped guide their work.

Ron Carlee emphasized the importance of crafting and communicating a clear purpose or mission to generate support from multiple stakeholders to mobilize around a specific plan. In many ways, that mission needs to be broad enough to accommodate the diverse interests of different participants. Carlee explained, "All parties need to understand and respect each other's goals, while moving forward to the broader mission." More specifically, the objective is to encompass the differing motives that would drive nonprofit and private sector organizations to mobilize around a single program or initiative.

Carlee provided Arlington County's General Land Use Plan as an example of achieving a broader mission. This program offers incentives for businesses to contribute to public purposes such as low-cost housing or community spaces. The primary objective is to provide appropriate incentives to the private sector (businesses) in order for them to participate. As Carlee explains, the role of the public manager is to create greater value for the community by partnering with the private sector to invest in cultural facilities, affordable housing, or other public purposes by providing incentives (such as selectively increasing community density) for the private sector to get involved.

As the head of a nonprofit association, Sue Russell provided some explanations for generating support from other organizations. Put bluntly, she stated that "it's rare that a nonprofit can fulfill its mission without a partnership. . . The world of the nonprofit is a 'bridge-world,' where we need to create new initiatives that are not provided by government." This involves building partnerships and networks with other nonprofits and with government agencies.

In an environment where nonprofit organizations operate with no formal obligations to one another, Russell mentioned the importance of leading by example. She pointed out that demonstrating a significant impact on the kinds of social issues that other potential partners are concerned with is one of the best ways to gain their support: "They don't do things because you are great, it's really about the difference you make." Building on this idea, she also discussed the value of demonstrating the measurable impact of potential collaboration. The stronger the message that potential collaboration can improve issues that other organizations care about (through your own example and impact), the better the potential for generating support from others.

Generating the support of potential partners can be challenging for a number of reasons. Collaborating with government can be difficult since the public sector often views nonprofits as little more than "beggars at the table," without immediately understanding their potential contributions. One of the ways Lori Kaplan discussed generating greater support from nonprofit and government providers is to frame the priorities of collaboration with respect to a shared interest among potential partners. She stated, "You have to be in a position where people trust that you're in it not just working for your own organization, but the mutual interest." She also indicated the importance of highlighting the potential "collective impact," or anticipated benefit to the missions of all of the parties involved, rather than simply describing one organization's interest in collaboration.

Leading Outside One's Formal Role

Cross-sector collaborations require those involved to see beyond their narrow job descriptions and examine the potential of working with others in a partnership, network, or other arrangement. Allen commented on the importance of seeing beyond one's individual role within the context of a wider response effort. He referenced Peter Senge and the importance of avoiding "getting caught up in the notion or definition of your job description [to the point where] you see your job description as a limitation on your action." A solution Allen suggested is "seeing the art of the possible," or the overall objectives of the activity involving collaborations. He elaborated on the point by stating that people "need to feel empowered to speak truth to power, to have an impact."

Allen provided an illustration with respect to frontline staff facing administrative constraints in carrying out rapid and context-specific requirements in disaster recovery and response. He indicated that during both the response to Hurricane Katrina and the Deepwater Horizon spill, he heard from staff that if they had the power to make decisions, they would have a bigger impact. For example, Coast Guard officers tasked with clearing homes and checking for survivors along the coast after Katrina required detailed explanations and authorization from higher authorities, leading to delays. Allen's response was to "go back" and ensure that "the people managing them gave them more discretion." By cutting back on the approval processes needed, frontline responders had more flexibility to act beyond their roles to address the needs of the disaster.

Encouraging public employees to work beyond their specific job descriptions is complicated for a number of reasons. Chief among them is the overall inclination toward risk aversion in the public sector and the tendency for many public employees to avoid behaviors and actions that could generate unfavorable press. For Ron Carlee, the key to encouraging public employees to go above and beyond the call of duty involves greater attention to the goals underlying the public interest. As he explained, "Public managers first and foremost need to focus on what is in the public interest."

Encouraging nonprofit employees to work beyond their individual roles also is complicated for a number of reasons—chief among them the reality that many professional positions already encompass a wide spectrum of responsibilities with little overhead support. Sue Russell described the importance of learning about the individual responsibilities and roles of employees in order to carry out this work. Specifically, she noted the value of understanding "their issues and priorities" to know how to encourage their contributions beyond their respective priorities. One important advantage is that serving a wider social cause is inherent in the social motivations of employees in the nonprofit sector.

Lori Kaplan described the importance of creating a greater "community orientation" for members of nonprofits to encourage them to act outside their respective roles and responsibilities. There is little question that the professionalization of the nonprofit sector has created a type of corporatization, where nonprofits often operate like franchises that branch out from a single entity. While this model offers great potential for capitalizing on organizational scale, it runs contrary to the grassroots orientations that other nonprofits have in the communities where they work. Kaplan emphasized the importance of "homegrown" and "place-based" orientations of nonprofit missions to help them to act beyond narrow scopes of work to better serve their populations. For her, the key is "changing values" of the staff working on the programs, so they can channel their contributions to the needs of the local population.

Understanding the Wider System

Systems thinking offers a perspective for viewing one's role within a wider structure of collaboration. Senge (2006) describes the concept as "a discipline for seeing the 'structures' that underlie complex situations, and for discerning high from low leverage change" (69). Systems thinking involves recognizing not only the wider span of interactions among multiple individuals or organizations, but also the influences that one's own actions have on behaviors in other parts of the system. Senge points out that too often, we focus on the individual points of interaction that we may have with one or more persons or organizations within a wider system. Instead, we need to understand how our own contributions set off ripple effects and influence flow processes among separate members.

Allen spoke on the importance of seeing the bigger picture in heterarchies by stating that "everything has to do with the notion of systems thinking." He explained the idea: "If you are working on [some kind of partnership] beyond your appropriations and your limitations, you need to work with people on similar outcomes." He suggested that part of the process of achieving systems thinking and a greater understanding of how different groups, persons, or organizations contribute to wider outcomes involves understanding how an individual mission fits into those larger goals. He elaborated the point by saying that "you can see . . . beyond the constraints of the organizational mission you are working on [that] you haven't violated anything by working together. You actually produce a better product for the American people."

Allen provided an example of this type of systems perspective with respect to the government's response to Hurricane Katrina. During the immediate aftermath of the storm, a number of fishing boats washed up into the trees along the Gulf Coast. There was a very real need to assist the local community in retrieving the boats, but in many cases the boats "did not have the threat of fuel discharge, [and] because of that it was beyond the jurisdiction of the federal government" to retrieve them. The constraints on the legal obligations of the federal response presented a picture where "it didn't appear that the federal government could address the need of bringing down the boats for the local fishermen." Allen worked with the Bush administration to create a grant program to allow the federal government to address similar problems. The issue demonstrates how a systems perspective can help to show the wider needs of a given response regardless of the existing legal constraints during a response.

Ron Carlee discussed the importance of building relationships among people involved in a wider system in order to better understand how their individual roles relate to the whole. Specifically, he discussed the importance of social capital and how it accumulated through repeated in-person interactions among those involved. He again referred to the planning programs of the county to explain how a wider perspective could be achieved. In this case, it involved what he called a "smart growth agenda" that worked to align business and nonprofit actors around goals in infrastructure and transportation through joint planning programs.

Sue Russell described the importance of regular meetings to achieve greater collaboration across involved organizations. Her point is that "collaboration takes time . . . [since] decisions are not quick and easy." It is only through the amount of time that they spend working together that professionals can learn more about how to understand their respective roles in the wider system of child care delivery. Russell described one interorganizational function, "chapter referral," with respect to this point. The organizations in the association, for example, determine processes for referral based on council decisions to find the best provider for the patients identified. Russell noted the role of allocating association resources through these decision-making councils as evidence of some of the ways that she and her colleagues generate an understanding of the wider system through their collective decision making.

The very nature of a grassroots approach to service delivery can also improve attention to the wider system of service delivery organizations, since the homegrown groups are more aware of their limitations of doing things on their own. Lori Kaplan describes the impacts on local policy change as an example. Along with her work for LAYC, Kaplan works for the DC Alliance for Nonprofits, which advocates for policy changes to improve youth services. She explains that the collective impact of advocating together is far beyond what any organization can do on its own. This kind of collective work provides access to public leaders that individual organizations would not have on their own and gives them more leverage over other leaders.

Building Trust

Navigating multiple relationships successfully, each operating within significant spheres of autonomy, requires an environment of trust. As discussed in earlier chapters, this is true of all forms of CSC: collaborative contracting, partnerships, networks, or IPSPs. There is well-established evidence that trust and information sharing are interdependent; they reinforce one another among organizations (Ratnasingam 2003). Trust, however, takes deliberate effort on the part of all members. In the field of emergency management, for example, training, exercises, and even social events can help to build familiarity and understanding among different groups (Carlee 2008). The process is to build bridges among different professional cultures of first responders, local businesses, and government planning officials.

The trust of citizens in their government is also important in any public service activity. A recent study of public-private partnerships (PPPs) for transportation infrastructure found that citizen engagement can foster public trust and improve public perceptions about the roles of the private sector in collaborations such as PPPs (Boyer 2012). If public trust erodes, the pressure for formal controls (often in the form of regulations) increases, constraining the potential for public leaders to engage in innovative collaborations with organizations outside government.

Citizen engagement through transparency, public hearings or town halls, and online forums can address misunderstanding surrounding the objective of cross-sectoral collaborations. This level of understanding can help to mitigate public outcries against controversial programs and can help public, private, and nonprofit organizations to align their interests by improving an understanding of how their contributions affect the circumstances of the citizens, customers, or clients they serve.

Allen discussed his approach to foster trust among multiple organizations by requiring representatives from the public and nonprofit sectors to work together in a shared workspace. He advised putting "them in the same place to work together. Create a command center. When they are using the same coffee pot, they begin talking to each other about their families, etc. When you work together, you start to challenge each other to create solutions together." His overall message in both the Katrina and Deepwater Horizon responses was "colocate."

Fostering trust is related to creating social capital. Ron Carlee advised, "You must respect the relationship to truly build trust." This involves "spending time together" on a regular and frequent basis. Examples include scenario planning in emergency management, where employees from local fire, police, and other safety departments enact a simulated response to a disaster. Not only do such events help the organizations to cultivate and craft their responses to disasters, they also give personnel from different workplaces the chance to get to know one another. The chief advantage of such "preneed" relationships is that when a disaster hits, they are not challenged to develop new relationships, but can instead reach out to people they already know (Whitehead 2005). Carlee also instituted periodic lunches with the Arlington County leaders from all sectors. "There was no agenda," he explained. "We just got together and discussed what was going on and the issues we were dealing with. This often led to joint initiatives that otherwise would not have occurred."

Fostering trust among nonprofit organizations is inherently difficult since organizations working in the same service area often compete for the same sources of funding. Sue Russell described overcoming these challenges by improving transparency in their operations so potential partners would have a better idea of what they did. She also mentioned the importance of candid debates and discussions through association-related functions to overcome areas of distrust. Russell stated the need to "welcome disagreement" among nonprofits involved in collective decision making. She indicated that this type of discussion led to better compromises among the different goals of the agencies involved, which ultimately led to better relations among the groups.

Lori Kaplan discussed the importance of cultivating trust by leading by example. Like Russell, she emphasized that nonprofit leaders are often challenged to establish trust since they compete with other nonprofits for the same pools of money. She pointed out that "it is not just about talking about trust, but it is your actions that actually make things happen."

IMPLICATIONS FOR PRACTICE: HOW TO ADAPT LEADERSHIP TO CSCs

Comments from the interviewees on each of the four leadership areas help to explain specific activities that can further working effectively in CSC. One of the challenges of leading in more heterarchical structures is the dependence on (or interdependence with) other semiautonomous actors in order to achieve a desired purpose. For Allen working in a federal system, it often meant soliciting cooperation from executives in state or local governments or from key representatives in the private or nonprofit sectors. Similarly, for Carlee it meant coordinating action among people and organizations from different levels of government and from the nonprofit and private sectors. In the nonprofit sector, the challenge was often to demonstrate the collective benefit achieved by working more closely with one another. Both Russell and Kaplan highlighted the importance of demonstrating individual contributions to a social issue of shared concern to generate this kind of collective support.

Interviewees also spoke about the importance of developing and communicating a wider vision (or mission or value) that can help to unify collective action in response to complex problems. As we have noted in earlier chapters, there must be mutuality among the collaborators; each must feel it has something to gain individually while also contributing to the broader collective goal. This message was particularly clear among the public sector leaders in the study. Specifically, this can involve clarifying a mission that is broad enough that it helps nonprofit and private sector organizations recognize how their roles contribute to wider goals of community development. In both public and nonprofit sectors, this often means learning more about individual organizations and cultivating shared values that can help to build greater cohesion among them.

Acting beyond one's formal roles or responsibilities is often needed in decentralized governance structures in order to solve collective problems and achieve success. Allen describes how increased administrative discretion can improve the potential for frontline workers to experiment and work beyond their assigned roles to address wider goals of an emergency response. Carlee mentioned the value of appealing to public interest objectives to encourage people to work outside their individual job descriptions to achieve collective goals.

The systems perspective encompasses viewing the wider environment of relations that underlie a collective course of action. Allen spoke about the

Table 9.1
Comparing Public and Nonprofit Leadership Perspectives

	Public Sector Perspective		Nonprofit Sector Perspective	
	Allen	**Carlee**	**Russell**	**Kaplan**
Generating support	Develop a value proposition; create a unity of effort.	Cultivate a mission that incorporates private and nonprofit interests in public goals.	Demonstrate your ability to make a difference to social issues of shared concern; demonstrate shared impact.	Demonstrate the collective impact achieved by working together.
Leading outside one's role	Give discretion to frontline responders; see the art of the possible.	Put the public interest above risk aversion.	Learn about the existing responsibilities of staff; encourage them to look beyond their defined roles.	Cultivate a grass-roots, homegrown, community orientation to delivery.
Understand the wider system	Overcome legal obstacles; see how individual mission fits into larger goals.	Focus on a wider agenda or purpose for cooperation; build social capital.	Foster collective decision making in association-related activities.	Illustrate the immediate benefits of collective action.
Building trust	Colocate network members to build relationships.	Build relationships prior to major events.	Welcome disagreement to build shared commitment.	Lead by example.

importance of communicating how collective action can help individual organizations better meet their goals rather than inhibiting their abilities. For Carlee, a wider perspective can be achieved through the planning process for a given locality. By engaging relevant nonprofits and private sector groups in community development plans, they can better understand how their roles relate to others. Nonprofit leaders discussed the importance of collective decision making through associations to cultivate greater understanding among the many parties involved in collaboration. In addition, reorienting nonprofit leaders to their grassroots relations in the communities where they serve can also increase their understanding of the need to work with others.

Trust is the glue in collaborations, particularly in less authoritative work structures. While the level of trust may vary depending on the specific CSC approach, trust is a factor in all successful collaborations. Believing in and counting on others allow people to cooperate more effectively when there are fewer formal rules guiding their actions. For Allen, trust can be cultivated through the simple design of cross-functional teams or related structures that bring people together from different organizational entities. Carlee also spoke about the importance of relationships and explained how the regularity of ongoing relationship building among key networked actors can facilitate more effective communication in a crisis. In the nonprofit sector, trust was often cultivated through a combination of relationship building, transparency, and examples of commitment to the social issues the group works toward. A summary of the interviewees' views is contained in table 9.1.

CONCLUSION

This chapter identifies the key leadership elements for public and nonprofit managers in a cross-sector, heterarchical environment. While the interviews were context specific, they confirm the growing literature on collaborations with respect to the leadership requirements. There are obvious limitations to any approach at attempting to find "the" answer to a complex subject, and other scholars may find other skills also relevant. Shadish, Cook, and Campbell (2002) remind us that analysis of relationships in any empirical study is context dependent, depending on sampling strategy and modes of analysis.

A review of the four identified leadership strategies, however, does explain many of the ways that collaboration takes place across public and nonprofit organizations. For government, the challenges of interorganizational functions are driven by the historic boundaries of the US federal system and the tendency for government agencies to seek to protect their own turf. For nonprofits, the fundraising imperative of their operational existence often creates barriers to aligning with others to achieve common purposes. Adhering to the techniques identified in this chapter can assist administrators across the public and nonprofit sectors to improve their leadership of heterarchical modes of collaboration.

Case Study for Discussion: State Employment Training

You are an assistant to the executive director of the Department of Social Services (DSS). The governor has campaigned on increasing job training in the state and moving individuals from receiving state welfare payments to working. Currently, the Division of Employment Training (DET) (within DSS) provides that service; however, the governor and the state legislature are unhappy with the current results. At an annual cost of $20 million, DET has found work for only a fraction of those on welfare. The program is operated out of twenty local offices, and the current annual success rate is less than 10 percent of the 500,000 adult recipients on welfare placed in a job. Welfare payments cost the state over $2 billion a year (averaging about $4,200 a person per year plus administrative costs of program administration).

Questions and Issues for Consideration

1. A nonprofit association with extensive experience providing job training and career services is located in the capital of your state. What strategies could you use for engaging the group? What are some of the advantages or disadvantages of engaging an association to help with this program?

2. What leadership characteristics should be considered in engaging the association?

3. Imagine that you are working for a member of the nonprofit association that has been approached for this job training program. What interests do you have in mind? What approaches to leadership are important for you to consider from the perspective of the nonprofit sector? Are the leadership needs similar to or different from those of your public sector counterparts? Explain.

chapter TEN

Fostering Democratic Accountability

Public accountability is the extent to which the government administration is answerable for its action within the context of a democratic system: it is an essential requirement for cross-sector collaborations (CSCs). Like any other delivery model for public services administered by government, CSC must meet citizens' expectations and create public value. Meeting citizen expectations through contracts, partnerships, networks, and independent public-services providers (IPSPs) requires new ways of conceptualizing citizen engagement and fostering democratic accountability.

The discretion accorded collaborators in CSC transforms the approaches with which public managers ensure accountability. Ensuring accountability for noncollaborative, traditional approaches to delivering public services is difficult enough, and efforts often fall well short of expectations. Cross-sector collaborations present even greater challenges; however, greater accountability will not come from just intensifying the use of conventional approaches, built around regulations and control. It also must come from the discretionary decisions that public managers make in crafting, negotiating, and monitoring cross-sector relationships and their ongoing dialogue with the citizens served by the collaboration.

In our discussions of each of the four types of CSC—collaborative contracting, partnerships, networks, and IPSPs—we have described factors that improve their performance. This chapter expands on a framework that was used to address the "accountability question" with respect to public-private partnerships (PPPs; Forrer et al. 2010) by broadening that discussion to address the accountability challenges presented by all CSCs.

The chapter is divided into five sections. First, it describes in greater detail why accountability is the linchpin for successful public management and for collaborative relationships. Second, the chapter provides a discussion of some important dimensions of democratic accountability and the concepts of leading authors in the field on this issue and their implications for CSC. Third, the chapter discusses how public managers can promote mutual, democratic accountability by addressing four aspects of collaborations: agreeing to common outcome measures, creating value, promoting a trusted partnership, and engaging citizens. Finally, it discusses in detail specific aspects of mutual accountability applicable to different types of CSC.

CSCs AND ACCOUNTABILITY

Accountability is long recognized as a keystone to successful public management. Kettl (2002) reminds us that "government's performance is only as good as its ability to manage its tools and to hold its tool users accountable" (421). In an environment of proliferating CSC, the tools of government needed to maintain accountability for these arrangements are not the same as those needed for conventional interagency or intra-agency activities. Cross-sector collaborations change the requirements for public accountability by involving business and nonprofits in traditionally governmental decision making and program delivery. The specific terms and conditions of such collaborations deserve careful scrutiny and understanding by public managers, since private and nonprofit participants are motivated to enter into and participate in these arrangements for different reasons than government is. Thus, public managers must exercise care to ensure that the public interest is achieved in any CSC.

In PPPs involving major transportation infrastructure projects, for example, governments attempt to serve the public interest by creating new capital projects: facilitating commerce, decreasing traffic congestion, and increasing mobility to specific communities. Private partners in such PPPs are understandably focused on issues such as the profitability of the project to the operators (from tolls or fees) and risk and return on investment for the investors. Thus, the accountability of PPPs for infrastructure requires the creation of standards of performance aligned with specific, agreed-to objectives, such as effective management, safety, and the availability of the road to traffic; it requires reliable oversight and monitoring mechanisms; and it requires proper safeguards to ensure that public services are not compromised for the sake of profits. In this way, the private partners can achieve their goals, while the public manager's focus is on achieving results in the public interest.

A central characteristic of collaboration is the discretion governments allow to other organizations. Cross-sector collaborations display a variety of horizontal relationships through collaborative mixing, consensual decision making, and other recognized characteristics of interorganizational cooperation. However, public managers also need to consider how to create collaborative accountability with their private and nonprofit partners. Specific approaches may vary across different cross-sector collaborations; in general, however, the nature of these arrangements must foster greater dialogue and organizational interdependence or, at a minimum, a sense that everyone in the collaboration is in it together.

Working together in CSCs, where public authority is diluted and power is diffused to the participants, members share the responsibility of providing an ongoing account of their actions. Accountable cross-sector collaborators see one another as partners. Partnership ensures that each participant stays focused, concentrates on results, and is productive. It is in their mutual self-interest to do so. If members do not value accountability, there is no assurance that they will stay committed to their promises or meet the obligations of their collaboration. However, because of the ability of collaborators to exit the relationship, such accountability cannot be mandated and imposed through fear and punishment; it must be jointly accepted by all collaborators. When accountability of CSCs is thought of in this way, public managers can play a critical role in ensuring it is achieved. Similar to Follett's (2003) concept of "power with" rather than "power over," public managers must foster a mutual accountability or an accountability "with" their collaborators, not "over" them.

Traditional Public Accountability

Traditionally public accountability has been achieved through mechanisms of control. Light (1998) claims that public accountability has long been narrowly defined as "limit[ing] bureaucratic discretion through compliance with tightly drawn rules and regulations" (12). Since public managers are not elected by the people, it is up to elected representatives (such as legislatures and chief executives) to ensure that public managers serve the needs of the people. Lynn (2006) identifies the root challenge of government accountability as "the delegation of sovereign authority to [nonelected] officials empowered to act in the name of the people and their representatives and the resulting necessity to maintain control over those officials' actions" (137).

From a more practical view of the public manager, however, public accountability means "addressing the public's expectations for government performance" (Posner 2002, 547). The key question is whether the government is accomplishing what citizens expect it to accomplish. Of course, that question is about more than just implementation. The reasonableness of a policy and its goals, the resources allotted to support it, the authority to take appropriate program actions, and the capacity and know-how to design and carry out the necessary steps all have a bearing on addressing the accountability question successfully. Yet at the end of the day, public accountability is a bottom-line issue: Did government successfully complete the job in a manner consistent with the public interest? Since the answer has political consequences, such a perspective compels public managers to use whatever administrative mechanisms are available to achieve a positive answer to that question.

Dimensions of Public Accountability Control

Public sector employees are called on to serve many (and sometimes conflicting) stakeholder interests through informal and formal control mechanisms (Romzek and Dubnick 1994). Informally, public managers report "not only to a multitude of elected officials, but also to a plethora of interest groups, clientele, media, and other actors" (Posner 2002, 524). Formally, mechanisms of control have evolved to address different dimensions of public accountability. Dicke and Ott (1999) identified three of them: accountability to other governmental bodies, hierarchical accountability, and accountability to impersonal standards. The result is that public agencies are asked to conform simultaneously to several legitimate but often competing accountability expectations.

The very division of power among executive, legislative, and judicial branches is one formalized approach to limiting the discretion of public managers and promoting accountability. Reforms enacted during the Progressive era in the United States also led to the establishment of independent government regulatory agencies, public commissions, and public corporations to oversee government bodies through the executive branch. Congress has a role in agency oversight through their authorizing and appropriation committees, public hearings, and indirectly through the semiautonomous US Government Accountability Office (GAO). The judicial branch also has a role in agency oversight by placing a check on the "arbitrary and capricious" behavior of agencies and their officials.

A second formal approach to accountability for public actions is advanced through vertical chains of authority within government. Echoing the views of Max Weber, Woodrow Wilson (1887) placed vertical reporting relationships at the center of his call for a separation of politics from administration. The concept purports that intraorganizational controls enhance adherence to the public interest by holding bureaucrats to the account of "higher authorities including elected and appointed officials who sit at the apex of institutional chains of command" (Kearns 1996, 11).

Finally, impersonal standards of performance also have emerged as a formal method for monitoring public managers. Freidrich's (1940) call for increased attention to technical standards provided the groundwork for much of the attention we see toward performance management in government today. Performance measures increase accountability to the public, and they encourage and codify shared commitments and responsibilities (Kettl 2005). In addition, Congress and many state legislatures have created procedural standards and safeguards to enforce bureaucratic accountability through such legislation as the federal Administrative Procedures Act (1946), which specifies processes through which government officials take certain actions.

The combination of these various control factors makes accountability anything but straightforward for public managers. The result is an "overlapping set of independent and competing mechanisms—and a variety of independently operating accountability holders" (Behn 2001, 60). Public managers working with CSCs are thus positioned within an existing set of complicated and often competing accountability mechanisms. Defining public accountability for CSCs not only demands attention to these existing constraints, but also requires new approaches to create mutual accountability and ensure democratic accountability.

Dimensions of Democratic Accountability

The central tension of democratic accountability is the question of how to ensure that the administrative arms of government implement policies and programs that are in line with the public interest. The issue revolves around the inherent challenge of government bureaucracy within a democracy and the extent to which unelected officials in administrative agencies carry out their duties in a manner that matches the public's expectations as expressed through their elected officials. Much of the foundational work on democratic accountability revolves around the question of the influence that bureaucratic agents have in policy outcomes through the process of implementation. There are a variety of views on that topic, including those who want to hold administrators accountable for specific goals and those who take a pragmatic view that dissolves the distinction between ends and means (Harmon 1995).

The seminal works by Dwight Waldo inform our understanding of democratic accountability and its importance to CSCs. Waldo's *The Administrative State* (1948) sets out a conceptual foundation for understanding the role of government managers in interpreting and shaping the policies they implement. He challenges the notion that policy direction alone can guide bureaucratic outcomes and claims that "any simple division of government into politics-and-administration is inadequate" (148). The drawback of the adoption of that simple dichotomy is the subsequent removal of the ideals of democracy from the discourse on public administration. Management within the public sector is more than simply accomplishing objectives; it also is about the active work of determining those objectives. He challenges Woodrow Wilson and others' suggestion that democracy "could only apply to the deciding phase of the two-fold governmental process." Instead, Waldo argues that democracy is a relevant value in the administration of those decisions.

Waldo's book provides an important contribution to our understanding of what makes management in government different from that in the private sector or nonprofit organizations. The very democratic nature of our government, and the underlying assumption that citizens have a voice in how it operates, permeates not only our electoral processes, but also our method of implementing government programs. His writings also remind us of the important influence that unelected agency leaders have in interpreting and shaping the nature of public policy.

O. C. McSwite's book, *Legitimacy in Public Administration: A Discourse Analysis* (1997), explains why accountability is particularly important to a democracy.[1] McSwite provides more evidence of why we need to take particular care in evaluating the work of government agencies. McSwite presents the term *legitimacy* (the government's appropriate representation of the public's goals) and relates it to the authority of government to carry out the public's will in a democracy. Rather than trying to solve the legitimacy question, McSwite asks "how administration fits within the scheme of American democratic government" (11).

McSwite claims that the founding fathers recognized that citizens would inevitably have different interests on policy issues and that the democratic form of government would have to accommodate different preferences in the construction of national policy. Madison's *The Federalist* Number 10 articulates this view of American federalism by arguing that in a country as large as the territory of the United States, direct democracy (or direct citizen input on policy decisions) is incompatible with national government (Hamilton, Jay, and Madison 2001). Instead, *The Federalist* authors recommended popularly elected representatives. The nature of their electoral responsibilities to diverse constituents would force elected officials to consider diverse citizen interests in policymaking.

McSwite, whose sympathy lies with the Anti-Federalists, suggests that the problem with relying solely on the legislative process to set the standards of government accountability is that it ignores the influence that administrators have in determining policy outcomes. He points out that determining the legitimacy of any given activity of the bureaucracy is not always clear; rather, it needs to be worked out among a group of interested parties in an ongoing dialogue or relationship. It is the same dynamic that is called for in CSC. Each of the parties to a collaboration may come in with individual "goals"; however, the interaction among the parties will determine the specific course of action, and the initial course may evolve during the collaboration. McSwite validates the concept that the activities of public administrators are potentially legitimate when they are contested and negotiated by public managers on behalf of the public they serve through collaborative interactions, as often occurs in CSC.

Robert Behn's contribution to our understanding of democratic accountability involves his attention to the varying institutional mechanisms that hold administrative behavior to account and complement legislative oversight. In *Rethinking Democratic Accountability* (2001), he highlights the historical influences that shaped the institutions and mechanisms designed to ensure that the public interest is not distorted through the process of implementation. He suggests that "our American concept of democratic accountability evolved from Madison's separation of powers to Wilson's separation of administration from policies, with Taylor and Weber justifying that separation by describing how an independent administrative apparatus could be both efficient and accountable" (58). He also points out the varied and at times layered pressures on bureaucratic behavior that are inherent in a system of government developed around the notion of separation of powers. He explains, "Our current system of democratic accountability is neither orderly, nor hierarchal, nor coherent" (60).

Behn presents a new concept of democratic accountability, suggesting that it must be a "compact of mutual, collective responsibility" (2001). The concept implies an ethos within administration that involves (1) a compact, or ethical commitment; (2) responsibility, or a willingness to accept constraints on administrative behavior for the public good; (3) mutual commitment to rules as a sense of duty to others; and (4) a collective duty to avoid narrowing in on scapegoats when things go wrong and to take responsibility as a team for all outcomes. This shift in attitude can create a more collective approach to accountability whereby public administrators consider the impacts of their actions (and other cross-sector collaborators) on the populations they serve within the constraints of the existing system.

In an environment of increasing involvement of nonstate organizations in the delivery of public programs, the question is how to ensure the public interest is served through CSCs. In addressing democratic accountability, it is important to consider the processes by which the public's expectations are defined, as well as concrete techniques for dialogue with citizens affected by any given program.

In *Public Values and Public Interest: Counterbalancing Economic Individualism* (2007), Barry Bozeman presents a standard by which CSCs could hold each other to account. For Bozeman, the public interest "refers to those outcomes best serving the long-run survival and well-being of a social collective construed as a public" (17). He addresses the challenge of identifying what exactly is the "public interest" for a given constituency, arguing that creating an understanding of what a jurisdiction wants requires a procedural approach to defining the public interest in terms of a process, not a predetermined set of ideals. The "procedural conception of the public interest makes virtually no distinction between political processes and the substance of the public interest" (94). Instead, the very nature of what should be designed for a health care program or a tax incentive, for example, is determined through a process of accommodation and compromise.

The needs of policy are often not known in advance and may require some level of deliberation, especially by those affected by a given program.[2]

In chapter 7, we discussed the importance of defining the nature of the public task or challenge to be implemented by government in order to identify the appropriate form of CSC (if any) to be applied to the effort. As Bozeman explained, determining the nature of the public interest may be a process in and of itself as different populations are likely to have different preferences for a particular program. Within the scope of democratic accountability, the ways by which the public interest is defined will be just as important as the institutional mechanisms designed to ensure that it is achieved.

Table 10.1 summarizes the contributions of this select group of scholars who are relevant to our thinking about democratic accountability, the public interest, and CSC. As we have discussed throughout this book, defining the nature of the public task to be implemented through a cross-sector approach and adapting the appropriate institutional approaches and leadership strategies for their implementation is essential for ensuring their accountability. There always will be a tension between trying to establish, measure, and achieve specific goals, objectives, or results of a government policy and the realization, especially in CSC, that these often emerge as the collaboration evolves. Public managers should come to collaboration with some sense of the public interest involved and results sought. However, they need to be flexible and allow the specific actions and tasks to evolve as collaborators interact with themselves and the public.

CSCs require flexibility on the part of public managers. Dictating policies and approaches as when public services are provided directly by government or a traditional contract will not work. Yet flexibility does not mean that standards are not set, expectations established, and outcomes monitored. A challenge in managing CSCs is to recognize when in the process of their design and management flexibility is best. For example, when working with a specific type of public-private partnership for infrastructure, flexibility is needed in the earliest stages, allowing new approaches to be considered and negotiated. Once the terms of the partnership are set, private sector partners should expect that they will accept some of the risks of unanticipated events, and change orders in contract modifications would not be an option. Such an arrangement improves the quality of bids. Alternatively, networks and IPSPs excel at adapting to changes and their environment. Public managers should anticipate that what was negotiated and set out for partners might be reassessed just six months out.

Table 10.1
Democratic Accountability, the Public Interest,
and Cross-Sector Collaboration

Author	Foundational Concepts of Democratic Accountability	Implications for Cross-Sector Collaboration
Dwight Waldo	Public managers play a role in interpreting and shaping the public interest and public policy—determining the boundaries of policy as they implement government programs.	Public managers are accountable to the populations they serve and need standards of performance against which they can be measured.
O. C. McSwite	Implementers affect policy outcomes. Public sector legitimacy derives from a dialogue among interested parties, and the government delivers the scope and scale of programs that constituents desire.	CSC arrangements negotiated by public managers are legitimate if they involve citizens and stakeholders in the decisions in a collaborative relationship.
Robert Behn	Democratic accountability is not orderly or hierarchical but an overlapping set of independent and competing mechanisms. It requires mutual, collective responsibility: 1. Ethical commitment or compact 2. Willingness to accept constraints for the public good 3. Mutual commitment to rules as a sense of duty to others 4. Collective duty, team responsibility for outcomes	Ensuring democratic accountability in CSC requires an understanding of the existing accountability of stakeholders involved in a given policy area. It also requires developing mutual accountability for shared outcomes.
Barry Bozeman	The public interest, or the standard of democratic accountability, can be defined by a social collective. The bounds of the public interest for a given program can be created through a process, not from a predetermined set of ideals.	Public administrators must engage the citizens they serve to determine the appropriate public interest or standard for the programs they implement, including those involving CSC.

FOSTERING DEMOCRATIC ACCOUNTABILITY IN CSCs

Ideas on how to improve democratic accountability in public sector–run programs provide a strong intellectual foundation for thinking about how to achieve mutual, democratic accountability in CSC. Waldo and McSwite stress the importance of implementers as shapers of policy and the necessity for public managers to engage in a continuing dialogue with citizens to ascertain what the public interest is in a particular case. Behn's description of the roles of checks and balances among different organizations and the impact of various regulatory bodies in public administration provides a perspective on organizational relations, particularly the role of independent monitoring groups. His notion of "mutual, collective responsibility" should inform the standard for any CSC. Furthermore, the procedural approaches to defining the public interest presented by Bozeman, combined with techniques for engaging citizens directly (discussed below), help provide the legitimacy of programs delivered through CSC.

Mutual accountability is a concept that reflects two dimensions of accountability distinctive to CSC. The first dimension is grounded in the need to institute both horizontal accountability, and the second is to be faithful to the requirements for traditional vertical hierarchy. The horizontal accountability responds to the relationships among the members in a CSC. The requirements for traditional vertical hierarchy are necessary to ensure that public managers are accountable to appointed and elected officials who establish public policy. A public manager must find a way to align the different demands of the two accountability structures and integrate them so they are mutually reinforcing.

While ensuring accountability is a hurdle for any organization, it is a substantial challenge when cross-sector collaborators have different cultures, organizational norms, and motivations. In addition, since the relationships are voluntary, participants lack an obvious enforcement mechanism in the event that members stray from their common purpose, as might occur in a hierarchical structure. To address these challenges to CSC accountability, we have identified four practical pillars or ways managers can help achieve mutual accountability: (1) agreeing on outcomes rather than goals, (2) understanding how value is created through collaboration, (3) emphasizing and developing a trusted partner relationship, and (4) engaging citizens in the design and implementation of CSCs. These concepts enable public managers to develop relationships that are self-sustaining and whose members are intrinsically motivated to achieve results.

Outcome-Based Performance

Shortly after his appointment as incident commander for the Hurricane Katrina response in Louisiana in 2004, Thad Allen was challenged to communicate a common mission among the multiple governmental and nongovernmental entities mobilized in the area. As we noted in the previous chapter, his approach was to call all members of the response teams to a large airplane hangar in the city and announce using a loudspeaker that he empathized with their efforts, thanked them for their work, and asked them to treat every victim they encountered "as a member of their family." The simple idea of treating storm victims with a level of familiarity that all responders could relate to helped to build a common purpose among the federal, state, and local government staff, as well as the nonprofit and private sector staff working in the region. While some common purposes are proffered to collaborators and others are cocreated among the participants, the key is to identify a frame of reference that drives people of different backgrounds toward a common outcome or result.

One pitfall of CSC is the failure of participants to acknowledge that the goals of business will seldom be the same ones as of government or nonprofit organizations. Each party to the transaction is hoping to achieve something different from their work together: for the public sector, it is often the advancement of policy objectives; for the nonprofit sector, it is to fulfill their social purpose; and for the private sector, it is often profits. What is important is not goal alignment but a common purpose that leads to a set of agreed-to results, outputs, or outcomes that advance the disparate interests of collaborators, which in turn become the mechanism to measure the effects of the collaboration and achieve shared accountability.

The PPP for the Port of the Miami Tunnel project, discussed in chapter 4, provides an interesting illustration of how the public and private sectors can support a common purpose for different reasons. The Florida Department of Transportation, in collaboration with the City of Miami, entered into a thirty-four-year PPP worth $1.4 billion to improve freight transportation around Miami (AECOM Technology Corporation 2007). The partnership helped the state and the city to achieve a roadway system that ensured cargo entering the nearby port would bypass the downtown area; the private vendor to the partnership received assurances of ongoing (availability) payments from the city over thirty-four years. Both the state and the private sector cared about the larger objective of building an effective and efficient tunnel system to transport freight. Yet the private and public partners had different reasons for this interest.

Clear goal setting by each CSC actor can facilitate cooperation as long as collaborators can maintain some flexibility. Goals in the public realm, for example, set boundaries about what government will and will not do from a policy perspective as they engage in CSCs. In CSCs, private and nonprofit actors are not setting policy but are interested collaborators. Different organizations can have different goals, but that does not mean that they cannot work together toward the same purpose, outcomes, or results.

By reframing the question of how to structure CSCs from goal alignment to specific result measurements, public managers and actors in these relationships establish a clear and straightforward method to jointly monitor progress through a specific and quantifiable set of results, outputs, or outcomes that the collaboration is accomplishing. For example, in the case of the Miami Tunnel PPP, outcomes included reduction in levels of traffic congestion and increased safety. The Department of Systems Management for Human Services in Fairfax County, Virginia, used a network to assist those in need in the county; among the outcome measures was "the percentage of need achieved," a concept readily acceptable to a variety of government and nonprofit organizations.

Shorter-term or intermediate measures that meet the performance measurement criteria indicated in chapter 7 provide near-term indicators of the success or failure of the CSC. For example, such an outcome measure might be to reduce the level of a certain urban pollutant. While the long-term goal would be to improve the health of urban residents, reducing pollution is an outcome that would help attain that long-term goal.

Coming to agreement on such results or outcomes can take time, and it is time that not all members want to spend, but it is essential for achieving shared accountability. Often collaborators have not thought of what specific outcomes their efforts should achieve. It is in the public manager's interest to focus the group on quantifying their anticipated outcomes as an essential basis for accountability and the success of the collaboration.

Creating Value in CSCs

Public managers should approach cross-sector relationships by understanding the value they can create. Consideration of the value that is created by the efforts of CSCs not only is a useful way to think about the impact these collaborations have, but it is an essential calculation by CSC members regarding the usefulness of their participation. Creating value that is judged to be important to CSC members is a key reason for them to remain with the CSC and make their best efforts to ensure its success. Creating value means that the actions of collaborators will not shift or reallocate resources from one group to another, but create value to all parties. Understanding the value stemming from the actions of the collaboration and how those benefits are captured by citizens and the collaborators makes it clearer what benefits are accrued. If public managers understand how much value each of the collaborators will capture, it is easier to engage the relationships.

A variety of theories approach the concept of value creation (Dobb 1973). For the purposes of CSC accountability, two ways are considered: public value and shared value. Public value is measured and assessed much differently from value in the private sector. Although private managers can gauge success through a variety of financial measures, public manager success is less clear because what they produce is more "ambiguous" (Moore 1995). Public value creation therefore revolves around the idea of justifying means to ends: there needs to be agreement around what outcomes public managers work toward in order to justify the resources used. Since management in the public sector occurs through the allocation of scarce resources, that allocation must be worth the effort. Adopting an understanding of the public value created enables us to "evaluate the efforts of public sector managers; not in the economic marketplace of individual consumers but in the political marketplace of citizens and the collective decisions of representative democratic institutions" (Moore 1995, 31).

In addition to the idea of public value, CSCs create shared value. Shared value lies at the "intersection between society and corporate performance" (Porter and Kramer 2011) and is defined as the "policies and operating practices that enhance the competitiveness of a company while simultaneously advancing the economic and social conditions in the communities in which it operates" (6). In this way, shared value "focuses on the connections between societal and economic progress" (4–5).

Inherent in this concept is the idea that businesses are compelled to think about the bottom-line or reputational benefits from corporate social responsibility. Companies should consider all aspects of their work by recognizing how social factors are just as important in defining a market as economic ones. Porter and Kramer argue that adopting a shared value approach benefits business, government, and citizens. The pursuit of shared value leads businesses to be more innovative and grow, government benefits from businesses that are responsive and open to collaboration, and citizens benefit from the value created by the CSC.

It is important to recognize that these ideas of shared value contradict traditional definitions of capitalism and neoclassical economic models, and they run counter to Milton Friedman's (1962) argument that a company is an entirely self-contained entity. Friedman advocated that society existed outside the scope of business considerations, and therefore pursuing only profit is important for firms. This perspective, however, is shortsighted. Businesses do not operate in a vacuum: they are highly responsive to the communities in which they operate and need to acknowledge their role within them. Adopting a shared value approach and engaging government and nonprofits in various collaborative arrangements not only makes good business sense but creates value that is a strong motivator for taking up collaborations in the first place.

Trusted Partners

As we noted in previous chapters, trust is essential for successful CSCs: trust means that participants have faith in one another's abilities and commitments to achieving a shared purpose. Successful collaborations are built on trust and often lead to greater collaborative productivity (Carnevale 1995). In chapter 3 we discussed three levels of trust when working in a collaborative contracting environment that are also important for any collaborative arrangement:

1. *Contractual trust*—adhering to the agreement. Hardin (2004) refers to this as "encapsulated interest"—the collaborator's interests align with governments because it is in the collaborator's interest to accomplish what it agreed to accomplish. This basic level of trust also must exist in any CSC.

2. *Competence trust*—recognition by the public manager of the special expertise or local knowledge of the collaborator and allowing them discretion within the confines of that competence area. Although this is not yet a partnership, there is genuine collaboration and a respect for each party's expertise and judgment, a necessary condition in any successful collaboration.

3. *Goodwill trust*—confidence that the collaborator will go beyond the minimum in order to achieve mutual objectives. As a result of repeated interaction and collaboration, the collaborator will have considerable latitude on how to proceed and on daily decision making. The collaboration now begins to resemble a true partnership.

To achieve democratic accountability, we add two additional dimensions of trust: social trust, which promotes mutual credibility, and fairness trust, that is, faith that the relationship will be ethical and fair:

4. *Social trust*—the interest and support of citizens in the efforts of their government. Social trust is built on a healthy amount of social capital, which is cultivated over time. One of the major responsibilities of public managers in CSC is to engage citizens to ensure that their views are heard and valued.

5. *Fairness trust*—citizen confidence that government will act for the benefit of all, not just a favored few. Trust in government also results from confidence that government will be fair and ethical, which is often predicated on past performance. When there is public cynicism about government, citizens are less willing to trust other people in general, which collectively lowers public trust (Brewer and Hayllar 2005; Wuthnow 1998; Berman 1997) and can erode confidence in collaborative projects. Developing a culture of trust creates an environment where information can be openly shared and actors can acquire sensitive information needed to make decisions on complex policy issues (Brewer and Hayllar 2005).

The public's trust is particularly important in CSCs because citizens often interact with direct service providers who operate outside government. For example, health programs provided through Medicaid and Medicare often involve many groups of nonprofit and private sector physicians who administer direct care to patients. Without a clear understanding of the nature of nongovernmental involvement, citizens may question the motives of other organizations that are operating in the name of the public.

Furthermore, the increased incorporation of user fees in social services provided by nonprofit organizations (National Center for Charitable Statistics 2012) means that the collaborators in both the public and the nonprofit sectors need to demonstrate the reasons for and value of the fees to end users. A similar trend is occurring in the transportation sector in the United States, where the increase in PPPs for roadways results in more toll roads. If the collaborators do not explain the benefits that are intended from these fees, public resentment can disrupt collaborations that are designed to serve the public.

Collaborators should strive to become "trusted partners" (Forrer et al. 2012), a notion that elaborates on relationships between partners within collaborations.

Participants need to have trust that they will benefit from the relationship; otherwise the collaboration will be unsustainable as members exit the relationship. Without trusted partners, the relationship falls apart because contributors begin to focus on the achievement of their own short-term goals without recognizing the achievement of wider social goals. Trusted partners recognize that different decisions by the CSC may have implications for the participants and their own organizations.

Trusted partners are empathetic in that they care about the other partner's problems and issues and work together to address those concerns when possible— even when the issue has little or no relevance to a partner. By collaborating to solve problems related to the CSC mission and in a way that addresses the problems and issues that the partners face, CSCs develop devoted and committed collaborators. The commitment to understanding success not just in terms of the CSC mission but also to the successful experiences of partners improves the chances that the CSC will accomplish what it set out to do, thereby being accountable to each collaborative partner and to the public.

In summary, trusted partners in CSC move beyond minimal adherence to contractual agreements toward acceptance of the competence of their partners in the CSC. The ultimate goal of trusted partners is achieving a level of goodwill trust, social trust, and fairness with each other that leads to joint efforts without detailed ongoing monitoring. Partners also are conscious of the need to develop social trust with the public at large through ethical dealings, communications, and citizen involvement.

One cautionary note: because cross-sector collaborators often have different motives for entering into a collaboration, CSC involves some melding or blurring of roles. It is the responsibility of the public manager to ensure that such melding is in the public interest and that public values are not sacrificed in the collaboration. Many in the public administration community are concerned that private and nonprofit interests may override public values and are skeptical that trust is a solid foundation for accountability. Public managers must build trusting partnerships in CSC, but in the final analysis, they have to demonstrate that the results of collaborations benefit the general public.

Enhancing Citizen Participation

Greater citizen participation in providing information about their needs, the quality of public services, and how that compares to their expectations is one way to enhance democratic accountability in CSCs. Public managers participating in CSCs play a central role in aligning policy objectives, public sector stakeholder interests, and citizen involvement in the shaping of policy outcomes.

Reenergizing the idea of citizenship is a key component of maintaining democratic accountability. Today public managers are increasingly turning to methods of engaging citizens directly to determine the scope and scale of government programs. At the federal level, for example, the Obama administration developed the Open Government Initiative in 2009 to solicit comments and feedback from constituents to guide federal decision making (White House 2009).

State and local governments are using social media to promote accountability in ways that could be adapted by networks, partnerships, and IPSPs. Nearly all city and county governments are embracing social media platforms to share information with residents. Town hall meetings are posted on YouTube or hosted entirely electronically, city council members Tweet with constituents to share their involvement in the community and receive feedback, and Facebook is used to promote local events and seek feedback on community initiatives.

Information and communication technology (ICT) offers citizens access to more information on public service delivery than ever before. The potential for government to engage citizens through social media and related forms of ICT is enormous. Government agencies have engaged citizens through various innovations, such as "e-government," presenting citizens with options for providing information or receiving administrative services. Examples of e-government include comments on the creation of public facilities, real-time information on the needs of victims of natural disasters, updates on traffic delays, and renewing driver's licenses or car registration. However, such uses of ICT generally distribute information in one direction, from government to citizens or from citizens to government, without further interactions.

The creation of a bus stop design in Salt Lake City provides one example of how public participation is improved through the use of ICT. In this case, the government adopted a crowdsourcing approach to generating ideas for the structure's design.[3] It created a website, outlined general expectations for the structure, and allowed citizen contributors to come up with their own ideas for how it should look. Over 4,654 unique visitors per day went to the site during the peak of the project, and a conceptual design for the bus stop that the government likely would not have envisioned on its own emerged (Brabham, Sanchez, and Bartholomew 2009).

Tina Nabatchi (2012) describes how a procedural approach to defining the public interest can be applied to government programs. Her explanations address themes that were raised earlier on the importance of building trust among relevant stakeholders in collaborations. Nabatchi addresses democratic accountability through the concept of public participation and the varied techniques of selecting among competing public values. She argues that engaging citizens in understanding and assessing public service outcomes entails citizens' power sharing with public managers and involvement in substantive decisions about program goals and expectations.

In this way, public participation expands our understanding of democratic participation from indirect participation, whereby citizens support representatives in public office or advocacy groups to make decisions for them, to include direct participation, whereby constituents directly influence public sector outcomes through in-person or technology-based forums.

Social Media and Citizen Engagement

The expansion of social media allows a richer type of interaction of government officials, CSCs, and citizens. Social media allow users to express their values and preferences within a public space and exchange ideas with others—both friends and strangers. The aftermath of the 2010 earthquake in Haiti demonstrated how social media assisted first responders in identifying immediate needs. In the wake of the disaster, an open source crisis-mapping program was adopted to translate social media comments into a picture of the parts of Port-au-Prince that were safe, those that needed water or other aid, and other related issues (Heinzelman and Waters 2010). A team of graduate students based in Boston collected text messages, reviewed Twitter posts, and collected Facebook data from the affected region to map out trends of what people were talking about on the ground. Both governments and nonprofits used this information to target relief where it was most needed.

Transportation officials are adopting social media to help them gauge roadway and transit traffic delays, as well as citizen perceptions of them. Collecting Twitter posts within a given metropolitan region or posts related to a specific transit system can help public managers identify trends in travel and gain a better understanding of citizen perceptions and travel patterns in response to delays. This monitoring function for public managers is particularly important in CSCs, where government may not be the direct service provider but still require monitoring to ensure democratic accountability. Another way that local governments have adopted social media to provide real-time responses to citizens is through the use of GPS devices on trash trucks and snowplows so citizens can individually track the locations of these vehicles.

The way in which citizens conceive their relationship with government and public services is changing dramatically. Rather than seeing themselves as mere taxpayers or clients, many citizens now expect to be treated as joint creators or partners of government services and expect a higher-quality experience (Osborne and Gaebler 1992; Thomas 2012). Social media are powerful tools for improving citizen engagement. The information that social media collect and report regarding the performance of an individual, group, or organization can be harnessed to review processes or strategies used by partnerships, networks, and IPSPs.

By generating an online community, social media broaden the access and participation of citizens in new ways. For example, social media enable local officials to engage with citizens from younger demographics, a group notoriously considered difficult to track down, in ways that were previously considered impossible (Brabham 2009). In addition, citizens who would not be able to attend critical governance meetings in person due to work or family obligations are now able to participate virtually by streaming sessions online or sending feedback and requesting information online.

An Integrated Approach to Mutual Accountability

The four pillars of mutual accountability are reinforcing. For CSCs, public managers need to focus on how they can work toward outcomes that generate value for each member, while maintaining trusted partnerships among collaborative partners and keeping communications open to the public. If members of the collaborations fail to adopt an integrated approach and concentrate on only a few of these aspects, the relationship may flounder. It is not enough for CSCs to focus on building trust without understanding the value created by their collective efforts. Alternatively, if they focus on creating a list of shared outcomes without understanding how they relate to the motivations of the partner organizations, the relationship may be short-lived.

The best collaborations are those that cultivate a culture of trust and openness to share information and best practices both vertically and horizontally within an organization and across collaborative partners. Each of the four components—outcome-based performance, public and shared value, trusted partners, and engaged citizens—contributes to developing an environment for collaboration that facilitates accountability by creating a climate where all participants can forecast and measure tangible results from their efforts.

SPECIFIC ACCOUNTABILITY ISSUES FOR CSCs

Vertical hierarchy structures and corresponding administrative processes have long been the principal method of controlling the acts of those who work within an organization, a scenario much different from the horizontal relationships of CSCs. The challenges that managing horizontal relationships present are becoming more familiar as public managers gain experience working in CSCs.

Accountability and Contracting Out

While the accountability demands with traditional contracting are similar to those with CSC, the mechanisms or approaches to maintain accountability for traditional government contractors generally do not apply in partnerships, networks, or IPSPs. In traditional contracts, governments generally can maintain defined standards of conduct because of their principal-agent relationship. Government is in charge of contracting relationships because it controls the way contracts are written and develops all the terms for the relationship. The private party is motivated to follow all of the specifications and rules in the agreement because that is the only way to ensure that the company will be paid. Examples of traditional methods include filing reports on certain activities and bookkeeping against specific standards to demonstrate that contractors are being held accountable. Dicke and Ott (1999) developed a list of techniques for managing government contracts with private and nonprofit organizations that included auditing, monitoring, licensure, markets, the courts, codes of ethics, whistleblowing, and outcomes-based assessments.

Even with these methods of control, contractors typically are not held to the same ethical standards as public employees. Furthermore, even an agreed-on ethical code of conduct or a contractors' agreement to abide by certain regulations can be difficult to enforce in government-contractor relationships. A Government Accountability Office report (2010) found that more than twenty federal contractors had violated federal labor laws yet continued to be awarded billions of dollars in government contracts.

Accountability in Partnerships and PPPs

Unlike accountability in contract management, keeping partners accountable requires more than being a smart buyer. In particular, partnerships and PPPs involve many joint responsibilities and commitments with a partner that are not easily severed, as is the case in a short-term contractual relationship. Cancelling contracts is one of the key means governments have to control the behavior of contractors—it is the ultimate sanction. Cancelling a partnership with a non-profit or with a private partner is one of the last things governments want to do except in the most extreme cases. For PPPs, a long-term perspective about partnership relationships is necessary.

PPPs require clear expectations and oversight both before and after contract formation. A major challenge in many complicated PPP arrangements is that public managers are often inexperienced in dealing with the private sector, including their inability to analyze private sector financial plans, markets, and available incentives to ensure appropriate oversight. Without prior experience, they will necessarily depend on consultants and advice from other governments (which have experience with PPPs) to assist them in the design of the contract. This is why organizational learning must be a part of the new collaborative environment, a topic discussed in chapter 11.

When effective expectations and oversight are not in place as part of the contract, public managers often must try to develop them as the partnership is evolving. However, as the Coast Guard Deepwater case clearly illustrates, the failure to develop appropriate performance measures at the start and the inability to monitor their partner effectively led to a significant failure and the ultimate termination of the partnership, at significant cost to the Coast Guard.

Once the contract has been awarded, the public and private partners are involved in ongoing negotiations about the delivery of services. Most PPPs last longer than election cycles or even the average tenure of many public managers. In such cases, accountability depends heavily on anticipating the ex post facto issues and relationships. Because of their long period of performance, the combination of thoughtful procedures and decision rules embedded in the agreement and developing a trusted partnership is a requirement for appropriate accountability.

Exercising accountability in PPPs ultimately depends on clarifying responsibilities in relationships. The director of the UK National Audit Office, James

Robertson (personal communication 2008), claimed that creating some flexibility is an essential component of PPP contracts. It signaled accommodation to the other partners and reassured them about the long-term prospects for the partnership. Transparency about performance standards and the PPP's actual performance are also critical. Negotiated standards need to be reasonable and reflect a proper balance of risk taking by both parties. The quality of the interactions between public and private partners affects the overall ability of an agency to monitor compliance by the contractor and adjust performance incentives accordingly.

In this respect, public managers can learn from their own interactions with other governmental units. Intergovernmental scholars have noted that when one level of government works with another level (e.g., federal to state) on grants or contracts, these relationships are not one-sided, with one government dictating to the other. The relationship often involves bargaining so that each side feels its priorities are reflected in the final agreement (Ingram 1977; Derthick 2013). Whether in a partnership or a network, each side can often exit the arrangement. Thus, public managers need to balance their own policy concerns and objectives with those of the collaborators and find methods to focus on the areas (such as key performance indicators) that are most important to maintain the public interest.

Performance standards and clear expectations for each partner create a basis for trust. The success of the PPP in its service delivery is tied to the success of each of the partners. The private sector strives to meet the standards based on a return on its expenditures. The government seeks to support the project and the private sector partner to ensure citizens are receiving the services they expect. Structuring PPPs properly creates the incentive for both parties to make their best efforts to provide quality public services.

Accountability in Networks

Eggers and Goldsmith (2004) identified four key issues in network governance to ensure public accountability: properly aligning the incentives, routinely measuring performance, building trust in the network, and appropriately sharing risk. Many of these same factors have been previously identified as important to PPPs. It makes sense that similar factors help ensure accountability in PPPs and networks. Both approaches represent government efforts to engage collaborators to carry out government responsibilities without having direct control over the actions of the PPP or the network.

With multiple collaborators in networks, the need to have specific shared outcomes identified and committed to at the start of the collaboration is critical. With just the government and a business involved, PPPs rely more on continual adjustments and accommodations with the aim of making sure the PPP meets its goals and objectives. The time it would take to use a similar approach with networks is overwhelming and not the best use of everyone's time and resources. Negotiating specific outcomes in advance is the best way for networks to deliver quality public services, leading to collaborative accountability. A critical role for public managers in network governance is to ensure that all network participants and the general public have meaningful input into the deliberations on outcomes.

In the Fairfax County human services project, county leaders used an effective formula of mutual accountability: shared values, outcome measures, and trust. The shared value was to assist those in need in the county, whether the aid came from the public, private, or nonprofit sectors. Among the outcome measures was "percentage of need achieved," a clear indicator of how successful the total network was in achieving their shared value. Trust was built in a number of ways: by involving nonprofit actors in developing the system and measuring performance, the widespread sharing of information among public and nonprofit agencies, and a "change-centric" environment where the door was always open to suggestions for improving the system. This approach led to a strong collaborative accountability among the network members.

Accountability in Independent Public-Services Providers

Accountability in IPSPs is the most challenging for public managers because they have considerable autonomy and independence from governments. There are twin accountability issues for IPSPs: participants need to establish accountability within their own collaboration, and public managers need to determine whether and to what extent the IPSP should be accountable to the public interest. However, because of the independent nature of

IPSPs, government cannot employ traditional accountability measures or approaches.

The best approach for public managers to take is to engage IPSPs in respectful, cooperative interactions. Public managers should consider what sources of leverage are available through government actions that might influence any given IPSP. There are four principal sources of influence of public managers:

1. *Permission:* The IPSP may be engaged in an activity that requires public sector permission or authorization, such as licenses, permits, or certifications.

2. *Information:* The IPSP might be more effective if government provided certain information, such as case files, and access to databases that are routinely collected by government agency.

3. *Funding:* The government may have discretionary funds that can be used to support the IPSP activity.

4. *Citizen interface:* Government has the political legitimacy that the IPSP might not have in terms of interactions with citizens and communities.

If public managers can influence an IPSP, what sort of accountability measures should be advocated? First, public managers should advocate for full transparency of its members and activities. Second, they should encourage the IPSP to establish clear performance measures to both hold members accountable and provide appropriate public accountability. Third, they might negotiate certain standards or activities consistent with meeting public policy goals and objectives. Fourth, they can monitor and report citizen concerns and broader effects on the public.

CONCLUSION

When working with CSCs, public managers have less control over partners than in the traditional contracting relationship. The level of control lessens as one considers the options from contracting to IPSPs. Therefore, establishing procedures to promote collaborative accountability that rely on government dictating terms is implausible. The voluntary nature of collaborative arrangement and the ability of collaborators to exit any arrangement make enforcement of specific rules and regulations problematic at best. If public managers attempt to institute the same types of strict rules and regulations for CSCs as exist for traditional contracting relationships, stakeholders from the private or nonprofit sectors would have less motivation to continue with the relationship. In the case of networks and IPSPs, if the collaboration becomes overly burdensome for any member to participate, then that member can just walk away.

Of course, most CSCs involve some type of agreement, for example, a contract or memorandum of understanding, so the notion of totally voluntary collaboration has its limits. Yet a central presumption of collaborative relationships is the effort to achieve a shared purpose. The achievement of that purpose requires cooperation and trust that cannot be specified or enforced through a legal document. We have stressed the importance of trust in this chapter and how it is vital to successful collaboration. Open and candid communication and transparency with both the internal and external stakeholders comprising the CSC is essential to engender trust.

Consistent and clear dialogue with all stakeholders in the collaboration and with the general public is vital to ensuring accountability. Effective communication and two-way dialogue build trust and encourage transparency, which can translate into increased buy-in from those whose support is needed. Effective project management is another key to success. The project manager's role will be to guide the project through its course to ensure that resources and processes work well and benchmarks are appropriately met along the way.

Despite the challenges, ensuring shared accountability is critical for garnering support for CSCs. There must be assurances for citizens that taxpayer money is spent wisely and used for public purposes that generate public value. Citizens and public managers alike want to know that the private and nonprofit organizations that partner with government will not act in ways that would jeopardize the public interest. Furthermore, any problems involving public service delivery that result from collaborating are likely to generate enormous blame toward the public manager involved. We believe that if public managers learn how to harness the four pillars of successful relationships—understanding public and shared value, focusing on outcomes, building trust, and engaging citizens—they will be well prepared to manage CSCs to benefit all involved.

Case Study for Discussion: Accountability in Job Training Networks

You are an assistant to the executive director of the Department of Social Services (DSS). The governor has campaigned on increasing job training in the state and moving individuals from receiving state welfare payments to working. Currently the Division of Employment Training (DET), within DSS, provides that service. The head of the DET has decided to launch a network of training with both private and non-profit social service organizations to provide training services. You have been asked to develop policies and agency procedures that will ensure the new network is publicly accountable.

Questions and Issues for Consideration

1. What would be your approach to ensuring mutual, democratic accountability?

2. How would you use social media to accomplish that goal?

Developing Government Capacity for Cross-Sector Collaboration

We explained in chapter 9 the challenges of public management in heterarchical structures where nonprofit and private sector organizations take on shared roles and responsibilities in delivering public goods and services. Whether engaging with networks, public-private partnerships (PPP), or independent public-service providers (IPSPs), significant attention and resources are needed in government to manage the horizontal and vertical relationships that underlie cross-sector collaborations (CSC).

This chapter draws from fieldwork and observations from two government agencies to explain how the public sector can improve its abilities to work with organizations outside government. The chapter reviews the importance of government capacity for CSC, discusses how knowledge development and learning can drive capacity building, and presents a framework to guide public managers in preparing their own agencies for more effective work in PPPs and other CSCs.

GOVERNMENT SKILLS FOR PPPs

As discussed in chapter 4, PPPs for infrastructure are a unique form of CSC—far more complex than traditional contracting and less relational forms of CSC. In many ways, PPPs of this kind are the extreme example of complexity in CSC, involving not only relational and incomplete conditions, but the added risk of private investment and financial forecasting over an extensive period of time, for which the public sector is not as accustomed to planning. The key areas of difference include planning and design development, bidding processes, construction monitoring, and long-term monitoring.

Planning and Design Development

The planning and design development stage for PPPs thoroughly assesses whether a particular type of infrastructure project is appropriate for a PPP. Tasks include determining whether the project requires a major capital investment, specifying services, considering services in terms of their whole-life costs (or estimated costs over the life cycle of the asset), forecasting technology change during the project life cycle, predicting user demand, and determining whether private sector expertise exists (Her Majesty's Treasury 2006). Project assessments and comparisons may follow the model of a public sector comparator to assess the overall costs that the public sector would incur if it conducted the effort and to establish a baseline of public sector project costs to compare against a PPP (PartnershipsVictoria 2001).

Risk analysis and allocation is critical for any infrastructure project, particularly PPPs. Understanding the various technical, construction, operational, revenue, political, and regulatory risks in PPPs is critical for aligning public and private incentives for a long-term project like a PPP (Grimsey and Lewis 2007). Unfortunately, the typical infrastructure planning process does not consider this spectrum of risks since government typically plans for construction alone and deals with long-term operational issues only after a project is completed.

Planning also requires an understanding of whether services can be measured through key performance indicators and whether the public sector has the in-house monitoring skills to measure and develop targets for program outputs and outcomes and to ensure that those targets are met. An understanding of the technical and operational dimensions of the project is needed to understand the potential for valuing the project in terms of whole-life-cycle costs—costs that combine design, construction, and operational project dimensions.

Bidding Process

Facilitating a bidding process for PPPs requires skills in maintaining competitive tension among all contractors in the negotiations. Competition is one of the primary drivers of cost reductions in PPPs (Morallos and Amekudzi 2008) and requires government to ensure that enough providers in the market will compete on a project. It is also necessary to ensure that private operators have the flexibility to create their own design solutions. The UK government, for example, uses a competitive dialogue approach to review bids, where public procurement teams negotiate the terms of all bidding designs simultaneously for a fixed period of time (Felipe 2003).

The flexibility in designing project solutions in PPP negotiations means that there is often greater variation among project designs that the public sector must vet. Reviews of PPP bids must consider technical elements (such as project designs), financial elements (including financing and revenue generation), allocation of risk (such as responsibility for forecasting demand), and legal elements (such as the public sector lending and supervisory potentials allowed by current legislation). Public agencies need skills in each area to evaluate the potentials of contractor bids. Evaluating bids also requires the ability to compare the private sector proposal to the alternative of government production.

A single project team that is capable of assessing all vendor proposals simultaneously is generally the best structure for evaluating competing bids (Her Majesty's Treasury 2009). The World Bank reports that single project teams, often in the form of PPP units, have been developed to address these responsibilities in Bangladesh, Jamaica, Philippines, Portugal, South Africa, Australia, and Korea, among other countries (World Bank 2007). The creation of PPP units is particularly important in low-income countries where the public sector is already short on administrative skills and resources.

Construction

During construction, public managers need to play a role in overseeing project deadlines and progress toward the completion of facility renovation or construction. Payment to private partners is often deferred until services begin to be delivered, placing more risk on the private sector to complete the project on time. Skills public managers generally need include monitoring construction deadlines and the overall quality standards of facilities created.

Monitoring and Evaluation

Post-construction responsibilities include monitoring and evaluation and ensuring that agreed-on standards of performance are achieved. Much like other forms of CSC, monitoring and evaluation is a critical stage of quality control.

Administratively, monitoring needs to be carried out through a contracting team with clear lines of authority, clear management standards, mechanisms for addressing contract variations, and the ability to detect problems at various stages of implementation (Robinson et al. 2010).

Contract managers also need to understand the financial dimensions of service provision by private contractors, including the nature of cash flows and revenue streams that repay the debt behind projects. Managers must be knowledgeable of indicators such as "dividend payouts, debt coverage, liquidity, [and] published accounts" to provide an indication of whether the business scheme is operating effectively (Grimsey and Lewis 2007, 212). Contract management therefore entails much more than monitoring regular performance; it also requires a thorough review of project operations (including estimates of future performance), as well as revenue and cost streams, to ensure adequate project delivery over a long-term time horizon.

GOVERNMENT SKILLS FOR NETWORK MANAGEMENT

Network management also involves a set of skills for leading multiple members around a shared purpose. Managing across organizations requires the creation of relationships beyond the scope of written agreements (Van Slyke 2009) and the building of social relations among organizational leaders to ensure cooperation and agreement around mutual objectives (Carlee 2008). A study of social service contracts in Georgia, for example, found that social norms and related interpersonal agreements were central to the performance of contracting networks (Gazley 2008).

Managers also need skills in persuasion and negotiation to achieve public service delivery objectives established for networks of multiple organizations (Kettl 2002). McGuire (2006) suggests that government administrators preserve a role as a central coordinating actor and bear the bulk of responsibility for achieving public objectives. Specific tasks needed include activation (identifying the right people and resources needed), framing (facilitating agreement on roles and responsibilities), mobilizing (building the support and commitment of everyone involved), and synthesizing (building trust and information exchange among involved participants). As with other forms of CSCs, network management also requires continual monitoring and evaluation of the outputs and outcomes of the network.

Recognizing all of the actors in CSC efforts, resolving conflicts, and managing relationships strategically also have been found to improve performance in networked governance. Conflict management skills are important in order to negotiate diverse interests among the varied organizations within a networked environment. Skills for ameliorating divergent priorities can include negotiation, bargaining, collaborative problem solving, and conflict management (Bingham and O'Leary 2007).

GOVERNMENT SKILLS FOR IPSPs

Independent public-services providers (IPSPs) pose another problem for public managers. They operate outside government control, and skills involved in interfacing with them are different from those of PPPs or networks, where government plays more of a participatory role. In general, public managers need some of the skills that we have referenced with respect to both networks and partnerships: negotiations, bargaining, collaborative problem solving, and building social capital and trust. Public managers also need to consider the operational health of IPSP members and their potential to contribute to long-term outcomes for the project.

Additional skills include scanning the environment of the IPSP and determining whether such organizations are acting in the public interest. How do public managers accomplish this? First, it is important for public managers to understand why a particular IPSP was created and what public problem or policy it is addressing. Second, managers must determine whether the IPSP is meeting a public need by addressing a known public problem that is not being addressed effectively by existing government mechanisms. Third, they need to attempt to provide avenues for citizens to weigh in on the work of the IPSP. This may or may not be easy. Where government has nothing to offer the IPSP, public managers have little leverage. A public manager's only recourse may be to develop a relationship with IPSP managers that might provide two-way information about IPSP activities and their impact on public problems.

As discussed in chapter 10, governments often have resources at their disposal that might be used as effective bargaining chips to enable public managers to shape the actions of the IPSP. Potential resources include the ability to permit or regulate the activity of the IPSP, providing information on the need or clients that are important for the success of the IPSP, and possibly providing some funding to support IPSP activities. In each of these cases, public managers need to exercise restraint in their bargaining and be seen as enablers of IPSP action rather than as roadblocks to effective IPSP activities.

GOVERNMENT LEARNING AND CSC

Learning how to improve government capacity for collaboration matters for government agencies interested in engaging in CSC since knowledge underlies the ability of government to control the potential risks of these projects and to capitalize on their financial and social benefits.

A review of infrastructure-based PPPs across policy sectors concluded that while many PPPs have performed effectively, many turned out terribly wrong (Hodge and Greve 2007). Specific failures of PPPs can involve improper technical designs by private operators who are unable to meet the building requirements of their projects. In one case, the private operator constructing a government laboratory for physicists in the United Kingdom was repeatedly unable to meet the highly sensitive building conditions that the facility required for conducting scientific experiments (National Audit Office 2006). The result was that the public sector was forced to take over the project, incurring costs far above those budgeted for the endeavor. Similarly, public service outcomes in networks can fail to deliver if government members are unprepared. Case studies of child care delivery through networks found problems with transparency and limited oversight of programs provided to the public (Vancoppenolle and Verschuere 2012). Much of the problem was due to complicated chains of accountability created among the varied nongovernmental members of the network, so that it was difficult to determine who was accountable for which outcomes. Kettl (2008) also explains how the many nonprofit and private sector organizations working in the network of health services delivered through the federal Medicare and Medicaid programs often fragment social services, denying clients a more comprehensive approach to addressing their unique needs.

BUILDING GOVERNMENT CAPACITY FOR COLLABORATION: A LEARNING FRAMEWORK

Government agencies can improve their transition to new skills areas needed for CSC by adopting practices to facilitate collective learning within their organizations. Knowledge derives from experience, such that organizations with more experience can generate more expertise from their past behavior to guide future action (Mahler 1997), demonstrating a learning curve of experience-based skill acquisition. The challenge for public agencies is that they have little CSC experience to draw on.

Core Issues in Government Learning

Organizational learning for CSC may be viewed as involving both structural and social dimensions of activities that support the adoption of skills, expertise, and systems related to the design and implementation of networks, partnerships, and IPSPs. Structural dimensions of learning include formally organized events like after-action reporting or structured trainings. Social dimensions of learning refer to interpersonal interactions among individuals that give meaning to knowledge derived from experience. Assigning a value to knowledge is central to the transfer of individual-level learning to organization-wide outcomes (Mahler 1997).

Considering structural dimensions alongside the social processes that underlie them explains how learning leads to changes in behavior. Social context, for example, has been found to have great influence over the potential for individuals to learn within activities designed for such purposes. In order for behavior to change, environments surrounding learning may need conditions such as voluntary participation, noncompetitive forums for sharing ideas, the welcoming of personal accounts of failures, and an iterative or ongoing approach to reflection (Blindenbacher and Nashat 2010). It is also important to ensure that employees do not feel incrimination for taking risks or sharing examples of past failures. Avoiding recriminations for mistakes helps to ensure that individuals are willing to share their ideas, consider alternate points of view, and reach collective solutions through an atmosphere of psychological safety (Edmondson 1999).

A Framework of Learning for CSCs

Figure 11.1 outlines four domains of government learning. The stages address activities and conditions that assess the current state of technical knowledge (assessing and assigning employees); identify sources of desired knowledge and adapt learning activities to transfer outside knowledge to internal employees (deciphering and integrating external knowledge); describe how to collect lessons

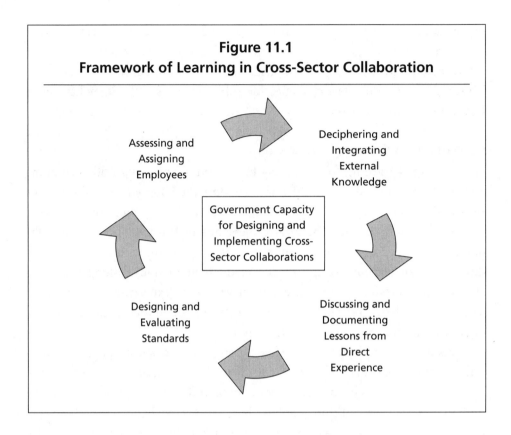

Figure 11.1
Framework of Learning in Cross-Sector Collaboration

Assessing and Assigning Employees

Deciphering and Integrating External Knowledge

Government Capacity for Designing and Implementing Cross-Sector Collaborations

Designing and Evaluating Standards

Discussing and Documenting Lessons from Direct Experience

from ongoing experimentation in new program areas (discussing and documenting lessons from direct experience); and explain how to capture ongoing knowledge through performance and evaluation systems (designing and evaluating standards) (Boyer 2013).

Dimensions of the Learning Framework

Each of the four stages explained in the theoretical framework, when considered in respect to empirical findings derived from studies of two government transportation agencies, reveal a number of activities and practices that public managers could adopt to improve their management of CSCs.

Assessing and Assigning Employees   The first stage refers to the multiple processes that underlie an organization's efforts to develop an understanding of what they already know about a new skill area. For an agency that has no experience working on collaborative projects, the list of required knowledge would presumably be quite long. The desired expertise can include a host of technical, financial, legal, and managerial skills for managing relationships with cross-sector partners.

Identifying employees with appropriate skills and assigning them to relevant roles is a critical part of any agency's effort to determine what its staff members already know about managing agreements with public and private sectors. The reality is that "organizations often do not know what they know" (Huber 1991, 100). Without clarifying analyses of existing knowledge, public managers are likely to encounter a knowing-doing gap where their organizations as a whole are unable to perform in line with what their employees already know (Smith, McKeen, and Singh 2006).

Analysis of semistructured interviews with twenty-four government officials and industry executives working on PPPs, for example, identified three areas related to an agency's approach to establishing a baseline of skills:

1. Dedicating staff to duties involving CSC

2. Identifying additional skill areas specific to the collaborative approach

3. Setting a clear policy strategy for the program

Assigning government staff to work on CSC can ensure that appropriate human capital is devoted to the administrative obligations in designing and implementing collaborative partnerships. One public manager commented, "There should be some kind of test for the staff to determine what they already know." The challenge is that many public employees are assigned responsibilities to design and implement collaborations on top of their existing responsibilities. The establishment of dedicated teams for the design and implementation of partnership and networks ensures governmental leadership commitment to these projects. Examples include the Secretary's Global Partnership Initiative at the US State Department (2012) and the Virginia Department of Transportation's Office of Transportation Public-Private Partnerships (OTP3 2012).

While a number of skills are identified as important for government leadership in networks and partnerships throughout this book, additional skills may be needed for the specific CSC adopted. Some of the most important skills needed for government staff managing PPPs for infrastructure are financial modeling, public engagement, and managing consultants. The design of PPPs encompasses complex financial forecasting, where predictions are made about project revenues and investments often forty to fifty years into the future. In addition, public managers are challenged to explain the perceived benefits of the project to relevant constituent groups through varied forms of public engagement. Involving the private sector in the operations of public assets like seaports or highways can generate public skepticism, which is often made worse when private sector operators collect fees from citizens in the form of tolls or related user fees. Preparing public sector staff to clearly communicate the goals of the project can help to appease public concern and adapt the CSC to local interests.

Finally, when public managers begin to assess the backgrounds of employees tasked with working on a CSC, having clear policies for the project in question is critical. For transportation projects, the policy goals may include reductions in traffic congestion, reduced vehicle accidents, or reduced costs in delivery. One person remarked, "The key is for the leadership of the agency to set a clear policy direction, then provide the resources for people to implement and execute." For public health programs, goals could include reduced costs of care or improvements in preventative medicine. The clearer the policy objectives are behind government programs, the better equipped public managers can be in adapting their knowledge development efforts to cultivate skills that are most directly related to improving collaborations to meet those objectives.

Deciphering and Integrating External Knowledge   Leveraging knowledge from outside one's agency to improve approaches to collaboration requires identifying the sources of knowledge desired and developing plans for incorporating that knowledge into one's own organization. It is widely recognized that "organizations can get a great deal accomplished that they do not know how to do, by drawing on the capabilities of others" (Nelson and Winter 1982, 125). Drawing from the lessons of other organizations can also reduce the costs of learning, since managers can learn from the mistakes of others without having to suffer the consequences of those same mistakes.

Three aspects of learning from others in forms of CSC are important:

1. Determining sources of desired knowledge

2. Determining the characteristics of desired knowledge

3. Applying learning techniques to adapt outside knowledge to existing practice

A wide range of organizations, for example, provide guidance to state and local governments on their implementation of PPPs for transportation, including federal agencies such the Federal Highway Administration and the Research and Innovative Technology Administration in the US Department of Transportation; nonprofit associations such as the National Council of Public-Private Partnerships and the American Association of State Highway and Transportation Officials; and industry groups such as InfraAmericas and Booz Allen Hamilton, which hold conferences on emerging topics related to PPPs. For any collaborative approach requiring some level of learning for the public sector, decisions will need to be made as to what outside sources of knowledge will help those working in the approach get the skills they desire.

Interviews with experts working on PPPs indicated that external consultants, public sector officials, and conferences and workshops were the best sources of knowledge related to designing and implementing PPPs. External consultants are often viewed as the most important source of knowledge for PPPs, since so many of the skills related to PPP management require personnel with the experience (and related salaries) that usually are beyond the reach of the public sector. One interviewee explained that reliance on outside consultants is particularly important since "there aren't any DOT's [staff] that have sufficient knowledge to do this on their own." In addition, other public sector organizations are often seen as particularly valuable (and less biased) partners since they can share experiences that are more applicable to public sector contexts.

Determining the sources of desired knowledge and their expected adaptations in the agency is also important. Knowledge, for example, can be divided into tacit knowledge, which requires interpersonal interaction to be shared, and explicit knowledge, which can be shared by reading written records (Argyris and Schön 1996). In the case of PPPs for transportation, for example, the knowledge related to PPPs is generally found to be tacit, since it is based so much on personal experience (Boyer 2013). The complicated and multifaceted aspects of PPPs demand that much of the knowledge about their design and implementation is learned only when public administrators work on them firsthand. In addition, the skills and knowledge needed for managing PPPs, networks, and IPSPs are so different from current practices in public organizations that it is difficult to scaffold new ideas onto existing systems.

Discussing and Documenting Lessons from Direct Experience Learning through direct experience generally refers to the process of learning by doing and the strategies organizations adopt to capture lessons learned from events that they have encountered themselves (Sheehan et al. 2005). Since experience with collaborative approaches to governance is often limited among government agencies, many of the insights they gain from projects will emerge as they are implementing them. Organizations need to adopt practices to capture and document lessons gleaned from experience of this kind before those experiences are forgotten (Carrillo et al. 2006).

Two aspects of learning by doing have been found to be particularly relevant in other CSCs:

1. Facilitating project reviews and documenting lessons from reviews during the design and implementation of a CSC

2. Cultivating social climates where employees feel comfortable speaking about their own mistakes and challenging their superiors during project reviews

Establishing formal practices for learning by doing helps government make ongoing learning consistent throughout designing and implementing forms of CSC. Examples include work groups, learning forums, and other processes designed to generate or share knowledge among employees in the same organization (Gibson and Vermeulen 2003). Government agencies implementing PPPs, for example, often implement project reviews and document lessons from those reviews to capture as much knowledge from practice as possible. Recognizing and documenting design-related lessons from project reviews can apply the lessons from these standards to future projects. One interviewee explained the importance of learning by doing in the following way: "What you see is that if a state agency has four of these projects, you begin to learn how to implement them. When you [are] done, you make adjustments in how you do it. The private sector says I want a deal like we had in year 2—but the public sector has learned." The public agency now has a better understanding of the key issues in PPPs and is better able to negotiate a good deal for the state. In this way, experiential learning improves the knowledge base for the public sector and reduces information asymmetries between public and private sectors on PPPs.

Since so much of learning from collaborations occurs through direct experience and the discussions within project reviews and related forums, it is critical to ensure that all employees within project reviews feel comfortable sharing lessons from their experience. One concept for understanding a social climate amenable to discussing errors is psychological safety, or a "shared belief that [a] team is safe for interpersonal risk taking" (Edmondson 1999, 354). The benefits of interactive learning derive from the deliberation among multiple individuals as they consider different points of view and different types of knowledge (Haunschild and Sullivan 2002). Since carving out social space for psychological safety can be difficult in government, specific practices could help to solicit employee feedback, such as a "free pass"—or the ability to discuss personal mistakes without fear of recrimination. Open discussions where all issues are on the table and anonymous reporting of project outcomes can improve the identification of important lessons from experience.

Cultivating an environment that welcomes different points of view and engages all members improves the potential for achieving adequate contributions from multiple individuals and, by extension, sources of knowledge that prove valuable. Furthermore, an environment where all members feel free to contribute can improve the potential for sharing experiences that led to failures as well as experiences or practices that led to successes. There is a very real danger to recognizing only project successes, which may slow adaptation and limit attention to alternative courses of action (Denrell and March 2001). Furthermore, recognizing failures and their causes can promote deeper levels of reflection among individuals and encourage them to seek out more innovative solutions to avoid such outcomes in the future (Sitkin 1992).

Designing and Evaluating Standards   Monitoring and evaluation provides mechanisms for ongoing data generation and reflection that can improve the development of skills in organizations and promote ongoing learning to improve organizational performance. Program evaluation refers to the "application of systemic methods to address questions about program operations and results" (Wholey, Hatry, and Newcomer 2010, 5). Recommended changes in operations, procedures, or practices contribute to organizational learning by drawing from analyses of experience to guide changes in collective behavior. Within the CSC context, information from evaluations can provide indications of how well activities are achieving desired results and how management changes can improve performance.

Three aspects of monitoring and evaluation are particularly relevant for knowledge development related to networks, PPPs, and IPSPs:

1. Designing measurement standards that will inform decision making in the future

2. Engaging evaluators in the design of project standards

3. Linking evaluation standards to public interest objectives

For both monitoring and evaluation to be useful, information must be gathered that can inform decisions. Performance data will only be deemed useful if they are credible and reliable and if they measure aspects of implementation that are important and remedial (Wholey et al. 2010). Furthermore, standards need to clearly capture information on the components of projects that public administrators may wish to adjust on future projects. For example, PPPs for transportation often include metrics on the design standards of bridges, roadways, or other facilities so that evaluators can trace back the design outcomes to compare decisions made earlier to operational outcomes that are apparent only later in the project. The key to creating appropriate standards is ensuring that what is being measured can inform decision making on future projects. One interviewee explained, for example, that "you have to set uniform metrics for the projects."

The value of incorporating managers in the development of evaluation criteria has been documented in other studies in public administration (Preskill and Torres 2000). Too often the public sector invests time and resources in developing the appropriate contracting or network structure without considering the administrative resources needed to ensure that those terms are met. Incorporating evaluators into the design reflects a wider need to ensure that public administrators creating CSCs look beyond contract design to the many government demands that emerge after a contract has been signed (Brown, Potoski, and Van Slyke 2011).

Too often public managers have little understanding of how the measures they evaluate link to wider policy outcomes. The challenge is that evaluators are asked to measure standards without understanding their link to the wider picture. Improving collective learning from monitoring and evaluation also requires the communication of wider policy objectives to the public managers involved in evaluation. The more that contract managers understand the wider goals behind performance standards, the greater their personal commitment will be to assessing their measurements. Government officials in state-level transportation departments, for example, indicated that they were more likely to glean lessons from evaluation of PPPs when they understood how those measures linked to wider policy objectives.

CONCLUSION: A SYSTEMS APPROACH TO LEARNING

The four domains of learning discussed in this chapter identify specific activities and arrangements that can improve government approaches to CSCs. They include a number of structural and social dimensions of learning that underlie collective learning and reinforce the importance of social conditions to facilitate collective understandings of new information and behavioral change.

The domains of learning derive from analyses of state government agencies with some experience working on CSCs. Implementing a process for learning skills related to CSC is likely to be different for government agencies with no prior experience in collaboration. Without direct personal experience, agencies will rely more on learning from others since they will not have the foundation of knowledge to assess from the outset. In addition, the process of learning from direct experience will be particularly relevant for public managers with little experience of CSC, since ongoing lessons will help them to avoid making repeat mistakes and can accelerate their accumulation of knowledge. In all cases, dedicating a team of public sector professionals to CSC work is recommended to enable them to begin accumulating and making use of lessons from CSC.

The interdependent and ongoing contributions of each of the four areas of learning (employee assessment and assignment, deciphering and integrating external knowledge, discussing and documenting lessons from direct experience, and designing and evaluating standards) imply that rather than considering each area as a step in a progression, the components formerly discussed as stages may instead be considered domains or subsystems of a larger system (Senge 2006). Theoretical models in public sector contexts often explain behavioral processes of subsystems, within larger systems, that interact to generate wider outcomes (Sabatier and Weible 2007). Government learning can therefore be considered a wider system of processes related to managing networks, partnerships, and IPSPs.

A number of specific activities related to each stage of learning also emerge as important to the process of organizational learning. Assessing and assigning employees, creating a dedicated team, identifying employees with skills in public engagement and managing consultants, and setting a clear policy strategy for the program are central to determining what the agency already knows in relation to managing complex collaborations. The establishment of a team of employees with the sole responsibility of working on partnerships or networks creates a specific division within the organization that can generate, store, and act on knowledge related to such collaborations. Furthermore, the creation of a clear policy directive for the program provides goals for learning to direct knowledge-based activities (Senge 2006).

Within the domain of deciphering and integrating external knowledge, a number of external sources of knowledge are important for improving agency learning. However, it is also important for government managers to understand the characteristics of outside knowledge (and their potential biases) in order to adopt practices that can best benefit internal transformations.

Discussing and documenting lessons from direct experience through learning by doing is likely to involve project reviews and a social climate amenable to discussions of failures and challenges to authority. The emphasis on challenges to authority by interviewees reinforces the importance of psychological safety for learning processes in organizations (Edmondson 1999). Attention to psychological safety also reinforces the importance of organizational culture in directing organizational behavior (Schein 1965) by highlighting the impact of social norms on the disclosure and recognition of project failures (Mahler and Casamayou 2009).

The prior discussion also highlights the importance of designing and evaluating standards for generating lessons to inform collective learning in organizations. Furthermore, engaging evaluators in the design of standards helps to explain how employees can better understand the meaning behind the measures they are tasked with measuring.

Considering both the integrated and overlapping nature of the stages of learning, as well as their social dimensions, helps to illustrate learning activities that can improve government capacity building for designing and implementing networks, partnerships, and IPSPs. The four stages, and their accompanying activities, can help public managers to improve their approaches to cross-sector collaboration.

Case Study for Discussion: Cross-Sector Collaboration in Transit Development

You are the project manager for a public works department within a local government agency in a large metropolitan area. The mayor has asked your division to explore the potentials for a PPP for infrastructure to support the expansion of a light-rail system to improve the mobility of citizens across the city. Your boss has asked you to develop a recommendation for how to evaluate the potential for a PPP delivery approach for this project.

The primary mode of transit in the city now is a public bus network, and most people rely on automobiles for their travel, causing a great deal of traffic congestion and limiting mobility for low-income travelers. The city is looking for ways to finance a new transit system and generate some innovative ideas for a project design. The new transit system would have to have enough coverage to allow travelers from both low-income urban neighborhoods and high-income suburban neighborhoods adequate access to the city center and major destinations like the airport and the sports center. In addition, the light-rail system would need to charge a fee that all segments of the city's population can afford.

Questions and Issues for Consideration

1. Based on what you know about PPPs for infrastructure, what do you think should be considered in comparing this approach to a contracting-out approach for the project?

2. What human capital issues do you think your division should consider for developing the appropriate expertise to carry out a PPP?

The Future of Cross-Sector Collaboration

The growing complexity of today's public policy problems and a lack of confidence by citizens in adopting government-only solutions have led to an expansion of a variety of governmental collaborations with private and nonprofit sector organizations. New approaches to governance—collaborative contracts, partnerships, networks, and independent public-services providers (IPSPs)—have emerged to fill the void left by ineffective, underperforming, and underfunded government agencies. Governments now are beginning to rely on the private and nonprofit sectors to bring to the table expertise, experience, and capacity that many public agencies lack.

A high-visibility example that underscores the need for effective cross-sector collaboration (CSC) is the stark failure associated with the initial implementation of the website for the Patient Protection and Affordable Care Act of 2010, popularly known as Obamacare. Once US government agencies sent astronauts to the moon; now the question is whether they can even build a website. If government agencies cannot properly design and establish something as basic as a customer-based website, what confidence can people have that government is able to take care of much more complex endeavors? CSC should not be viewed as a luxury or a governance add-on; it may, in some instances, be the only viable option to deliver quality public services. The urgency of the challenges we face, however, has motivated practice to race ahead of theory. It is fair to say that the collaborative cart is out in front of the governance framework horse.

This book makes the case that sufficient experience and research exist to guide public managers to engage all forms of CSC successfully. Like any other public service delivery model administered by federal, state, or local governments, CSCs should meet citizens' expectations for performance and create public value. Meeting citizen expectations for performance through CSCs requires new ways of conceptualizing citizen engagement and reinvigorating the values of democratic accountability. Creating public value through CSCs means reimagining the ways public services can be produced and distributed and rethinking how innovative approaches can generate mutual benefits to citizens and to all collaborators.

Some public managers, public administration scholars, and citizens are not convinced about the merits of CSC, particularly when they involve the private sector. Part of the explanation for the antagonism toward such collaborations is embedded in a philosophy that does not approve of nongovernmental entities operating in what is viewed as the public sphere. From this perspective, government is the proper and only legitimate actor to conduct and mediate certain collective actions that aim to meet the public interest. It is government that has the authority and responsibility to decipher and serve the public interest for the benefit of all. This is an interesting debate and one that is likely to continue for a long time.

Skepticism of CSC involving both private and nonprofit organizations also is rooted in more practical concerns: Will fees for services be imposed on users? Will government officials be less responsive to citizens' complaints and problems? Will the quality or availability of services decrease? Will access to services become restricted and unavailable to particular groups in society, such as low-income, rural residents or minorities? Will public officials be able to control their collaborators, or will they be co-opted or even corrupted? Will our government "sell out" our national interests to foreign companies? These are all good questions and should be addressed fully by public managers before engaging in CSC. In earlier chapters, this book examined numerous issues that can arise when engaging different forms of CSC and offered guidance to public managers on how to ensure accountability and to protect the public interest.

Before considering the various forms of CSC, public managers need to recognize their strengths and weaknesses. While in some cases, public managers may have no choice because of lack of capacity to address the problem solely through agency actions, in other cases, deciding to engage in CSC is a strategic decision or deliberate choice about the best way to maximize public resources to achieve a public purpose (and create public value). Table 12.1 provides a summary of the major advantages and disadvantages of public managers engaging in CSCs.

Table 12.1

Advantages and Disadvantages to Public Sector Use of CSC

	Advantages	Disadvantages/Cautions
Innovation	Private and nonprofit actors have more flexibility and incentives to experiment and try innovative solutions.	Public managers lose direct control; innovations may create a backlash from the public.
Interactions with citizens	Private providers typically are more customer focused and responsive to customer needs, providing more choices to citizens. Nonprofits are able to respond to particular constituencies that often are underserved by the public sector.	Public managers have a broader interest than serving "customers"; they have equity concerns; the democratic process provides a means for negotiating citizen interests, indirectly and directly; and the process of delivery of goods and services to citizens may be important.
Access to funding	The private sector can access private funding and may be able to borrow more easily than government. Nonprofits have access to foundations, donors, and others sources of support. Use of volunteers may lower the cost of service.	Government can usually borrow at rates lower than the private sector, though such borrowing may be subject to constitutional or statutory limitations or voter approval.
Expertise	The private sector can engage specialized expertise more easily than government because of its flexible hiring policies and ability to provide upward mobility. Nonprofits may have access to volunteers or have local knowledge that is valuable in serving a certain clientele.	The reliance on outside expertise can result in a public sector that is unable to appropriately manage and supervise cross-sector relationships. It also can create undesirable information asymmetries between government and potential CSC partners.

(Continued)

Table 12.1

Advantages and Disadvantages to Public Sector Use of CSC (*Continued*)

	Advantages	Disadvantages/Cautions
Motivation	The private sector is motivated by efficient operation of programs and by creating shared value. Nonprofits are motivated to fulfill their mission in a cost-effective manner; their mission often aligns with government policies and goals.	Private and nonprofit goals and objectives may not align with public sector goals and objectives. Negotiating divergent goals is a challenge, and the risk is that public interests may be co-opted by private or nonprofit interests.
Ownership relations	Private sector ownership creates an incentive for efficient and profitable execution of programs. Donors encourage efficient allocation of nonprofit resources, and nonprofit members can influence program priorities.	Public sector ownership is diffused among the citizens; however, ultimately public managers are responsible for stewarding public resources and achieving the public interest.
Moving to principal-principal relations	Private and nonprofit organizations no longer see themselves as mere agents but as trusted partners with public organizations in solving public problems.	Public managers are used to working in an arm's-length principal-agent environment and are challenged to move beyond hierarchical controls to negotiated principal-principal relations.

EVOLVING NATURE OF THE GOVERNANCE CHALLENGE

The challenges of governance today are substantial enough when governments operate within the framework of the traditional bureaucratic model, let alone when they move to more collaborative arrangements that anticipate less direct government control. Figure 12.1 shows how different approaches to collaboration have evolved over time as governments (and others involved in governance) seek new ways to gain access to resources, expertise, and market-driven management as a way to solve the emerging complex problems that public managers face.

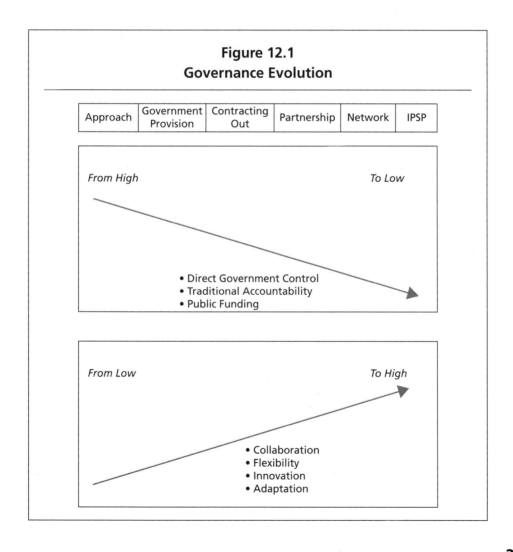

Figure 12.1
Governance Evolution

Approach	Government Provision	Contracting Out	Partnership	Network	IPSP

From High   *To Low*

- Direct Government Control
- Traditional Accountability
- Public Funding

From Low   *To High*

- Collaboration
- Flexibility
- Innovation
- Adaptation

As public managers have moved from the traditional provision of services, to contracting out, to partnerships, networks, and now IPSPs, each form of collaboration is seen as having some additional benefits to public service delivery. At the same time, these engagements mean an incremental loss of direct control by government and greater discretion and autonomy on the part of the collaborators. The IPSP is the extreme case—near autonomy from government, but with the greatest potential for responsiveness, flexibility, and innovation.

The evolution of these alternative approaches produces interesting choices for public managers: promising for their potential and threatening for what they take away. The paradox for public managers is that in order to gain full access to the benefits of these new approaches—collaboration, flexibility, innovation, and adaptation—public managers must relinquish the very essence of the conventional idea of what it has come to mean to act as government managers: formal control over the production and delivery of public services. Even public managers who endorse CSC are reluctant to step back from the view that government's prerogative should prevail in all such arrangements—even under the most extreme circumstances, where government is contributing minimal or no resources at all.

CONTRIBUTIONS TO NEW PUBLIC GOVERNANCE

A governance framework to guide expectations for engagements with CSC is now emerging, with a variety of opinions and proposals that do not yet represent a fully formed concept (Eggers and Goldsmith 2004; Salamon 2002; McGuire 2006; Osborne 2010; Hale and Held 2011). CSCs are growing as routine practice, yet a governance model to address them is still developing. Under such circumstances, some might counsel caution and argue it is best to wait until a more complete governance framework has been developed before embracing CSC.

New Public Governance seeks to address many of the issues raised in this book. CSCs have emerged out of the pressure to provide public services that are more responsive to citizens, but they have created a governance gap—between policy problems and mechanisms to address them—that has become a permanent fixture on the government/governance landscape. While New Public Management (NPM) proponents have presented some interesting ideas and challenges to conventional thinking about governance, New Public Governance scholars see NPM as an incomplete set of theories and research that do not fully address the governance challenges public managers now face. NPM may serve as a transition from "the statist and bureaucratic tradition of public administration and the embryonic plural and pluralist tradition of new public management" (Osborne 2010, 2); however, it is inadequate to fully explain the expansions and governance challenges involved in collaboration.

New Public Governance scholars continue to develop new concepts and practical approaches for public policy implementation and public service delivery, incorporating CSC theory and practice. Earlier chapters of the book advance several key propositions as contributions to a future New Public Governance paradigm:

1. *A continuum of four CSC options or models.* Three of the four CSC options of contracting, partnerships, and network governance have been studied by public administration scholars. We propose that these forms of collaboration, plus IPSPs, are better viewed as four related approaches public managers may choose for collaboration based on the existing conditions and expectations. The four forms of CSCs are related in the extent to which public managers seek to draw on collaborators' expertise, government capacity, and the complexity that is part of service delivery.

2. *IPSPs.* These entities are being established and operated to provide public services like government but are independent and self-directed collaborations, bringing together multiple organizations across sectors to address public policy problems. Typically IPSPs organize themselves as networks, but their autonomy from government direction and their commitment to collaboration are distinctive characteristics that distinguish them from the other forms of CSCs.

3. *Principal-principal relationships in CSC.* The tradition of viewing relationships involving government and collaborators as principal-agent is challenged by CSCs that often involve principal-principal relationships; this is explicitly the case for IPSPs, and it is true in most partnerships and networks. Principal-principal relationships complicate fundamental ideals of public accountability, but that is often a more accurate description of the relationship between governments and collaborators in CSCs.

4. *The bureaucratic model's incompatibility with CSCs.* CSCs have emerged in part due to frustrations with the classic public administration approach

to governance and its inability to consistently provide high-quality and responsive public services. The innovativeness, flexibility, and dynamism that are the appeal of CSC are incompatible with the requirements for traditional methods of control and accountability that are the foundation of the bureaucratic model.

5. *A new accountability structure for CSC.* To gain the optimum benefit for CSC, a new model of administrative governance needs promulgating. Because traditional forms of accountability are not as successful in CSC, we propose four pillars of mutual accountability: agreeing to common outcome measures, creating value, promoting a trusted partnership, and engaging citizens.

6. *The importance of citizen engagement to ensure legitimacy and accountability.* CSCs, perhaps more than any other form of government public service delivery, place public managers in a position where they must represent the views of citizens served by these arrangements. Thus, managers must find ways to engage citizens through social media and other formats to ensure that the collaboration is producing public value for the constituents they serve.

These propositions are consistent with looking at CSC as part of a pluralistic form of governance that depends more on successful collaborations among entities with different missions and values and less on the formal authorities granted government agencies through legislation and executive order. With these issues in mind, we make one more proposition that may aid the development of a New Public Governance paradigm: the significance of public value.

CSC AND PUBLIC VALUE

Prior presentations on CSCs have positioned them as an extension of traditional modes of public governance. Experts on contracting, partnerships, and networks acknowledge the challenges in collaborating in ways that advance the public interest. A central theme of this book is the natural tension between the expectations for governments to control and maintain close accountability for collaborations and the expectations for CSCs to be responsive, flexible, and innovative. One approach for public managers who develop and work with CSCs and must manage the tensions between expectations and performance is the concept of public value.

Defining Public Value

The idea of public value is a relatively new concept in public administration. We build off the foundational ideas of Moore (1995), discussed in chapter 10, in developing a rationale for the role that public value can play in helping public managers gauge the success of CSCs. Just as the goal of private managers is to create private (economic) value, the goal of public managers can be seen as creating public (social) value. The definition of public value provides a unifying idea of what public managers should aspire to in CSCs and can guide decisions on the appropriate collaborative solution to meet a public need.

The idea of public value, however, remains elusive. Moore's (1995) definition of public value equates managerial success in the public sector with initiating and reshaping public sector enterprises in ways that increase their value to the public in both the short run and the long run. Many have found the idea interesting but difficult to pin down. Much of the debate has been predicated on the assumption that public value is created, or at least identified, by public agencies. Examining CSC contributions to public value allows greater flexibility in determining what constitutes public value and where it originates. Talbot's (2006) economical consolidation of a complex set of considerations over what public value means may work best: "Public value is what the public values" (7). It allows the concept to be debated and resolved within any given CSC, with the presumption that most, if not all, participants will have a sense of what the public values in their communities. Public managers thus play a key role in helping CSCs to better understand how to translate their activities into public value. This recognizes that ultimately citizens do determine public values either directly, through citizen participation, or indirectly, through elections.

Moore's concept of public value as an analogy to private value remains the most useful touchstone for assessing CSC performance. For business, creating private value is the goal, but one with a purpose. Private value created and captured by firms can be passed along to the buyers of their products and captured in various measures of financial return. Firms attempt to create private value that is useful and profitable, but there is no guarantee of success. For CSCs, creating public value is the goal, but one with a purpose as well. Public value can be created and captured by citizens, whether through the services provided by CSCs or by additional spillover impacts that CSCs have on society. By applying Moore's concept to CSCs, public managers make a pragmatic assessment of the value of a CSC. Public managers might assess public value through four different lenses:

1. *A public policy perspective.* To what extent is the CSC advancing goals and objectives already adopted as public policy? It is reasonable to assume that public value is generated when public policy goals are furthered. Through this lens, public managers can work to maximize the extent to which CSCs meet articulated public policy goals.

2. *The organizational perspective.* To what extent has the CSC accomplished the purposes and results it has set for itself? The core rationale for CSCs is their capacity to provide public services, meeting some unmet public policy need. Through this lens, public managers can work to make sure that the efforts of CSCs do not drift from a generally accepted view of what is in the public interest.

3. *The better governance perspective.* To what extent has the CSC created innovative and adaptive approaches to providing public services? The public value created by such innovations is not limited to the specific CSC, but in its potential replications and adoption as regular practice by other CSCs and by government agencies.

4. *The citizen perspective.* To what extent do citizens perceive that the CSC is creating public value for them, either directly or indirectly? It is reasonable to assert that the efforts of CSCs are likely aligned with public policy. Active engagements of citizens, through various phases of a CSC (not only in the lead-up to a project but also once a project has begun), can provide an answer to whether citizens' expectations are met.

In all four aspects, public value becomes a touchstone for public managers to assess the contributions of CSCs and a guide for influencing the design, decisions, and operations of CSCs. As a practical matter, the assessment may have to come as CSCs are operating, and the values identified can provide useful evaluative tools. Examining public value created by CSCs becomes an approach for public managers to compare and contrast the efforts.

Illustration: A PPP for Infrastructure

The DC Capital area I-495 Beltway Hot Lanes project represents an effective use of a PPP in many respects and can be assessed in terms of public value. This project built fourteen miles of new express lanes (two in each direction) on I-495 between the Springfield Interchange and roadways north of the Dulles Toll Road—one of the busiest stretches of the Capital Beltway. These express lanes allow the beltway to offer high-occupancy vehicle lanes (HOV-3) connections with I-95/395, I-66, and the Dulles Toll Road for the first time, with enormous potential for reducing traffic congestion. It also made a significant contribution to the beltway's forty-five-year-old infrastructure, replacing more than fifty aging bridges and overpasses, upgrading ten interchanges, and improving new bike and pedestrian access. Toll prices for the 495 Express Lanes change according to traffic conditions, which regulate demand for the lanes to keep them congestion free even during peak hours (Virginia Department of Transportation 2013). Some of the values for traveling citizens include reduced travel times, improved safety on modernized infrastructure, and expanded pricing options to meet their individual traveling needs.

The private sector partner (Capital Beltway Express LLC) committed $349 million in equity financing (matching state and federal government financing) of the total $2 billion project costs, which was seen as essential for adding the new lanes (AASHTO 2014). Capital Beltway Express LLC also took on the risk that the fees and tolls they collect from managing the road would be sufficient to provide an attractive return on investment. Capital Beltway Express has experience financing and managing other highway projects and brought that expertise to this project. The expansion of that portion of the beltway meant the repair and replacement of numerous overpasses along that stretch, a significant and pressing capital improvement cost that the State of Virginia shifted in part to private partners.

Examining this project through a public value perspective, public managers could respond positively that they were fulfilling a clear Virginia public policy objective and creating an innovative approach to expanding highway capacity. If everyone involved in the CSC achieves their objectives and the mutual outcomes of the collaboration are achieved as well, we would consider the CSC to be a success.

Citizen acceptance of this PPP remains to be seen. Users of the 495 Express Lanes pay a variable congestion toll, depending on the length of the trip and the amount of traffic—generally ranging from about $1.50 to $5.00, but there is no cap on the maximum toll that could be charged. Carpools and taxis with three or more passengers, motorcycles, emergency vehicles, and some hybrids and buses are exempt from the tolls. The congestion fares have taken many drivers by surprise—despite public relations efforts by VDOT to inform the public of how the rates can speed up travel times. Paying a fee for what some may consider a reasonable commute time will seem a burden to many drivers—one they are likely to feel they have already paid for through their taxes. However, even for those who do not use the express lanes, the expansion should reduce overall commuting time, taking some travelers off the existing lanes and onto the express lanes. This PPP structure is similar to many under consideration nationally and internationally; tolls are critical to cover the interest and principal on the borrowed funds, whether publicly or privately financed, that paid for the expanded highway. Public managers will need to examine whether citizen expectations were met and whether they perceive that the public value created is commensurate with the tolls paid.

Illustration: An International IPSP

The self-direction and financial independence of the Global Network for Neglected Tropical Disease (GNNTD), discussed in chapter 6, is a reflection of the public value offered by IPSPs. The GNNTD established its own mission and goals consistent with its members' view that neglected tropical diseases (NTDs) had not received enough attention from global health care funders. US programs directed at global diseases and pandemics had settled on the priorities of HIV/AIDS, malaria, and tuberculosis. GNNTD has received funding support from the Gates Foundation and is implementing in-country programs that cure NTDs. The program efforts are consistent with the global health community's recognition of the importance of NTDs, but GNNTD supports programs well beyond those that the US government supports. For those who advocate greater attention to NTDs, an IPSP approach fits very well and creates value to the affected populations served.

However, GNNTD's relative independence also means its efforts may be seen as separate from a larger global policy context. Would the funding generated by GNNTD have been better spent on priorities already recognized by the United States and the global health community? The GNNTD also strives to be the strongest advocate for NTD support, but other organizations (such as the UK

Coalition against NTDs) remain active, and it is not clear how to resolve mission overlap among the different groups.

Can public managers assess the public value created by GNNTD? In a broad sense, GNNTD is fulfilling a public policy goal of improving the health of people in developing nations. While not supporting the specific priorities of US health care spending for developing nations, it is not inconsistent with broad policy objectives, and it is providing services in an innovative, cost-effective manner. Because of its independence, it is not a public manager's responsibility to monitor outcomes. A public manager's advocacy for public assistance for GNNTD, however, would center on the idea of the results achieved and maximizing the public's dollars through the use of this IPSP.

MOVING FORWARD WITH CSC

CSCs have the potential to help governments do their jobs better by creating more public value. It is a way to close the gap between what politicians promise and what governments deliver. Accomplishing this goal successfully means building long-term relationships among the public, private, and nonprofit sectors in CSCs as trusted partners. Such collaborations should be built around basic tenets: allocating risks to the partners in the best position to manage them and to ensure that all partners have a stake in the game, sharing information voluntarily to help partners make collaborative decisions in the public interest, agreeing on measurable outcomes for the collaboration to create public value, productive engagements with citizens, and a willingness of all collaborators to hold themselves accountable for their performance.

CSCs at their best are not mere extensions of government programs but a fundamental change in the way public services are provided. They offer opportunities to create innovative and responsive public service: those that create more public value than other approaches. With the proper design, CSC participants are motivated to generate the maximum public and shared value possible. However, such an approach calls on public managers to rethink the way public services are identified and provided and to manage the feedback and expectations of citizens regarding the quality, access, and cost of those services.

We should all insist on public services that are responsive to citizens' needs and of the highest quality regardless of one's wealth or influence. The notion that government provides a one-size-fits-all, take-it-or-leave-it kind of service is not only unacceptable but violates democratic principles. Increasingly, the lack of innovation found in the government's delivery of public services contrasts with the adaptive customer-oriented modes of service delivery found in the private and nonprofit sectors, with their strong motivations to serve their customers and clients. One has only to think of the kind of customer service received at Amazon versus most state departments of motor vehicles to appreciate the difference. Successful businesses continually seek to provide value to their customers. Public agencies should be no different in a quest for increasing public value.

With this in mind, CSCs are rightly understood as one way of organizing for better governance that improves the public services provided to citizens (Milburn 2007). CSCs have the potential to transform the way in which we view and deliver public services when guided by the appropriate vision and principles. Although there is no one best approach, Milburn argues for three principles: (1) choice and voice, emphasizing customer services and making standards matter; (2) empowerment, or allowing partners to be innovative and responsive; and (3) diversity of supply, or encouraging a robust market and entrepreneurial nonprofit organizations to test new ideas.

At the operational level, CSCs must employ approaches that spotlight their performance in creating public value. It is achieved through monitoring and evaluating services based on an agreed level of performance. Using new capabilities available through ICTs and social media, monitoring and evaluation could be done daily, or hourly, or in real time, not annually. Technology also expands the options for considering citizen input on projects after a CSC is up and running. Monitoring and evaluation could be repositioned to explain how well a CSC is achieving public value, improving transparency and accessibility for citizens. Such real-time accountability provides a prospect for adjustments and modifications of CSCs, with new opportunities to create more public value and develop more ongoing relationships and trust between government and citizens. Transparency throughout this process is key. The level and quality of public services provided, their costs, and the extent to which they meet expectations can be recorded and provided through websites and other social media so that the public can see exactly what they are paying for and what they are receiving.

As the use of CSCs expands, they exacerbate the tensions that already exist within public administration over the best way to deliver public services. CSCs challenge government to consider citizen interests beyond direct and indirect public sector involvement, to also include values for citizens identified and addressed from outside government. The four CSC approaches described and analyzed in this book have emerged and evolved during the past few decades. The strains they place on traditional ideas of accountability, public interest, and public values are growing pains as a slow but steady transformation takes place. Until a new public governance paradigm emerges, however, CSC will continue to face the challenge of being an innovative form of public service delivery that does not comport with traditional principles and ideals most familiar to public managers. Regardless, it is clear that CSCs are here to stay. They have the potential to deliver public services in ways that satisfy citizens' needs otherwise unimaginable.

CONCLUSION

A century ago, public administration principles and practices were codified in legislation and formalized through academic curricula to safeguard democratic accountability as public governance was revolutionized in response to a transforming society. Today public administration needs to be reconceptualized again to adapt to the reality of a new approach to governance: cross-sector collaborations.

We have emphasized throughout this book the challenges public managers face in identifying which form of CSC will be of greatest value in meeting their goals. One practical way to think about engaging CSC is to draw on Kettl's (1993) notion of government as a "smart buyer." He cites three basic prerequisites:

1. Government must know what it wants to buy.

2. Government must know who can sell what it wants.

3. Government must know how to judge what it bought.

Kettl's smart buyer approach is an apt lesson for public managers considering using CSC. Privatization and public-private relationships have been emerging, and public managers have been encouraged to find more market-based approaches to solving public policy problems since at least the 1980s. Kettl's advice fits well with an analogous awareness of government being asked to embrace methods of governance for which it may lack the capacity. We propose three parallel prerequisites for engaging CSCs:

1. Government must know what public value outcomes are achievable through CSC.

2. Government must know which participants can make the best contributions to a CSC.

3. Government must know how to monitor and evaluate public value in CSC.

Kettl's concern over the government's shortcomings in the procurement skills and acumen should be heeded for CSCs as well. Master's programs of public administration and public policy should be educating future public managers with the skills and analytics required to design and manage CSCs. Public managers will find the following skills increasingly important: understanding how to negotiate successfully with private and nonprofit organizations, managing and inspiring collaborative relationships, generating and measuring public value, engaging citizens and their preferences through social media and in-person events, developing innovative solutions that gain buy-in from collaborators, and participating in CSCs using the right level of government participation to optimize success.

This book has documented experiences of successful (and unsuccessful) CSCs and provided analytics that public managers can use to assess the trade-offs of using one form of CSC over another. The overall approach we advise public managers to take regarding the use of CSCs is *trust but verify*. The phrase, made famous by President Ronald Reagan when describing his approach to nuclear arms negotiations with the Soviet Union, captures the need to balance enthusiasm with caution and the need to monitor results.

Public value as envisioned by Moore (1995) presents an inspiration for public and nonprofit managers engaged in CSCs. Considering public value as a metric has caused public administration scholars no shortage of consternation as they struggle to conceptualize what such a thing as public value is and how to account for it in practice. At some point in the future, perhaps all public managers will be measuring the public value of government and nongovernment CSC programs just as we now do revenues and costs.

NOTES

INTRODUCTION

1. The concept of the public enterprise was discussed in Newcomer and Kee (2011). Some materials in this Introduction are drawn from that article.

CHAPTER ONE

1. This is close to the definition found in Bryson, Crosby, and Stone (2006), while adding the concepts of voluntariness, decision making, and risk.

2. The screeners are overseen by Transportation Security Administration supervisors; they use the same X-ray and scanning equipment and wear similar uniforms, but they work for a private company.

CHAPTER TWO

1. In a few days Walmart provided $20 million in cash donations, 1,500 truckloads of free merchandise, food for 100,000 meals, and the promise of a job for every one of its displaced workers (Barbaro and Gillis 2005).

2. This view is reflected in a widely circulated quote by economist Milton Friedman, who was noted for his skepticism of corporate social responsibility. He argued the points in "The Social Responsibility of Business Is to Increase Its Profits" (1970).

CHAPTER THREE

1. The most famous example is the apostle Matthew in the New Testament.

2. *Managed competition* also is a term used in the health care industry and has a different application from the discussion in this chapter on contracting and outsourcing.

3. The Bell Report was named after Budget Bureau Director David Bell.

CHAPTER FOUR

1. Thirty-four states have adopted legislation to authorize a special form of partnerships (called P3s) that promote public infrastructure.

CHAPTER SEVEN

1. For a more detailed discussion of these cases, see Kee and Newcomer (2007, 2008) and Brown, Potoski, and Van Slyke (2013) for the Deepwater case. These materials were supplemented with additional interviews of key actors by the authors.

2. *Interoperability* refers to the capacity to easily coordinate assets to carry out variable tasks across the Coast Guard's operational divisions and units and sometimes in concert with the Department of the Navy. For example, sea assets must be able to coordinate their actions with air assets.

3. Shadow tolls involve payments by the government based on use. Instead of the users paying actual tolls, the government pays tolls based on the number of users of the road or facility. Payments based on accessibility are made based on the availability of the road or facility for users, without any tolling—actual or shadow.

4. For a detailed ten-step process for conducting cost-benefit and cost-effectiveness analysis, see Cellini and Kee (2010). For cost-benefit analysis, see also Boardman et al. (2006), and for cost-effectiveness analysis, see Levin and McEwan (2000).

CHAPTER EIGHT

1. Deming's total quality management movement (TQM) is an integrative philosophy of management for continuously improving the quality of products

and processes. It functions on the premise that the quality of products and processes is the responsibility of everyone who is involved with the creation or consumption of the products or services offered by an organization.

CHAPTER TEN

1. O. C. McSwite is a pseudonym for Orion F. White, professor emeritus of public administration at the Center for Public Administration and Policy at Virginia Polytechnic Institute and State University, and Cynthia J. McSwain, former professor of public administration at the George Washington University.

2. Bozeman's process approach focuses on procedures, whereas McSwite argues for a more organic collaborative dialogue built around relationships and shared responsibility.

3. *Crowdsourcing* is an organized attempt to leverage the knowledge of thousands (in some cases, millions) of Internet users with disparate interests toward a common goal (Brabham, Sanchez, and Bartholomew 2009). The more people involved, the greater its value.

REFERENCES

INTRODUCTION

Bobbitt, Philip. 2002. *The Shield of Achilles: War, Peace, and the Course of History.* New York: Knopf.

Goldstein, Mark. 1992. *America's Hollow Government: How Washington Has Failed the People.* Homewood, IL: Irwin.

Kee, James Edwin, and Kathryn E. Newcomer. 2008. *Transforming Public and Nonprofit Organizations: Stewardship for Leading Change.* McLean, VA: Management Concepts.

Kettl, Donald. 1997. "The Global Revolution in Public Management: Driving Themes, Missing Links." *Journal of Policy Analysis and Management* 16(3):446–62.

Milward, H. Brinton, and Keith G. Provan. 2000. "Governing the Hollow State." *Journal of Public Administration Research and Theory* 10(2):359–79.

Newcomer, Kathryn E., and James Edwin Kee. 2011. "Federalist 23: Can the Leviathan Be Managed?" *Public Administration Review* 71(Supp. 1):537–46.

Salamon, Lester M. 2002. "The Tools Approach and the New Governance: Conclusions and Implications." In *The Tools of Government: A Guide to the New Governance*, edited by L. M. Salamon. New York: Oxford University Press.

Savas, E. S. 2000. *Privatization and Public-Private Partnerships.* New York: Chatham House.

CHAPTER ONE

Agranoff, Robert. 2003. *Leveraging Networks: A Guide to Public Managers Working Across Organizations.* Washington, DC: IBM Endowment for the Business of Government.

AidMatrix. 2013. http://www.aidmatrix.org/.

Bill and Melinda Gates Foundation. 2013. "Foundation Fact Sheet." http://www.gatesfoundation.org/.

Boris, Elizabeth T., Erwin de Leon, Katie L. Roeger, and Milena Nikolova. 2010. *Human Service Nonprofits and Government Collaboration: Findings of the 2010 National Survey of Nonprofit Government Contracts and Grants.* Washington, DC: Urban Institute.

Bowman, Ann, and Richard C. Kearney. 2011. *State and Local Government: The Essentials.* 5th ed. Boston: Wadsworth, Cengage Learning.

Brown, Trevor L. 2008. "The Dynamics of Government-to-Government Contracts." *Public Performance and Management Review* 31(3):364–86.

Bryson, John, Barbara C. Crosby, and Mellissa Middleton Stone. 2006. "The Design and Implementation of Cross-Sector Collaborations: Propositions from the Literature." *Public Administration Review* 66(Suppl. 1):44–55.

Center for Climate and Energy Solutions. 2014. "Historical Global CO_2 Emissions." http://www.c2es.org/facts-figures/international-emissions/historical.

Conlan, Timothy J., and Paul Posner, eds. 2008. *Intergovernmental Management for the 21st Century.* Washington, DC: Brookings Institution.

Derthick, Martha. 1996. *Whither Federalism?* Washington DC: Urban Institute.

Donahue, John D., and Richard J. Zeckhauser. 2011. *Collaborative Governance: Private Roles for Public Goals in Turbulent Times.* Princeton, NJ: Princeton University Press.

Gallup Politics. 2012. "In U.S., Trust in State, Local Governments Up." September 26. http://www.gallup.com/poll/157700/trust-state-local-governments.aspx.

Gallup Politics. 2013. "Americans' Satisfaction with U.S. Gov't Drops to New Low." http://www.gallup.com/poll/165371/americans-satisfaction-gov-drops-new-low.aspx.

Global Alliance for Improved Nutrition. 2011. "About Gain." http://www.gainhealth.org/about-gain.

Global Network for Neglected Tropical Diseases. 2013. http://www.globalnetwork.org/.

Goldstein, Mark. 1992. *America's Hollow Government: How Washington Has Failed the People.* Homewood, IL: Irwin.

International Federation of Red Cross and Red Crescent Societies. 2013. "History." http://www.ifrc.org/history.

Kee, James Edwin, and Kathryn E. Newcomer. 2008. *Transforming Public and Nonprofit Organizations: Stewardship for Leading Change.* McLean, VA: Management Concepts.

Kettl, Donald. 1997. "The Global Revolution in Public Management: Driving Themes, Missing Links." *Journal of Policy Analysis and Management* 16(3):446–62.

Kettl, Donald. 2006. "Managing Boundaries in American Administration: The Collaboration Imperative." *Public Administration Review* 66(Suppl. 1):10–19.

Koliba, Christopher, Jack Meek, and Asim Azia. 2011. *Governance Networks in Public Administration and Public Policy.* Baton Raton, FL: CRC Press.

Light, Paul. 1999. *The True Size of Government.* Washington, DC: Brookings Institution.

Milward, H. Brinton, and Keith C. Provan. 2006. *A Manager's Guide to Choosing and Using Networks.* Washington, DC: IBM Center for the Business of Government.

National Center for Charitable Statistics. 2012. "NCCS Databases and Tools." Washington, DC: Urban Institute. http://nccs.urban.org/NCCS-Databases-and-Tools.cfm.

National Council for Public-Private Partnerships. 1999. *City of Dallas/Dallas Public Library.* http://www.ncppp.org/cases/dallas.shtml.

National Council for Public-Private Partnerships. 2009. *Yuma Desert Proving Grounds, Yuma,* Arizona. http://ncppp.org/cases/YumaProvingGrounds.shtml.

National Council for Public-Private Partnerships. 2012. *PPP Case Studies.* http://www.ncppp.org/cases/index.shtml.

National Geographic. 2011. "Effects of Global Warming: Signs Are Everywhere." http://environment.nationalgeographic.com/environment/global-warming/gw-effects/.

Newcomer, Kathryn E., ed. 1997. *Using Performance Measurement to Improve Public and Nonprofit Programs.* San Francisco: Jossey-Bass.

Newcomer, Kathryn E., and James Edwin Kee. 2011. "Federalist 23: Can the Leviathan Be Managed?" *Public Administration Review* 71(Suppl. 1):537–46.

O'Toole, Laurence J., ed. 2006. *American Intergovernmental Relations.* 4th ed. Washington DC: CQ Press.

O'Toole, Laurence J., and Kenneth I. Hanf. 2002. "American Public Administration and Impacts of International Governance." *Public Administration Review* 62(1):158–69.

Pachauri, R. K., and A. Reisinger, eds. 2008. *Climate Change 2007: Synthesis Report.* Geneva, Switzerland: Intergovernmental Panel on Climate Change. http://www.ipcc.ch/pdf/assessment-report/ar4/syr/ar4_syr_cover.pdf.

Provan, Keith G., and Howard B. Milward. 1995. "A Preliminary Theory of Interorganizational Effectiveness: A Comparative Study of Four Community Mental Health Systems." *Administrative Science Quarterly* 40(1):1–33.

Rainforest Alliance. 2013. http://www.rainforest-alliance.org/.

Ridley-Duff, R. J., and M. Bull. 2011. *Understanding Social Enterprise: Theory and Practice*. London: SAGE.

Rosenau, James N. 1990. *Turbulence in World Politics: A Theory of Change and Continuity*. Princeton, NJ: Princeton University Press.

Salamon, Lester M. 2002. "The Tools Approach and the New Governance: Conclusions and Implications." In *The Tools of Government: A Guide to the New Governance*, edited by Lester M. Salamon. New York: Oxford University Press.

Savas, E. S. 2000. *Privatization and Public-Private Partnerships*. New York: Chatham House.

Scholte, Jan Aart. 2005. *Globalization: A Critical Introduction*. 2nd ed. London: Palgrave Macmillan.

US Environmental Protection Agency. 2011. *Climate Change: Health and Environmental Effects*. http://epa.gov/climatechange/effects/health.html.

US Office of Personnel Management. 2011. *Historical Federal Workforce Tables: Executive Branch Civilian Employment Since 1940*. Washington, DC: Office of Personnel Management.

Verkuil, Paul R. 2007. *Why Privatization of Government Functions Threatens Democracy and What We Can Do About It*. Cambridge: Cambridge University Press.

Wettenhall, Roger. 2003. "The Rhetoric and Reality of Public–Private Partnerships." *Public Organization Review* 3:77–107.

Wolfe, Martin. 2004. *Why Globalization Works*. New Haven, CT: Yale University Press.

CHAPTER TWO

Adams, Guy B., and Danny L. Balfour. 2004. *Unmasking Administrative Evil*. Armonk, NY: M. E. Sharpe.

Agranoff, Robert. 2012. *Collaborating to Manage: A Primer for the Public Sector*. Washington, DC: Georgetown University Press.

Allen, Thad W. 2010. "Unprecedented Events: Unprecedented Leadership Challenges." Speech presented at George Washington University, Washington, DC.

Axelrod, Nancy R. 1994. "Board Leadership and Board Development." In *The Jossey-Bass Handbook of Nonprofit Leadership and Management*, edited by Robert D. Herman. San Francisco: Jossey-Bass.

Barbaro, Michael, and Justine Gillis. 2005. "Wal-Mart at Front in Hurricane Relief." *Washington Post*, September 6.

Baron, David. 2013. *Business and Its Environment*. 7th ed. Boston: Pearson.

Baur, Dorothea, and Hans Peter Schmitz. 2012. "Corporations and NGOs: When Accountability Leads to Co-optation." *Journal of Business Ethics* 106(1):9–21.

Behn, Robert D. 2001. *Rethinking Democratic Accountability*. Washington, DC: Brookings Institution.

Bozeman, Barry. 2002. "Public-Value Failure: When Efficient Markets May Not Do." *Public Administration Review* 62(2):145–61.

Bozeman, Barry. 2007. *Public Values and Public Interest: Counterbalancing Economic Individualism*. Washington, DC: Georgetown University Press.

Brooks, A. C. 2002. "Can Nonprofit Management Help Answer Public Management's 'Big Questions'?" *Public Administration Review* 62(3):259–66.

Bryson, John M., Barbara C. Crosby, and Melissa Middleton Stone. 2006. "The Design and Implementation of Cross-Sector Collaborations: Propositions from the Literature." *Public Administration Review* 66(Suppl. 1):44–55.

Buchanan, James M., and Richard E. Wagner. 1977. *Democracy in Deficit: The Political Legacy of Lord Keynes*. New York: Academic Press.

Centers for Disease Control and Prevention. 2013. *Overweight and Obesity: Data and Statistics*. http://www. cdc.gov/obesity/data/childhood.html/.

Centers for Disease Control and Prevention. 2014. "New CDC Data Show Encouraging Development in Obesity Rates Among 2 to 5 Year Olds." Press release. http://www.cdc.gov/media/releases/2014/p0225-child-obesity.html.

Chandler, David, and William Werther, Jr. 2014. *Strategic Corporate Social Responsibility: Stakeholders, Globalization, and Sustainable Value Creation*. 3rd ed. Thousand Oaks, CA: SAGE.

Childhood Obesity Prevention Coalition. 2014. "Shared-Use Toolkit." http://copcwa.org/.

Cooper, Terry L. 1990. *The Responsible Administrator: An Approach to Ethics for the Administrative Role*. 3rd ed. San Francisco: Jossey-Bass.

Crosby, B. C., and J. M., Bryson. 2005. *Leadership for the Common Good: Tackling Public Problems in a Shared-Power World*. 2nd ed. San Francisco: Jossey-Bass.

Demsetz, Harold. 1967. "Toward a Theory of Property Rights." *American Economic Review* 57(2):347–59.

DiMaggio, Paul J., and Walter W. Powell. 1983. "The Iron Cage Revisited: Institutional Isomorphism and Collective Rationality in Organizational Fields." *American Sociological Review* 48:147–60.

Donahue, John D., and Richard J. Zeckhauser. 2011. *Collaborative Governance: Private Roles for Public Goals in Turbulent Times*. Princeton, NJ: Princeton University Press.

Downs, Anthony. 1967. *Inside Bureaucracy*. Longrove, IL: Waveland Press.

Entwistle, T., and S. Martin. 2005. "From Competition to Collaboration in Public Service Delivery: A New Agenda for Research." *Public Administration* 83(1):233–42.

Feigenbaum, Harvey, Jeffrey Henig, and Chris Hamnett. 1998. *Shrinking the State: The Political Underpinnings of Privatization*. Cambridge: Cambridge University Press.

Forrer, John, James Edwin Kee, Kathryn Newcomer, and Eric Boyer. 2010. "Public-Private Partnerships and the Accountability Question." *Public Administration Review* 70(3):475–84.

Fox, Elliot M., and L. F. Urwick. 1973. *Dynamic Administration: The Collective Papers of Mary Parker Follett*. London: Camelot Press.

Friedman, Milton. 1970. "The Social Responsibility of Business Is to Increase Its Profits." *New York Times Magazine,* September 13.

Gazley, Beth. 2008. "Beyond the Contract: The Scope and Nature of Informal Government-Nonprofit Partnerships." *Public Administration Review* 68(1):141–54.

Guttman, Dan. 2011. *Government by Contract: Considering a Public Service Ethics to Match the Reality of the "Blended" Public Workforce*. Washington, DC: Johns Hopkins University, Center for Advanced Government Studies.

Hodge, Graeme. A., and Ken Coghill. 2007. "Accountability in the Privatized State." *Governance: An International Journal of Policy Administration and Institutions* 20(4):675–702.

Hoffman, E., K. McCabe, K. Shachat, and V. Smith. 1994. "Preferences, Property Rights, and Anonymity in Bargaining Games." *Games and Economic Behavior* 7(3):346–80.

Huxham, Chris, and Siv Vangen. 2005. *Managing to Collaborate: The Theory and Practice of Collaborative Advantage*. London: Routledge.

Kale, Prashant, and Harbir Singh. 2007. "Building Firm Capabilities Through Learning: The Role of the Alliance Learning Process in Alliance Capability and Firm-Level Alliance Success." *Strategic Management Journal* 28(10):981–1000.

Kanter, Rossbeth Moss. 1994. "Collaborative Advantage: The Art Of Alliances." *Harvard Business Review* 72(4):96–108.

Kass, H. D. 1990. "Stewardship as a Fundamental Element." In *Image and Identity in Public Administration*, edited by H. D. Kass and Bayard L. Catron. Newbury Park, CA: SAGE.

Kee, James Edwin, and Kathryn Newcomer. 2008. *Transforming Public and Nonprofit Organizations: Stewardship for Leading Change*. Vienna, VA: Management Concepts.

Kettl, Donald. 2006. "Managing Boundaries in American Administration: The Collaboration Imperative." *Public Administration Review* 66(Suppl. 1):10–19.

Lawrence, Anne, and James Weber. 2014. *Business and Society: Stakeholders, Ethics, Public Policy*. New York: McGraw-Hill.

Lipsky, Michael. 1980. *Street Level Bureaucracy: Dilemmas of the Individual in Public Services*. New York: Russell Sage Foundation.

Lynn, Laurence E., Jr., 2006. *Public Management: Old and New*. New York: Routledge.

Milward, H. Brinton, and Keith G. Provan. 2006. *A Manager's Guide to Choosing and Using Collaborative Networks*. Washington, DC: IBM Center for the Business of Government. http://www.businessofgovernment. org/report/managers-guide-choosing-and-using-collaborative-networks.

Moe, Ronald. 1994. "The 'Reinventing Government' Exercise: Misinterpreting the Problem, Misjudging the Consequences. *Public Administration Review* 54(4):446–62.

Moe, Ronald. 2001. "The Emerging Federal Quasi Government: Issues of Management and Accountability." *Public Administration Review* 61(3):290–312.

Mowla, Mohammad Masrurul. 2012. "An Overview of Strategic Alliance: Competitive Advantages in Alliance Constellations." *Journal of Business Management and Corporate Affairs* 1(1):1–10.

National Commission on the BP Deepwater Horizon Oil Spill and Offshore Drilling. 2011. *Deepwater: The Gulf Oil Disaster and the Future of Offshore Drilling. Report to the President*. Washington, DC: National Commission on the BP Deepwater Horizon Oil Spill and Offshore Drilling.

Nelson, Jane. 2005. *Averaging the Development Impact of Business in the Fight Against Global Poverty*. Washington, DC: Brookings Institution.

Niskansen, William A. 1971. *Bureaucracy and Representative Government*. Chicago: Aldine-Atherton.

Norris-Tirrell, Dorothy, and Joy A. Clay, eds. 2010. *Strategic Collaboration in Public and Nonprofit Administration*. Boca Raton, FL: CRC Press.

O'Leary, Rosemary, and Nidhi Vij. 2012. "Collaborative Public Management: Where Have We Been and Where Are We Going?" *American Review of Public Administration* 42(5):507–22.

Osborne, David, and Ted Gaebler. 1993. *Reinventing Government: How the Entrepreneurial Spirit Is Transforming the Public Sector*. Reading, MA: Addison-Wesley.

Pollitt, Christopher, and Geert Bouckaert. 2011. *Public Management Reform: A Comparative Analysis—New Public Management and the Neo-Weberian State*. 3rd ed. Oxford: Oxford University Press.

Porter, Michael E., and Mark R. Kramer. 2011. "Creating Shared Value." *Harvard Business Review* 89(1/2):62–77.

Rittel, Horst W. J., and Melvin M. Webber. 1973. "Dilemmas in a General Theory of Planning." *Policy Sciences* 4(2):55–69.

Salamon, Lester M. 1987. "Of Market Failure, Voluntary Failure, and Third-Party Government: Toward a Theory of Government-Nonprofit Relations in the Modern Welfare State." *Journal of Voluntary Action Research* 16(1–2):29–49.

Salamon, Lester M. 2002. "The Tools Approach and the New Governance: Conclusions and Implications." In *The Tools of Government: A Guide to the New Governance*, edited by L. M. Salamon. New York: Oxford University Press.

Schooner, Steven L. 2001. "Fear of Oversight: The Fundamental Failure of Business-Like Government." *American University Law Review* 50(3):627–723.

Sclar, Elliott D. 2000. *You Don't Always Get What You Pay For: The Economics of Privatization*. Ithaca, NY: Cornell University Press.

Selden, S., J. E. Sowa, and J. Sandfort. 2002. "The Impact of Nonprofit Collaboration in Early Child Care and Education on Management and Program Outcomes." *Public Administration Review* 66(3):412–25.

Senge, Peter M. 2006. *The Fifth Discipline: The Art and Practice of the Learning Organization*. New York: Doubleday.

Shiffman, Jeremy. 2008. "Has Donor Prioritization of HIV/AIDS Displaced Aid for Other Health Issues?" *Health Policy and Planning* 23(2):95–100.

Steensma, H. Kevin, Laszlo Tihanyi, Marjorie A. Lyles, and Charles Dhanaraj. 2005. "The Evolving Value of Foreign Partnerships in Transitioning Economies." *Academy of Management Journal* 48(2):213–35.

Steinberg, Richard. 2006. "Economic Theories of Nonprofit Organizations." In *The Nonprofit Sector: A Research Handbook*, edited by Walter W. Powell and Richard Steinberg. New Haven, CT: Yale University Press.

Terry, Larry D. 1995. *Leadership of Public Bureaucracies: The Administrator as Conservator.* Thousand Oaks, CA: SAGE.

Thomson, Ann M., and James. L. Perry. 2006. "Collaboration Processes: Inside the Black Box." *Public Administration Review* 66(Suppl. 1):20–32.

Tiebout, Charles M. 1956. "A Pure Theory of Local Expenditures." *Journal of Political Economy* 64(5):416–24.

Uddin, Mohammed Belal, and Bilkis Akhter. 2011. "Strategic Alliances and Competitiveness: Theoretical Framework." *Journal of Arts, Science, and Commerce* 2(1):43–55.

US National Aeronautics and Space Administration. 2008. *Tunnel of Terror: Systems Failure Case Studies.* http://pbma.nasa.gov/docs/public/pbma/images/msm/big_dig_sfcs.pdf.

Weber, Edward P., and Anne M. Khademian. 2008. "Wicked Problems, Knowledge Challenges, and Collaborative Capacity Builders in Network Settings." *Public Administration Review* 68(2):334–49.

Wolf, Charles. 1978. *A Theory of Nonmarket Failure: Framework for Implementation Analysis.* Santa Monica, CA: Rand. http://130.154.3.14/content/dam/rand/pubs/papers/2006/P6034.pdf.

Wolf, Charles. 2001. "The Emerging Federal Quasi Government: Issues of Management and Accountability." *Public Administration Review* 61(3):290–312.

Wood, Donna J., and Barbara Gray. 1991. "Toward a Comprehensive Theory of Collaboration." *Journal of Applied Behavioral Science* 27(2):139–62.

CHAPTER THREE

American Federation of State, County, and Municipal Employees. 2014. *Government for Sale.* 8th ed. http://www.afscme.org/newspublication/publication/privitization/pdf/GovernmentSale.pdf.

Bell, David. 1962. *Report to the President on Government Contracting for Research and Development.* Document No. 94. Washington, DC: US Senate, 87th Congress, 2nd Session.

Bertelli, Anthony, and Craig R. Smith. 2009. "Relational Contracting and Network Management." *Journal of Public Administration Research and Theory* 20 (1):21–40.

Boston, Jonathon. 1994. "Purchasing Policy Advice." *Governance* 7(1):1–30.

Brown, Trevor L., and Matthew Potoski. 2003. "Transaction Costs and Institutional Explanations for Government Service Production Decisions." *Journal of Public Administration Research and Theory* 13(4):441–68.

Brown, Trevor L., Matthew Potoski, and David M. Van Slyke. 2008. *The Challenge of Contracting for Large Complex Projects: A Case Study of the Coast Guard's Deepwater Program.* Washington, DC: IBM Center for the Business of Government.

Brown, Trevor L., Matthew Potoski, and David M. Van Slyke. 2010, "Contracting for Complex Products." *Journal of Public Administration Research and Theory* 20(Suppl. 1):41–58.

Brown, Trevor L., Matthew Potoski, and David M. Van Slyke. 2011. "Accountability Challenges in Public Sector Contracting for Complex Products." In *Accountable Governance: Problems and Promises*, edited by Melvin J. Dubnick and H. George Frederickson. New York: M. E. Sharpe.

Bryson, John M. 2011. *Strategic Planning for Public and Nonprofit Organizations.* 4th ed. San Francisco: Jossey-Bass.

Cooper, Phillip J. 2003. *Governing by Contract: Challenges and Opportunities for Public Managers.* Washington, DC: Congressional Quarterly Press.

DeHoog, Ruth Hoogland, and Lester M. Salamon. 2002. "Purchase-of-Service Contracting." In *The Tools of Government: A Guide to the New Governance*, edited by Lester M. Salamon. New York: Oxford University Press.

Domberger, S., and P. Jensen. 1997. "Contracting Out by the Public Sector: Theory, Evidence, Prospects." *Oxford Review of Economic Policy* 13(4):67–78.

Forrer, John, and James Edwin Kee. 2004. "Public Servants as Contract Managers?" *Public Contract Law Journal* 33(2):361–68.

Foster Care Kansas. 2013. "Foster Care in Kansas." http://www.fostercarekansas.org/.

Freundlich, Madelyn, and Sarah Gerstenzang. 2003. *Privatization of Child Welfare Services: Challenges and Successes*. Washington, DC: Child Welfare Services of America.

Gazley, Beth. 2008. "Beyond the Contract: The Scope and Nature of Informal Government-Nonprofit Partnerships." *Public Administration Review* 68(1):141–54.

Gietzmann, M. B. 1996. "Incomplete Contracts and the Make or Buy Decision: Governance Design and Attainable Flexibility." *Accounting Organizations and Society* 21(6):611–26.

Gore, Albert. 1993. *Creating a Government That Works Better and Costs Less*. Report of the National Performance Review. Washington, DC: US Government Printing Office.

Guttman, Daniel. 2000. "Public and Private Service: The Twentieth Century Culture of Contracting Out and the Evolving Law of Diffused Sovereignty." *Administrative Law Review* 52(3):859–926.

Guttman, Daniel. 2002. "Who's Doing Work for Government? Monitoring, Accountability and Competition in the Federal and Service Contract Workforce." Testimony before the US Senate, Committee on Governmental Affairs, March 6. http://www.gpo.gov/fdsys/pkg/CHRG-107shrg79883/html/CHRG-107shrg79883.htm.

Hardin, Russell. 2002. *Trust and Trustworthiness*. New York: Russell Sage.

Johnston, Jocelyn M., and Barbara S. Romzek. 2005. "Traditional Contracts as Partnerships: Effective Accountability in Social Services Contracts in the American States." In *The Challenge of Public-Private Partnerships*, edited by Graeme Hodge and Carsten Greve. Cheltenham, UK: Edward Elgar.

Kee, James Edwin. 2005. "Evaluating Contracting-Out and PPPs." PowerPoint presentation at The Evaluators Institute, Washington, DC.

Kelman, Steven J. 2002. "Contracting." In *The Tools of Government: A Guide to the New Governance*, edited by L. M. Salamon. New York: Oxford University Press.

Kettl, Donald. 1993. *Sharing Power: Public Governance and Private Markets*. Washington, DC: Brookings Institution.

Lonsdale, Chris. 2005. "Post-Contractual Lock-In and the UK Private Finance Initiative (PFI): The Cases of National Savings and Investments and the Lord Chancellor's Department." *Public Administration* 83(1):67–88.

Mayer, Holly A. 1999. *Belonging to the Army: Camp Follower and Community During the American Revolution*. Columbia: University of South Carolina Press.

Moten, Matthew. 2010. *The Army Officer's Professional Ethic—Past, Present, and Future*. http://www.dtic.mil/cgibin/GetTRDoc?AD=ADA514082&Location=U2&doc=GetTRDoc.pdf.

Organization for Economic Co-operation and Development. 2010. *Guidelines for Performance-based Contracts Between Water Utilities and Municipalities: Lessons Learnt from Eastern Europe, Caucasus and Central Asia*. Paris: Organization for Economic Co-operation and Development.

Petrie, Murray. 2002. *A Framework for Public Sector Performance Contracting*. Paris: Organization for Economic Co-operation and Development.

Price, Don K. 1965. *The Scientific Estate*. Cambridge, MA: Harvard University Press.

Savas, E. S. 2000. *Privatization and Public-Private Partnerships*. New York: Chatham House.

Sclar, Elliott D. 2000. *You Don't Always Get What You Pay For: The Economics of Privatization*. Ithaca, NY: Cornell University Press.

Tirole, Jean. 1999. "Incomplete Contracts: Where Do We Stand?" *Econometrica* 76(4):741–81.

US General Accountability Office. 2004. *Competitive Sourcing: Greater Emphasis Needed on Increasing Efficiency and Improving Performance* (GAO 04–367). Washington, DC: General Accountability Office.

US General Accountability Office. 2011. *High Risk Series: An Update* (GAO 11–278). Washington, DC: General Accountability Office.

US Office of Management and Budget. 2008. *Competitive Sourcing: Report on Competitive Sourcing Results, FY 2007*. Washington, DC: Executive Office of the President.

US Office of Management and Budget. 2011. "Policy Letter 11–01." *Federal Register* 76:176, September 12.

Van Slyke, David M. 2009. "Collaboration and Relational Contracting." In *The Collaborative Public Manager: New Ideas for the 21st Century*, edited by Rosemary O'Leary and Lisa Blomgren Bingham. Washington, DC: Georgetown University Press.

Walker, David. 2002. *Commercial Activities Panel: Final Report* (GAO 02–866T). Washington, DC: US Government Accountability Office.

Zaheer, Akbar, and N. Venkatraman. 1995. "Relational Governance as an Interorganizational Strategy: An Empirical Test of the Role of Trust in Economic Exchange." *Strategic Management Journal* 16(5):373–92.

CHAPTER FOUR

Abadie, Richard. 2008. "Using Private Finance to Fund Public Infrastructure." In *Presentation to Vancouver Board of Trade*. Vancouver, BC: Pricewaterhouse Coopers, LLP.

Alexander, Rob. 2012. "Network Structures and the Performance of Brownfield Redevelopment PPPs." *Public Performance and Management Review* 35(4):753–68.

American Society of Civil Engineers. 2013. *Report Card for America's Infrastructure*. http://www.infrastructurereportcard.org/a/#p/grade-sheet/americas-infrastructure-investment-needs.

Andrews, Rhys, and Tom Entwistle. 2010. "Does Cross-Sectoral Partnership Deliver? An Empirical Exploration of Public Service Effectiveness, Efficiency, and Equity." *Journal of Public Administration Research and Theory* 20(3):679–701.

Bain, David Howard. 1999. *Empire Express: Building the First Transcontinental Railroad*. New York: Viking Press.

Blau, P. M. 1964. *Exchange and Power in Social Life*. New York: Wiley.

Boardman, Anthony E., Finn Poschmann, and Aidan R. Vining. 2005. "North American Infrastructure P3s: Examples and Lessons Learned." In *The Challenge of Public-Private Partnerships: Learning from International Experience*, edited by Graeme Hodge and Carsten Greve. Cheltenham, UK: Edward Elgar.

Bovaird, Tony. 2004. "Public-Private Partnerships: From Contested Concepts to Prevalent Practice." *International Review of Administrative Sciences* 70(2): 199–215.

Boyer, Eric. 2012. "Building Capacity for Cross-Sector Collaboration: How Transportation Agencies Build Skills and Systems to Manage Public-Private Partnerships." Ph.D. diss., George Washington University.

Boyer, Eric. 2013. "Government Learning in Public-Private Partnerships: Lessons from the Field." Working paper, Georgia Institute of Technology, Atlanta.

Boyer, Eric J., Gordon Kingsley, and Christopher M. Weible. 2013. "Evaluating Prime and Subcontractor Relations in the Georgia Department of Transportation." Working paper, Georgia Institute of Technology, Atlanta.

Brabham, Daren C. 2009. "Crowdsourcing the Public Participation Process for Planning Projects." *Planning Theory* 8(3):242–62.

Brabham, Daren C. 2010. "Crowdsourcing: A Model for Leveraging Online Communities." In *The Routledge Handbook of Participatory Cultures*, edited by Aaron Dewwiche and Jennifer Henderson. New York: Routledge.

Brown, Trevor L., Matthew Potoski, and David M. Van Slyke. 2006. "Managing Public Service Contracts: Aligning Values, Institutions, and Markets." *Public Administration Review* 66(3):323–31.

Buxbaum, Jeffrey N., and Iris N. Ortiz. 2009. "Public Sector Decision Making for Public-Private Partnerships: A Synthesis of Highway Practice." National Cooperative Highway Research Program. Washington, DC: Transportation Research Board.

Chen, Bin, and Elizabeth A. Graddy. 2010. "The Effectiveness of Nonprofit Lead-Organization Networks for Social Service Delivery." *Nonprofit Management and Leadership* 20(4):405–22.

Delmon, Jeffrey. 2010. *Understanding Options for Public-Private Partnerships in Infrastructure—Sorting Out the Forest from the Trees: BOT, DBFO, DCMF, Concession, Lease.* Washington, DC: World Bank.

Eggers, William, and Stephen Goldsmith. 2004. *Government by Networks: The New Public Management Imperative.* Cambridge, MA: Ash Institute for Governance and Innovation, Harvard Kennedy School.

Entwistle, T., and S. Martin. 2005. "From Competition to Collaboration in Public Service Delivery: A New Agenda for Research." *Public Administration* 83(1):233–42.

Forrer, John, James Edwin Kee, Kathryn Newcomer, and Eric Boyer. 2010. "Public Private Partnerships and the Public Accountability Question." *Public Administration Review* 70(3):475–84.

Forrer, J., J. E. Kee, and Z. Zhang. 2002. "Private Finance Initiative: A Better Public-Private Partnership. *Public Manager* 31(2):43–47.

Garvin, M. J. 2010. "Enabling Development of the Transportation Public-Private Partnership Market in the United States." *Journal of Construction Engineering and Management–ASCE* 136:402–11.

Gazley, Beth. 2008. "Beyond the Contract: The Scope and Nature of Informal Government-Nonprofit Partnerships." *Public Administration Review* 68(1):141–54.

Gazley, Beth, and Jeffrey L. Brudney. 2007. "The Purpose (and Perils) of Government-Nonprofit Partnership." *Nonprofit and Voluntary Sector Quarterly* 36(3):389–415.

Geddes, R. Richard. 2011. *The Road to Renewal: Private Investment in US Transportation Infrastructure.* Washington, DC: AEI Press.

Goldfarb, Zachary A. 2013. "Obama Visits Miami Port to Push Plan to Rebuild Roads, Bridges, Other Infrastructure." *Washington Post*, March 29. http://www.washingtonpost.com/business/economy/obama-visits-miami-port-to-push-plan-to-rebuild-roads-bridges-other-infrastructure/2013/03/29/3dacb07e-98a1-11e2-b68f-dc5c4b47e519_story.html.

Grimsey, Darrin, and Mervyn K. Lewis. 2007. *Public Private Partnerships: The Worldwide Revolution in Infrastructure Provision and Project Finance.* Northampton, MA: Edward Elgar.

Gulati, Ranjay, Dovev Lavie, and Harbir Singh. 2009. "The Nature of Partnering Experience and the Gains from Alliances." *Strategic Management Journal* 30(11):1213–33.

Hodge, G. A., and K. Coghill. 2007. "Accountability in the Privatized State." *Governance: An International Journal of Policy, Administration, and Institutions* 20(4):675–702.

International Finance Corporation. 2013. *Emerging Partnerships.* Washington, DC: World Bank. http://www.ifc.org/wps/wcm/connect/511912004ebc2c059d48bd45b400a808/EmergingPartnerships_FINAL_Web.pdf?MOD=AJPERES.

Istrate, Emilia, and Robert Puentes. 2011. *Moving Forward with Public Private Partnerships: US and International Experience with PPP Units.* Washington, DC: Brookings Institution.

Johnston, Jocelyn M., and Barbara S. Romzek. 2005. "Traditional Contracts as Partnerships: Effective Accountability in Social Services Contracts in the American States." In *The Challenge of Public-Private Partnerships*, edited by Graeme Hodge and Carsten Greve. Cheltenham, UK: Edward Elgar.

Jooste, S. F., and W. R. Scott. 2012. "The Public-Private Partnership Enabling Field: Evidence from Three Cases." *Administration and Society* 44(2):149–82.

Kanter, R. M. 1994. "Collaborative Advantage—The Art of Alliances." *Harvard Business Review* 72(4):96–108.

Kapucu, Naim. 2006. "Public-Nonprofit Partnerships for Collective Action in Dynamic Contexts of Emergencies." *Public Administration* 84(1):205–20.

Kee, James Edwin, and Kathryn Newcomer. 2008. *Transforming Public and Nonprofit Organizations: Stewardship for Leading Change.* Vienna, VA: Management Concepts.

Kettl, Donald. 2002. "Managing Indirect Government." In *The Tools of Government*, edited by Lester M. Salamon, 490–510. New York: Oxford University Press.

Klijn, Erik-Hans, and Geert R. Teisman. 2003. "Institutional and Strategic Barriers to Public-Private Partnership: An Analysis of Dutch Cases." *Public Money and Management* 23(3):137–46.

Mendel, S. C., and J. L. Brudney. 2012. "Putting the NP in PPP: The Role of Nonprofit Organizations in Public-Private Partnerships." *Public Performance and Management Review* 35(4):617–42.

Nabatchi, Tina. 2012a. *A Manager's Guide to Evaluating Citizen Participation*. Washington, DC: IBM Center for the Business of Government.

Nabatchi, Tina. 2012b. "Putting the 'Public' Back in Public Values Research: Designing Participation to Identify and Respond to Values." *Public Administration Review* 72(5):699–708.

National Association of State Budget Officers. 2011. *Fall 2010 Fiscal Survey of States*. Washington, DC: National Association of State Budget Officers.

Ni, A. Y. 2012. "The Risk-Averting Game of Transport Public-Private Partnership: Lessons from the Adventure of California's State Route 91 Express Lanes." *Public Performance and Management Review* 36(2):253–74.

North, Douglass C. 1990. *Institutions, Institutional Change and Economic Performance*. Cambridge: Cambridge University Press.

Office of Government Commerce. 2003. *Effective Partnering: An Overview of Customers and Providers*. London, UK: Office of Government Commerce.

Ostrom, Elinor. 2000. "Collective Action and the Evolution of Social Norms." *Journal of Economic Perspectives* 14(3):137–58.

Patterson, Jean A. 2004. "What's the Bottom Line? Corporate Involvement in an Early Childhood Initiative." *Urban Review* 36(2):147–68.

Pfeffer, Jeffrey, and Gerald Salancik. 1978. *The External Control of Organizations: A Resource Dependence Perspective*. New York: Harper.

Pongsiri, Nutavoot. 2002. "Regulation and Public-Private Partnerships." *International Journal of Public Sector Management* 15(6):487–95.

Provan, Keith G., and Patrick Kenis. 2008. "Modes of Network Governance: Structure, Management, and Effectiveness." *Journal of Public Administration Research and Theory* 18(2):229–52.

Rainey, Hal. 2003. *Understanding and Managing Public Organizations*. 3rd ed. San Francisco: Jossey-Bass.

Rall, Jaime, James B. Reed, and Nicholas J. Farber. 2010. *Public-Private Partnerships for Transportation: A Toolkit for Legislators*. Denver: NCSL Partners Project on Public-Private Partnerships for Transportation, National Conference of State Legislatures.

Rittel, Horst W. J., and Melvin M. Webber. 1973. "Dilemmas in a General Theory of Planning." *Policy Sciences* 4(2):155–69.

Robinson, Herbert, Patricia Carrillo, Chimay J. Anumba, and Manju Patel. 2010. *Governance and Knowledge Management for Public Private Partnerships*. Oxford, UK: Wiley-Blackwell.

Saavedra, P., and B. Bozeman. 2004. "The 'Gradient Effect' in Federal Laboratory–Industry Technology Transfer Partnerships." *Policy Studies Journal* 32(2):235–52.

Savas, E. S. 2000. *Privatization and Public-Private Partnerships*. New York: Chatham House.

Suarez, D. F. 2010. "Collaboration and Professionalization: The Contours of Public Sector Funding for Nonprofit Organizations." *Journal of Public Administration Research and Theory* 21(2):307–26.

Te'eni, Dov, and Dennis R. Young. 2003. "The Changing Role of Nonprofits in the Network Economy." *Nonprofit and Voluntary Sector Quarterly* 32(3):397–414.

Thompson, J. D. 1967. *Organizations in Action*. New York: McGraw-Hill.

Van Slyke, David M. 2003. "The Mythology of Privatization in Contracting for Social Services." *Public Administration Review* 63(3):296–315.

Velotti, Lucia, Antonio Botti, and Massimiliano Vesci. 2012. "Public-Private Partnerships and Network Governance." *Public Performance and Management Review* 36(2): 340–65.

Whitaker, G. P. 1980. "Coproduction: Citizen Participation in Service Delivery." *Public Administration Review* 40(3):240–46.

Whitaker, G. P., L. Altman-Sauer, and M. Henderson. 2004. "Mutual Accountability Between Governments and Nonprofits: Moving Beyond Surveillance to Service." *American Review of Public Administration* 34(2):115–33.

Wholey, Joseph, Harry Hatry, and Kathryn E. Newcomer. 2010. *The Handbook of Practical Program Evaluation.* 3rd ed. San Francisco: Jossey-Bass.

Yescombe, E. R. 2007. *Public-Private Partnerships: Principles of Policy and Finance.* Oxford: Elsevier.

Zaheer, Akbar, and N. Venkatraman. 1995. "Relational Governance as an Interorganizational Strategy: An Empirical Test of the Role of Trust in Economic Exchange." *Strategic Management Journal* 16(5):373–92.

Zhang, X. 2005. "Paving the Way for Public-Private Partnerships in Infrastructure Development." *Journal of Construction Engineering and Management* 131(1):71–80.

CHAPTER FIVE

Agranoff, Robert. 2007. *Managing Within Networks: Adding Value to Public Organizations.* Washington, DC: Georgetown University Press.

Agranoff, Robert. 2012. *Collaborating to Manage: A Primer for the Public Sector.* Washington, DC: Georgetown University Press.

Hale, Thomas, and David Held, eds. 2011. *The Handbook of Transnational Governance: Institutions and Innovations.* Malden, MA: Polity.

Kapucu, Naim, and Montgomery van Wart. 2006. "The Evolving Role of the Public Sector in Managing Catastrophic Disasters." *Administration and Society* 38(3):279–308.

Kee, James Edwin, and John Forrer. 2012. "PPPs: E-SCAD or Partners in Service." *Public Integrity* 14(2):193–202.

Kennedy School of Government. 2006. *Hurricane Katrina (A): Preparing for "The Big One" in New Orleans.* Boston: Kennedy School of Government Case Program, Harvard University.

Lee, E.W.Y., and H. K. Liu. 2012. "Factors Influencing Network Formation Among Social Service Nonprofit Organizations in Hong Kong and Implications for Comparative and China Studies." *International Public Management Journal* 15(4):454–78.

McGuire, Michael. 2002. "Managing Networks: Propositions on What Managers Do and Why They Do It." *Public Administration Review* 62(5):599–609.

McGuire, Michael. 2006. "Collaborative Public Management: Assessing What We Know and How We Know It." *Public Administration Review* 66(6):33–43.

Milward, H. Brinton, and Keith G. Provan. 2003. "Managing Networks Effectively." Paper presented at the Seventh National Public Management Research Conference, Washington, DC, October. http://www.pmranet.org/conferences/georgetownpapers/Milward.pdf.

Milward, H. Brinton, and Keith G. Provan. 2006. "A Manager's Guide to Choosing and Using Collaborative Networks." Washington, DC: IBM Center for the Business of Government, 2006.

Moore, Jan. 2005. *Collaborations of Schools and Social Services Agencies.* Finalized draft, National Center for Homeless Education, Greensboro, NC. http://files.eric.ed.gov/fulltext/ED491199.pdf.

Provan, Keith G., and Patrick Kenis. 2008. "Modes of Network Governance: Structure, Management, and Effectiveness." *Journal of Public Administration Research and Theory* 18(2):229–52.

Provan, Keith G., and H. Brinton Milward. 1995. "A Preliminary Theory of Interorganizational Network Effectiveness: A Comparative Study of Four Community Mental Health Systems." *Administrative Science Quarterly* 40(1):1–33.

Provan, Keith G., and H. Brinton Milward. 2001. "Do Networks Really Work? A Framework for Evaluating Public-Sector Organizational Networks." *Public Administration Review* 61(4):414–23.

Silvia, Chris, and Michael McGuire. 2010. "Leading Public Sector Networks: An Empirical Examination of Integrative Leadership Behaviors." *Leadership Quarterly* 21(2):264–77.

Small Community Water Infrastructure Exchange. 2014. *The Small Community Water Infrastructure Exchange.* http://www.scwie.org/.

Turrini, Alex, Daniela Cristofoli, Francesca Frosini, and Greta Nasi. 2010. "Networking Literature About Determinants of Network Effectiveness." *Public Administration* 88(2):528–50.

United Nations Environmental Programme. 2001. *United Nations Environmental Programme Dams and Development Project.* http://www.unep.org/dams/.

US Department of Education. 2008. *Lessons Learned from School Crises and Emergencies.* Washington, DC: National Center for Educational Evaluation and Regional Assistance. http://rems.ed.gov/docs/LL_Vol3Issue2.pdf.

Zaheer, A., V. McEvily, and V. Perrone. 1998. "Does Trust Matter? Exploring the Effects of Interorganizational and Interpersonal Trust on Performance." *Organization Science* 9(2):141–59.

CHAPTER SIX

American Hospital Association. 2010. *AHA Research Synthesis Report: Accountable Care Organization.* Chicago: American Hospital Association.

Business Civic Leadership Center. 2012. *National Network for Sustainable Urban Mobility.* http://csr.bclcmaps.com/#!/projects/national-network-for-sustainable-urban-mobility.

Caterpillar. 2012. *First Response Team Uses Caterpillar Equipment to Save Lives.* http://www.caterpillar.com/cda/layout?m=412995&x=7&id=3265721.

Channel Industries Mutual Aid. 2014. "About CIMA." http://www.cimatexas.org/.

Congressional Budget Office. 2011. *Reducing the Deficit: Spending and Revenue Options: A CBO Study.* CBO Publication No. 4212. Washington, DC: US Government Printing Office.

Fisher, Elliot S. 2006. *Creating Accountable Care Organizations: The Extended Hospital Medical Staff.* http://content.healthaffairs.org/content/26/1/w44.abstract.

Fisher, Elliot S. 2009. *Slowing the Growth of Health Care Costs: Lessons from Regional Variation.* http://www.nejm.org/doi/full/10.1056/NEJMp0809794#t=article.

Forrer, John, Ridhima Kapur, and Leilani Greene. 2012. "Understanding Global Governance Networks: Organization and Leadership." Working Paper, Institute for Corporate Responsibility, George Washington University, Washington, DC.

Global Network for Neglected Tropical Diseases. 2013. "Mission Statement." http://www.globalnetwork.org/about.

Joint Venture—Silicon Valley Network. 2014. *Joint Venture—Silicon Valley Network: About Us.* http://www.jointventure.org/.

Kaiser Commission on Medicaid and the Uninsured. 2009. *Community Care of North Carolina: Putting Health Reform Ideas into Practice in Medicaid.* http://www.kff.org/medicaid/upload/7899.pdf.

Kosar, Kevin R. 2011. *The Quasi-Government: Hybrid Organizations with Both Government and Private Sector Legal Characteristics.* Washington, DC: Congressional Research Service.

Nelson, Bryn. 2009. "Quality over Quantity." *Hospitalist.* http://www.the-hospitalist.org/details/article/477391/Quality_over_Quantity.html.

Oregon Environmental Council. 2011. *Overview Report 2010–2011.* Portland: Oregon Environmental Council. http://www.oeconline.org/resources/publications/reportsandstudies/oec-overview-report-2010–201.

Peters, B. G., and John Pierre. 1998. "Governance Without Government? Rethinking Public Administration." *Journal of Public Administration Research and Theory* 8(2):223–43.

Rainforest Alliance. 2012. *2011 Annual Report.* Rainforest Alliance. http://www.rainforest-alliance.org/sites/default/files/about/annual_reports/annual-report2011.pdf.

Simmons, J. 2010. "The Medical Home as Community Effort." *Health Leaders.* http://www.healthleadersmedia. com/content/MAG-249300/Quality-The-Medical-Home-as-Community-Effort.

US General Accountability Office. 2008. "Surface Transportation: Restructured Approach Needed for More Focused Performance-based and Sustainable Program" (GAO-08-400). Washington, DC: U.S. General Accountability Office.

US Health and Human Services. 2014. "Medicare's Delivery System Reform Initiatives Achieve Significant Savings and Quality Improvements—Off to a Strong Start." Press release, January 30. http://www.hhs.gov/ news/press/2014pres/01/20140130a.html.

White House. 2013. "The President's Climate Action Plan." Executive Office of the President. http://www. whitehouse.gov/sites/default/files/image/president27sclimateactionplan.pdf.

CHAPTER SEVEN

Balanced Scorecard Institute. 2012. "Balanced Scorecard Basics." http://www.balancedscorecard.org/ BSCResources/AbouttheBalancedScorecard/tabid/55/ Default.aspx.

Boardman, A. A., D. H. Greenberg, A. R. Vining, and D. L. Veimer. 2006. *Cost-Benefit Analysis: Concepts and Practice.* 3rd ed. Upper Saddle River, NJ: Prentice Hall.

Brown, Trevor, Matthew Potoski, and David M. Van Slyke. 2013. *Complex Contracting: Government Purchasing in the Wake of the US Coast Guard's Deepwater Program.* Cambridge: Cambridge University Press.

Cellini, Stephanie Riegg, and James Edwin Kee. 2010. "Cost-Effectiveness and Cost-Benefit Analysis." In *Handbook of Practical Program Evaluation,* edited by Harry Hatry, Kathryn Newcomer, and Joseph Wholey. 3rd ed. San Francisco: Jossey-Bass.

Congressional Budget Office. 2011. *Reducing the Deficit: Spending and Revenue Options: A CBO Study.* CBO Publication No. 421. Washington, DC: US Government Printing Office.

Hatry, Harry. 2007. *Performance Management: Getting Results.* 2nd ed. Washington, DC: Urban Institute.

Her Majesty's Treasury. 2006. *Value for Money Assessment Guidance.* London: Her Majesty's Treasury.

Kee, James Edwin, and John Forrer. 2008. "Private Finance Initiative: The Theory and the Practice." *International Journal of Public Administration* 31(2):151–67.

Kee, James Edwin, and Kathryn E. Newcomer. 2007. *Leading Change, Managing Risk: The Leadership Role in Public Sector Transformation.* Washington, DC: Center for Innovation in Public Service, George Washington University.

Kee, James Edwin, and Kathryn E. Newcomer. 2008. *Transforming Public and Nonprofit Organizations: Stewardship for Leading Change.* McLean, VA: Management Concepts.

Kerali, Henry. 2012. "Public Sector Comparator for Highway PPP Projects." Presentation at the World Bank. http://siteresources.worldbank.org/INTTRANSPORT/Resources/336291–1122908670104/1504838– 1151587673078/PSCforHighwayPPPProjects-v2.pdf.

Koliba, Christopher, Jack W. Meek, and Asim Zia. 2011. *Governance Networks in Public Administration and Public Policy.* Boca Raton, FL: CRC Press.

Levin, Henry M., and Patrick J. McEwan. 2000. *Cost-Effectiveness Analysis.* 2nd ed. Thousand Oaks, CA: SAGE.

Milward, H. B., and K. G. Provan. 2000. "Governing the Hollow State." *Journal of Public Administration Research and Theory* 10(2):359–80.

N Street Village. 2011. "Mission Statement." http://www.nstreetvillage.org/about/.

Neely, Andy, Chris Adams, and Mike Kennerley. 2002. *The Performance Prism: The Scorecard for Measuring and Managing Business Success.* Bedford, UK: Cranfield University, School of Management.

Newcomer, Kathryn E., ed. 1997. *Using Performance Measurement to Improve Public and Nonprofit Programs.* San Francisco: Jossey Bass.

Newcomer, Kathryn E., ed. 2002. *Meeting the Challenges of Performance Oriented Government.* Washington, DC: American Society for Public Administration.

Newcomer, Kathryn E., Harry Hatry, and Joseph Wholey, eds. 2010. *Handbook of Practical Program Evaluation.* 3rd ed. San Francisco: Jossey-Bass.

Parker, David. 2009. "Editorial: PPP/PFI: Solution or Problem?" *Economic Affairs*, March, 2–6.

Sclar, Elliott D. 2000. *You Don't Always Get What You Pay For: The Economics of Privatization.* Ithaca, NY: Cornell University Press.

US General Accountability Office. 1997. *Privatization: Questions State and Local Decisionmakers Used When Considering Privatization Options.* Washington, DC: US General Accountability Office.

Way, Jerry. 2012. "Interview with Brandon Key," April 23, George Washington University.

Wyden, Ron, and Paul Ryan. 2011. "Guaranteed Choices to Strengthen Medicare and Health Security for All: Bipartisan Options for the Future." US House, Budget Committee. http://budget.house.gov/uploadedfiles/wydenryan.pdf.

Yasutani, Satoru. 2010. "Interview with Leon Corbett, Manager, and Diane Flowers, Project Finance Team, Financial Development Office, and Gary Drzewiecki, Finance and Revenue Manager, Financial Development Office, Florida Department of Transportation." March 4, Tallahassee, FL. Report from the GW Center for the Study of Globalization, George Washington University.

Yescombe, E. R. 2007. *Public-Private Partnerships: Principles of Policy and Finance.* Oxford: Elsevier.

CHAPTER EIGHT

Adler, Paul S., and Bryan Borys. 1996. "Two Types of Bureaucracy: Enabling and Coercive." *Administrative Science Quarterly* 41(1):61–89.

Agranoff, Robert. 2007. *Managing Within Networks: Adding Value to Public Organizations.* Washington, DC: Georgetown University Press.

Agranoff, Robert, and Michael McGuire. 2003. *Collaborative Public Management: New Strategies for Local Governments.* Washington, DC: Georgetown University Press.

Allan, Kenneth D. 2005. *Explorations in Classical Sociological Theory: Seeing the Social World.* Thousand Oaks, CA: Pine Forge Press/SAGE.

Amy, Douglas J. 2011. "Government Is Good: The Case for Bureaucracy." http://governmentisgood.com/articles.php?aid=20&print=1.

Barzelay, M., and Armajani, B. J. 1992. *Breaking Through Bureaucracy: A New Vision for Managing in Government.* Berkeley: University of California Press.

Behn, Robert. 1998. "What Right Do Public Managers Have to Lead?" *Public Administration Review* 58(3):209–24.

Bresser Pereira, Luiz Carlos, and P. Spink. 1999. *Reforming the State: Managerial Administration in Latin America.* Boulder, CO: Lynne Rienner.

Deming, W. Edward. 1986. *Out of Crisis.* Cambridge, MA: MIT Center for Advanced Engineering Study.

Denhardt, Janet V., and Robert B. Denhardt. 2011. *The New Public Service.* 3rd ed. Armonk, NY: M. E. Sharp.

Diver, Colin. 1982. "Engineers and Entrepreneurs: The Dilemma of Public Management." *Journal of Policy Analysis and Management* 1(3):402–406.

Follett, Mary Parker. 2003. In *Mary Parker Follett: Prophet of Management*, edited by Pauline Graham. Washington, DC: Beard Books.

Follett, Mary Parker. 2007. "The Giving of Orders." In *Classics of Public Administration*, edited by Jay M. Shafritz and Albert C. Hyde. 6th ed. Belmont, CA: Wadsworth.

Forrer, John, and James Edwin Kee. 2008. "Private Finance Initiative: The Theory Behind the Practice." *Journal of International Public Administration* 31(2):151–67.

Freedberg, Syndey J. Jr. 2005. "In One Louisiana Parish, Flexibility Trumps Bureaucracy." *National Journal*, "Daily Briefing," October 11.

Friedman, Milton. 1962. *Capital and Freedom.* Chicago: University of Chicago Press.

Goldsmith, Stephen, and William D. Eggers. 2004. *Governing by Network: The New Face of the Public Sector.* Washington, DC: Brookings Institution Press.

Goodsell, Charles T. 2004. *The Case for Bureaucracy: A Public Administration Polemic.* 4th ed. Washington, DC: CQ Press.

Gore, Albert. 1993. *Creating a Government That Works Better and Costs Less.* Washington DC: US Government Printing Office.

Hayek, Friedrich. 1944. *The Road to Serfdom.* London: Routledge.

Hooghe, Liesbet. 2001. *The European Commission and the Integration of Europe: Images of Governance.* Cambridge: Cambridge University Press.

Kee, James Edwin, and Kathryn E. Newcomer. 2008. *Transforming Public and Nonprofit Organizations: Stewardship for Leading Change.* McLean, VA: Management Concepts.

Kettl, Donald. 1997. "The Global Revolution in Public Management: Driving Themes, Missing Links." *Journal of Policy Analysis and Management* 16(3):446–62.

Kettl, Donald. 1999. "The Future of Public Administration." *Journal of Public Affairs Education* 5:127–33.

Kettl, Donald, and Steven Kelman. 2007. *Reflections on 21st Century Government Management.* Washington, DC: IBM Center for the Business of Government.

Light, Paul C. 1997. *The Tides of Reform: Making Government Work, 1945–1995.* New Haven, CT: Yale University Press.

Lynn, Laurence E. Jr. 2003. "Public Management." In *Handbook of Public Administration,* edited by B. Guy Peters and Jon Pierre. Thousand Oaks, CA: SAGE.

Moe, Ronald. 1994. "The 'Reinventing Government' Exercise: Misinterpreting the Problem, Misjudging the Consequences." *Public Administration Review* 54(2): 446–62.

Mumby, D. K. 1996. "Feminism, Postmodernism, and Organizational Communication Studies: A Critical Reading." *Management Communication Quarterly* 9(3):259–95.

Osborne, David, and Ted Gaebler. 1992. *Reinventing Government: How the Entrepreneurial Spirit Is Transforming the Public Sector.* Reading, MA: Addison-Wesley.

Peters, B. Guy. 1996. *The Future of Governing: Four Emerging Models.* Lawrence: University Press of Kansas.

Rohr, John A. 1986. *To Run a Constitution: The Legitimacy of the Administrative State.* Lawrence: University Press of Kansas.

Salamon, Lester M. 2002. "The Tools Approach and the New Governance: Conclusions and Implications." In *The Tools of Government: A Guide to the New Governance,* edited by L. M. Salamon. New York: Oxford University Press.

Syed, Jawad, and Peter A. Murray. 2008. "A Cultural Feminist Approach Towards Managing Diversity in Top Management Teams." *Equal Opportunities International* 27(5):413–32.

Terry, Larry D. 1998. "Administrative Leadership, Neo-Managerialism, and the New Public Management Movement." *Public Administration Review* 58(3):194–200.

Weber, Max. 1947. *The Theory of Social and Economic Organization.* Translated by A. M. Henderson and Talcott Parsons. London: Collier Macmillan.

Wilson, James Q. 1989. *Bureaucracy.* New York: Basic Books.

CHAPTER NINE

Agranoff, Robert. 2012. *Collaborating to Manage: A Primer for the Public Sector.* Washington, DC: Georgetown University Press.

Agranoff, Robert, and Michael McGuire. 2001. "American Federalism and the Search for Models of Management." *Public Administration Review.* 61(6):671–81.

Allen, Thad W. 2010. "Unprecedented Events: Unprecedented Leadership Challenges." Speech presented at George Washington University, Washington, DC.

Austin, James E. 2000. "Strategic Collaboration Between Nonprofits and Business." *Nonprofit and Voluntary Sector Quarterly* 29(1):69–97.

Barnard, Chester Irving. 1938. *The Functions of the Executive.* Cambridge, MA: Harvard University Press.

Berinato, Scott. 2010. "You Have to Lead from Everywhere: An Interview with Admiral Thad Allen." *Harvard Business Review* 88(11):76–79.

Berry, J. M. 2002. "Validity and Reliability Issues in Elite Interviewing." *PS: Political Science and Politics* 35(4):679–682.

Bertelli, Anthony, and Craig R. Smith. 2009. "Relational Contracting and Network Management." *Journal of Public Administration Research and Theory* 20(1):21–40.

Boyer, Eric. 2012. "Building Capacity for Cross-Sector Collaboration: How Transportation Agencies Build Skills and Systems to Manage Public-Private Partnerships." PhD diss., George Washington University.

Carlee, Ron. 2008. "Leadership in Emergency Management Networks." In *Transforming Public and Nonprofit Organizations: Stewardship for Leading Change*, James Edwin Kee and Kathryn E. Newcomer. McLean, VA: Management Concepts.

Cooper, David E. 2005. *Hurricanes Katrina and Rita: Preliminary Observations on Contracting for Response and Recovery Efforts* (GAO 06–246). Washington, DC: US Government Accountability Office.

Denhardt, Janet V., and Robert B. Denhardt. 2003. *The New Public Service.* Armonk, NY: M. E. Sharp.

Gazley, Beth. 2010. "Linking Collaborative Capacity to Performance Measurement in Government-Nonprofit Partnerships." *Nonprofit and Voluntary Sector Quarterly* 39(4):653–73.

George, Alexander L., and Andrew Bennett. 2004. *Case Studies and Theory Development in the Social Sciences.* Cambridge, MA: MIT Press.

Goldsmith, Stephen, and William D. Eggers. 2004. *Governing by Network: The New Face of the Public Sector.* Washington, DC: Brookings Institution Press.

Jenkins, W. O. 2006. "Collaboration over Adaptation: The Case for Interoperable Communications in Homeland Security." *Public Administration Review* 66(3): 319–21.

Johansen, M., and K. LeRoux. 2013. "Managerial Networking in Nonprofit Organizations: The Impact of Networking on Organizational and Advocacy Effectiveness." *Public Administration Review* 73(2):355–63.

Kee, James Edwin, and Kathryn E. Newcomer. 2008. *Transforming Public and Nonprofit Organizations: Stewardship for Leading Change.* McLean, VA: Management Concepts.

Kettl, Donald. 2006. "Managing Boundaries in American Administration: The Collaboration Imperative." *Public Administration Review* 66(1):10–19.

Kettl, Donald. 2008. *The Next Government of the United States: Why Our Institutions Fail Us and How to Fix Them.* New York: Norton.

Kettl, Donald, and Steven Kelman. 2007. *Reflections on 21st Century Government Management.* Washington, DC: IBM Center for the Business of Government.

Kennedy School of Government. 2006. *Hurricane Katrina (A): Preparing for "The Big One" in New Orleans.* Boston: Kennedy School of Government Case Program, Harvard University.

Landy, Marc. 2008. "Mega-Disasters and Federalism." *Public Administration Review* 68(1):S186–S198.

Milward, H. Brinton, and Keith G. Provan. 2006. *A Manager's Guide to Choosing and Using Collaborative Networks.* Washington, DC: IBM Center for the Business of Government.

Moynihan, Donald P. 2005. *Leveraging Collaborative Networks in Infrequent Emergency Situations.* Washington, DC: IBM Center for the Business of Government.

Provan, Keith G., and Robin H. Lemaire. 2012. "Core Concepts and Key Ideas for Understanding Public Sector Organizational Networks: Using Research to Inform Scholarship and Practice." *Public Administration Review* 72(5):638–48.

Ratnasingam, Pauline. 2003. "Inter-Organizational Trust in Business to Business E-Commerce: A Case Study in Customs Clearance." *Journal of Global Information Management* 11(1):1–19.

Reihlen, Markus. 1996. "The Logic of Hierarchies: Making Organizations Competitive for Knowledge-Based Competition." Working Paper 91. Cologne, Germany: University of Cologne.

Salamon, Lester M. 2002. "The Tools Approach and the New Governance: Conclusions and Implications." In *The Tools of Government: A Guide to the New Governance*, edited by L. M. Salamon. New York: Oxford University Press.

Schein, E. H. 1992. *Organization Culture and Leadership*. 2nd ed. San Francisco: Jossey-Bass.

Senge, Peter M. 2006. *The Fifth Discipline: The Art and Practice of the Learning Organization*. New York: Doubleday.

Shadish, William R., Thomas D. Cook, and Donald T. Campbell. 2002. *Experimental and Quasi-Experimental Designs*. Boston: Houghton Mifflin.

Soda, Giuseppe, and Akbar Zaheer. 2012. "A Network Perspective on Organizational Architecture: Performance Effects of the Interplay of Formal and Informal Organization." *Strategic Management Journal* 33(6):751–771.

Stephenson, Karen. 2009. "Neither Hierarchy nor Network: An Argument for Heterarchy." *People and Strategy* 32(1):4–7.

Tansey, O. 2007. "Process Tracing and Elite Interviewing: A Case for Non-Probability Sampling." *PS: Political Science and Politics*. 40(4):765–72.

Titan Systems Corp. 2002. *After-Action Report on the Response to the September 11th Terrorist Attack on the Pentagon*. San Diego, CA: Arlington County.

Varley, Pamela. 2003. *Command Performance: County Firefighters Take Charge of the 9/11 Pentagon Emergency*. Cambridge, MA: John F. Kennedy School of Government, Harvard University.

Whitehead, Joel. 2005. Remarks at George Washington University, October 22, Washington, DC.

CHAPTER TEN

AECOM Technology Corporation. 2007. *Case Studies of Transportation Public-Private Partnerships in the United States*. http://www.fhwa.dot.gov/ipd/pdfs/us_ppp_case_studies_final_report_7-7-07.pdf.

Behn, Robert D. 2001. *Rethinking Democratic Accountability*. Washington, DC: Brookings Institution.

Berman, Sheri. 1997. "Civil Society and Political Institutionalization." *American Behavioral Scientist* 40(5):562–74.

Bozeman, Barry. 2007. *Public Values and Public Interest: Counterbalancing Economic Individualism*. Washington, DC: Georgetown University Press.

Brabham, Daren C. 2009. "Crowdsourcing the Public Participation Process for Planning Projects." *Planning Theory* 8(3):242–62.

Brabham, Daren C., Thomas W. Sanchez, and Keith Bartholomew. 2009. *Crowdsourcing Public Participation in Transit Planning: Preliminary Results from the Next Stop Design*. Washington, DC: Transportation Research Board Conference.

Brewer, B., and M. R. Hayllar. 2005. "Building Public Trust Through Public-Private Partnerships." *International Review of Administrative Sciences* 71(3):475–92.

Carnevale, David. 1995. *Trustworthy Government: Leadership and Management Strategies for Building Trust and High Performance*. San Francisco: Jossey-Bass.

Derthick, Martha. 2013. "Ways of Achieving Federal Objectives." In *American Intergovernmental Relations*, edited by Lawrence J. O'Toole and Robert K Christensen. 5th ed. Thousand Oaks, CA: SAGE/CQ Press.

Dicke, L. A., and J. S. Ott. 1999. "Public Agency Accountability in Human Service Contracting." *Public Productivity and Management Review* 22(4):502–16.

Dobb, Maurice. 1973. *Theories of Value and Distribution Since Adam Smith: Ideology and Economic Theory*. Cambridge: Cambridge University Press.

Eggers, William, and Stephen Goldsmith. 2004. *Government by Networks: The New Public Management Imperative*. Washington, DC: Deloitte Research and the Ash Institute for Democratic Governance and Innovation.

Follett, Mary Parker. 2003. In *Mary Parker Follett: Prophet of Management*, edited by Pauline Graham. Washington, DC: Beard Books.

Forrer, John, James Edwin Kee, Kathryn Newcomer, and Eric Boyer. 2010. "Public-Private Partnerships and the Accountability Question." *Public Administration Review* 70(3):475–84.

Friedman, Milton. 1962. *Capitalism and Freedom*. Chicago: University of Chicago Press.

Friedrich, Carl J. 1940. "Public Policy and the Nature of Administrative Responsibility." In *Public Policy: A Yearbook of the Graduate School of Public Administration*, edited by C. J. Friedrich and E. S. Mason. Cambridge, MA: Harvard University Press.

Hamilton, Alexander, John Jay, and Jay Madison. 2001. *The Federalist*, edited by G. W. Carey and J. McClellan. Indianapolis: Indianapolis Liberty Fund.

Hardin, Russell. 2004. *Trust and Trustworthiness*. New York: Russell Sage Foundation.

Harmon, Michael M. 1995. *Responsibility as Paradox: A Critique of Rational Discourse on Government*. Thousand Oaks, CA: SAGE.

Heinzelman, Jessica, and Carol Waters. 2010. "Crowdsourcing Crisis Information in Disaster-Affected Haiti." *Special Report*. Washington, DC: US Institute of Peace.

Ingram, Helen. 1977. "Policy Implementation Through Bargaining: The Case of Federal Grant-in-Aid." *Public Policy* 25(4):499–526.

Kearns, K. P. 1996. *Managing for Accountability: Preserving the Public Trust in Public and Nonprofit Organizations*. San Francisco: Jossey-Bass.

Kettl, Donald. 2002. *The Transformation of Governance: Public Administration for Twenty-First Century America*. Baltimore, MD: Johns Hopkins University Press.

Kettl, Donald. 2005. *The Global Public Management Revolution*. 2nd ed. Washington, DC: Brookings Institution Press.

Light, Paul C. 1998. *The Tides of Reform: Making Government Work, 1945–1995*. New Haven, CT: Yale University Press.

Lynn, L. E. 2006. *Public Management: Old and New*. New York: Routledge.

McSwite, O. C. 1997. *Legitimacy in Public Administration: A Discourse Analysis*. Thousand Oaks, CA: SAGE.

Moore, M. 1995. *Creating Public Value*. Cambridge, MA: Harvard University Press.

Nabatchi, Tina. 2012. "Putting the 'Public' Back in Public Values Research: Designing Participation to Identify and Respond to Values." *Public Administration Review* 72(5):699–709.

National Center for Charitable Statistics. 2012. *Quick Facts About Nonprofits*. http://nccs.urban.org/statistics/quickfacts.cfm.

Osborne, David, and Ted Gaebler. 1992. *Reinventing Government: How the Entrepreneurial Spirit Is Transforming the Public Sector*. Reading, MA: Addison-Wesley.

Porter, Michael E., and Mark R. Kramer. 2011. "Creating Shared Value." *Harvard Business Review* 89(1–2):2–17.

Posner, Paul L. 2002. "Accountability Challenges of Third-Party Government." In *The Tools of Government*, edited by L. M. Salamon. New York: Oxford University Press.

Romzek, Barbara, and Melvin Dubnick. 1994. "Issues of Accountability in Flexible Personnel Systems." In *New Paradigms for Government: Issues for the Changing Public Services*. edited by Patricia Ingraham and Barbara Romzek. San Francisco: Jossey-Bass.

Thomas, John. 2012. *Citizen, Customer, Partner: Engaging the Public in Public Management*. Armonk, NY: M. E. Sharpe.

US Government Accountability Office. 2010. *Assessments and Citations of Federal Labor Law Violations by Selected Federal Contractors*. Washington, DC: US Government Accountability Office.

Waldo, Dwight. 1948. *The Administrative State*. New Brunswick, NJ: Transaction Publishers.

White House. 2009. *Memorandum for the Heads of Executive Departments and Agencies: Open Government Directive*. Washington, DC: Executive Office of the President, Office of Management and Budget.

Wilson, Woodrow. 1887. "The Study of Administration." *Political Science Quarterly* 2(2):197–222.

Wuthnow, R. 1996. *Poor Richard's Principle: Recovering the American Dream Through the Moral Dimension of Work, Business, and Money.* Princeton, NJ: Princeton University Press.

CHAPTER ELEVEN

Argyris, Chris, and Donald A. Schön. 1996. *Organizational Learning II: Theory, Method, and Practice.* Reading, MA: Addison-Wesley.

Bingham, Lisa Blomgren, and Rosemary O'Leary. 2007. *A Manager's Guide to Resolving Conflicts in Collaborative Networks.* Washington, DC: IBM Center for the Business of Government.

Blindenbacher, Raoul, and Bidjan Nashat. 2010. *The Black Box of Governmental Learning: The Learning Spiral—A Concept to Organize Learning in Governments.* Washington, DC: World Bank, Independent Evaluation Group.

Boyer, Eric. 2012. "Building Capacity for Cross-Sector Collaboration: How Transportation Agencies Build Skills and Systems to Manage Public-Private Partnerships." PhD dissertation, George Washington University.

Boyer, Eric. 2013. "A Preliminary Framework of Collaborative Learning." Working paper, Georgia Institute of Technology.

Brown, Trevor L., Matthew Potoski, and David M. Van Slyke. 2011. "Accountability Challenges in Public Sector Contracting for Complex Products." In *Accountable Governance: Problems and Promises*, edited by Melvin J. Dubnick and H. George Frederickson. Armonk, NY: M. E. Sharpe.

Carlee, Ron. 2008. "Leadership in Emergency Management Networks." In *Transforming Public and Nonprofit Organizations: Stewardship for Leading Change*, by James Edwin Kee and Kathryn E. Newcomer. McLean, VA: Management Concepts.

Carrillo, Patricia, Herbert Robinson, Chimay Anumba, and Nasreddine Bouchlaghem. 2006. "A Knowledge Transfer Framework: The PFI Context." *Construction Management and Economics* 24(10):1045–56.

Denrell, Jerker, and James March. 2001. "Adaptation as Information Restriction: The Hot Stove Effect." *Organization Science* 12(5):523–38.

Edmondson, Amy C. 1999. "Psychological Safety and Learning Behavior in Work Teams." *Administrative Science Quarterly* 44(2):350–83.

Felipe, Jesus. 2003. *Public-Private Partnership for Competitiveness.* Manila: Asian Development Bank.

Gazley, Beth. 2008. "Beyond the Contract: The Scope and Nature of Informal Government-Nonprofit Partnerships." *Public Administration Review* 68(1):141–54.

Gibson, Cristina, and Freek Vermeulen. 2003. "A Healthy Divide: Subgroups as a Stimulus for Team Learning Behavior." *Administrative Science Quarterly* 48(2): 202–39.

Grimsey, Darrin, and Mervyn K. Lewis. 2007. *Public Private Partnerships: The Worldwide Revolution in Infrastructure Provision and Project Finance.* Northampton, MA: Edward Elgar.

Haunschild, Pamela R., and Bilian Ni Sullivan. 2002. "Learning from Complexity: Effects of Prior Accidents and Incidents on Airlines' Learning." *Administrative Science Quarterly* 47(4):609–43.

Her Majesty's Treasury. 2006. *Value for Money Assessment Guidance.* London: Her Majesty's Treasury.

Her Majesty's Treasury. 2009. *Competitive Dialogue in 2008: OGC/HMT Joint Guidance on Using the Procedure.* London: Her Majesty's Treasury.

Hodge, Graeme A., and Carsten Greve. 2007. "Public-Private Partnerships: An International Performance Review." *Public Administration Review* 67(3):545–58.

Huber, George P. 1991. "Organizational Learning: The Contributing Processes and the Literatures." *Organization Science* 2(1):88–115.

Kettl, Donald. 2002. "Managing Indirect Government." In *The Tools of Government*, edited by Lester M. Salamon. New York: Oxford University Press.

Kettl, Donald. 2008. *The Next Government of the United States: Why Our Institutions Fail Us and How to Fix Them.* New York: Norton.

Mahler, Julianne. 1997. "Influences of Organizational Culture on Learning in Public Agencies." *Journal of Public Administration Research and Theory* 7(4):519–40.

Mahler, Julianne, and Maureen Hogan Casamayou. 2009. *Organizational Learning at NASA: The Challenger and Columbia Accidents.* Washington, DC: Georgetown University Press.

McGuire, Michael. 2006. "Collaborative Public Management: Assessing What We Know and How We Know It." *Public Administration Review* 66(Suppl. 1):33–43.

Morallos, Dorothy, and Adjo Amekudzi. 2008. "The State of the Practice of Value for Money Analysis in Comparing Public Private Partnerships to Traditional Procurements." *Public Works Management Policy* 13(2):114–25.

National Audit Office. 2006. *The Termination of the PFI Contract for the National Physics Laboratory.* London: National Audit Office.

Nelson, R. R., and S. G. Winter. 1982. *An Evolutionary Theory of Economic Change.* Cambridge, MA: Belknap Press.

Newcomer, Kathryn E., Harry Hatry, and Joseph Wholey. 2010. "What You Need to Know About Program Evaluation." In *The Handbook of Practical Program Evaluation*, 3rd ed., edited by Joseph Wholey, Harry Hatry and Kathryn E. Newcomer. San Francisco: Jossey-Bass.

OTP3. 2012. Office of Transportation Public-Private Partnerships, Virginia Department of Transportation (OTP3). http://www.vappta.org/.

PartnershipsVictoria. 2001. "Public Sector Comparator." Technical note, Department of Treasury and Finance, State of Victoria, Victoria, Australia.

Preskill, H., and R. T. Torres. 2001. "The Learning Dimension of Evaluation Use." *New Directions for Evaluation* (88):25–37.

Robinson, Herbert, Patricia Carrillo, Chimay J. Anumba, and Manju Patel. 2010. *Governance and Knowledge Management for Public Private Partnerships.* Oxford: Wiley-Blackwell.

Sabatier, Paul A., and Christopher M. Weible. 2007. "The Advocacy Coalition Framework: Innovations and Clarifications." In *Theories of the Policy Process*, edited by Paul A. Sabatier. Boulder, CO: Westview Press.

Schein, E. H. 1965. *Organizational Psychology.* Englewood Cliffs, NJ: Prentice Hall.

Secretary's Global Partnership Initiative. 2012. U.S. State Department, Global Partnership Initiative (S/GPI). http://www.state.gov/s/partnerships/.

Senge, Peter M. 2006. *The Fifth Discipline: The Art and Practice of the Learning Organization.* New York: Doubleday.

Sheehan, Tony, Dominique Poole, Ian Lyttle, and Charles O. Egbu. 2005. "Strategies and Business Case for Knowledge Management." In *Knowledge Management in Construction*, edited by Chimay J. Anumba, Charles Egbu, and Patricia Carrillo. Oxford: Blackwell.

Sitkin, Sim B. 1992. "Learning Through Failure: The Strategy of Small Losses." In *Research in Organizational Behavior*, edited by Barry Staw and L. L. Cummings. Greenwich, CT: JAI Press.

Smith, Heather A., James D. McKeen, and Satyendra Singh. 2006. "Making Knowledge Work: Five Principles for Action-Oriented Knowledge Management." *Knowledge Management Research and Practice* 4:116–24.

Van Slyke, David M. 2009. "Collaboration and Relational Contracting." In *The Collaborative Public Manager: New Ideas for the Twenty-First Century*, edited by Rosemary O'Leary and Lisa Blomgren Bingham. Washington, DC: Georgetown University Press.

Vancoppenolle, Diederik, and Bram Verschuere. 2012. "Failure in Service Delivery by Public-Private Networks: The Case of Flemish Childcare." *Public Policy and Administration* 27(1):31–48.

Wholey, Joseph, Harry Hatry, and Kathryn E. Newcomer. 2010. *The Handbook of Practical Program Evaluation.* 3rd ed. San Francisco: Jossey-Bass.

World Bank. 2007. *Public-Private Partnership Units: Lessons for Their Design and Use in Infrastructure.* Washington, DC: Public-Private Infrastructure Advisory Facility, World Bank.

CHAPTER TWELVE

AASHTO Center for Excellence in Project Finance. 2014. "I-495 Capital Beltway HOT Lanes." http://www.trans-portation-finance.org/projects/i495_capital_beltway_hotlanes.aspx.

Eggers, William, and Stephen Goldsmith. 2004. *Government by Networks: The New Public Management Imperative.* Deloitte Research and the Ash Institute for Democratic Governance and Innovation. Cambridge, MA: Harvard Kennedy School of Government.

Goldsmith, S., and W. D. Eggers. 2004. *Governing by Network: The New Shape of the Public Sector.* Washington, DC: Brookings Institution Press.

Hale, T., and D. Held. 2011. *Handbook of Transnational Governance: Institutions and Innovations.* Cambridge, MA: Polity.

Kettl, D. F. 1993. *Sharing Power: Public Governance and Private Markets.* Washington, DC: Brookings Institution.

McGuire, M. 2006. "Intergovernmental Management: A View from the Bottom." *Public Administration Review* 66(5):677–79.

Milburn, Alan. 2007. "A 2020 Vision for the Public Services." Lecture at the London School of Economics, London.

Moore, M. H. 1995. *Creating Public Value: Strategic Management in Government.* Cambridge, MA: Harvard University Press.

Osborne, S. P. 2010. *The New Public Governance: Emerging Perspectives on the Theory and Practice of Public Governance.* London: Routledge.

Salamon, L. M. 2002. *The Tools of Government: A Guide to the New Governance.* Oxford: Oxford University Press.

Talbot, C. 2011. "Paradoxes and Prospects of 'Public Value.'" *Public Money and Management* 31(1):27–34.

Virginia Department of Transportation. 2013. *495 Express Lanes: Virginia Megaprojects Current Alerts.* http://www.vamegaprojects.com/about-megaprojects/i495-hot-lanes/#overview.

John J. Forrer is a research professor of strategic management and public policy and associate director of the Institute for Corporate Responsibility at the School of Business and associate faculty at the Trachtenburg School of Public Policy and Public Administration at the George Washington University (GW). Prior to joining GW in 1997, Forrer worked for the US federal government and nonprofit and for-profit organizations as an energy and environmental analyst. At GW he has held university positions including executive director of the Institute for Global Management and Research and founder and director of the GW Center for the Study of Globalization. He has researched, taught, and written on cross-sector collaborations and partnerships for fifteen years, emphasizing in particular the role the private sector can play in advancing public policy goals. Other research areas are global governance, sustainable global supply chains, and business and peace. He has coauthored two books on economic sanctions and more than twenty book chapters and journal articles.

James Edwin (Jed) Kee is a professor emeritus of public policy and public administration at the Trachtenberg School of Public Policy and Public Administration. He joined George Washington University (GW) in 1985 after a seventeen-year career in government in New York State and Utah. In New York, Kee served as a legal assistant in the office of Senator Robert F. Kennedy and later became a legislative counsel to the New York State Assembly. In Utah, he held a series of cabinet positions including budget director and executive director of the Department of Administrative Services, the umbrella finance and management department of the state. At GW, Kee was senior associate dean of the School of Business and Public Management from 1993 to 1997. From 1997 to 2003, he was the Giant Food Inc. Professor of Public/Private Management. His teaching and research interests are in the areas of leadership, cross-sector collaborations, contracting out, and public financial management. He has authored or coauthored two other books and more than forty book chapters and journal articles. Kee has conducted a variety of training programs in finance, evaluation, and public leadership throughout the world.

Eric Boyer is an assistant professor of public administration at the University of Texas–El Paso. He was a postdoctoral researcher in the School of Public Policy at the Georgia Institute of Technology, where he conducted a study on communities of practice within the Georgia Department of Transportation (GDOT). Within GDOT, he advised officials in the human resource department on issues in training and knowledge management, and he conducted workshops on knowledge-sharing practices for professionals across the agency. His PhD is from the Trachtenberg School of Public Policy and Public Administration, and his MPA is from the Maxwell School of Syracuse University. Before graduate school, Boyer spent nearly seven years in the former Soviet Union, working for humanitarian programs and international nonprofits. His publications explore issues in cross-sector collaboration, public participation, knowledge management, nonprofit leadership, disaster management, and public-private partnerships. Boyer contributes to the Transportation Research Board's Taskforce on Knowledge Management and Subcommittee on Public-Private Partnerships.

INDEX

A

accountability
  analyzing in CSCs, 180–181
  in bureaucratic administration, 211–212
  citizen participation and, 267–269
  comparing heterarchies and hierarchies, 231
  comparing options for delivery of goods and
    services, 24
  contracting out and, 271
  controls in, 254–255
  CSCs and, 252–253
  dimensions of democratic accountability, 255–259
  ensuring, 196
  fostering democratic accountability, 261
  foundation concepts of democratic
    accountability, 260
  future of CSCs and, 309
  heterarchical leadership and, 234
  integrated approach to mutual accountability,
    270–271
  IPSPs and, 274–275
  networks and, 130, 273–274
  New Public Governance paradigm and, 304
  New Public Management and, 218
  overview of, 251–252
  partnerships/PPPs and, 272–273
  review, 275–276
  social media and citizen engagement and,
    269–270
  state employment training case study, 277
  traditional, 253–254
  trust and, 265–267
  twenty-first century government, 222–223

value creation and, 263–265
  vertical nature of traditional, 262–263
Accountable Care Organizations (ACO)
  mutuality in approach of, 158
  response to health care crisis and, 152–154
action networks
  in delivery of services for the homeless, 117
  types of networks, 116
activation skills
  government skills needed for network
    management, 282
  needed for New Public Governance model, 221
ad hoc collaboration
  moving beyond, 40
  policy and delivery options available to public
    managers, 16–17
adaptation (change management)
  advantages of IPSPs for public managers, 162
  risk allocation and, 186
administration, public. *See* public administration
administrative organization, of networks, 121–122
administrative reform
  network management approach, 220–221
  New Public Governance model, 220–221
  New Public Management reform movement,
    215–217
  reactions to New Public Management (NPM)
    reform, 217–219
  reforming bureaucratic state, 214–215
  reframing approaches to administration, 219–220
  transformational stewardship (Kee and
    Newcomer), 221–222
  twenty-first century orientation, 222–223

The Administrative State (Waldo), 256

Affordable Care Act. See Patient Protection and Affordable Care Act (2010)

agency dilemma. See principal-agent problem

AidMatrix, IPSP example, 19

air quality, role of IPSPs in meeting environmental challenges, 147

Allen, Thad W.
   adapting leadership areas to CSCs, 245–247
   brief biography of work in public service, 235
   on building trust, 244
   on gaining wider perspective, 241–242
   on generating support, 237–238
   on leading outside of formal roles, 239–240
   outcome-based performance in Hurricane Katrina response, 262

allocation efficiency, competition achieving, 39

allocation of risk. See risk allocation

analytical framework
   accountability and, 180–181, 196
   analytical approaches, 189–191
   best value analysis, 188–189
   case studies, 168–169
   communication needs, 180
   contracting strength and weaknesses, 197–198
   determining nature of task or challenge, 170
   IPSP strengths and weaknesses, 200–202
   monitoring and evaluation and, 181
   networks strengths and weaknesses, 199–200
   one sector vs. multisector solutions, 170–172
   organizational capacity, 177–178
   overview of, 167–168
   partnership strengths and weaknesses, 198–199
   performance measures in, 194–195
   political factors, 174–175
   private market vs. nonprofit solutions, 172–173
   program or project design, 179
   program or project planning, 177
   public interest considerations, 191–193
   resources needs, 176–177, 181–183
   review, 197
   risk allocation, 185–187
   risk analysis, 179–180, 187–188
   risk identification, 183–184
   state employment training case study, 205
   summary of, 202–204

Anti-Federalists, 257

assessment
   advantages/disadvantages of contracting, 79–80

applying to Kansas foster care and adoption program, 78–79
   of contracting, 68–72
   of employee skills, 286–288
   of partnerships, 108–109

assigning employees, to collaborative partnerships, 287

asymmetrical information
   agency dilemma and, 37–38
   market failure and, 36

attributes, of partnerships, 106–107

authority
   comparing heterarchies and hierarchies, 230–231
   vertical nature in traditional accountability, 255

autonomy, flexibility of IPSPs and, 157–158

B

balanced scorecards
   for accountability, 194–195
   emphasizing outcomes in public sector, 11

BCBSM (Blue Shield of Michigan), role of IPSPs in responding to health care crisis, 153

Behn, Robert, 257–258, 260

benchmarks, in evaluating contracting, 76

best-value analysis
   cost-benefit analysis, 190
   cost-effectiveness analysis, 190–191
   overview of, 188–189
   value for money analysis, 190–191

bidding process, PPPs and, 280–281

Bill and Melinda Gates Foundation: The Family Homelessness Project, 19, 308

Blue Shield of Michigan (BCBSM), role of IPSPs in responding to health care crisis, 153

Boyer, Eric, about the authors section, 346

Bozeman, Barry, 258–260, 261

bureaucratic model
   advantages of, 211–212
   control-based accountability in, 253
   disadvantages of, 213–214
   historic origins of, 210–211
   Hurricane Katrina example, 225
   incompatibility with CSCs, 303–304
   reforming bureaucratic state, 214–215

Bush, George W., 63

C

capacity
   assessing organizational capacity, 177–178
   balancing control with, 219

government capacity as issue in partnerships, 92–94

government capacity for CSC. *See* government, creating capacity for CSC

needs and capacity analysis, 176

strategic objectives of CSC and, 41

Carlee, Ron

adapting leadership areas to CSCs, 245–247

brief biography of work in public service, 235–236

on building trust, 244

on gaining wider perspective, 242

on generating support, 238–239

on leading outside of formal roles, 240

Caterpillar Corporation, role in First Response Team of America, 151

CCSA (Child Care Services Association), 236

Centers for Disease Control (CDC), 32–33

challenges

analyzing nature of, 170

to bureaucratic model, 209

to contemporary governments, 146–147

creating need for collaborative approach, 5–6

creating need for new administrative models, 210

evolving nature of governance and, 301–302

facing local, state, and federal governments, 3–4

facing public managers, 5

to governance of CSCs, 51–55, 132–134

of involving private and nonprofit sectors in CSCs, 49–50

natural disasters, 32–33

change management (adaptation)

advantages of IPSPs for public managers, 162

risk allocation and, 186

Channel Industries Mutual Aid (CIMA), 150–151

charitable organizations, 12

Child Care Services Association (CCSA), 236

childhood obesity, illustrating need for collaboration, 32–33

Childhood Obesity Prevention Coalition, 33

Children and Homeless Collaborative, 116

CIMA (Channel Industries Mutual Aid), 150–151

citizen participation/engagement

advantages of networks, 129

enhancing, 267–269

leadership in heterarchical structures and, 234

New Public Governance paradigm and, 304

social media and citizen engagement, 269–270

twenty-first century government, 223

citizens

perspective on creation of public value, 306

responsiveness to needs of, 309–311

sources of influence for public managers, 275

City of Dallas, partnership example, 25

civil service, hierarchical (Weberian), 211–212

Clean Air Act (1970), 147

Climate Action Plan, 147

climate change

challenges facing governments, 5–6

IPSPs in meeting challenges of, 147

Joint Venture-SV initiatives, 148

one sector vs. multisector solutions, 172

Oregon Environmental Council mission, 148–149

coalition building, leadership in heterarchical structures and, 234

Coalition for the Homeless, 116–117

Coast Guard. *See* US Coast Guard (USCG)

collaboration

benefits of IPSPs, 139

benefits of networks, 111–112

building government capacity for, 284–285

leadership in heterarchical structures and, 234

moving from contracting to, 64–65

networks in facilitation of, 115

in successful partnerships, 98–99

collaborative communication, 214

collaborative contracts

characteristics of, 59–60

public managers and, 65–66

command-and-control solutions, 209

communications

analyzing CSC options, 180

building trust between partners, 99

in bureaucratic model, 214

disadvantages of IPSPs, 162–163

elements of network governance, 125–126

in heterarchies and hierarchies, 231–233

Community Care of North Carolina

innovation in approach of IPSPs, 159

IPSPs responding to health care crisis, 153

COMPARE method. *See* assessment

compensation methods, in contracts, 73

competence, strategic objectives of CSC and, 41

competence trust, 75, 265

competition

allocation efficiency and, 39

competitive advantage of nonprofits in meeting some social needs, 39–40 competition (*continued*)

consumer power and, 5

driving force in cost reduction, 280–281

managed competition, 60–61

complexity

risk allocation, 186

risk identification, 184

conservatives, advocating market mechanisms over government programs, 217

construction

examples of traditional contracts, 58

PPPs and, 281

risk allocation, 186

risk identification, 184

consultants, managing, 288–289

contracting out

accountability, 271

advantages/disadvantages of, 79–80, 197–198

applying to public health example, 20

assessing pros/cons of, 68–72

clarity of expectations and, 68

collaborative contracts, 59–60, 65–66

comparing options for delivery of goods and services, 22–23

criteria in contract design, 72–73

efforts to reduce government role, 217–218

emerging structures filling void in government services, 9

EPA example, 77–78

evaluation during and following, 76

evolution of governance and, 301–302

global implications of, 80–82

history in U.S., 62–64

inherently governmental and critical functions and, 70–72

Kansas foster care and adoption program, 78–79

monitoring, 74–76

moving to collaboration, 64–65

moving to principal-principal relationships, 45–47

overview of, 18, 57

policy and delivery options available to public managers, 16

process of, 67

rationale for, 61–62

state employment training case study, 83–84

traditional contracts, 57–58

transitioning between public service delivery options, 26–27

transparency in avoiding fraud and abuses, 73–74

vs. outsourcing, 60–61

contractual trust, 75, 265

control

balancing with administrative capacity, 219

command-and-control solutions, 209

comparing options for delivery of goods and services, 22

leadership in heterarchical structures and, 233

traditional public accountability based on, 253–255

coordination, moving to collaboration, 46

corporate social responsibility (CSR)

examples, 42

overview of, 41–42

private sector and, 12

corruption, ways to avoid in contracting process, 74

cost-benefit analysis (CBA)

analyzing CSCs, 190

managing partnerships and, 96–97

types of analytical approaches, 189

cost-effectiveness analysis (CEA)

analysis of CSCs, 190–191

comparing with CBA and VfM analysis, 192

comparing with CEA and VfM analysis, 192

types of analytical approaches, 189

cost-reimbursement contracts, 73

costs

competition as driving force in cost-reduction, 280–281

disadvantages of networks, 131

rationale for partnerships, 91–92

cross-sector collaboration (CSC)

analyzing options in. *See* analytical framework

contracting. *See* contracting out

cross-sector partnerships. *See* partnerships

defined, 9–11

future of. *See* future of CSCs

government capacity for. *See* government, creating capacity for CSC

imperative for. *See* imperative for CSCs

IPSPs. *See* independent public services providers (IPSPs)

networks. *See* networks

nonprofit role, 12–15

partnerships. *See* partnerships

PPPs and. *See* public-private partnerships (PPPs)

private role of, 11–12

public role of, 11
rationales for. *See* rationales, for CSC
CSR. *See* corporate social responsibility (CSR)
customers service, 310

D

Dallas Public Library, partnership example in delivery of goods and services, 25
DC Capital area Hot Lanes program, example of PPP for infrastructure, 198–199, 307–308
debt, issues facing U.S. government, 7
decision making, in hierarchies, 230
Deepwater Horizon oil spill, Coast Guard response, 235
Deepwater Program (USCG)
    assessing resources and capacity, 181–183
    best-value analysis, 193
    communication needs, 180
    performance measurement system, 196
    public task/challenge of, 175
    risk identification and allocation, 187
defense contracts, collaborative nature of, 59–60
deliverables (outcomes), strategic objectives of CSC, 41
democratic accountability
    creating value and, 263–265
    dimensions of, 255–259
    enhancing citizen participation, 267–269
    fostering, 261
    foundation concepts, 260
    integrated approach to mutual accountability, 270–271
    outcome-based performance in, 262–263
    social media and citizen engagement, 269–270
    trust in, 265–267
democratic values, NPM concepts as threat to, 218
Department of Homeland Security (DHS), network response to Hurricane Katrina, 122
Department of Systems Management for Human Services (DSMHS)
    cutting across silos, 128
    Fairfax county example, 121–122
    measuring network performance, 127
deregulation, neoliberalism and, 35
design
    financial forecasting and, 288
    planning and design development stage for PPPs, 280

of programs or projects, 179
of request for proposal (RFP), 62
specifications in contracting criteria, 72
developmental networks
    in delivery of services for the homeless, 116–117
    types of networks, 115
direct government provision
    applying to public health, 20
    comparing options for delivery of goods and services, 21–23
    overview of, 17–18
    policy and delivery options available to public managers, 16
    responses to market failure, 36
    transitioning between public service delivery options, 26–27
disaster response/recovery
    clearing roadways, 160
    heterarchies in, 231
    social media in response to Haiti earthquake, 269
    transformational stewardship model (Kee and Newcomer) model, 222
disease, challenges facing governments, 6
dispute resolution, in contracts, 76
divergent interests
    managing partnerships, 94–95
    negotiating motivational differences in collaboration, 50
diversity of supply, benefits of CSCs, 310
documentation, of lessons learned, 290–291
Drug Abuse Resistance Education, network example, 25
Dunford Bridge, PPP example in UK, 187

E

EAP (Environmental Action Programme), 81
Eastern Europe, Caucasus Central Asia (EECCA), 81
economic rationales, for CSC
    agency dilemma and, 37–39
    competition and, 39
    competitive advantage of nonprofits, 39–40
    market failure and, 35–36
    overview of, 35
    ownership structures impact on employee incentive and behavior, 36–37
economics
    of partnerships, 104
    risk allocation, 186
    risk identification, 184

fixed-price contracts, 73
flexibility
    bureaucracies and, 225
    in heterarchies, 231
    leadership in heterarchical structures and, 233–234
    need for new administrative models and, 210
Florida Department of Transportation (FDOT),
    example of outcome-based performance, 101,
    193, 262
food shortages, challenges facing governments, 6
formalization, control and, 46–48
for-profit sector. *See* private (for-profit) sector
Forrer, John J., about the authors section, 345
forums, learning by doing, 290
foster care and adoption (FCA), contracting example,
    78–79
framework for learning
    assessing and assigning employees, 286–288
    deciphering and integrating external knowledge,
    288–289
    discussing and documenting lessons from direct
    experience, 290–291
    monitoring and evaluation and, 291–293
    overview of, 285–286
framing (facilitation) skills, government skills needed
    for network management, 282
free trade, neoliberalism and, 35
Friedman, Milton, 216, 265
FRTA (First Response Team of America), examples
    of IPSPs, 151–152, 156
funding, sources of influence for public
    managers, 275
future of CSCs
    advantages/disadvantages to public sector,
    299–300
    challenges of governance and, 301–302
    example applying IPSP to neglected tropical
    diseases, 308–309
    example applying PPP to infrastructure, 307–308
    improving public services, 309–311
    New Public Governance paradigm, 302–304
    overview of, 297
    public value and, 304–306
    review, 311–312

G

GAO (Government Accountability Office). *See*
    Government Accountability Office (GAO)

gender-bias, criticisms of bureaucratic model,
    213–214
GHG (greenhouse gases), reducing, 147–148
Global Alliance for Improved Nutrition (GAIN), 26,
    163–164
Global Fund, example of global network, 134–135
Global Network for Neglected Tropical Disease
    (GNNTD)
    characteristics and approaches of IPSPs, 156
    coordination of resources, 160
    emergency response and, 151–152
    example of IPSP, 20, 308–309
    large scale social issues illustrating pragmatic need
    for collaboration, 33
    private sector collaboration with federal
    government, 34–35
    public health and, 21
    response to natural disasters, 32
    role of IPSPs in, 151–152
    strengths and weaknesses of IPSPs and, 201
Global Partnership Initiative, US State
    Department, 98
Global Sustainable Tourism Council, 147–148
global warming. *See* climate change
globalization
    challenges facing public managers, 5
    IPSPs and, 163–164
    networks and, 134–135
    PPPs and, 102–103
goodwill trust, 75, 265
governance
    challenges in, 53–55, 301–302
    complexity of network governance, 131
    consequences of CSC, 48
    elements of network governance, 123–127
    failure of network governance, 113–114
    hollowed-out government and, 52–53
    involving nonprofit sector in CSC, 49–50
    involving private sector in CSC, 49
    IPSPs in meeting challenges of, 146
    lead organization networks, 120–121
    legal issues in CSC, 51
    loss-of-control problem and, 51–52
    modes of network governance, 118–119
    moving to principal-principal relationships, 45–47
    negotiating divergent interests, 50–51
    networks and, 121–122
    New Public Governance paradigm, 221, 302–304

network response to, 122
network strengths and weaknesses, 199–200
Hurricane Rita, 235
Hurricane Sandy, 32–33
hybrid organizations, 142–144

I

ICT (Information and communication technology)
 future of CSCs and, 310
 supporting citizen participation, 268–269
imperative for CSCs
 challenges creating need for collaborative
  approach, 5–6
 lack of resources, 7–8
 overview of, 4
 public dissatisfaction with public sector, 6–7
 societal expectations and transformations, 5
impermanence, disadvantages of IPSPs for public
 managers, 163
incentives, contract negotiation and, 73
independent public services providers (IPSPs)
 accountability in, 274–275
 addressing global issues, 163–164
 advantages/disadvantages for public managers,
  161–163
 applying to public health, 21
 approach of, 155–156
 challenges of governance and, 146
 characteristics of, 140–142
 comparing options for delivery of goods and
  services, 23–24
 comparing with other CSCs, 145–146
 comparing with quasi-governmental entities,
  144–145
 emergency response and, 151–152
 environmental protection and, 147–149
 evolution of governance and, 301–302
 flexibility of, 157–158
 government capacity for, 283–284
 growth of quasi-governmental and hybrid
  organizations, 142–144
 health care crisis and, 152–155
 innovation in approach of, 159
 measuring performance of, 160–161
 monitoring and evaluation and, 292
 mutuality in approach of, 158–159
 New Public Governance paradigm and, 303
 overview of, 19–20, 139–140

policy and delivery options available to public
 managers, 16
principal-principal relationships and, 45–47
public managers and, 156
review, 164–165
risk allocation and, 160
sharing expertise and resources, 159–160
state employment training case study, 166
strengths and weaknesses, 200–202
transitioning between public service delivery
 options, 27–28
transportation infrastructure and, 149–151
India, international experience with PPPs, 102–103
Indiana Economic Development Council, 25
informal networks, 115–116
information. *See also* knowledge
 asymmetrical. *See* asymmetrical information
 comparing information exchange in heterarchies
  and hierarchies, 231–233
 importance of transparency in IPSPs, 159
 sources of influence for public managers, 275
Information and communication technology (ICT)
 future of CSCs and, 310
 supporting citizen participation, 268–269
infrastructure
 challenges facing governments, 5
 DC Capital area Hot Lanes program, 198–199
 helping local government implement
  transportation infrastructure, 289
 IPSPs in transportation infrastructure, 149–151
 operating environment in infrastructure
  partnerships, 104–105
 PPPs for, 48, 99–101, 307–308
innovation
 advantages of IPSPs, 159
 advantages of networks, 129
 criticisms of bureaucratic model and, 214
 leadership in heterarchical structures and, 234
integration, in collaborative structures, 46
intermediate-term partnerships, 87–89
International Finance Corporation, of World
 Bank, 103
investment, in U.S. infrastructure, 100–101

J

Joint Venture-Silicon Valley (Joint Venture-SV)
 IPSPs in environmental protection, 148–149
 mutuality in approach of, 159

Manhattan Project, example of private
contracting, 63
market failure, economic rationales for CSC, 35–36
markets
advocates of market mechanisms over government
programs, 217
benefits of CSCs and, 310
shared value and, 42
McSwite, O. C., 256–257, 260–261
Medicaid, crisis in health care, 152–154
Medicare
crisis in health care, 152–154
one sector vs. multisector solutions, 170–171
partnership applied to public health, 21
military, contracting approach in, 64
mission drift
IPSP issues, 163
partnership issues, 92
mobilization, government skills needed for network
management, 282
models, for public administration, 209–210
modulation skills, New Public Governance model
and, 221
monitoring and evaluation
analyzing in CSCs, 181
contracting and, 74–76
designing government standards for, 291–293
future of CSCs and, 310
government skills needed for network
management, 282
partnerships and, 99
PPPs and, 281–282
traditional accountability and, 255
monopolistic/oligopolistic effects, competition and
allocation efficiency and, 39
moral hazard, managing divergent interests in
partnerships, 94–95
motivation, bureaucratic model and, 213
multisector aspect, of IPSPs, 140–142
multisector solutions, 170–172
mutual accountability
citizen participation, 266–270
four pillars of, 261
integrated approach to, 270–271
outcome-based performance, 262–263
overview of, 261
trust, 265–266
value creation, 263–265

mutuality
advantages of IPSPs, 158–159
elements of network governance, 124

N
N Street Village (NSV), 173
National Aeronautics and Space Administration
(NASA), 53
National Performance Review, 61
NDOs. *See* nonprofit sector
Neglected Tropical Disease (NTDs)
applying IPSP to, 308–309
IPSP strengths and weaknesses and, 201
negotiation, government skills needed for network
management, 282
neoliberalism
advocating market mechanisms over government
programs, 217
economics of, 35
network capture, disadvantages of networks, 131
networks
accountability, 273–274
administrative organization of, 121–122
advantages/disadvantages of, 127–131, 199–200
as alternative approach to public administration,
220–221, 224
communications and, 125–126
comparing IPSPs with, 145–146
comparing options for delivery of goods and
services, 23–25
definitions, 113–115
evolution of governance and, 301–302
in facilitation of collaboration, 115
globalization and, 134–135
governance of, 123–124
government skills needed for managing, 282–283
lead organization network, 120–121
leadership in, 234
measuring performance of, 126–127
monitoring and evaluation and, 292
mutuality and, 124
overcoming challenges to good governance of,
132–134
overview of, 18–19, 111–113
policy and delivery options available to public
managers, 16
political support and, 124–125
principal-principal relationships and, 45–47

horizontal relationships compared with traditional hierarchical structures, 22

impact of ownership structures on employee incentive and behavior, 36–37

networks and, 118–119

partnerships and, 106

outcome-based performance, in democratic accountability, 262–263

outcomes (deliverables)

measuring performance of IPSPs, 160–161

operational outcomes in partnerships, 107

strategic objectives of CSC, 41

outreach networks

in delivery of services for the homeless, 117

types of networks, 115

outsourcing, contracting compared with, 60–61

ownership structures, impact on employee incentive and behavior, 36–37

ownership theory (property rights theory), 36–37

P

pandemics, challenges facing governments, 6

partisanship, issues facing U.S. government, 7

partners in network, securing buy-in, 132

partnerships. *See also* public-private partnerships (PPPs)

accountability in, 272–273

applying to public health example, 21

aspects of, 89–90

assessing, 108–109

attributes of, 106–107

collaboration in, 98–99

collaborative contracts compared with, 66

comparing options for delivery of goods and services, 23, 25

contextualizing collaborative practices, 103–104

costs and benefits of, 96–97

evolution of governance and, 301–302

expertise in, 98

government capacity and, 92–94

IPSPs compared with, 145–146

issues with, 92

managing divergent interests, 94–95

measuring performance, 99

networks compared with, 111

operating environment and, 104–105

organizational characteristics, 106

outcomes, 107

overview of, 18, 85–87

policy and delivery options available to public managers, 16

Port of Miami Tunnel (POMT) example, 101–102

pragmatic rationales for CSC, 34–35

principal-principal relationships and, 45–47

rationales for, 90–92

review, 109

risk allocation in successful, 95–96

social and political impact of successful, 97–98

state employment training case study, 110

strengths and weaknesses, 198–199

transitioning between public service delivery options, 27–28

types of, 87–89

Pathways to Health, role of IPSPs in responding to health care crisis, 153

Patient Protection and Affordable Care Act (2010), 152, 297

performance

criteria for evaluating, 195

criticisms of bureaucratic model, 213

evaluating contacting, 76

evaluating partnerships, 99

measures, 194–195

measuring in IPSPs, 160–161

measuring in networks, 126–127

measuring in partnerships, 99

monitoring and evaluation and, 292

outcome-based, 262–263

performance budgeting, emphasis on outcomes in public sector, 11

performance contracts, 73

permission, sources of influence for public managers, 275

Perspectives, outreach network delivering services for homeless, 117

persuasion, government skills needed for network management, 282

PFI (Private Finance Initiative), in UK, 105, 188–189

philanthropy, 49–50

planning and design development stage, for PPPs, 280

planning programs/projects, 177, 179

policies

CSC advancing goals and objectives of public policy, 306

government skills in setting clear, 287–288

in network governance, 114

public value
  creating, 263–265
  CSCs in creation of, 298
  defining, 305–306
  future of CSCs and, 304–305, 311–312
  role of CSCs in supporting governments and, 309
Public Values and Public Interest: Counterbalancing Economic Individualism (Bozeman), 258–259
public-private partnerships (PPPs). *See also* partnerships
  accountability in, 252, 272–273
  adoption of NPM ideas in UK, 216–217
  advantages/disadvantages of, 108–109, 198–199
  bidding process, 280–281
  comparing trade-offs in options for delivery of goods and services, 23
  construction and, 281
  Dunford Bridge project in UK, 187
  evolution of governance and, 301–302
  examples, 25
  external consultants in, 289
  government skills needed for, 279–282
  improving services offered by public sector, 28
  for infrastructure, 48, 99–101, 307–308
  international experience with, 102–103
  issues in managing, 93–94
  learning from failures, 284
  monitoring and evaluation and, 281–282, 292
  networks compared with, 111
  operating environment in infrastructure partnerships, 104–105
  outcome-based performance example, 262–263
  planning and design development stage for, 280
  Port of Miami Tunnel (POMT) example, 101–102
  Private Finance Initiative (in U.K.), 105
  private market vs. nonprofit solutions, 173
  privatization and, 16
  skills needed by government staff, 287–288
  stakeholder relationships, 90
  trust and, 24
  United Way of New York City (UWNYC), 86
purchasing agreements, examples of traditional contracts, 58

Q

quality, price vs. quality tradeoff in contracting, 64
quasi-governmental organizations
  comparing IPSPs with, 144–145

emerging structures filling void in government services, 9
growth of, 142–144
U.S. examples, 143–144

R

Rainforest Alliance
  autonomy of, 158
  partnership example in delivery of goods and services, 25
  role of IPSPs in environmental protection, 147–148
  work in forest conservation, 149
rationales, for CSC
  addressing governance challenges, 53–55
  agency dilemma and, 37–39
  competition and, 39
  competitive advantage in meeting some social needs, 39–40
  economic, 35
  governance and, 48–51
  hollowed-out government and, 52–53
  impact of ownership structures on employee incentive and behavior, 36–37
  loss-of-control problem and, 51–52
  market failure and, 35–36
  overview of, 31–32
  pragmatic examples, 32–33
  principal-principal relationships and, 45–47
  private and nonprofit perspectives, 34–35
  strategic perspectives of private sector, 41–43
  strategic perspectives of public and nonprofit sectors, 43–45
Reagan, Ronald, 63
Reagan Revolution, decline in support for federal government, 8
recessions, 104
reform
  administrative. *See* administrative reform
  efforts at contract reform, 63
regulation
  creation of regulatory agencies, 254
  CSR and, 42
  responses to market failure, 36
relational contracting, 66
relationships, managing in partnerships, 93
Report Card of America's Infrastructure, 100
request for information (RFI), in contracting, 68
request for proposal (RFP), in contracting, 58, 62

social responsibility, of private sector. *See* corporate
  social responsibility (CSR)
Social Security System (US)
  as example of success of bureaucratic model, 212
  one sector vs. multisector solutions, 170
social trust, democratic accountability and, 266
societal expectations and transformations, factors
  creating cross-sector imperative, 5
SOEs (state-owned enterprises), 216
spillovers
  risk allocation, 186
  risk identification, 184
stability, disadvantages of networks, 130
staff, assigning to CSC tasks, 287–288
stakeholders
  analyzing, 174
  building trust and, 99
  CSR and, 42
  multisector aspect of IPSPs, 142
  partnerships and, 90
  public employees serving diverse interests of, 254
  social and political involvement of, 97–98
state employment training case study
  accountability, 277
  analyzing in CSCs and, 205
  contracting out and, 83–84
  IPSPs and, 166
  leadership, 248–249
  networks and, 136–137
  overview of, 29
  partnerships and, 110
state government
  challenges facing, 3–4
  in definition of public sector, 11
  dynamics of collaboration, 10
  federal government shifting responsibilities to, 9
  foster care and adoption program example, 78–79
  legal issues related to collaboration, 51
  managed competition, 61
state-owned enterprises (SOEs), 216
statutory procedures, contract transparency and,
  73–74
stewardship, transformational stewardship (Kee and
  Newcomer), 221–222
strategic rationales, for CSC
  private sector and, 41–43
  public and nonprofit sectors and, 43–45
structure, of networks, 118–119

structures, organizational. *See* organizational
  structures
subsidies, responses to market failure, 36
support
  critical elements of CSC leadership, 234
  leaders generating, 237–239
Supreme Court (U.S.), ruling on limits on
  government contracting, 70–71
sustainability
  Oregon Environmental Council mission, 148–149
  Rainforest Alliance work in, 147–148
  role of IPSPs in meeting challenges of, 147
synthesizing skills, government skills needed for
  network management, 282
system thinking
  critical elements of CSC leadership, 234
  leader viewing issues from broad perspective,
    241–243
  learning and, 293–294

T
Taft Commission on Economy and Efficiency
  (1912), 215
tasks. *See also* challenges
  analyzing nature of, 170
  case studies, 175
  one sector vs. multisector solutions, 170–172
  overview of, 170
  political factors, 174–175
  private market vs. nonprofit solutions, 172–173
teams
  developing dedicated teams for CSC projects, 287
  new governance model and, 221
television, example of overlap of private and public
  sectors, 15
termination
  risk allocation, 186
  risk identification, 184
timeliness, price vs. timeliness tradeoff in
  contracting, 64
total quality movement (Deming), 217
tourism, Global Sustainable Tourism Council,
  147–148
traditional contracts, 57–58
transaction costs, rationales for partnerships, 91–92
transformational stewardship (Kee and Newcomer),
  221–222, 224
transit development case study, 295

transparency
  advantages of networks, 129
  avoiding fraud and abuses in contracting, 73–74
  building trust between partners, 99
  IPSPs and, 159
transportation infrastructure
  DC Capital area Hot Lanes program example, 198–199
  helping local government implement, 289
  monitoring and evaluation and, 292
  role of IPSPs in, 149–151
trust
  among partners, 99
  building, 76
  comparing options for delivery of goods and services, 24
  critical elements of CSC leadership, 234
  democratic accountability and, 265–267
  in effective collaboration, 174
  government skills needed for network management, 282
  leaders building, 243–244
  leadership in heterarchical structures and, 234
  levels of, 75
  network management and, 222
  trust but verify concept, 312
"trusted partners" (Forrer et al.), 266–267
twenty-first century government, 222–224

U

uncontrollable risks
  allocation, 186
  identification, 184
United Kingdom (U.K.)
  adoption of NPM ideas, 216–217
  Dunford Bridge project, 187
  Neglected Tropical Disease (NTDs), 201
  Private Finance Initiative (PFI), 105, 188–189
United Nations Millennium Development Goals, 134
United Way of New York City (UWNYC), 86
urban congestion, role of IPSPs in, 150
U.S. (United States)
  examples of quasi-governmental organizations, 143–144
  historic origins of bureaucratic model and, 210
  history of contracting in, 62–64
  history of partnerships with government, 85
  low level of confidence in government, 6–7

Supreme Court ruling on limits on government contracting, 70–71
US Agency for International Development (USAID), partnerships with governments, 85
US Coast Guard (USCG)
  Admiral Allen's roles in, 235
  Deepwater Program, 168–169
  response to Hurricane Katrina, 222
US State Department, Global Partnership Initiative, 98
UWNYC (United Way of New York City), 86

V

value
  best value analysis. *See* best-value analysis
  creating, 263–265
  public. *See* public value
  shared value, 42–43
value-for-money analysis (VfM)
  analysis of CSCs, 190–191
  comparing with CBA and CEA analysis, 192
  Florida Department of Transportation example, 193
  types of analytical approaches, 189
values-based leadership, 234
vendors, traditional contracts and, 58
verify, trust but verify concept, 312
vertical relationships
  in hierarchies, 230
  traditional accountability and, 255
Veterans Health Administration, example of direct government provision of public health, 20
vision
  negotiating motivational differences and, 50
  in network governance, 114

W

Waldo, Dwight, 256, 260–261
Weber, Max, 210–211
welfare state, opponents of, 216
work groups, learning by doing, 290
World Bank
  adoption of NPM ideas, 215
  international experience with PPPs, 103
  partnerships with governments, 85

Y

Yuma Desert Proving Grounds, public-private partnership, 25